Understanding Aspects of the Law

Understanding Aspects of the Law

A GUIDE TO CRIMINAL, TORT, AND REGULATORY LAW

FIRST EDITION

Written and edited by Carl F. Cranor

cognella®
SAN DIEGO

Bassim Hamadeh, CEO and Publisher
Mieka Portier, Senior Acquisitions Editor
Tony Paese, Project Editor
Celeste Paed, Associate Production Editor
Asfa Arshi, Graphic Design Assistant
Alexa Lucido, Licensing Manager
Natalie Piccotti, Director of Marketing
Kassie Graves, Vice President of Editorial
Jamie Giganti, Director of Academic Publishing

Printed in the United States of America.

cognella® | ACADEMIC PUBLISHING
3970 Sorrento Valley Blvd., Ste. 500, San Diego, CA 92121

TABLE OF CONTENTS

LIST OF CASES

PREFACE

This book, based on a course I have taught for many years since completing a Master of Studies in Law at Yale Law School, seeks to introduce readers to several aspects of our legal system: the US criminal law, the tort or personal injury law, and some regulatory or administrative law, as well as strengths and shortcomings of each area. I seek to introduce these areas of law from "the ground up"; that is, by introducing some basic components of each area of the law to assist understanding in how each area of law functions, how component parts bring about these functions, and how some of them impose limitations and restrictions on the functioning of the law. The elements of crimes and their sanctions differ from the elements of torts and their sanctions and more substantially from many aspects of administrative law.

The book's emphasis developed from my philosophical background, which emphasizes the understanding of basic ideas and has also been influenced by the study of law at UCLA and Yale, considerable legal research, and some testifying in court cases. I have acquired an interest in assisting students to understand the law in a more granular manner than merely reviewing many different kinds of crimes or torts, for example. Instead, the focus is on basic elements of several different areas of law and some legal procedures, especially in civil litigation, with major emphases on the law revealed by legal cases (one needs understanding of civil procedure to see why courts address tort cases as they do).

At present, the text is based on a quarter-system course because that is what I have taught. Thus, it is possible that it might need some augmentation for semester-length classes. Despite this cautionary note, since there is a raft of information in each case, many fascinating in their own right, and how long one spends teaching it is flexible, there may well be sufficient material for a longer course. However, if the topics seem too short for a semester system, it would be easy to augment the readings with articles or other legal cases illustrating a broader range of crimes, torts, regulatory issues, or other topics because the students should have the basic concepts of these areas of law, which in turn could be utilized to illustrate and develop them with other topics. This text is not a casebook as that might be understood in a law school aiming to be comprehensive in some areas of the law because such a volume would be inappropriate for undergraduate courses. Also, as an introductory text, it does not seek to be comprehensive in the criminal law or torts, but to give students major conceptual tools to understand the foundations of these areas of law with some introduction to some major cases and ideas from each area.

My teaching has been assisted and influenced by graduate students who served as teaching assistants over the years, with Heinrik Hellwig meriting special mention because of our conversations during courses, about his dissertation on the tort law, and over many years about teaching this and other classes. He has additionally provided extensive and quite helpful comments on the text that follows. My daughter, Taylor J. Cranor, Yale Law graduate and now a practicing tax lawyer, also provided important comments over time as well as reviewing aspects of this volume. I am also grateful in a much broader sense for conversations about the law and related issues with Joe Cecil of the Federal Judicial Center; Herbert Morris, a mentor at UCLA Law School and in subsequent discussion groups; Morty Schwartz, UCLA Law School; Doug Kysar, Yale Law School; Tony Kronman, Yale Law School; George Priest, Yale Law School; Harold Koh, Yale Law School; Fred Lawrence, Georgetown Law School; Robert Taylor, National Oceanic and Atmospheric Administration; Steve Baughman Jensen, Dallas, Tx, plaintiffs' attorney, Tom McGarity, Texas Law School; Wendy Wagner, Texas Law School; Sid Shapiro, Wake Forest Law School; Raphael Metzger, plaintiffs' attorney; and numerous others with whom I interacted in litigation in some tort law cases.

INTRODUCTION

A legal system, or "the law," is an institution that has a number of functions in a larger society. To some extent it represents an instrument of social control, or perhaps better, keeping the peace, and seeks to guide and also restrain the behavior of citizens who are subject to it. There are other institutions of social control. To some extent broadly shared conceptions of morality guide how we behave, place restrictions on our conduct, provide protections for one another, and make some activities possible that would not be available without certain moral conceptions.

Moral views typically have prohibitions against assaulting one another (e.g., don't hit or kill) or against cheating in business or personal relationships because of the harm each can do. Promises and their widespread acceptance can help us predict the future and make agreements with others in terms that seem acceptable to us. Law-recognized promises concern buying and selling, facilitating commercial transactions, and assisting the transfer of property from one person to another or from one generation to another. The very idea of mine and thine concerning ownership of things and ideas is developed in property law and provides guidance to what we own and what is ours to keep, trade, give away, or sell.

Rudimentary ideas such as these in either moral views or accepted social practices facilitate our collective lives together. And yet, more is needed. While informal views and practices such as these have their place and provide grounds for living with one another, for guiding our behavior, and for criticizing others who don't abide by the rules, they provide only limited recourse if someone is tempted to violate the practices and does. The law has more formalized rules in various parts of our lives to assist our living together, and it brings more precise rules in most instances, with those rules backed by formal procedures and sanctions to help persuade those tempted to violate the rules to follow them or face formal institutional consequences. Sanctions in the law are more formal and likely more serious than informal critiques, guilt trips, shaming, or, perhaps in extreme instances in some communities, ostracism.

One area in which this is obvious concerns promises. We are quite familiar with promises and how they can facilitate our lives, but what we might think of as the moral practice of making, keeping, and enforcing promises seems quite vague. However, they are so important that we have an entire area of the law based on promises; it's called "contract law." It concerns how to make and keep promises, enforce them if the promisor defaults on the promise, or vice versa, as well as what one of the parties can do about it and what remedies exist for defaulted contracts. Where our informal practices are vague and a lot is left to be worked out in particular cases, and there may be no adjudicator to tell or guide us in what to do, the contract law is enormously extensive, exceedingly precise about how things should be done, what breaches of contracts will be enforced, who must do it, and what likely consequences there would be to the violator of a contract (but even here vagueness remains). I recall seeing a body of contract law by a single author on the shelves of the Yale Law School library that was perhaps 8 or 10 feet long in many different volumes addressing the myriad details of contracts, or one might say, promises.

Promises and contract law are just one example of relations between informal conceptions of moral or social practices and their more formal legal instantiation. This is not my topic, only a means to illustrate that the law tends to be much more precise in ordering our relationships, backing violations of them with various kinds of sanctions to discourage violations or to inflict some kind of unpleasant consequence (e.g., monetary penalty) on the person or persons who violate the laws.

The study of the law provides insights into some of the institutional structures of the community in which one lives: what is forbidden, permitted, facilitated, encouraged, and so on. The law provides a major part of the "bones" of the society in which one lives. As one studies the law one begins to learn more about the structure of the community in which they live.

It is also fun to study the law. In many circumstances the legal cases themselves are stories or fragments of stories about interactions between people, involving assaults, homicides, or complicated interactions between people that lead to legal consequences. One should not take them to be the entire history of what occurred even in the circumstances of a particular case, but it is part of the story. At least some of the legal cases are sufficiently compelling that you may long remember them and be able to recall them years later. Some of the legal cases may surprise or even seem quite implausible to us—perhaps this occurs more often with some of the unusual tort law cases we consider; what a crazy circumstance developed in interactions between two or more people! Watch for these. Sometimes events in the world present such unusual circumstances that legal doctrines need to be reformulated to properly address what occurred within the broader doctrine of the law. You probably have not considered that a train bumping a guy-wire support for an electric line could kill someone miles away or that two interacting negligent drivers could lead to a person's derangement, resulting in his shooting a third party who was only seeking to offer assistance at an accident scene. Enjoy the cases as you study them, but also learn what they have to reveal about the legal system—the legal cases we read are the "data" about the law and what they tell us about the doctrines, presuppositions, and guidance of the law.

Perhaps one other preliminary point should be mentioned. We often think of legal cases as occurring in trials in different areas of the law (e.g., the criminal law, tort law, family law, or contract law). We will read none of these. Instead, we will read and discuss decisions from appellate courts to which one side or another in a trial case has appealed because the legal party thought one or more legal mistakes had occurred at the trial court.

The general structure of courts in either state jurisdictions (e.g., California, Illinois, or South Carolina) or the federal court system is as follows. Trials occur in first-level trial courts. If a litigant thinks legal errors occurred in that court, that party might try to appeal what the party believes is a "mistaken" legal decision to an *intermediate* appellate court. Such courts only rule on the law as interpreted or applied by the trial judge at the first level. Less commonly we will discuss some cases that have been heard by the *highest appellate* in a jurisdiction; in many state jurisdictions and in the federal law, these are called the "Supreme Court" of that jurisdiction. New York is an outlier, dubbing its highest court of appeal, the "Court of Appeals."

In what follows, I present some major aspects of the criminal law, the tort law, and some regulatory laws, supported by components that go into each of the areas of law, so that the reader has an improved understanding of what the law is at a more detailed level, how it can function, how it may protect a variety of important interests we might have as citizens, and some of its limitations. I think of this as a somewhat granular view of these areas of the law. Toward the latter sections of the book, I also suggest that, while all the areas I consider seek to protect various central interests we each might have under an area of the law (they could be called "rights"), they carry out these tasks in different ways, have different strengths and weaknesses as institutions, and can support one another in some ways. This too, I believe, gives us insights into these areas of our legal system, as well as some insights about how we could think about our legal system more broadly.

We begin with the criminal law and some of its components, then turn to the tort law and its components, providing an approximate side-by-side comparison of these two institutions that seek to protect us and our central interests from invasions by others. Similar tasks are carried out in different ways and supported by different sanctions seeking to ensure that the provisions of these two areas of the law are followed. Some are more successful than others. Some aspects of administrative or regulatory law have many of the same objectives, but, on the face of it, seem less similar to us than the criminal law and torts, and achieve their aims by different means. Administrative law also has different strengths and weakness compared to the other two areas of the law. I focus on these because the tort law and regulatory law have been an object of much of my research, and one can learn much from comparing their strengths and weaknesses in pursuit of similar goals.

One other point is important for teaching purposes. At my own institution it seems many law courses focus on constitutional law. While this is an important area of our legal system and has been followed to one extent or another by other countries, the law has a much broader reach than constitutional law. After I returned to campus from studying some law as a PhD student at UCLA and a year immersed in law at Yale Law School, I realized that important areas of the law were being ignored in the few departments that offered some kind of law course, with different units retaining a major focus on constitutional law. Every law school regards two of its most important courses as the criminal law and tort law, yet for undergraduates interested in the law, they could graduate from our campus not knowing much about either area, except perhaps what they gleaned from newspapers and TV, not the best grounding for understanding these topics. Consequently, I created and have taught a course with these emphases for decades, and the students seem very appreciative of what they learn from courses that have little discussion of constitutional law. The criminal law and torts remain quite important areas, central to the legal system as they have been for some time; perhaps one might think of them as two of the most basic areas of the law. For contrasts and expanding ideas about the law I also introduce administrative law, an important and more recent component of this field.

■ CHAPTER 1

The Criminal Law

Some Basics

The criminal law is a most important area of the law. It is the oldest area of law that we will consider, since it has literally been around in one form or another for centuries (which I do not consider). However, by focusing on the criminal law "from the ground up" as it were, we will see that some typical descriptions of it can be misleading and need amendment.

On the internet, for example, various shorthand descriptions are given of the criminal law by several websites. Also, an encyclopedic text on the law, *Black's Law Dictionary*, says it is, "The body of law defining offenses against the community at large, regulating how suspects are investigated, charged and tried, and establishing punishments for convicted offenders."[1]

Broader claims sometimes assert that the criminal law aims to protect people from threatening, harmful, or other endangering behavior and is established by statute, which is to say that the laws are enacted by a legislature.

While some of these statements about the criminal law are roughly correct, they can be misleading. The criminal law does seek to protect citizens from threatening, harmful, or other endangering conduct, but so do other areas of the law, including the tort law and aspects of administrative law that we will consider. Much criminal law has been and is established by statute. However, considerable criminal law has entered the US legal system from judicial decisions, or case law, issued in jurisdictions in the United States over many years, with some quite old, and others tracing their existence to early judicial decisions in British law. We will see a few examples of British decisions and some legal cases reference early US or sometimes British legal decisions. It is correct to point out that what we think of as the

1 *Black's Law Dictionary* (8th ed.) (2004), p. 493. Bryan A. Garner, Ed. West Publishing.

quintessentially major sanction of the criminal law is punishment, but there are other possibilities that should be mentioned. This sanction is so critical to the criminal law that it has contributed to several components of this area of the law that are not present in other areas. Other areas of the law also have sanctions, but they are different, and this makes a difference in elements of other areas of the law and how they function.

Salient Features of the Criminal Law

The criminal law has a number of what we might call "salient features" that are typical of the criminal law and help contrast it with other areas of the law.

As do many other areas of the law, the criminal law seeks to protect people or perhaps institutions in the community from various kinds of legally protected "border crossings" by others, often but not always resulting in harms. Many different areas of the law provide protection from border crossings. Perhaps, without being too misleading, we can consider the border crossings as violations of rights, or perhaps central interests, that we think we should have, or rights already provided by the area of law, whether we consider the tort law, contract law, property law, family law, and so on. What legal "borders" we have under different areas of the law are specified by the content of a particular area of the law. For example, both the criminal law and tort law protect us against attacks against our person, but they do it in different ways.

This area of law aims to secure the rightful "borders" of our possessions and ourselves by **penalizing** those who cross our legally protected borders. We are invited to visualize an imaginary space around our possessions and ourselves that are legally protected from invasions by others.

In contrast, the tort law seeks to secure the rightful borders of our possessions and ourselves **by requiring the defendant who violated them to put matters right (or make us whole)** should we suffer damages from the "border crossings." The criminal law imposes a penalty or punishment on a defendant who has violated our legal borders, while the tort law requires that a defendant who violated us must repair the damage by putting matters "right," preferably as they were before we were harmed by his or her behavior. Sometimes, in the tort law it is claimed that a defendant found liable for harming us should "make us whole." We will consider more about the tort law when we take up that topic; the important point here is just to note the different sanctions in criminal and tort laws to legal violations.

The "legally authorized borders" that an area of law seeks to protect depends upon the content of each area and will differ to some or a great extent from other areas of the law, and I do consider some of these items. Of course, often there is overlap between the criminal and tort laws in violations of boundaries they seek to prevent, and we will consider some of these as we go along.

Different areas of the law impose different **standards of behavior** for who should obey the criminal, tort, or contract law. The criminal law imposes a *public* standard of conduct, roughly speaking, on all adult members of the public to abide by it and refrain from violating the borders of every person in the community, although there can be some exceptions. Every adult has to follow the requirements of the criminal law toward others. The tort law has analogous *public* standards of conduct every adult has to observe. However, this is not necessarily true of other legal areas. If I enter into a **contract** with you to buy your car, under provisions of the contract law, you and I create a legal relationship that exists just between the two of us. I seek to buy your car for a certain price and you agree to sell it to me at that price. The legal rights and duties are between you and me; other adult members of the public are not part of this relationship. If I pay you the agreed price for your car, other things equal under contract law, you legally must transfer it to me, and after it is transferred, I own it. My offer to buy your car does not mean that I must offer to buy the cars of anyone else in the community. Your agreement to sell to me does not oblige you to sell to any other member of the public. In the criminal law, I must not only refrain from assaulting, or killing or burglarizing or robbing you, but also to refrain from assaulting, or killing or burglarizing or robbing every other person in the community. *Everyone* in the community is entitled to my restraint from crossing their legal borders. The criminal law sets, one might say "public," standards of conduct for (nearly) all adults that must be observed toward all others, and (nearly) all adults must observe the same restraints vis-à-vis me.

What kind of harm is suffered when there are violations of the criminal law? This may seem to be a strange question, but I pose it to draw attention to a misleading idea with ancient credentials. Of course, if persons are robbed, burglarized, raped, assaulted, or killed, they are harmed. But according to *Black's Law Dictionary*, crimes are the wrongs which the government notices *as injurious to the public*.[2] The idea seems to be that the government (or state) with the criminal law legally regards some wrongs done to individuals as in some way injurious to the public as a whole.

This aphorism seems misleading in some respects. Although it might directly apply to crimes such as the actions of serial killers, rapists, robbers, or burglars, not every crime threatens or may even disturb or upset or injure the public as a whole. If Jones embezzles money from Smith's small business, that is the crime of embezzlement, but it seems a stretch to say that it is injurious (or represents any threat) to the community as a whole. Would we even be inclined to say that the community as a whole "notices or regards this as injurious to the public?" There are subsets of crimes that might be regarded as injurious to the public or even threatening to the public, such as the serial crimes noted above. Even some non-serial crimes may be so disturbing to the broad public that they become matters of wide concern and "injurious" in that sense.

An important characteristic of the criminal law that provides better insights are answers to the question, "Who enforces the standard of conduct specified by the content of the criminal law when the law has been violated?" A clearer statement is, "**Who** has to establish that a law has been violated and bring a legal case?" The answer here is clear and different from several other areas of the law. A public prosecutor, district attorney, or attorney general *acting in the name of the appropriate community* must **initiate** legal action against a defendant suspected of violating the criminal law. The appropriate public official must bring a legal action against the suspect.

This is quite different from the tort law. In torts, the **party who believes they have been injured by another must initiate** legal action against a tort law defendant who is believed to have committed the injury. The difference just articulated points to another one. An injured party in the criminal law, e.g., someone who has been assaulted and battered, can inform law enforcement officials that he or she has been harmed and provide evidence of any injuries. However, a prosecutor acting in the name of the community would initiate legal action based on an initial complaint after considering whether there is sufficient evidence against the defendant suspected of committing the assault and battery. If the same act were considered in the tort law, the injured party—the victim (not an agent of the state or the community as a whole)—would have to find a lawyer and initiate legal action against the defendant.

---

2 *Black's Law Dictionary*, *ibid.*, 493.

The adversaries in the criminal law, somewhat echoing *Black's Law Dictionary*, are considered the community as a whole versus the defendant. That is, it might be the Commonwealth of Pennsylvania or the People of the State of California or, in a federal case, the United States versus the defendant. Thus, a typical name of a criminal case might be "The Commonwealth of Pennsylvania versus Sam Jones," or "The State of California v. Sam Jones," or shortened versions of these titles, such as, State v. Jones, "People v. Jones," or U.S. v. Jones. A legal officer representing the community as a whole, who is seen as the complaining party, acts against the alleged defendant who is believed to be the law violator. In the tort law, it's just an injured party, which, for example, might be an individual, a group, or a company, *inter alia*, versus the alleged tortfeasor (the party alleged to have committed the harm). If Sally is alleged to have damaged Jane's garage, Jane must initiate any legal action against Sally if she wants compensation for the injuries she suffered. Typically, she would do this by finding an appropriate lawyer to take on the case and try to recover any damages she might have suffered.

In bringing a legal action, the issues of the "burden of proof" and the "standard of proof" arise. Too often the term "burden of proof" is used for both concepts, but they should be distinguished because these can be confusing.

The **burden of proof**, properly so called, is the legal assignment of ***who* has to initiate legal action** and **change the legal status quo of the parties**. In other terms, before Smith assaulted and battered Jones, roughly speaking, both were equal citizens before the law in the sense that both had full legal rights and neither was in legal trouble. If a prosecutor seeks to successfully find Smith guilty of the assault and battery, the prosecutor must change Smith's legal standing (or status quo ante) in the community from being a free citizen with a normal complement of full legal rights to being charged, tried, and found guilty of the crime of assaulting and battering Jones, provided the evidence supports the finding. Consequently, if the prosecutor obtains a guilty verdict against Smith, this changes the legal status quo between him and the community; he will forfeit some of his complement of legal rights and likely some freedoms as a result.

The **standard of proof**, properly so called, is the legal assignment within an area of law specifying how difficult it is **to change the legal status quo of the parties and hold a defendant accountable for a legal violation**. To convict Smith for battering and assaulting Jones, the prosecutor must satisfy a specified **standard of proof** to find Smith guilty of the crime. He must be found guilty to the satisfaction of the *finder of fact* of assault and battery **beyond a reasonable doubt**. The finder of fact in the vast majority of instances is a jury of one's peers, but in rare cases a judge may serve as the finder of fact, serving as both judge and jury, because neither party requested a jury trial (to which both sides in a jury trial are constitutionally entitled). This is called a "bench trial" because a judge at his or her bench in the courtroom both interprets the law and makes a factual finding under that interpretation whether or not the defendant violated the law.

The criminal law's standard of proof is quite demanding: if a jury has "reasonable doubt" about the charges brought against Smith based on the evidence and reasons (not merely gut feelings), because of the standard of proof, they are legally required to find him not guilty of the alleged crime. The phrase *reasonable doubt*, like many in the law, is vague with some things left to interpretation or filling in (if that can even be done). Unfortunately, often it remains vague: if a juror or a whole jury has reasonable doubt that the law and facts do not support a finding that an alleged defendant committed the crime, it should find him or her "not guilty." However, if a juror or the entire jury has "unreasonable doubt"—e.g., because of prejudices or similar attitudes it brings to a case—in principle it may not find the defendant "not guilty."

That is, just because a judge gives a jury instructions on what proof beyond a reasonable or unreasonable doubt means, a jury might not follow the guidance. Assessing each of these is not easy. Another heuristic or phrase sometimes used is that for jurors to find criminal guilt, they "must have an abiding conviction to a moral certainty in the truth of the charge." This still contains some vagueness, but it does suggest that the belief that a defendant is guilty has staying power—it must be an abiding conviction.

The major way in which the law protects our rights or central interests is to **threaten a legal sanction to discourage a legal violation or actually enforce a sanction for one found guilty**. While many people abide by the criminal law and tort law out of general moral beliefs, social practice, or decency, not all do so. In order to address this issue, there not only have to be norms from the law to guide how one should treat fellow citizens—what to do and not do. Those norms must be enforced, because some people will likely be tempted to violate them. Sanctions serve this purpose. For a violation in the criminal law, the typical sanction would be a **punishment** of the defendant that may involve jail or prison time, or a suspended sentence with parole, as well as a kind of social condemnation associated with the convicted defendant for the crime in question. For less serious offenses, the sanction may be a fine paid by the defendant to the state. We will discuss some general features of punishment in later sections.

In contrast, in the tort law when defendants are found accountable for a tortious conduct that harms others, or a tort violation, they are required to **compensate the injured party for the injuries**. Another point sometimes made is that defendants must make tort plaintiffs whole or restore them as near as possible to their status quo ante. Sometimes this metaphor seems difficult to achieve; if a person is seriously injured in a car accident, becoming a quadriplegic, that person cannot be "made whole again" or "restored to the status quo ante," because nearly all physical capabilities the person previously had would be gone. Typical sanctions in the tort law consist of the transfer of money or other resources from the tort law defendant to the successful plaintiff. Sometimes a plaintiff might request a different sanction from a court, such as a temporary or permanent injunction or other alternatives.

A criminal defendant cannot be found guilty without having exhibited an appropriate **culpable state of mind for the crime in question** (with a major exception we discuss in Chapter 2 regarding strict liability offenses), as well as satisfying other needed **elements** of a criminal offense that we will soon consider. We will have an extensive discussion of culpable states of mind that are typically required in the criminal law. The American Law Institute's Model Penal Code regards four states of mind important for the criminal law.[3]

A person may act **purposely** or **intentionally** *in a narrow sense*, which means that the person makes it his or her **conscious object** to engage in conduct of that nature or to cause such a particular result. If it involves circumstances attending the act he or she must be **aware** of the existence of such circumstances or **believes or hopes** that they exist.[4]

---

3 The Model Penal Code is just what the name conveys. It is an independent organization in the United States that produces "scholarly work to clarify, modernize, and otherwise improve the law." (Located at https://www.ali.org/about-ali/.) The Model Penal Code clarifies and seeks to improve various aspects of the criminal law.

4 American Law Institute Model Penal Code Official Draft, 1962: Section 2.02. General requirements of culpability. In Sanford H. Kadish & Stephen J. Schulhofer (1989). *Criminal law and its processes: Cases and materials* (5th ed.), p. 1190. Little, Brown.

A person acts **knowingly** with respect to a material element of an offense when he or she is **aware** that his or her conduct is of that nature or that such circumstances exist: and if the element involves a *result of the conduct*, he or she is aware that it is **practically certain** that the conduct will cause such a result.[5]

A person acts **recklessly** with respect to a material element of an offense when he or she ***consciously disregards* a substantial and unjustifiable risk** that the material element exists or will result from the conduct. The risk must be of such a nature and degree that, considering the nature and purpose of the actor's conduct and the circumstances known to them, its disregard involves a **gross deviation** from the standard of conduct that a law-abiding person aware of risks to others would observe in the actor's situation.[6]

A person acts **negligently** with respect to a material element of an offense **when he or she *should be aware* of a substantial and unjustifiable risk** that the material element exists or will result from his or her conduct. The risk must be of such a nature and degree that the actor's failure to perceive it, considering the nature and purpose of his or her conduct and the circumstances known to them, involves a **deviation from the standard of care** that would be exercised by a reasonable person in his or her situation.[7]

These different culpability states of mind were adopted by the American Law Institute's Committee on the Model Penal Code to create some common standards of culpable behavior to be used in defining various crimes. The idea was to endorse codes of culpability that were utilized across jurisdictions. These efforts have been quite successful and seemingly widely adopted.

To illustrate some of these different culpability conditions, consider several examples. Suppose you have a friend who is in prison and you want to get him out. You concoct a scheme whereby you will be waiting in a getaway car outside the prison wall with a sufficient amount of dynamite to blow up the wall. You know when he's going to be in the recreation yard for one hour and plan to blow up the wall at that time. You also understand that there are risks to others.

Now imagine three different circumstances. Example 1: If you make it your **conscious object** to both destroy the prison wall and help your friend escape, but also to kill other people in the exercise yard (some of whom you know and quite dislike), if you succeed, you would have **purposely** destroyed the wall, assisted the escape, and **purposely killed others in the yard**. Thus, you would have both purposely assisted a prison escape and purposely committed what would be murder in the first degree.

Example 2: If the object of your action was merely to destroy the prison wall to help your friend escape, but you were **practically certain** that your conduct would cause deaths of others in the yard, but you don't wish this to occur, you might only have **knowingly** killed anyone who died. Now the distinction between purposely killing and knowingly killing may not make much difference in a particular legal system, but there are slightly different culpability connotations between the two. In one instance you make it your explicit goal to kill and in the other you are practically certain that people will die because of what you do. In some jurisdictions you might be guilty of murder in the first degree in both examples, but there might be other jurisdictions in which there could be a subtle difference in the final judgment between the two. The Model Penal Code regards both killing purposely and knowingly to be murder (in contrast to manslaughter).[8]

5 *Ibid.*

6 *Ibid.*

7 *Ibid.*

8 American Law Institute Model Penal Code: Section 210.2: Murder. In Kadish & Schulhofer,1225–1226.

Example 3: If the object of your action was merely to destroy the prison wall to help your friend to escape, but you were aware that there were risks to others, but continued your plan, we likely would say that you acted **recklessly** with regard to causing deaths to others. You did not *know* that your actions would kill others, nor were you practically certain that it would occur, but you **consciously disregarded a substantial and unjustifiable risk that harm to others would result**. And the risk must be of such a nature and degree that its disregard involves a **gross deviation** from the standard of conduct that a reasonable citizen would exercise in that circumstance, being aware of risks to others. And, of course, no reasonable law-abiding citizen would consider blowing up a wall and putting the lives of others at great risk.

Example 4 comes with a different set of facts. Suppose I want to burn the leaves on my property, so I rake them into a pile. Suppose I had not paid attention to the forecast that there would be high winds at 11:00 a.m. And I start a fire on this windy day but had heard little about it and had not read the weather report. Now suppose I pile my leaves not far from your house and ignite them. The wind suddenly picks up and blows from my burning leaves toward your house. It becomes so strong that the fire is blown to your house and burns it down. Suppose I was not aware of a substantial and unjustifiable risk of burning down your house, but suppose that a reasonable person in the community would have been aware of the fire risks. Suppose I was not reckless, not consciously disregarding a substantial and unjustifiable risk, but suppose a law-abiding citizen would have been alert to the weather forecast, not wanting to put your house at risk. However, I failed to be as careful as a reasonable law-abiding citizen might have been. In this circumstance I might be judged to have **negligently** burned down your house or perhaps **grossly negligently** burned it down. The difference between the two depends upon whether my failure to appreciate the fire risk to your house constitutes **a mere deviation** from the standard of care toward others in the community or is **a gross deviation from the appropriate standard of care**. In the first instance, I would merely have exhibited **simple negligence**; in the second, I would have exhibited **gross negligence**. We will use both concepts in the criminal, and one is especially important in the tort law. There may be fuzzy borderlines between some of these culpable states of mind. Acting recklessly in some circumstances may blur into being practically certain (acting knowingly) that one might cause harm to another. And at some point, gross negligence may approach acting recklessly.

With the above as background, consider the standard elements of a criminal offense.

The Elements of a Criminal Offense

Generic components that must be satisfied to hold a person accountable for a crime under the criminal law are considered the elements of a criminal offense. In summary, to be held accountable under the criminal law, a person (defendant) must commit an *actus reus* (illegal act) and concurrently have the appropriate *mens rea* (guilty mind). These devolve into four elements that reveal their components.

To be convicted of an offense, the defendant must

a) act or omit to perform an act of which he is physically capable that **breaches (or violates) a legal duty**;
b) the act or omission **must be voluntary;** and
c) at the time of the offense, the defendant must have acted with the appropriate guilty mind: exhibiting **general *mens rea*** (defendant must have been sane and must have had the general capacity

to understand the law and obey it, which children up to some age would lack) and committing the act with the **specific *mens rea*** required as part of the definition of the crime.

A prosecutor must show each element of a criminal offense **beyond a reasonable doubt**. What is called general *mens rea* often does not have to be shown in each case about a defendant because every adult human being is legally presumed to be sane and not to have the mental state of a child. We return to this point in the next chapter in the discussion of insanity as a defense to murder.

In order to be convicted for committing a crime, an individual must have a legal duty under the criminal law and act in violation of it or *breach* the law. This may not be a problem in many crimes if a person carries out an act that obviously harms another. If Sam punches James, we could probably quickly and approximately identify the legal breach; Sam committed assault and battery against James. If Fred invades Sally's home at night by breaking and entering, he likely committed burglary.

However, what if Jones fails or omits to act and someone is injured? Such omissions can raise more difficult issues, as illustrated in *Mary Jones v. the United States*. What does the prosecutor at trial have to show in this case? Did the prosecutor succeed in this? Did the trial judge require that Ms. Jones had a duty to the young children living in her house? This case nicely illustrates the need to show that a legal violation occurred. It's not enough that a person does something we might think is wrong or bad or exhibits a moral failure, such as failing to take sufficient care of children in one's home. In the law, a person must act or fail to act in a manner that **violates or breaches the law**. In general, if a person omits to act and someone is harmed, there would be no legal violation, unless the omission is expressly made sufficient by the law or the law imposes legal duty to perform the omitted act. For example, suppose a man and woman were having an affair and a third party gave an illegal drug to the woman, which she took, causing her to die. Her companion failed to act to save her. The Michigan Supreme Court held that her companion had no legal duty to intervene to help her, so there would be no conviction for his omission.[9] If the law doesn't require that the person had a *legal duty* and violated it, there is no criminal offense.

Actus Reus: The Breach of a Legal Duty

Jones v. United States

United States Court of Appeals District of Columbia Circuit

308 F.2d 307 (1960)

Opinion: WRIGHT, Circuit Judge.

Appellant, together with one Shirley Green, was tried on a three-count indictment charging them jointly with (1) abusing and maltreating Robert Lee Green (2) abusing and maltreating Anthony Lee Green, and (3) involuntary manslaughter through failure to perform their legal duty of care for Anthony Lee Green, which failure resulted in his death. At the close of evidence, after trial to a jury, the first two counts were dismissed as to both

9 *People v. Beardsley*, 150 Mich. 206, 113 N.W. 1128 (Supreme Court of Michigan, 1907).

defendants. On the third count, appellant was convicted of involuntary manslaughter. Shirley Green was found not guilty.

Appellant urges several grounds for reversal. We need consider but two. … [A]ppellant argues that the trial court committed plain error in failing to instruct the jury that it must first find that appellant was under a legal obligation to provide food and necessities to Anthony Lee before finding her guilty of manslaughter in failing to provide them. [We reverse the manslaughter finding by the jury.]

A summary of the evidence, which is in conflict upon almost every significant issue, is necessary for the disposition of both arguments. In late 1957, Shirley Green became pregnant, out of wedlock, with a child, Robert Lee, subsequently born August 17, 1958. Apparently patently to avoid the embarrassment of the presence of the child in the Green home, it was arranged that appellant, a family friend, would take the child to her home after birth. Appellant did so, and the child remained there continuously until removed by the police on August 5, 1960. Initially appellant made some motions toward the adoption of Robert Lee, but these came to nought, and shortly thereafter it was agreed that Shirley Green was to pay appellant $72 a month for his care. According to appellant, these payments were made for only five months. According to Shirley Green, they were made up to July, 1960.

Early in 1959 Shirley Green again became pregnant, this time with the child Anthony Lee, whose death is the basis of appellant's conviction. This child was born October 21, 1959. Soon after birth, Anthony Lee developed a mild jaundice condition, attributed to a blood incompatability with his mother. The jaundice resulted in his retention in the hospital for three days beyond the usual time, or until October 26, 1959, when, on authorization signed by Shirley Green, Anthony Lee was released by the hospital to appellant's custody. Shirley Green, after a two or three day stay in the hospital, also lived with appellant for three weeks, after which she returned to her parents' home, leaving the children with appellant. She testified she did not see them again, except for one visit in March, until August 5, 1960. Consequently, though there does not seem to have been any specific monetary agreement with Shirley Green covering Anthony Lee's support, appellant had complete custody of both children until they were rescued by the police.

With regard to medical care, the evidence is undisputed. In March, 1960, appellant called a Dr. Turner to her home to treat Anthony Lee for a bronchial condition. Appellant also telephoned the doctor at various times to consult with him concerning Anthony Lee's diet and health. In early July, 1960, appellant took Anthony Lee to Dr. Turner's office where he was treated for "simple diarrhea." At this time the doctor noted the "wizened" appearance of the child and told appellant to tell the mother of the child that he should be taken to a hospital. This was not done.

On August 2, 1960, two collectors for the local gas company had occasion to go to the basement of appellant's home, and there saw the two children. Robert Lee and Anthony Lee at this time were age two years and ten months respectively. Robert Lee was in a "crib" consisting of a framework of wood, covered with a fine wire screening, including the top which was hinged. The "crib" was lined with newspaper, which was stained, apparently with feces, and crawling with roaches. Anthony Lee was lying in a bassinet and was described as having the appearance of a "small baby monkey." One collector testified to seeing roaches on Anthony Lee.

On August 5, 1960, the collectors returned to appellant's home in the company of several police officers and personnel of the Women's Bureau. At this time, Anthony Lee was upstairs in the dining room in the bassinet, but Robert Lee was still downstairs in his "crib." The officers removed the children to the D. C. General Hospital where Anthony Lee was diagnosed as suffering from severe malnutrition and lesions over large portions of his body, apparently caused by severe diaper rash. Following admission, he was fed repeatedly, apparently with no difficulty, and was described as being very hungry. His death, 34 hours after admission, was attributed without dispute to malnutrition. At birth, Anthony Lee weighed six pounds, fifteen ounces—at death at age ten months, he weighed seven pounds, thirteen ounces. Normal weight at this age would have been approximately 14 pounds.

Appellant argues that nothing in the evidence establishes that she failed to provide food to Anthony Lee. She cites her own testimony and the testimony of a lodger, Mr. Wills, that she did in fact feed the baby regularly. At trial, the defense made repeated attempts to extract from the medical witnesses opinions that the jaundice, or the condition which caused it, might have prevented the baby from assimilating food. The doctors conceded this was possible but not probable since the autopsy revealed no condition which would support the defense theory. It was also shown by the disinterested medical witnesses that the child had no difficulty in ingesting food immediately after birth, and that Anthony Lee, in the last hours before his death, was able to take several bottles, apparently without difficulty, and seemed very hungry. This evidence, combined with the absence of any physical cause for nonassimilation, taken in the context of the condition in which these children were kept, presents a jury question on the feeding issue.

Moreover, there is substantial evidence from which the jury could have found that appellant failed to obtain proper medical care for the child. Appellant relies upon the evidence showing that on one occasion she summoned a doctor for the child, on another took the child to the doctor's office, and that she telephoned the doctor on several occasions about the baby's formula. However, the last time a doctor saw the child was a month before his death, and appellant admitted that on that occasion the doctor recommended hospitalization. Appellant did not hospitalize the child, nor did she take any other steps to obtain medical care in the last crucial month. Thus, there was sufficient evidence to go to the jury on the issue of medical care, as well as failure to feed.

Appellant also takes exception to the failure of the trial court to charge that the jury must find beyond a reasonable doubt, as an element of the crime, that appellant was under a legal duty to supply food and necessities to Anthony Lee. Appellant's attorney did not object to the failure to give this instruction, but urges here the application of Rule 52(b).

The problem of establishing the duty to take action which would preserve the life of another has not often arisen in the case law of this country. The most commonly cited statement of the rule is found in People v. Beardsley.

"The law recognizes that under some circumstances the omission of a duty owed by one individual to another, where such omission results in the death of the one to whom the duty is owing, will make the other chargeable with manslaughter. * * * This rule of law is always based upon the proposition that the duty neglected must be a legal duty, and not a mere moral obligation. It must be a duty imposed by law or by contract, and the omission to perform the duty must be the immediate and direct cause of death. * * *"

There are at least four situations in which the failure to act may constitute breach of a legal duty. One can be held criminally liable:

first, where a statute imposes a duty to care for another; second, where one stands in a certain status relationship to another; third, where one has assumed a contractual duty to care for another; and fourth, where one has voluntarily assumed the care of another and so secluded the helpless person as to prevent others from rendering aid.

It is the contention of the Government that either the third or the fourth ground is applicable here. However, it is obvious that in any of the four situations, there are critical issues of fact which must be passed on by the jury—specifically in this case, whether appellant had entered into a contract with the mother for the care of Anthony Lee or, alternatively, whether she assumed the care of the child and secluded him from the care of his mother, his natural protector. On both of these issues, the evidence is in direct conflict, appellant insisting that the mother was actually living with appellant and Anthony Lee, and hence should have been taking care of the child herself, while Shirley Green testified she was living with her parents and was paying appellant to care for both children.

In spite of this conflict, the instructions given in the case failed even to suggest the necessity for finding a legal duty of care. The only reference to duty in the instructions was the reading of the indictment which charged, inter alia, that the defendants "failed to perform their legal duty." A finding of legal duty is the critical element of the crime charged and failure to instruct the jury concerning it was plain error.

Reversed and remanded.

[...]

(Citations omitted)

Why does the appellate court reverse the case? What errors did the appellate court find that occurred at the trial court? Who committed these errors? What would have to be corrected on a retrial? What large lesson does one learn about the legal system from the case?

Actus Reus: The Voluntary Act Requirement

To be held accountable, a criminal defendant must act **voluntarily** in committing a crime. According to the Model Penal Code

1. A person is not guilty of an offense unless his liability is based on conduct which includes a voluntary act or the omission to perform an act of which he is physically capable.
2. The following **are not voluntary acts**. ... a) a reflex or convulsion; b) a bodily movement during unconsciousness or sleep; c) conduct during hypnosis or resulting from hypnotic suggestion; d) a bodily movement that otherwise is not a product of the effort or determination of the actor, either conscious or habitual; ...[10]

Why is this condition important for criminal accountability, and what conduct would be potentially criminal and what not? Consider an implausible example. Suppose I have guests for dinner and a number of us are in the kitchen preparing food. Suppose I am busy chopping up a pile of vegetables with my meat cleaver (a big, heavy chopping tool) on a moderately high table. A short person is standing nearby,

10 American Law Institute Model Penal Code: Section 210.2, 1189.

watching my activity and helping out. Suddenly, I suffer an unanticipated convulsion resulting from a condition about which I had no knowledge. During the first stages of the convulsion, my arm holding the cleaver jerks downward, hits the short person in the head, splitting his skull open, and he dies as a consequence. Should I be charged with some form of homicide because of this event?

Obviously not. Why? A common answer is that because my movement was not intended, I should not be held accountable. This is mistaken. While the words "acting intentionally" are ambiguous and especially so in the law, by implicitly assuming that in the criminal law when a person acts, the person intentionally does the harmful act in question, in this case, death to another person. This is mistaken. A variety of different "criminally faulty" or "culpable" states of mind are the basis of liability and punishable, as already noted from the Model Penal Code: one may purposely, knowingly, recklessly, grossly negligently, or negligently violate the law and cause harm to others, whether it is an assault or actual killing, and acting with some of these states of mind would or could be the basis of criminal liability depending on the offense.

An answer that brings us closer to a correct view is that to be held accountable in the criminal law, one must have a "guilty mind." This vague idea will be described further below, but it at least suggests that at the time of acting to be found guilty of a crime and punished, a person must exhibit some *faulty* or *culpable* state of mind recognized by the criminal law. Involuntary acts, bodily movements that are not consciously willed, do not necessarily reveal one's state of mind, and they do not show the appropriate (or any) criminal fault needed for conviction. Note what the Model Penal Code (above) rules out as possible bases of a crime: "reflexes, convulsions, a mere bodily movement, movement during sleep or unconsciousness, conduct from hypnotic suggestion, or a movement that is *not the 'product of the effort or determination of the actor.'*" When one of these obtains, a person does not consciously will a bodily movement and may or may not have some appropriate culpable state of mind (or at least one cannot be sure about the state of mind), and there is no obvious connection between the actor's state of mind and subsequent action.

A much better answer to our question is that the voluntary act requirement serves two purposes. First, a voluntary act provides the possibility of a "window" into a person's mind at the time of acting because the actor *chose* to carry out the act; and second, it also requires that the actor's mind must be in control of their bodily movements or their actions; they must be consciously willed. But what do these answers point to?

One is that a person must *choose* to act as he or she did and the actor's bodily movement must be the product or outcome of what the actor chose to do. However, in choosing, *what was the actor's state of mind* in making the choice? When one acts voluntarily, one makes a choice. Was the actor's choice one that reveals a state of mind that is culpable and punishable by the law for the act committed? Did he or she purposely, knowingly, recklessly, or grossly negligently act? Or was it an accident, a choice made in excusable ignorance that is recognized in the criminal law, or some other state of mind that is not criminally culpable?

The voluntary act requirement is merely a necessary background condition of criminal responsibility. As the preceding paragraph shows, just because a person has acted voluntarily and violated a legal duty, this is not sufficient for a finding of criminal liability.

Mens Rea, or Guilty Mind

To be held criminally accountable, one must also exhibit the appropriate "guilty mind." This has two components. In order to be held accountable for a specific crime, a person must exhibit (or have) a) "general *mens rea*," or the minimal requirements needed for understanding the requirements of the law and the needed ability to conform one's conduct to it; and b) the state of mind that is part of the definition of the crime charged, or "specific *mens rea*."

General *Mens Rea*

General *mens rea* characterizes the difference between a **responsible versus a non-responsible** person. A person who lacks general *mens rea* is absolved from criminal responsibility because his or her **deficiencies** of **temperament, personality**, or **maturity** distinguish them so utterly from the rest of us that we do not expect them to comply with the law. (After the voluntary act condition, this is a second background condition that must obtain for legal responsibility.) All adult human beings are **rebuttably presumed** to be responsible persons in this sense. However, this presumption can be rebutted or overcome by evidence in a specific case by the presentation of evidence.

A person may fail to exhibit general *mens rea* because the person is found to be *insane* or to lack the minimal mental capacities of an adult to be fairly held accountable, to appreciate the consequences of his or her action, or to deliberate properly about it. There are different accounts of legal insanity that we consider in Chapter 2, but the general idea expressed by a version of the Model Penal Code is, "A person is not responsible for criminal conduct if at the time of such conduct as a result of mental disease or defect he lacks substantial capacity either to appreciate the criminality of his conduct or to conform his conduct to the requirements of law."[11]

The obvious idea is that even an adult may not be held criminally accountable if that person lacks substantial capacities to appreciate the criminality of what he or she did or lacks the ability to abide by the law. However, every adult is presumed to have the minimal conditions to understand the law and conform to its requirements. If a particular defendant wants to plead differently, he or she must raise the issue and then, depending upon the law in different jurisdictions, there are different approaches to adjudicating the issue.

With regard to infancy, clearly children below a certain age are simply incapable of understanding or appreciating that what they might do could harm another or violate a law. In the United States, the lower age for charging a child with a crime varies considerably. The Model Penal Code states, "A person shall not be tried for or convicted of an offense if: at the time of the conduct charged to constitute the offense he was less than sixteen years of age [in which case the Juvenile Court shall have exclusive jurisdiction] ..."[12] However, a variety of states have much lower ages at which children can be charged with a crime. Thirty-three of 51 jurisdictions have no lowest age for holding a person criminally accountable. Most of the 18 other jurisdictions set the lowest age for a child to be charged with a crime at 10 years of age. The state of Florida with no lowest age for criminal responsibility charged one 6-year-old with misdemeanor battery when she lashed out as a result of a sleep disorder. The policeman who arrested and

---

11 *Ibid.*, 1204.

12 *Ibid.*, 1209.

cuffed her was fired for his efforts.[13] Children 16 years old, but less than 18, typically would be addressed by the Juvenile System, but some at that age may be charged as adults (this separate "legal system" is sufficiently self-contained and complicated that I do not consider it here).

Consequently, if an adult lacks the minimal mental capacities needed to hold a child criminally accountable, he or she would not be held accountable for a crime. For example, one might have a 30-year-old, 6-foot-5-inch neighbor weighing 250 pounds who has the mental capacities of a 3-year old. Depending upon the legal jurisdiction, if that person were to harm another, he likely could not be held accountable for a crime, despite his age and size, because he would lack the appropriate mental capacity.

Specific *Mens Rea*

Specific *mens rea* refers to various mental state terms that define a crime. Thus, if a person exhibits the state of mind needed to be held accountable for a specific crime, and all other conditions of criminal liability are satisfied, including proof beyond a reasonable doubt, the person could be held criminally accountable for that crime. (Note the mental state terms in the definition of several crimes that follow.) Larceny is "the appropriation of another's property **knowing** it is not one's own with the **intent** to deprive the owner of it." Receiving stolen goods is "receiving goods from another person **knowing** that they have been stolen." Manslaughter is "killing another person by an act done with the **awareness of a substantial and unjustifiable risk** of doing so."

Consider some examples of persons who satisfy all the requirements for particular crimes, and for comparison, some who lack them. Imagine the following scenarios.

A. Standard cases of criminal responsibility: Standard illegal, voluntary act with **full capacity responsibility** (***mens rea*** in the general sense) and **standard specific *mens rea***(s).

   - Malicious Manny, with full mental capacities, lies in wait and **purposely** kills another with **malice aforethought** (which, in many jurisdictions, would be murder in the first degree).
   - Larcenous Larry, with full mental capacities, takes the property of another **knowing** it is not one's own with the **intent** to deprive the owner of it (a typical account of larceny).
   - Reckless Ruth, with full mental capacities, acts in such a way that she kills another with the **awareness** that such an act creates **a substantial and unjustifiable risk** of the death of others (in many jurisdictions, this would be manslaughter).

B. Example in which *mens rea* in a specific sense is not satisfied:

   - Inattentive Ike, with full mental capacities, **voluntarily**, but mistakenly, picks up a portable computer belonging to another and is charged with **larceny**. His defense: he did not **know** the computer belonged to someone else and did not **intend** to deprive him of it. In short, he does not have ***mens rea*** in the **specific sense** required of the particular crime of larceny.

C. Example in which the voluntary act requirement is not satisfied:

   - Epileptic Edith, with full mental capacities, suffers a first-time **epileptic seizure** while holding a knife and kills a nearby person as a result of a convulsion from the epilepsy.

---

13 John Donovan (September 24, 2019). How young is too young to be arrested? How Stuff Works. https://people.howstuffworks.com/too-young-to-be-arrested.htm.

- Spastic Saul, with full mental capacities, **suffers a spasm** while holding a knife and kills another. He was fully aware of what his body was doing, but **could not control it** and does not engage in the behavior purposely, knowingly, recklessly, or negligently.
- Spastic Evil Ed, with full mental capacities, **suffers a spasm** while holding a knife and kills another. He was fully aware of what his body was doing, could not control it, but strongly desires that the person die.

D. Example in which the **illegal act** requirement might not be satisfied: *Jones v. U.S.*

E. Example in which, because a person is **insane**, ***mens rea* in the general sense** is not satisfied (the person has inadequate ***capacity responsibility***).

- Delusional Debbie, because of extreme delusion, believes that Sam is the devil in disguise and voluntarily and intentionally kills him.

Next, two English cases raise an interesting issue about the criminal law and provide some important comparisons between the US and UK criminal law regarding specific *mens rea*. Suppose a person commits a crime, such as stealing a gas meter from a house, but when doing this, the action releases a gaseous substance that sickens people living upstairs. Does the fact that the defendant maliciously stole the meter imply that he also maliciously gassed the upstairs residents? This is the issue in the next case.

Regina v. Cunningham

Court of Criminal Appeal, 1957

41 Crim. App. R. 155, [1957]

Byrne, J., read the following judgment. The appellant was convicted at Leeds Assizes upon an indictment framed under section 23 of the Offences against the Person Act, 1861, which charged that he unlawfully and maliciously caused to be taken by Sarah Wade a certain noxious thing, namely, coal gas, so as thereby to endanger the life of the said Sarah Wade.

The facts were that the appellant was engaged to be married and his prospective mother-in-law was the tenant of a house, No. 7 A, Bakes Street, Bradford, which was unoccupied, but which was to be occupied by the appellant after his marriage. Mrs. Wade and her husband, an elderly couple, lived in the house next door. At one time the two houses had been one, but when the building was converted into two houses a wall had been erected to divide the cellars of the two houses, and that wall was composed of rubble loosely cemented.

On the evening of January 17, 1957, the appellant went to the cellar of No. 7 A, Bakes Street, wrenched the gas meter from the gas pipes and stole it, together with its contents, and in a second indictment he was charged with the larceny of the gas meter and its contents. To that indictment he pleaded guilty and was sentenced to six months' imprisonment. In respect of that matter, he does not appeal.

The facts were not really in dispute, and in a statement to a police officer the appellant said: "All right, I will tell you. I was short of money. I had been off work for three days, I got eight shillings from the gas meter. I tore it off the wall and threw it away." Although there was a stop tap within two feet of the meter the appellant did not turn off the gas, with the result that a very considerable volume of gas escaped, some of which seeped through the wall of the cellar and partially asphyxiated Mrs. Wade, who was asleep in her bedroom next door, with the result that her life was endangered.

At the close of the case for the prosecution, Mr. Brodie, who appeared for the appellant at the trial and who has appeared for him again in this court, submitted that there was no case to go to the jury, but the judge, quite rightly in our opinion, rejected this submission. The appellant did not give evidence.

The act of the appellant was clearly unlawful and therefore the real question for the jury was whether it was also malicious within the meaning of section 23 of the Offences against the Person Act, 1861.

Before this court Mr. Brodie has taken three points, all dependent upon the construction of that section. Section 23 provides:

> "Whosoever shall unlawfully and maliciously administer to or cause to be administered to or taken by any other person any poison or other destructive or noxious thing, so as thereby to endanger the life of such person, or so as thereby to inflict upon such person any grievous bodily harm, shall be guilty of felony ..."

Mr. Brodie argued, first, that mens rea of some kind is necessary. Secondly, that the nature of the mens rea required is that the appellant must intend to do the particular kind of harm that was done, or, alternatively that he must foresee that that harm may occur yet nevertheless continue recklessly to do the act. Thirdly, that the judge misdirected the jury as to the meaning of the word "maliciously." ...

... [T]he following principle was propounded by the late Professor C.S. Kenny in the first edition of his Outlines of Criminal Law published in 1902 and repeated at p. 186 of the 16th edition edited by Mr. J.W. Cecil Turner and published in 1952:

> "In any statutory definition of a crime, malice must be taken not in the old vague sense of wickedness in general but as requiring either (1) an actual intention to do the particular kind of harm that in fact was done; or (2) recklessness as to whether such harm should occur or not (i.e., the accused has foreseen that the particular kind of harm might be done and yet has gone on to take the risk of it). It is neither limited to nor does it indeed require any ill will towards the person injured."

The same principle is repeated by Mr. Turner in his 20th edition of Russell on Crime at p. 1592.

We think that this is an accurate statement of the law. It derives some support from the judgments of Lord Coleridge, C.J., and Blackburn, J., in Pembliton's case. In our opinion the word "maliciously" in a statutory crime postulates foresight of consequence.

In his summing up Oliver, J., directed the jury as follows:

> "You will observe that there is nothing there about 'with intention that that person should take it.' He has not got to intend that it should be taken: it is sufficient that by his unlawful and malicious act he causes it to be taken. What you have to decide here, then, is whether, when he loosed that frightful cloud of coal gas into the house which he shared with this old lady, he caused her to take it by his unlawful and malicious action. 'Unlawful' does not need any definition. It is something forbidden by law. What about 'malicious'? 'Malicious' for this purpose means wicked—something which he has no business to do and perfectly well knows it. 'Wicked' is as good a definition as any other which you would get."

"The facts which face you (and they are uncontradicted and undisputed; the prisoner has not gone into the box to seek to give any particular explanation) are these. Living in the house, which was now two houses but which had once been one and had been rather roughly divided, the prisoner quite deliberately, intending to steal the money that was in the meter … broke the gas meter away from the supply pipes and thus released the main supply of gas at large into that house. When he did that he knew that this old lady and her husband were living next door to him. The gas meter was in a cellar. The wall which divided his cellar from the cellar next door was a kind of honeycomb wall through which gas could very well go, so that when he loosed that cloud of gas into that place he must have known perfectly well that gas would percolate all over the house. If it were part of this offence—which it is not—that he intended to poison the old lady, I should have left it to you to decide, and I should have told you that there was evidence on which you could find that he intended that, since he did an action which he must have known would result in that. As I have already told you, it is not necessary to prove that he intended to do it; it is quite enough that what he did was done unlawfully and maliciously."

With the utmost respect to the judge, we think it is incorrect to say that the word "malicious" in a statutory offence merely means wicked. We think the judge was, in effect, telling the jury that if they were satisfied that the appellant acted wickedly—and he had clearly acted wickedly in stealing the gas meter and its contents—they ought to find that he had acted maliciously in causing the gas to be taken by Mrs. Wade so as thereby to endanger her life.

In our view, it should have been left to the jury to decide whether, even if the appellant did not intend the injury to Mrs. Wade, he foresaw that the removal of the gas meter might cause injury to someone but nevertheless removed it. We are unable to say that a reasonable jury, properly directed as to the meaning of the word "maliciously" in the context of section 23, would without doubt have convicted.

In these circumstances this court has no alternative but to allow the appeal and quash the conviction.

Appeal allowed.

Mr. Cunningham was charged with two different crimes. The first was a charge of larceny or theft of the gas meter and its monetary contents. The second charge was for maliciously gassing Mrs. Wade. The trial judge says that under this statute, Mr. Cunningham had to act maliciously. But the trial judge also says acting maliciously means he acted "wickedly." If he acted wickedly in stealing the meter, he also acted wickedly in gassing Mrs. Wade.

The judge made several errors. First, he substituted a word from common moral use, *wickedly*, for a technical legal word, *maliciously*. Second, he did not permit defendant Cunningham to present his objections to the jury; namely, to argue at a minimum that this was the wrong interpretation of "malicious." Third, he failed to follow the language of the law with his linguistic substitution. And fourth, he transferred the language for theft, "maliciously" stealing the meter, to a causal consequence of breaking the gas line when stealing the meter. He assumed because the first action was malicious, so was the consequence of the theft without requiring proof for all the elements of the second act, maliciously gassing Mrs. Wade. The court finds this to be an error as the "**transference of specific *mens rea* from**

one act in committing a crime to a causal consequence of the first act," or the transference of *mens rea* for short. (Such transference might be permitted in other jurisdictions, but one should regard this of concern.) What are the consequences of permitting the trial court's reasoning versus the appellate court's approach of requiring that the evidence for the two events (stealing the gas meter and gassing Mrs. Wade) be independently established? What would be some legal consequences if such transference were generally permitted? Finally, in an effort to clean up the trial court's rulings, the appellate court suggests two different interpretations one might have for better addressing the consequences of the first illegal act. What are their solutions?

The next case, *Regina v. Faulkner*, raises a similar issue.

Regina v. Faulkner

13 Cox Crim. Cas. 550 (1877)

Defendant was a sailor aboard the ship Zemindar. While on the high seas he went to the forecastle hold to steal some rum and lit a match in order to see better in the dark hold. Some of the rum caught fire and the fire spread, injuring him and completely destroying the ship. He was convicted by a jury of violating the Malicious Damage Act by maliciously setting fire to the ship (arson) upon an instruction by the judge that "although the prisoner had no actual intention of burning the vessel, still, if they found he was engaged in stealing the rum, and that the fire took place in the manner above stated, they ought to find him guilty." In stating the case for the Court for Crown Cases Reserved, the judge observed: "It was conceded that the prisoner had no actual intention of burning the vessel, and was not asked to leave any question to the jury as to the prisoner's knowing the probable consequences of his act, or as to his reckless conduct." It was held that the conviction for arson of the ship should be quashed. Portions of the opinions of two of the judges follow.

Barry, J. "A very broad proposition has been contended for by the Crown, namely, that if, while a person is engaged in committing a felony, or, having committed it, is endeavouring to conceal his act, or prevent or spoil waste consequent on that act, he accidentally does some collateral act, which if done willfully would be another felony either at common law or by statute, he is guilty of the latter felony. I am by no means anxious to throw any doubt upon, or limit in any way, the legal responsibility of those who engage in the commission of felony, or acts mala in se; but I am not prepared without more consideration to give my assent to so wide a proposition. I shall not pronounce any opinion, as I shall consider myself bound for the purpose of this case by the authority of Reg. v. Pembliton. That case must be taken as deciding that to constitute an offence under the Malicious Injuries to Property Act, sect. 51, the act done must be in fact intentional and willful, although the intention and will may (perhaps) be held to exist in, or be proved by, the fact that the accused knew that the injury would be the probable result of his unlawful act, and yet did the act reckless of such consequences. The present indictment charges the offence to be under the 42nd section of the same Act, and it is not disputed that the same construction must be applied to both sections. The jury were, in fact, directed to give a verdict of guilty upon the simple ground that the firing of the ship, though accidental, was caused by an act done in the course of, or immediately consequent upon, a felonious operation, and no question of the prisoner's malice, constructive or otherwise, was left to the jury. I am of opinion that, according to Reg. v. Pembliton, that direction was erroneous, and that the conviction should be quashed."

Fitzgerald, J. "I concur in opinion with my brother Barry, and for the reasons he has given, that the direction of the learned judge cannot be sustained in law, and that therefore the conviction should be quashed. Counsel for the prosecution in effect insisted that the defendant, being engaged in the commission of, or in an attempt to commit a felony, was criminally responsible for every result that was occasioned thereby, even though it was not a probable consequence of his act or such as he could have reasonably foreseen or intended. No authority has been cited for a proposition so extensive, and I am of opinion that it is not warranted by law."

(Citations omitted)

What do these two cases reveal about the United Kingdom's criminal law? First, *Faulkner* poses issues similar to those in *Cunningham*. In both, the primary crime, theft of liquor and theft of a gas meter, respectively, led to further causal consequences that could also be crimes. Both UK courts held that the specific *mens rea* of the first crime did not *automatically* "transfer" to a causal effect of the first crime. Whether or not the causal consequence in each case was a crime had to be established independently of proof of the original crime. The original crime and its consequence had to be *individuated* from each other, treated individually; proof of each violation had to be established separately and the jury needed to consider evidence of the consequential effect of the original crime separately. The fire that destroyed the ship in *Faulkner* might have been an "accident," with no evidence of a specific *mens rea* on Faulkner's part to burn the ship. He and his lawyers must have the opportunity to present this point to the jury and expect an independent finding of arson. The trial judge denied this chance, thus erring in his ruling.

In contrast to these UK decisions, many jurisdictions in the United States have so-called "felony murder" rules: if a person is engaged in committing a crime classified as a felony and someone dies as a causal consequence, even if the death was not intended or desired, the defendant may be convicted for murder in addition to the original offense. For instance, if two of us rob a bank and during the robbery, my gun goes off, accidentally resulting in the death of a bystander in the bank, you and I would likely both be charged with bank robbery and with murder because the death occurred during the robbery. This does invite consideration of some other implausible circumstances, such as a bank guard shooting at the robbers and killing an employee or customer accidentally. Or suppose a guard fired a warning shot into the air that ricocheted and killed a customer. An older conception of felony murder in California permitted a person to be convicted of felony murder, if during the commission of a felony, the victim died, even though the defendant did "not intend to kill a person," the defendant did not know a homicide occurred or the killing was an accident.[14] Felony murder doctrines in effect extend the scope of murder, so that individuals that do not directly cause the murder can be charged with it.

The contrast with the UK cases should be clear; under the older California law, if one were engaged in a felony and someone died, one could be convicted of murder without an independent legal assessment

---

14 *People v. Stamp*, 2 Cal. App. 3d 203 (1969).

of the culpability conditions of murder. Participation in the felony was sufficient in many cases for a conviction of murder. This likely remains the law in many jurisdictions.

A nice example of an older felony murder is exhibited by *People v. Stamp*, a 1969 California murder case. Mr. Stamp and others robbed Mr. Honeyman's business. At one point he led Honeyman from his office and told him to lie on the floor for 10 minutes after he left the business. Being obese with a history of heart disease, shortly after Stamp left the premises, Honeyman began experiencing chest pain, collapsed, was taken to the hospital, and died there. Even though Stamp and codefendants were not present and did not intend to kill Honeyman, and even though Honeyman had a number of medical conditions that made him more vulnerable to heart attacks, Stamp was convicted of first-degree murder that was upheld on appeal. You should recall this case when we consider the "eggshell skull" cases in the tort law. Honeyman had physical conditions that made him particularly vulnerable to a heart attack when he was under pressure.

People v. Stamp

Court of Appeal, Second District, Division 3, California.

82 Cal. Rptr. 598 (1969)

Opinion: COBEY, Associate Justice.

These are appeals by Jonathan Earl Stamp, Michael John Koory and Billy Dean Lehman, following jury verdicts of guilty of robbery and murder, both in the first degree. Each man was given a life sentence on the murder charge together with the time prescribed by law on the robbery count.

Defendants appeal their conviction of the murder of Carl Honeyman who, suffering from a heart disease, died between 15 and 20 minutes after Koory and Stamp held up his business, the General Amusement Company, on October 26, 1965, at 10:45 a.m. Lehman, the driver of the getaway car, was apprehended a few minutes after the robbery; several weeks later Stamp was arrested in Ohio and Koory in Nebraska.

Broadly stated, the grounds of this appeal are: (1) insufficiency of the evidence on the causation of Honeyman's death; (2) inapplicability of the felony-murder rule to this case; (3) errors in the choice of instructions given and refused; and (4) erroneous admission in evidence of the extrajudicial confessions of Stamp and Koory and the incriminating statement of Lehman.

On this appeal appellants primarily rely upon their position that the felony-murder doctrine should not have been applied in this case due to the unforeseeability of Honeyman's death.

THE FACTS

Defendants Koory and Stamp, armed with a gun and a blackjack, entered the rear of the building housing the offices of General Amusement Company, ordered the employees they found there to go to the front of the premises, where the two secretaries were working. Stamp, the one with the gun, then went into the office of Carl Honeyman, the owner and manager. Thereupon Honeyman, looking very frightened and pale, emerged from the office in a "kind of hurry." He was apparently propelled by Stamp who had hold of him by an elbow.

The robbery victims were required to lie down on the floor while the robbers took the money and fled out the back door. As the robbers, who had been on the premises 10 to 15 minutes, were leaving, they told the victims to remain on the floor for five minutes so that no one would "get hurt."

Honeyman, who had been lying next to the counter, had to use it to steady himself in getting up off the floor. Still pale, he was short of breath, sucking air, and pounding and rubbing his chest. As he walked down the hall, in an unsteady manner, still breathing hard and rubbing his chest, he said he was having trouble "keeping the pounding down inside" and that his heart was "pumping too fast for him." A few minutes later, although still looking very upset, shaking, wiping his forehead and rubbing his chest, he was able to walk in a steady manner into an employee's office. When the police arrived, almost immediately thereafter, he told them he was not feeling very well and that he had a pain in his chest. About two minutes later, which was 15 to 20 minutes after the robbery had occurred, he collapsed on the floor. At 11:25 he was pronounced dead on arrival at the hospital. The coroner's report listed the immediate cause of death as heart attack.

The employees noted that during the hours before the robbery Honeyman had appeared to be in normal health and good spirits. The victim was an obese, sixty-year-old man, with a history of heart disease, who was under a great deal of pressure due to the intensely competitive nature of his business. Additionally, he did not take good care of his heart.

Three doctors, including the autopsy surgeon, Honeyman's physician, and a professor of cardiology from U.C.L.A., testified that although Honeyman had an advanced case of atherosclerosis, a progressive and ultimately fatal disease, there must have been some immediate upset to his system which precipitated the attack. It was their conclusion in response to a hypothetical question that but for the robbery there would have been no fatal seizure at that time. The fright induced by the robbery was too much of a shock to Honeyman's system. There was opposing expert testimony to the effect that it could not be said with reasonable medical certainty that fright could ever be fatal.

SUFFICIENCY OF THE EVIDENCE RE CAUSATION

Appellants' contention that the evidence was insufficient to prove that the robbery factually caused Honeyman's death is without merit. The test on review is whether there is substantial evidence to uphold the judgment of the trial court, and in so deciding this court must assume in the case of a jury trial the existence of every fact in favor of the verdict which the jury could reasonably have deduced from the evidence. … A review of the facts as outlined above shows that there was substantial evidence of the robbery itself, that appellants were the robbers, and that but for the robbery the victim would not have experienced the fright which brought on the fatal heart attack.[2]

APPLICATION OF THE FELONY-MURDER RULE

Appellants' contention that the felony-murder rule is inapplicable to the facts of this case is also without merit. Under the felony-murder rule of section 189 of the Penal Code, a killing committed in either the perpetration of or an attempt to perpetrate robbery is murder of the first degree. This is true whether the killing is wilfull, deliberate and premeditated, or merely accidental or unintentional, and whether or not the killing is planned as a part of the commission of the robbery […]

The doctrine presumes malice aforethought on the basis of the commission of a felony inherently dangerous to human life. … This rule is a rule of substantive law in California and not merely an evidentiary shortcut to finding malice as it withdraws from the jury the requirement that they find either express malice or the implied malice which is manifested in an intent to kill. … Under this rule no intentional act is necessary other than the attempt to or the actual commission of the robbery itself. When a robber enters a place with a deadly weapon with the intent to commit robbery, malice is shown by the nature of the crime. …

There is no requirement that the killing occur, "while committing" or "while engaged in" the felony, or that the killing be "a part of" the felony, other than that the few acts be a part of one continuous transaction. … Thus the homicide need not have been committed "to perpetrate" the felony. There need be no technical inquiry as to whether there has been a completion or abandonment of or desistence from the robbery before the homicide itself was completed. (People v. Chavez)

The doctrine is **not limited to those deaths which are foreseeable**. … Rather a felon is **held strictly liable for All killings committed by him or his accomplices in the course of the felony.** … As long as the homicide is **the direct causal result of the robbery the felony-murder rule applies whether or not the death was a natural or probable consequence** of the robbery. So long as a victim's **predisposing physical condition, regardless of its cause, is not the Only substantial factor bringing about his death, that condition**, and the robber's ignorance of it, **in no way destroys the robber's criminal responsibility for the death. … So long as life is shortened as a result of the felonious act, it does not matter that the victim might have died soon anyway. … In this respect, the robber takes his victim as he finds him.** […]

(Citations omitted)

A major concern with felony murder laws is that they can convert what could be accidental deaths into first-degree murder without a showing of typical specific *mens rea* for murder. (I am not claiming that this is an issue in *Stamp* because it's not.) Felony murder does undermine the idea that the criminal law should allocate just punishment proportional to wrongdoing, making the punishment quite disproportionate to the crime of murder under felony-murder laws. Is another concern that the crime aimed at and committed, namely robbery, and the outcome to Honeyman (death) are quite different from one another?

Under California's quite recently passed felony murder law, to be found guilty of murder, a defendant may be found guilty if he or she "directly kills a person in the commission of a felony, aids and abets the killing or is a major participant in the killing, or the victim was a peace officer."[15] This ties the murder portion of the conviction more closely to defendant's actions that plausibly contribute to the death.[16]

15 *Ibid.*

16 Shouse California Law Group. California's new felony murder laws. Located at https://www.shouselaw.com/ca/defense/laws/felony-murder-rule/#:~:text=Under%20the%20new%20felony%20murder%20law%2C%20a%20person,principle%20set%20forth%20under%20Penal%20Code%2031%20PC.

Strict Liability in the Criminal Law

Up to this point, we have considered the importance of specific *mens rea* that defines a particular crime, and this is quite important. However, there is a small class of crimes for which a person might be punished under federal or state law that does not require a showing of specific *mens rea*; these are so-called "strict liability laws." Under these, a person may be held accountable for simply *doing the act forbidden by the law* without a prosecutor needing to show that the person did the act purposely, knowingly, recklessly, grossly negligently, or even negligently. It is enough that an alleged defendant simply did the prohibited act. For instance, if Sally works at a bar, it is illegal to sell alcohol to an underage person. If John enters her bar and orders a beer and she sells it to him, if he is underage, she has violated the law, even if she carefully reviewed his identification, asked for a second form of identification, and he looks the age of a person above the age of majority. However, if John's uncle, employed by the Alcoholic Beverage Commission, responsible for ensuring that bars do not sell alcohol to underaged persons, happens to be in the bar and sees Sally serving John, whom he knows to be underage, he can arrest both people. Sally violates the law for selling alcohol to an underage person, and John violates the law as an underage person for purchasing it. Both would be punished for their actions.

A good history of some of these laws is provided by the *Morrisette* case. Such laws have been directed at tavern owners who serve alcohol to already inebriated customers, the owners of unsafe tenement buildings, those who commit statutory rape, businesses that sell adulterated drugs, people that sell illegal drugs without a proper form from the Internal Revenue Service, and businesses that sell spoiled or diseased food, *inter alia*.

We will consider rationales for these laws, especially after reading *Morrisette*, but these laws strike knowledgeable people as inconsistent with core crimes that require a showing of a specific *mens rea*, because they do not require a showing of criminal culpability or fault like the vast majority of crimes. Reconsider Sally's selling alcohol to underage John. Even if Sally does not sell him alcohol purposely because he is underage, knowing that he is underage, or is reckless or even negligent in reviewing his identification documents, the *mere act* of taking his money and delivering alcohol to him is a criminal violation. Sally's simple act of selling John alcohol is sufficient for a criminal violation and punishable.

Before considering the extensive and excellent case of *U.S. v. Morrisette*, we first have two cases decided about the same time concerning individuals who a) sold illegal drugs, but not in pursuance of an order on a form issued by the IRS required for such sales, or b) sold pharmaceutical that were mislabeled. For actually selling illegal drugs, a prosecutor likely would have had to show that the defendant had knowledge that the drugs were illegal, which sometimes might be difficult to establish. However, to hold defendants accountable for selling illegal drugs without the needed IRS form, they can be held criminally accountable even if they did not know the drugs were illegal.

United States v. Balint

U.S. Supreme Court.

258 U.S. 250 (1922)

This is a writ of error to the District Court under the Criminal Appeals Act of March 2, 1907. Defendants in error were indicted for a violation of the Narcotic Act of December 17, 1914. The indictment charged them with unlawfully selling to another a certain amount of a derivative of opium and a certain amount of a derivative of coca leaves, not in pursuance of any written order on a form issued in blank for that purpose by the Commissioner of Internal Revenue, contrary to the provisions of section 2 of the act. The defendants demurred to the indictment on the ground that it failed to charge that they had sold the inhibited drugs knowing them to be such. The statute does not make such knowledge an element of the offense. The District Court sustained the demurrer and quashed the indictment. The correctness of this ruling is the question before us.

While the general rule at common law was that the scienter [knowledge] was a necessary element in the indictment and proof of every crime, and this was followed in regard to statutory crimes even where the statutory definition did not in terms include it (Reg v. Sleep,), there has been a modification of this view in respect to prosecutions under statutes the purpose of which would be obstructed by such a requirement. It is a question of legislative intent to be construed by the court. It has been objected that punishment of a person for an act in violation of law when ignorant of the facts making it so, is an absence of due process of law. But that objection is considered and overruled in ShevlinCarpenter Co. v. Minnesota, in which it was held that in the prohibition or punishment of particular acts, the state may in the maintenance of a public policy provide "that he who shall do them shall do them at his peril and will not be heard to plead in defense good faith or ignorance." Many instances of this are to be found in regulatory measures in the exercise of what is called the police power where the emphasis of the statute is evidently upon achievement of some social betterment rather than the punishment of the crimes as in cases of mala in se. Commonwealth v. Mixer. So, too, in the collection of taxes, the importance to the public of their collection leads the Legislature to impose on the taxpayer the burden of finding out the facts upon which his liability to pay depends and meeting it at the peril of punishment. Again, where one deals with others and his mere negligence may be dangerous to them, as in selling diseased food or poison, the policy of the law may, in order to stimulate proper care, require the punishment of the negligent person though he be ignorant of the noxious character of what he sells. Hobbs v. Winchester Corporation (1910).

The question before us, therefore, is one of the construction of the statute and of inference of the intent of Congress. The Narcotic Act has been held by this court to be a taxing act with the incidental purpose of minimizing the spread of addiction to the use of poisonous and demoralizing drugs.

Section 2 of the Narcotic Act (38 Stat. 786) we give in part in the margin.[1] It is evident from a reading of it that the emphasis of the section is in securing a close supervision of the business of dealing in these dangerous drugs by the taxing officers of the Government and that it merely uses a criminal penalty to secure recorded evidence of the disposition of such drugs as a means of taxing and restraining the traffic. Its manifest purpose is to require every person dealing in drugs to ascertain at his peril whether that which he sells comes within the inhibition of the statute, and if he sells the inhibited drug in ignorance of its character, to penalize him. Congress weighed the possible injustice of subjecting an innocent seller to a penalty against the evil of exposing innocent purchasers to danger from the drug, and concluded that the latter was the result preferably to be avoided. Doubtless considerations as to the opportunity of the seller to find out the fact and the difficulty of proof of knowledge contributed to this conclusion. We think the demurrer to the indictment should have been overruled. [Defendant may be prosecuted for this offense.]

Judgment reversed.

(Citations omitted)

[…]

[1] Part of § 2 of the Narcotic Act … "Sec. 2. It shall be unlawful for any person to sell, barter, exchange, or give away any of the aforesaid drugs except in pursuance of a written order of the person to whom such article is sold, bartered, exchanged, or given, on a form to be issued in blank for that purpose by the Commissioner of Internal Revenue. Every person who shall accept any such order, and in pursuance thereof shall sell, barter, exchange, or give away any of the aforesaid drugs, shall preserve such order for a period of two years in such a way as to be readily accessible to inspection by any officer, agent, or employee of the Treasury Department duly authorized for that purpose, and the state, territorial, district, municipal, and insular officials named in section five of this and insular officials named in section five of this provided to any other person for any of the aforesaid drugs shall, at or before the time of giving such order, make or cause to be made a duplicate thereof on a form to be issued in blank for that purpose by the Commissioner of Internal Revenue, and in case of the acceptance of such order, shall preserve such duplicate for said period of two years in such a way as to be readily accessible to inspection by the officers, agents, employees, and officials hereinbefore mentioned."

United States v. Dotterweich

Supreme Court of the United States

320 U.S. 277 (1943)

Opinion: Mr. Justice FRANKFURTER delivered the opinion of the Court.

This was a prosecution begun by two informations, consolidated for trial, charging Buffalo Pharmacal Company, Inc., and Dotterweich, its president and general manager, with violations of the Act of Congress of June 25, 1938… known as the Federal Food, Drug, and Cosmetic Act. The Company, a jobber in drugs, purchased them from their manufacturers and shipped them, **repacked under its own label, in interstate commerce**. (No question is raised in this case regarding the implications that may properly arise when, although the manufacturer gives the jobber a guaranty, the latter through his own label makes representations.) The informations were based on § 301 of that Act, which prohibits **"The introduction or delivery for introduction into interstate commerce of any *** drug *** that is adulterated or misbranded". "Any person" violating this provision is made "guilty of a misdemeanor"**. Three counts went to the jury—two, for shipping misbranded drugs in interstate commerce, and a third, for so shipping an adulterated drug. The jury disagreed as to the corporation and found Dotterweich guilty on all three counts. …

The court below drew its conclusion not from the provisions defining the offenses on which this prosecution was based (§§ 301(a) and 303(a), but from the terms of § 303(c). That section affords immunity from prosecution if certain conditions are satisfied. The condition relevant to this case is a guaranty from the seller of the innocence of his product. [Thus]:…

"No person shall be subject to the penalties of subsection (a) of this section * * * (2) for having violated section 301(a) or (d), **if he establishes a guaranty** or undertaking signed by, and containing the name and address of, the person residing in the United States from whom he received in good faith the article, **to the effect, in case of an alleged violation of section 301(a), that such article is not adulterated or misbranded, within the meaning of this Act, designating this Act** ***."

This Circuit Court of Appeals found it "difficult to believe that Congress expected anyone except the principal to get such a guaranty, or to make the guilt of an agent depend upon whether his employer had gotten one." … And so it cut down the scope of the penalizing provisions of the Act to the restrictive view, as a matter of language and policy, it took of the relieving effect of a guaranty.

The guaranty clause cannot be read in isolation. The Food and Drugs Act of 1906 was an exertion by Congress of its power to keep impure and adulterated food and drugs out of the channels of commerce. By the Act of 1938, Congress **extended the range of its control over illicit and noxious articles and stiffened the penalties for disobedience**. The purposes of this legislation thus touch phases of the lives and health of people which, in the circumstances of modern industrialism, are largely beyond self-protection. Regard for these purposes should infuse construction of the legislation if it is to be treated as a working instrument of government and not merely as a collection of English words. … The prosecution to which **Dotterweich** was subjected is based on a now familiar type of legislation whereby penalties serve as effective means of regulation. Such **legislation dispenses with the conventional requirement for criminal conduct—awareness of some wrongdoing**. In the interest of the larger good it puts **the burden of acting at hazard upon a person otherwise innocent but standing in responsible relation to a public danger**. (United States v. Balint). … And so it is clear that shipments like those now in issue are "punished by the statute if the article is misbranded (or adulterated), and that the article may be misbranded (or adulterated) without any conscious fraud at all. It was natural enough to throw this risk on shippers with regard to the identity of their wares * * *[…]"

The statute (§ 303) makes "any person" who violates § 301(a) guilty of a "misdemeanor". It specifically defines "person" to include "corporation". § 201(e). But **the only way in which a corporation can act is through the individuals who act on its behalf** … And the historic conception of a "misdemeanor" makes all those responsible for it equally guilty, … If, then, Dotterweich is not subject to the Act, it must be solely on the ground that individuals are immune when the "person" who violates § 301(a) is a corporation, although from the point of view of action the individuals are the corporation. As a matter of legal development, it has taken time to establish criminal liability also for a corporation and not merely for its agents. … The history of federal food and drug legislation is a good illustration of the elaborate phrasing that was in earlier days deemed necessary to fasten criminal liability on corporations. Section 12 of the Food and Drugs Act of 1906, 21 U.S.C.A. § 4, provided that, "the act, omission, or failure of any officer, agent, or other person acting for or employed by any corporation, company, society, or association, within the scope of his employment or office, shall in every case be also deemed to be the act, omission, or failure of such corporation, company, society, or association as well as that of the person." … To **hold that the Act of 1938 freed all individuals**, except when proprietors, **from the culpability under which the earlier legislation had placed them is to defeat the very object of the new Act**. Nothing is clearer than that the later legislation was designed to enlarge and stiffen the penal net and not to narrow and loosen it. This purpose was unequivocally avowed by the two committees which reported the bills to the Congress. … If the 1938 Act were construed as it was below, the penalties of the law could be imposed only in the rare case where the corporation is merely an individual's alter ego. Corporations carrying on an illicit trade would be subject only to what the House Committee described as a "license fee for the conduct of an illegitimate business."[2] A corporate officer, who even with "intent to defraud or mislead" (§ 303(b), introduced adulterated or misbranded drugs into interstate commerce could not be held culpable for conduct which was indubitably outlawed by the 1906 Act. See, e.g., United States v. Mayfield, D.C. ... This argument proves too much. It is not credible that Congress should by implication have exonerated what is probably a preponderant number of persons involved in acts of disobedience—for the number of non-corporate proprietors is relatively small. …, [T]he history of the present Act, its purposes, its terms, and extended practical construction lead away from such a result once "we free our minds from the notion that criminal statutes must be construed by some artificial and conventional rule". …

The Act is concerned not with the proprietary relation to a misbranded or an adulterated drug but with its distribution. **In the case of a corporation such distribution must be accomplished, and may be furthered, by persons standing in various relations to the incorporeal proprietor**. If a guaranty immunizes shipments of course it immunizes all involved in the shipment. But simply because if there had been a guaranty it would have been received by the proprietor, whether corporate or individual, as a safeguard for the enterprise, the want of a guaranty does not cut down the scope of responsibility of all who are concerned with transactions forbidden by § 301. To be sure, that casts the risk that there is no guaranty upon all who according to settled doctrines of criminal law are responsible for the commission of a misdemeanor. To read the guaranty section, as did the court below, so as to restrict liability for penalties to the only person who normally would receive a guaranty—the proprietor—disregards the admonition that "the meaning of a sentence is to be felt rather than to be proved". … It also reads an exception to an important provision safeguarding the public welfare with a liberality which more appropriately belongs to enforcement of the central purpose of the Act.

… To speak with technical accuracy, under § 301 a corporation may commit an offense and all persons who aid and abet its commission are equally guilty. Whether an accused

shares responsibility in the business process resulting in unlawful distribution depends on the evidence produced at the trial and its submission—assuming the evidence warrants it—to the jury under appropriate guidance. The offense is committed, unless the enterprise which they are serving enjoys the immunity of a guaranty, by all who do have such a responsible share in the furtherance of the transaction which the statute outlaws, namely, to put into the stream of interstate commerce adulterated or misbranded drugs. Hardship there doubtless may be under a statute **which thus penalizes the transaction though consciousness of wrongdoing be totally wanting.** Balancing relative hardships, Congress has preferred to place it upon those who have at least the opportunity of informing themselves of the existence of conditions imposed for the protection of consumers before sharing in illicit commerce, rather than to throw the hazard on the innocent public who are wholly helpless.

It would be too treacherous to define or even to indicate by way of illustration the class of employees which stands in such a responsible relation. … In such matters the good sense of prosecutors, the wise guidance of trial judges, and the ultimate judgment of juries must be trusted. Our system of criminal justice necessarily depends on "conscience and circumspection in prosecuting officers," … even when the consequences are far more drastic than they are under the provision of law before us. See United States v. Balint, … (involving a maximum sentence of five years). …

Judgment reversed.

Mr. Justice MURPHY, dissenting.

Our prime concern in this case is whether the criminal sanctions of the Federal Food, Drug, and Cosmetic Act of 1938 plainly and unmistakably apply to the respondent in his capacity as a corporate officer. He is charged with violating § 301(a) of the Act, which prohibits the introduction or delivery for introduction into interstate commerce of any adulterated or misbranded drug. There is no evidence in this case of any personal guilt on the part of the respondent. There is no proof or claim that he ever knew of the introduction into commerce of the adulterated drugs in question, much less that he actively participated in their introduction. Guilt is imputed to the respondent solely on the basis of his authority and responsibility as president and general manager of the corporation.

It is a fundamental principle of Anglo-Saxon jurisprudence that guilt is personal and that it ought not lightly to be imputed to a citizen who, like the respondent, has no evil intention or consciousness of wrongdoing. … [I]n the absence of clear statutory authorization it is inconsistent with established canons of criminal law to rest liability on an act in which the accused did not participate and of which he had no personal knowledge. Before we place the stigma of a criminal conviction upon any such citizen the legislative mandate must be clear and unambiguous. Accordingly that which Chief Justice Marshall has called "the tenderness of the law for the rights of individuals"[1] entitles **each person, regardless of economic or social status, to an unequivocal warning from the legislature as to whether he is within the class of persons subject to vicarious liability.** Congress cannot be deemed to have intended to punish anyone who is not "plainly and unmistakably" within the confines of the statute. …

Moreover, the fact that individual liability of corporate officers may be consistent with the policy and purpose of a public health and welfare measure does not authorize this Court to impose such liability where Congress has not clearly intended or actually done so. Congress alone has the power to define a crime and to specify the offenders. … It is not our function to supply any deficiencies in these respects, no matter how grave the consequences. …

Looking at the language actually used in this statute, we find a complete absence of any reference to corporate officers. …

The dangers inherent in any attempt to create liability without express Congressional intention or authorization are illustrated by this case. Without any legislative guides, we are confronted with the problem of determining precisely which officers, employees and agents of a corporation are to be subject to this Act by our fiat. To erect standards of responsibility is a difficult legislative task and the opinion of this Court admits that it is "too treacherous" and a "mischievous futility" for us to engage in such pursuits. But the only alternative is a blind resort to "the good sense of prosecutors, the wise guidance of trial judges, and the ultimate judgment of juries." Yet that situation is precisely what our constitutional system sought to avoid. Reliance on the legislature to define crimes and criminals distinguishes our form of jurisprudence from certain less desirable ones. The legislative power to restrain the liberty and to imperil the good reputation of citizens must not rest upon the variable attitudes and opinions of those charged with the duties of interpreting and enforcing the mandates of the law. I therefore cannot approve the decision of the Court in this case.

Mr. Justice ROBERTS, Mr. Justice REED, and Mr. Justice RUTLEDGE join in this dissent. (Citations omitted)

In *Balint,* the defendants were charged with selling illegal drugs without the proper IRS forms, leading to a sentence of 5 years in prison. Defendants thought they could defend their actions by claiming that they did not know the drugs were illegal, but that is to no avail. That sellers must have the proper IRS form for selling the listed drugs is a strict liability law; they need not know the drugs they were peddling were illegal. They were held accountable for selling them without the proper form.

Similarly, in *Dotterweich*, Mr. Dotterweich, president and general manager of a corporation that purchased pharmaceuticals wholesale and then repackaged them with its own label, was found guilty of three misdemeanors. This firm resold and distributed mislabeled pharmaceuticals into interstate commerce. The Supreme Court held that Congress anticipated that individuals who participated in such activities should be held accountable in strict liability for distributing mislabeled drugs. Note the dissent and contrast it with the majority opinion to feel the tension between standard criminal offenses and strict liability laws. In a much later case, *United States v. Park,*[17] the Court held that "the duty imposed … on responsible corporate agents … requires the highest standard of foresight and vigilance, …, but it does not require that which is objectively impossible … Congress has [imposed on corporate agents] dealing with products which may affect the health of consumers by penal sanction cast in rigorous terms, and [the courts must give them effect] so long as they do not violate the Constitution."[18]

The next case, *Morissette v. United States*, is one of the most important cases we will read for understanding the criminal law. The US Supreme Court provides a nice review of aspects of the history and rationale of the criminal law, as well as why it has some of the features we have considered in this chapter; i.e., the illegal act and guilty mind requirements, how strict liability laws that are inconsistent with core

17 *United States v. Park*, 421 U.S. 658 (1975).

18 *United States v. Park*, 421 U.S. 658 (1975).

crimes in the United States but are permitted under the Constitution in certain instances. It also provides a theoretical apparatus for better understanding when strict liability laws will be permitted.

You will have to read this case carefully. The manner in which Congress drafted a law designed to assimilate disparate laws prohibiting theft of government property, omitted a critical word in the definition of "conversion of government property," otherwise a traditional aspect of common-law theft. Conversion is appropriation of another's property for one's own use, excluding or defying the owner's choice. The law forbade "knowing conversion of government property," but it left out a critical phrase, "knowing conversion of governmental property, *knowing* that it was governmental property." That is, one might sell governmental property, knowing it was removed from governmental property, but not *know* that it was still governmental property. By eliminating this critical term, Congress by legislation turned an aspect of the common law of theft into what was in effect a strict liability law, which in this case prevented a trial judge from permitting Mr. Morissette to present to a jury that he did not *know* the property he picked up and sold was still governmental property.

The bottom-line finding of *Morissette* is that Congress, in consolidating clusters of theft (or other common law crimes) may not exclude specific *mens rea* elements from definitions of traditional common law crimes as they existed prior to the legislation, or if it does, a legal duty of a trial judge is to "read in" what would have been the specific *mens rea* provisions of the law. The Court held that Mr. Morrisette should have been permitted to present evidence to a jury that he believed that shell casings had been "abandoned" and did not belong to any particular person or the federal government. At least he could have given his side of the story regarding what he thought was ownership of the shell casings. Read this carefully. It would be helpful to outline the main sections of the opinion to better guide your understanding.

Morissette v. United States

Supreme Court of the United States

72 S.Ct. 240 (1952)

Opinion: Mr. Justice JACKSON delivered the opinion of the Court.

This would have remained a profoundly insignificant case to all except its immediate parties had it not been so tried and submitted to the jury as to raise questions both fundamental and far-reaching in federal criminal law, for which reason we granted certiorari.

On a large tract of uninhabited and untilled land in a wooded and sparsely populated area of Michigan, the Government established a practice bombing range over which the Air Force dropped simulated bombs at ground targets. These bombs consisted of a metal cylinder about forty inches long and eight inches across, filled with sand and enough black powder to cause a smoke puff by which the strike could be located. At various places about the range signs read "Danger—Keep Out—Bombing Range." Nevertheless, the range was known as good deer country and was extensively hunted.

Spent bomb casings were cleared from the targets and thrown into piles "so that they will be out of the way." They were not sacked or piled in any order but were dumped in heaps, some of which had been accumulating for four years or upwards, were exposed to the weather and rusting away.

Morissette, in December of 1948, went hunting in this area but did not get a deer. He thought to meet expenses of the trip by salvaging some of these casings. He loaded three tons of them on his truck and took them to a nearby farm, where they were flattened by driving a tractor over them. After expending this labor and trucking them to market in Flint, he realized $84.

Morissette, by occupation, is a fruit stand operator in summer and a trucker and scrap iron collector in winter. An honorably discharged veteran of World War II, he enjoys a good name among his neighbors and has had no blemish on his record more disreputable than a conviction for reckless driving.

The loading, crushing and transporting of these casings were all in broad daylight, in full view of passers-by, without the slightest effort at concealment. When an investigation was started, Morissette voluntarily, promptly and candidly told the whole story to the authorities, saying that he had no intention of stealing but thought the property was abandoned, unwanted and considered of no value to the Government. He was indicted, however, on the charge that he "did unlawfully, wilfully and knowingly steal and convert" property of the United States of the value of $84, in violation of 18 U.S.C. § 641, which provides that "whoever embezzles, steals, purloins, or knowingly converts" government property is punishable by fine and imprisonment. Morissette was convicted and sentenced to imprisonment for two months or to pay a fine of $200. The Court of Appeals affirmed, one judge dissenting.

On his trial, Morissette, as he had at all times told investigating officers, testified that from appearances he believed the casings were cast-off and abandoned, that he did not intend to steal the property, and took it with no wrongful or criminal intent. The trial court, however, was unimpressed, and ruled: "(H)e took it because he thought it was abandoned and he knew he was on government property. * * * That is no defense. * * * I don't think anybody can have the defense they thought the property was abandoned on another man's piece of property." The court stated: "I will not permit you to show this man thought it was abandoned. * * * I hold in this case that there is no question of abandoned property." The court refused to submit or to allow counsel to argue to the jury whether Morissette acted with innocent intention. It charged: "And I instruct you that if you believe the testimony of the government in this case, he intended to take it. * * * He had no right to take this property. * * * (A)nd it is no defense to claim that it was abandoned, because it was on private property. * * * And I instruct you to this effect: That if this young man took this property (and he says he did), without any permission (he says he did), that was on the property of the United States Government (he says it was), that it was of the value of one cent or more (and evidently it was), that he is guilty of the offense charged here. If you believe the government, he is guilty. * * * The question on intent is whether or not he intended to take the property. He says he did. Therefore, if you believe either side, he is guilty." Petitioner's counsel contended, "But the taking must have been with a felonious intent." The court ruled, however: "That is presumed by his own act."

The Court of Appeals suggested that "greater restraint in expression should have been exercised", but affirmed the conviction because, "As we have interpreted the statute, appellant was guilty of its violation beyond a shadow of doubt, as evidenced even by his own admissions." Its construction of the statute is that it creates several separate and distinct offenses, one being knowing conversion of government property. The court ruled that this particular offense requires no element of criminal intent. This conclusion was thought to be required by the failure of Congress to express such a requisite and this Court's decisions in United States v. Behrman, ... and United States v. Balint [...]

I

In those cases this Court did construe mere omission from a criminal enactment of any mention of criminal intent as dispensing with it. If they be deemed precedents for principles of construction generally applicable to federal penal statutes, they authorize this conviction. Indeed, such adoption of the literal reasoning announced in those cases would do this and more—it would sweep out of all federal crimes, except when expressly preserved, the ancient requirement of a culpable state of mind. We think a resume of their historical background is convincing that an effect has been ascribed to them more comprehensive than was contemplated and one inconsistent with our philosophy of criminal law.

The contention that an injury can amount to a crime only when inflicted by intention is no provincial or transient notion. It is as universal and persistent in mature systems of law as belief in freedom of the human will and a consequent ability and duty of the normal individual to choose between good and evil.[4] A relation between some mental element and punishment for a harmful act is almost as instinctive as the child's familiar exculpatory "But I didn't mean to," and has afforded the rational basis for a tardy and unfinished substitution of deterrence and reformation in place of retaliation and vengeance as the motivation for public prosecution. Unqualified acceptance of this doctrine by English common law in the Eighteenth Century was indicated by Blackstone's sweeping statement that to constitute any crime there must first be a "vicious will." Common-law commentators of the Nineteenth Century early pronounced the same principle, although a few exceptions not relevant to our present problem came to be recognized.[8]

Crime, as a compound concept, generally constituted only from concurrence of an evil-meaning mind with an evil-doing hand, was congenial to an intense individualism and took deep and early root in American soil.[9] As the state codified the common law of crimes, even if their enactments were silent on the subject, their courts assumed that the omission did not signify disapproval of the principle but merely recognized that intent was so inherent in the idea of the offense that it required no statutory affirmation. Courts, with little hesitation or division, found an implication of the requirement as to offenses that were taken over from the common law. The unanimity with which they have adhered to the central thought that wrongdoing must be conscious to be criminal is emphasized by the variety, disparity and confusion of their definitions of the requisite but elusive mental element. However, courts of various jurisdictions, and for the purposes of different offenses, have devised working formulae, if not scientific ones, for the instruction of juries around such terms as "felonious intent," "criminal intent," "malice aforethought," "guilty knowledge," "fraudulent intent," "wilfulness," "scienter," to denote guilty knowledge, or "mens rea," to signify an evil purpose or mental culpability. By use or combination of these various tokens, they have sought to protect those who were not blameworthy in mind from conviction of infamous common-law crimes.

However, the Balint and Behrman offenses belong to a category of another character, with very different antecedents and origins. The crimes there involved depend on no mental element but consist only of forbidden acts or omissions. This, while not expressed by the Court, is made clear from examination of a century-old but accelerating tendency, discernible both here and in England,[12] to call into existence new duties and crimes which disregard any ingredient of intent. The industrial revolution multiplied the number of workmen exposed to injury from increasingly powerful and complex mechanisms, driven by freshly discovered sources of energy, requiring higher precautions by employers. Traffic of velocities, volumes and varieties unheard of came to subject the wayfarer to intolerable casualty risks if owners and drivers were not to observe new cares and uniformities of conduct. Congestion of cities and crowding of quarters called for health and welfare regulations undreamed of in simpler times. Wide distribution of goods became an instrument of wide distribution of harm when those who dispersed food, drink, drugs, and even securities, did not comply with reasonable standards of quality, integrity, disclosure and care. Such dangers have engendered increasingly numerous and detailed regulations which heighten the duties of those in control of particular industries, trades, properties or activities that affect public health, safety or welfare.

While many of these duties are sanctioned by a more strict civil liability, lawmakers, whether wisely or not, have sought to make such regulations more effective by invoking criminal sanctions to be applied by the familiar technique of criminal prosecutions and convictions. This has confronted the courts with a multitude of prosecutions, based on statutes or administrative regulations, for what have been aptly called "public welfare offenses." These cases do not fit neatly into any of such accepted classifications of common-law offenses, such as those against the state, the person, property, or public morals. Many of these offenses are not in the nature of positive aggressions or invasions, with which the common law so often dealt, but are in the nature of neglect where the law requires care, or inaction where it imposes a duty. Many violations of such regulations result in no direct or immediate injury to person or property but merely create the danger or probability of it which the law seeks to minimize. While such offenses do not threaten the security of the state in the manner of treason, they may be regarded as offenses against its authority, for their occurrence impairs the efficiency of controls deemed essential to the social order as presently constituted. In this respect, whatever the intent of the violator, the injury is the same, and the consequences are injurious or not according to fortuity. Hence, legislation applicable to such offenses, as a matter of policy, does not specify intent as a necessary element. The accused, if he does not will the violation, usually is in a position to prevent it with no more care than society might reasonably expect and no more exertion than it might reasonably exact from one who assumed his responsibilities. Also, penalties commonly are relatively small, and conviction does no grave damage to an offender's reputation. Under such considerations, courts have turned to construing statutes and regulations which make no mention of intent as dispensing with it and holding that the guilty act alone makes out the crime. This has not, however, been without expressions of misgiving.

The pilot of the movement in this country appears to be a holding that a tavernkeeper could be convicted for selling liquor to an habitual drunkard even if he did not know the buyer to be such. … Later came Massachusetts holdings that convictions for selling adulterated milk in violation of statutes forbidding such sales require no allegation or proof that defendant knew of the adulteration. … Departures from the common-law tradition, mainly of these general classes, were reviewed and their rationale appraised by Chief Justice Cooley, as follows: "I agree that as a rule there can be no crime without a criminal intent, but this is not by any means a universal rule. * * * Many statutes which are in the nature of police regulations, as this is, impose criminal penalties irrespective of any intent to violate them, the purpose being to require a degree of diligence for the protection of the public which shall render violation impossible." People v. Roby, 1884.

After the turn of the Century, a new use for crimes without intent appeared when New York enacted numerous and novel regulations of tenement houses, sanctioned by money penalties. Landlords contended that a guilty intent was essential to establish a violation. Judge Cardozo wrote the answer: "The defendant asks us to test the meaning of this statute by standards applicable to statutes that govern infamous crimes. The analogy, however, is deceptive. The element of conscious wrongdoing, the guilty mind accompanying the guilty act, is associated with the concept of crimes that are punished as infamous. * * * Even there it is not an invariable element. * * * But in the prosecution of minor offenses there is a wider range of practice and of power. Prosecutions for petty penalties have always constituted in our law a class by themselves. * * * That is true, though the prosecution is criminal in form."

Soon, employers advanced the same contention as to violations of regulations prescribed by a new labor law. Judge Cardozo, again for the court, pointed out, as a basis for penalizing violations whether intentional or not, that they were punishable only by fine "moderate in amount", but cautiously added that in sustaining the power so to fine unintended violations "we are not to be understood as sustaining to a like length the power to imprison. We leave that question open."

Thus, for diverse but reconcilable reasons, state courts converged on the same result, discontinuing inquiry into intent in a limited class of offenses against such statutory regulations.

Before long, similar questions growing out of federal legislation reached this Court. Its judgments were in harmony with this consensus of state judicial opinion, the existence of which may have led the Court to overlook the need for full exposition of their rationale in the context of federal law. In overruling a contention that there can be no conviction on an indictment which makes no charge of criminal intent but alleges only making of a sale of a narcotic forbidden by law, Chief Justice Taft, wrote: "While the general rule at common law was that the scienter was a necessary element in the indictment and proof of every crime, and this was followed in regard to statutory crimes even where the statutory definition did not in terms include it * * *, there has been a modification of this view in respect to prosecutions under statutes the purpose of which would be obstructed by such a requirement. It is a question of legislative intent to be construed by the court. * * *" United States v. Balint, supra.

He referred, however, to "regulatory measures in the exercise of what is called the police power where the emphasis of the statute is evidently upon achievement of some social betterment rather than the punishment of the crimes as in cases of mala in se," and drew his citation of supporting authority chiefly from state court cases dealing with regulatory offenses. Id.

On the same day, the Court determined that an offense under the Narcotic Drug Act does not require intent, saying, "If the offense be a statutory one, and intent or knowledge is not made an element of it, the indictment need not charge such knowledge or intent." United States v. Behrman, supra.

Of course, the purpose of every statute would be "obstructed" by requiring a finding of intent, if we assume that it had a purpose to convict without it. Therefore, the obstruction rationale does not help us to learn the purpose of the omission by Congress. And since no federal crime can exist except by force of statute, the reasoning of the Behrman opinion, if read literally, would work far-reaching changes in the composition of all federal crimes. Had such a result been contemplated, it could hardly have escaped mention by a Court which numbered among its members one especially interested and informed concerning the importance of intent in common-law crimes. This might be the more expected since the Behrman holding did call forth his dissent, in which Mr. Justice McReynolds and Mr. Justice Brandeis joined, omitting any such mention.

It was not until recently that the Court took occasion more explicitly to relate abandonment of the ingredient of intent, not merely with considerations of expediency in obtaining convictions, nor with the malum prohibitum classification of the crime, but with the peculiar nature and quality of the offense. We referred to "* * * a now familiar type of legislation whereby penalties serve as effective means of regulation", and continued, "such legislation dispenses with the conventional requirement for criminal conduct—awareness of some wrongdoing. In the interest of the larger good it puts the burden of acting at hazard upon a person otherwise innocent but standing in responsible relation to a public danger." But we warned: "Hardship there doubtless may be under a statute which thus penalizes the transaction though consciousness of wrongdoing be totally wanting." United States v. Dotterweich [...]

Neither this Court nor, so far as we are aware, any other has undertaken to delineate a precise line or set forth comprehensive criteria for distinguishing between crimes that require a mental element and crimes that do not. We attempt no closed definition, for the law on the subject is neither settled nor static. The conclusion reached in the Balint and Behrman cases has our approval and adherence for the circumstances to which it was there applied. A quite different question here is whether we will expand the doctrine of crimes without intent to include those charged here.

Stealing, larceny, and its variants and equivalents, were among the earliest offenses known to the law that existed before legislation; they are invasions of rights of property which stir a sense of insecurity in the whole community and arouse public demand for retribution, the penalty is high and, when a sufficient amount is involved, the infamy is that of a felony, which, says Maitland, is "* * * as bad a word as you can give to man or thing." State courts of last resort, on whom fall the heaviest burden of interpreting criminal law in this country, have consistently retained the requirement of intent in larceny-type offenses. If any state has deviated, the exception has neither been called to our attention nor disclosed by our research.

Congress, therefore, omitted any express prescription of criminal intent from the enactment before us in the light of an unbroken course of judicial decision in all constituent states of the Union holding intent inherent in this class of offense, even when not expressed in a statute. Congressional silence as to mental elements in an Act merely adopting into federal statutory law a concept of crime already so well defined in common law and statutory interpretation by the states may warrant quite contrary inferences than the same silence in creating an offense new to general law, for whose definition the courts have no guidance except the Act. Because the offenses before this Court in the Balint and Behrman cases were of this latter class, we cannot accept them as authority for eliminating intent from offenses incorporated from the common law. Nor do exhaustive studies of state court cases disclose any well-considered decisions applying the doctrine of crime without intent to such enacted common-law offenses, although a few deviations are notable as illustrative of the danger inherent in the Government's contentions here.[21]

The Government asks us by a feat of construction radically to change the weights and balances in the scales of justice. The purpose and obvious effect of doing away with the requirement of a guilty intent is to ease the prosecution's path to conviction, to strip the defendant of such benefit as he derived at common law from innocence of evil purpose, and to circumscribe the freedom heretofore allowed juries. Such a manifest impairment of the immunities of the individual should not be extended to common-law crimes on judicial initiative.

The spirit of the doctrine which denies to the federal judiciary power to create crimes forthrightly[22] admonishes that we should not enlarge the reach of enacted crimes by constituting them from anything less than the incriminating components contemplated by the words used in the statute. And where Congress borrows terms of art in which are accumulated the legal tradition and meaning of centuries of practice, it presumably knows and adopts the cluster of ideas that were attached to each borrowed word in the body of learning from which it was taken and the meaning its use will convey to the judicial mind unless otherwise instructed. In such case, absence of contrary direction may be taken as satisfaction with widely accepted definitions, not as a departure from them.

We hold that mere omission from § 641 of any mention of intent will not be construed as eliminating that element from the crimes denounced.

II

It is suggested, however, that the history and purposes of § 641 imply something more affirmative as to elimination of intent from at least one of the offenses charged under it in this case. The argument does not contest that criminal intent is retained in the offenses of embezzlement, stealing and purloining, as incorporated into this section. But it is urged that Congress joined with those, as a new, separate and distinct offense, knowingly to convert government property, under circumstances which imply that it is an offense in which the mental element of intent is not necessary.

Congress has been alert to what often is a decisive function of some mental element in crime. It has seen fit to prescribe that an evil state of mind, described variously in one or more such terms as "intentional," "wilful," "knowing," "fraudulent" or "malicious," will make criminal an otherwise indifferent act,[23] or increase the degree of the offense or its punishment. Also, it has at times required a specific intent or purpose which will require some specialized knowledge or design for some evil beyond the common-law intent to do injury. The law under some circumstances recognizes good faith or blameless intent as a defense, partial defense, or as an element to be considered in mitigation of punishment. And treason—the one crime deemed grave enough for definition in our Constitution itself—requires not only the duly witnessed overt act of aid and comfort to the enemy but also the mental element of disloyalty or adherence to the enemy. In view of the care that has been bestowed upon the subject, it is significant that we have not found, nor has our attention been directed to, any instance in which Congress has expressly eliminated the mental element from a crime taken over from the common law.

The section with which we are here concerned was enacted in 1948, as a consolidation of four former sections of Title 18, as adopted in 1940, which in turn were derived from two sections of the Revised Statutes. The pertinent legislative and judicial history of these antecedents, as well as of § 641, is footnoted. We find no other purpose in the 1948 re-enactment than to collect from scattered sources crimes so kindred as to belong in one category. Not one of these had been interpreted to be a crime without intention and no purpose to differentiate between them in the matter of intent is disclosed. No inference that some were and some were not crimes of intention can be drawn from any difference in classification or punishment. Not one fits the congressional classification of the petty offense; each is, at its least, a misdemeanor, and if the amount involved is one hundred or more dollars each is a felony. If one crime without intent has been smuggled into a section whose dominant offenses do require intent, it was put in ill-fitting and compromising company. The Government apparently did not believe that conversion stood so alone when it drew this one-count indictment to charge that Morissette "did unlawfully, wilfully and knowingly steal and convert to his own use."

Congress, by the language of this section, has been at pains to incriminate only "knowing" conversions. But, at common law, there are unwitting acts which constitute conversions. In the civil tort, except for recovery of exemplary damages, the defendant's knowledge, intent, motive, mistake, and good faith are generally irrelevant.[31] If one takes property which turns out to belong to another, his innocent intent will not shield him from making restitution or indemnity, for his well-meaning may not be allowed to deprive another of his own.

Had the statute applied to conversions without qualification, it would have made crimes of all unwitting, inadvertent and unintended conversions. Knowledge, of course, is not identical with intent and may not have been the most apt words of limitation. But knowing conversion requires more than knowledge that defendant was taking the property into his possession. He must have had knowledge of the facts, though not necessarily the law, that made the taking a conversion. In the case before us, whether the mental element that Congress required be spoken of as knowledge or as intent, would not seem to alter its bearing on guilt. for it is not apparent how Morissette could have knowingly or intentionally converted property that he did not know could be converted, as would be the case if it was in fact abandoned or if he truly believed it to be abandoned and unwanted property.

It is said, and at first blush the claim has plausibility, that, if we construe the statute to require a mental element as part of criminal conversion, it becomes a meaningless duplication of the offense of stealing, and that conversion can be given meaning only by interpreting it to disregard intention. But here again a broader view of the evolution of these crimes throws a different light on the legislation.

It is not surprising if there is considerable overlapping in the embezzlement, stealing, purloining and knowing conversion grouped in this statute. What has concerned codifiers of the larceny-type offense is that gaps or crevices have separated particular crimes of this general class and guilty men have escaped through the breaches. The books contain a surfeit of cases drawing fine distinctions between slightly different circumstances under which one may obtain wrongful advantages from another's property. The codifiers wanted to reach all such instances. Probably every stealing is a conversion, but certainly not every knowing conversion is a stealing. "To steal means to *take away from one* in lawful possession without right with the *intention to keep wrongfully*." (Italics added.). Conversion, however, may be consummated without any intent to keep and without any wrongful taking, where the initial possession by the converter was entirely lawful. Conversion may include misuse or abuse of property. It may reach use in an unauthorized manner or to an unauthorized extent of property placed in one's custody for limited use. Money rightfully taken into one's custody may be converted without any intent to keep or embezzle it merely by commingling it with the custodian's own, if he was under a duty to keep it separate and intact. It is not difficult to think of intentional and knowing abuses and unauthorized uses of government property that might be knowing conversions but which could not be reached as embezzlement, stealing or purloining. Knowing conversion adds significantly to the range of protection of government property without interpreting it to punish unwitting conversions.

The purpose which we here attribute to Congress parallels that of codifiers of common law in England and in the States[33] and demonstrates that the serious problem in drafting such a statute is to avoid gaps and loopholes between offenses. It is significant that the English and State codifiers have tried to cover the same type of conduct that we are suggesting as the purpose of Congress here, without, however, departing from the common-law tradition that these are crimes of intendment.

We find no grounds for inferring any affirmative instruction from Congress to eliminate intent from any offense with which this defendant was charged.

III

As we read the record, this case was tried on the theory that even if criminal intent were essential its presence (a) should be decided by the court (b) as a presumption of law, apparently conclusive, (c) predicated upon the isolated act of taking rather than upon all of the circumstances. In each of these respects we believe the trial court was in error.

Where intent of the accused is an ingredient of the crime charged, its existence is a question of fact which must be submitted to the jury. State court authorities cited to the effect that intent is relevant in larcenous crimes are equally emphatic and uniform that it is a jury issue. The settled practice and its reason are well stated by Judge Andrews in People v. Flack, …: "It is alike the general rule of law, and the dictate of natural justice, that to constitute guilt there must be not only a wrongful act, but a criminal intention. Under our system, (unless in exceptional cases,) both must be found by the jury to justify a conviction for crime. However clear the proof may be, or however incontrovertible may seem to the judge to be the inference of a criminal intention, the question of intent can never be ruled as a question of law, but must always be submitted to the jury. Jurors may be perverse, the ends of justice may be defeated by unrighteous verdicts; but so long as the functions of the judge and jury are distinct, the one responding to the law, the other to the facts, neither can invade the province of the other without destroying the significance of trial by court and jury. * * *"

It follows that the trial court may not withdraw or prejudge the issue by instruction that the law raises a presumption of intent from an act. It often is tempting to cast in terms of a "presumption" a conclusion which a court thinks probable from given facts. The Supreme Court of Florida, for example, in a larceny case, from selected circumstances which are present in this case, has declared a presumption of exactly opposite effect from the one announced by the trial court here: "* * * But where the taking is open and there is no subsequent attempt to conceal the property, and no denial, but an avowal, of the taking, a strong presumption arises that there was no felonious intent, which must be repelled by clear and convincing evidence before a conviction is authorized. * * *" Kemp v. State.

We think presumptive intent has no place in this case. A conclusive presumption which testimony could not overthrow would effectively eliminate intent as an ingredient of the offense. A presumption which would permit but not require the jury to assume intent from an isolated fact would prejudge a conclusion which the jury should reach of its own volition. A presumption which would permit the jury to make an assumption which all the evidence considered together does not logically establish would give to a proven fact an artificial and fictional effect.[34]

In either case, this presumption would conflict with the overriding presumption of innocence with which the law endows the accused and which extends to every element of the crime. Such incriminating presumptions are not to be improvised by the judiciary. Even congressional power to facilitate convictions by substituting presumptions for proof is not without limit. Tot v. United States.

Moreover, the conclusion supplied by presumption in this instance was one of intent to steal the casings, and it was based on the mere fact that defendant took them. The court thought the only question was, "Did he intend to take the property?" That the removal of them was a conscious and intentional act was admitted. But that isolated fact is not an adequate basis on which the jury should find the criminal intent to steal or knowingly convert, that is, wrongfully to deprive another of possession of property. Whether that intent existed, the jury must determine, nor only from the act of taking, but from that together with defendant's testimony and all of the surrounding circumstances.

Of course, the jury, considering Morissette's awareness that these casings were on government property, his failure to seek any permission for their removal and his self-interest as a witness, might have disbelieved his profession of innocent intent and concluded that his assertion of a belief that the casings were abandoned was an afterthought. Had the jury convicted on proper instructions it would be the end of the matter. But juries are not bound by what seems inescapable logic to judges. They might have concluded that the heaps of spent casings left in the hinterland to rust away presented an appearance of unwanted and abandoned junk, and that lack of any conscious deprivation of property or intentional injury was indicated by Morissette's good character, the openness of the taking, crushing and transporting of the casings, and the candor with which it was all admitted. They might have refused to brand Morissette as a thief. Had they done so, that too would have been the end of the matter.

Reversed.

Mr. Justice DOUGLAS concurs in the result.

Mr. Justice MINTON took no part in the consideration or decision of this case.

(Citations omitted)

Notes

4 [For some history], "Historically, **our substantive criminal law is based upon a theory of punishing the vicious will. It postulates a free agent confronted with a choice between doing right and doing wrong and choosing freely to do wrong**." Pound, Introduction to Sayre, Cases on Criminal Law (1927).

8 Exceptions came to include sex offenses, such as rape, in which the victim's actual age was determinative despite defendant's reasonable belief that the girl had reached age of consent. Absence of intent also involves such considerations as lack of understanding because of insanity, subnormal mentality, or infancy, lack of volition due to some actual compulsion, or that inferred from doctrines of coverture. Most extensive inroads upon the requirement of intention, however, are offenses of negligence, such as involuntary manslaughter or criminal negligence and the whole range of crimes arising from omission of duty. Cf. Commonwealth v. Welansky, 1944, 316 Mass. 383, 55 N.E.2d 902.

9 Holmes, The Common Law, considers intent in the chapter on The Criminal Law, and earlier makes the pithy observation: "Even a dog distinguishes between being stumbled over and being kicked." P. 3. Radin, Intent, Criminal, … points out that in American law "mens rea is not so readily constituted from any wrongful act" as elsewhere.

12 The changes in English law are illustrated by Nineteenth Century English cases. In 1814, it was held that one could not be convicted of selling impure foods unless he was aware of the impurities. ... However, thirty-two years later, in an action to enforce a statutory forfeiture for possession of adulterated tobacco, the respondent was held liable even though he had no knowledge of, or cause to suspect, the adulteration. Countering respondent's arguments, Baron Parke said, "It is very true that in particular instances it may produce mischief, because an innocent man may suffer from his want of care in not examining the tobacco he has received, and not taking a warranty; but the public inconvenience would be much greater, if in every case the officers were obliged to prove knowledge. They would be very seldom able to do so." Regina v. Woodrow, 15 M. & W. 404, 417 (Exch. 1846). Convenience of the prosecution thus emerged as a rationale. In 1866, a quarry owner was held liable for the nuisance caused by his workmen dumping refuse into a river, in spite of his plea that he played no active part in the management of the business and knew nothing about the dumping involved. His knowledge or lack of it was deemed irrelevant. Regina v. Stephens, L.R. 1 Q.B. 702 (1866). ... After these decisions, statutes prohibiting the sale of impure or adulterated food were enacted. Adulteration of Food Act (1872); Sale of Food and Drugs Act of 1875. A conviction under the former was sustained in a holding that no guilty knowledge or intent need be proved in a prosecution for the sale of adulterated butter, Fitzpatrick v. Kelly, (1873), and in Betts v. Armstead, (1888), involving the latter statute, it was held that there was no need for a showing that the accused had knowledge that his product did not measure up to the statutory specifications.

The *Morissette* case is quite insightful in characterizing some major features of the criminal law and its requirements. One issue worth considering is, "Would it be good legal policy to have all criminal laws strict liability laws?" What would be gained, but also what would be lost? What would it be like to live in a world in which every criminal law was a strict liability law? By thinking about this question and contrasting it with the criminal law that we have—where it requires voluntary violation of the law, excuses for those who are insane or have the mentality of infants, and generally requires various culpable states of mind to be held accountable under the law—how different would a world of strict liability laws be compared with existing laws?

The Court asserts that the historical criminal law—with its "compound concept, generally constituted only from concurrence of an evil-meaning mind with an evil-doing hand, was congenial to an intense individualism"—is quite important. How does this "compound concept" ensure an "intense individualism?"

One way to think about it is that for core common-law crimes, a person may not be convicted without voluntarily choosing between a legal versus illegal course of action and carrying it out with a particular culpable state of mind (required by the law). That is, one must *make a choice*—act voluntarily—with a sound mind to engage in behavior that purposely, knowingly, or recklessly (with some place of negligent or grossly negligent behavior) violates the law, and in many cases causes harm to another or others. Choices as the Court said preserve a kind of individualism that is represented by freedom from legal interference, if one does not *choose* a legal violation with a culpable ("evil-meaning") state of mind. Without going into great detail, the voluntary act requirement, the requirement of action with a sound mind, and the requirement that one exhibit the appropriate culpable state of mind seek to limit legal encroachment with one's life. The centrality of choice preserves one kind of individualism; to the extent that the law ensures this, one can have considerable confidence that one does not run afoul of the law unless one chooses to do so. Requirements for culpable states of mind preserve other aspects of protection from the law—it is much worse to intentionally harm others than doing so recklessly or grossly negligently (these may still be legal wrongs, but less serious ones). That is, one, as it were, chooses how seriously to violate the law and perhaps cause harm to others. Of course, this is a kind of oversimplification that needs the support of other doctrines (some in the US Constitution) and evenhanded administration of the law that we cannot discuss here, but it points to some of the protections provided by basic elements of existing criminal law and what might be different if some of these requirements were eliminated in favor of strict liability laws.

Sweet v. Parsley

House of Lords, 1969

[1969] 2 W.L.R. 470; [1969] 1 All E.R. 347

Lord Reid:

The Appellant was convicted at Woodstock Petty Sessions on 14th September 1967 on a charge that on the 16th June 1967 she was concerned in the management of certain premises at Fries Farm, Oxfordshire, which were used for the purpose of smoking cannabis contrary to section 5(6) of the Dangerous Drugs Act 1965. She was fined £25 and ordered to pay £12 18s. 0d. costs. It appears from the Case Stated by the Justices that the tenant of this farm had sublet the farmhouse to her at a rent of £28 per four weeks. She was a teacher at a school in Oxford and she had intended to reside in this house and travel daily by car to Oxford. This proved to be impracticable so she resided in Oxford and let rooms in the house at low rents to tenants allowing them the common use of the kitchen. She retained one room for her own use and visited the farm occasionally to collect her letters, to collect rent from her tenants and generally to see that all was well. Sometimes she stayed overnight but generally she did not.

On 16th June, while she was in Oxford, the police went to the premises with a search warrant. They found receptacles hidden in the garden which contained cannabis resin and L.S.D. They also found in the kitchen cigarette ends containing cannabis, and an ornamental hookah pipe which belonged to the Appellant and which had, admittedly without her knowledge, been used for smoking this substance.

The Justices found that "she did not enter the rooms of tenants except by invitation and she had no reason to go into their rooms. Her own room was occasionally used in her absence by other persons who lived in the house. She had no knowledge whatever that the house was being used for the purpose of smoking cannabis or cannabis resin. Once or twice when staying overnight at the farmhouse the Appellant shouted if there was excessive noise late at night but otherwise she did not exercise any control over the tenants except that she collected rent from them."

A Divisional Court dismissed her appeal, holding that she had been concerned in the management of those premises. The reasons given for holding that she was managing the property were that she was in a position to choose her tenants:

that she could put them under as long or as short a tenancy as she desired: and that she could make it a term of any letting that smoking of cannabis was not to take place. All these reasons would apply to every occupier who lets out parts of his house or takes in lodgers or paying guests. But this was held to be an absolute offence following the earlier decision in Yeandel v. Fisher [1966]. How has it come about that the Court of Appeal has felt bound to reach such an obviously unjust result? It has in effect held that it was carrying out the will of Parliament because Parliament has chosen to make this an absolute offence. And of course if Parliament has so chosen the Courts must carry out its will, and they cannot be blamed for any unjust consequences. But has Parliament so chosen?

[…] Our first duty is to consider the words of the Act: if they shew a clear intention to create an absolute offence that is an end of the matter. But such cases are very rare. Sometimes the words of the section which creates a particular offence make it clear that mens rea is required in one form or another. Such cases are quite frequent. But in a very large number of cases there is no clear indication either way. In such cases there has for centuries been a presumption that Parliament did not intend to make criminals of persons who were in no way blameworthy in what they did. That means that whenever a section is silent as to mens rea there is a presumption that, in order to give effect to the will of Parliament, we must read in words appropriate to require mens rea. […]

In the absence of a clear indication in the Act that an offence is intended to be an absolute offence, it is necessary to go outside the Act and examine all relevant circumstances in order to establish that this must have been the intention of Parliament […]

What, then, are the circumstances which it is proper to take into account? In the well known case of Sherras v. de Rutzen [1895]. Wright J. only mentioned the subject matter with which the Act deals. But he was there dealing with something which was one of a class of acts which "are not criminal in any real sense but are acts which in the public interest are prohibited under a penalty". It does not in the least follow that when one is dealing with a truly criminal act it is sufficient merely to have regard to the subject matter of the enactment. One must put oneself in the position of a legislator. It has long been the practice to recognise absolute offences in this class of quasi-criminal acts, and one can safely assume that, when Parliament is passing new legislation dealing with this class of offences, its silence as to mens rea means that the old practice is to apply. But when one comes to acts of a truly criminal character, it appears to me that there are at least two other factors which any reasonable legislator would have in mind. In the first place a stigma still attaches to any person convicted of a truly criminal offence, and the more serious or more disgraceful the offence the greater the stigma. So he would have to consider whether, in a case of this gravity, the public interest really requires that an innocent person should be prevented from proving his innocence in order that fewer guilty men may escape. And equally important is the fact that fortunately the Press in this country are vigilant to expose injustice and every manifestly unjust conviction made known to the public tends to injure the body politic by undermining public confidence in the justice of the law and of its administration. But I regret to observe that, in some recent cases where serious offences have been held to be absolute offences, the Court has taken into account no more than the wording of the Act and the Character and seriousness of the mischief which constitutes the offence.

The choice would be much more difficult if there were no other way open than either mens rea in the full sense or an absolute offence; for there are many kinds of case where putting on the prosecutor the full burden of proving mens rea creates great difficulties and may lead to many unjust acquittals. But there are at least two other possibilities. Parliament has not infrequently transferred the onus as regards mens rea to the accused, so that, once the necessary facts are proved, he must convince the jury that on balance of probabilities he is innocent of any criminal intention. I find it a little surprising that more use has not been made of this method … The other method would be in effect to substitute in appropriate classes of cases gross negligence for mens rea in the full sense as the mental element necessary to constitute the crime. It would often be much easier to infer that Parliament must have meant that gross negligence should be the necessary mental element than to infer that Parliament intended to create an absolute offence … It may be that none of these methods is wholly satisfactory but at least the public scandal of convicting on a serious charge persons who are in no way blameworthy would be avoided.

If this section means what the Court of Appeal have held that it means, then hundreds of thousands of people who sublet part of their premises or take in lodgers or are concerned in the management of residential premises or institutions are daily incurring a risk of being convicted of a serious offence in circumstances where they are in no way to blame. For the greatest vigilance cannot prevent tenants, lodgers or inmates or guests whom they bring in from smoking cannabis cigarettes in their own rooms. It was suggested in argument that this Appellant brought this conviction on herself because it is found as a fact that when the police searched the premises there were people there of the "beatnik fraternity". But surely it would be going a very long way to say that persons managing premises of any kind ought to safeguard themselves by refusing accommodation to all who are of slovenly or exotic appearance, or who bring in guests of that kind. And unfortunately drug taking is by no means confined to those of unusual appearance.

Speaking from a rather long experience of membership of both Houses, I assert with confidence that no Parliament within my recollection would have agreed to make an offence of this kind an absolute offence if the matter had been fully explained to it. So, if the Court ought only to hold an offence to be an absolute offence where it appears that that must have been the intention of Parliament, offences of this kind are very far removed from those which it is proper to hold to be absolute offences.

I must now turn to the question what is the true meaning of section 5 of the 1965 Act. It provides: "If a person: (a) being the occupier of any premises, permits those premises to be used for the purpose of smoking cannabis or cannabis resin or of dealing in cannabis or cannabis resin (whether by sale or otherwise); or (b) is concerned in the management of any premises used for any such purpose as aforesaid: he shall be guilty of an offence against this Act."

We are particularly concerned with paragraph (b), and the first question is what is meant by "used for any such purpose". Is the "purpose" the purpose of the smoker or the purpose of the management? … [A]n identical provision occurs in section 8(d) which deals with opium. This latter provision has been carried on from the Dangerous Drugs Act 1920 and has obviously been copied into the later legislation relating to cannabis. It would require strong reasons—and there are none—to justify giving this provision a new meaning in section 5 different from that which it had in the 1920 Act and now has in section 8 of the 1965 Act. I think that in section 8 it is clear that the purpose is the purpose of the management. The first purpose mentioned is the purpose of the preparation of opium for smoking which can only be a purpose of the management. I believe that opium cannot be smoked casually anywhere at any time as can a cannabis cigarette. The section is dealing with "opium dens" and the like when the use of opium is the main purpose for which the premises are used. But it is a somewhat strained use of language to say that an ordinary room in a house is "used for the purpose" of smoking cannabis when all that happens is that some visitor lights a cannabis cigarette there. Looking to the origin and context of this provision, I have come to the conclusion that it cannot be given this wide meaning. No doubt this greatly reduces the scope of this provision when applied to the use of cannabis. But that is apt to happen when a draftsman simply copies an existing provision without regard to the different circumstances in which it is to operate. So if the purpose is the purpose of the management the question whether the offence with regard to opium in 1920 and now with regard to cannabis can hardly arise. It could only arise if, although the manager not only knew about cannabis smoking but conducted the premises for that purpose, some person concerned in the management had no knowledge of that. One would first have to decide whether a person who is not actually assisting in the management can be regarded as being "concerned in the management" although ignorant of the purpose for which the manager was using the premises. Even if such a person could be regarded as "concerned in the management" I am of opinion that, for the reasons which I have given, he could not be convicted without proof of mens rea.

I would allow the appeal and quash the Appellant's conviction.

Lord Morris of Borth-y-Gest

It is said that the intention of Parliament was to impose a duty on all persons concerned in the management of any premises to exercise vigilance to prevent the smoking of cannabis. If that had been the intention of Parliament different words would have been used. It would be possible for Parliament to enact, though it would be surprising if it did, that if anyone should at any time smoke cannabis on any premises then all those concerned in the management of those premises, whether they knew of the smoking or not, should automatically be guilty of a criminal offence. Yet this is in effect what it is now said that Parliament has enacted. The implications are astonishing. Parliament would not only be indirectly imposing a duty upon persons concerned in the management of any premises requiring them to exercise complete supervision over all persons who enter the premises to ensure that no one of them should smoke cannabis, but Parliament would be enacting that the persons concerned in the management would become guilty of an offence if, unknown to them, someone by surreptitiously smoking cannabis eluded the most elaborately devised measures of supervision. There would not be guilt by reason of anything done nor even by reasons of any carelessness, but by reason of the unknown act of some unknown person whom it had not been found possible to control. When the range of possible punishments is remembered the unlikelihood that Parliament intended to legislate in such a way becomes additionally apparent.

For the reasons that I have indicated I consider that on a fair reading of the phrase "concerned in the management of premises used for the purpose of" a link is denoted between management and user for a purpose. To say that someone is concerned in the management of premises used for the purpose of smoking cannabis involves, in my view, that his management is with knowledge that the premises are so used. The wording of section 5(b) contains positive indications that mens rea is an essential ingredient of an offence.

Even if, contrary to my view, it is not affirmatively enacted that there must be mens rea I cannot read the wording as enacting that there need not be mens rea. I find it wholly impossible to say that the statute has either clearly, or by necessary implication, ruled out mens rea as a constituent part of guilt.

On the findings of the magistrates it follows that the Appellant was not guilty. I would, therefore, allow the appeal. Accordingly in my view the case should be remitted to the Divisional Court with a direction to quash the conviction.

[The concurring judgments of the other law lords are omitted.]

The United Kingdom's *Sweet v. Parsley* echoes some aspects of *Morissette*, but with some crucial differences. For one thing, the House of Lords addresses a statutory issue similarly as the *Morissette* court. However, it adds the proviso that all statutory offenses are presumed to have a *mens rea* requirement unless there is clear evidence that the legislature (Parliament) intended otherwise. *Morissette* doesn't go quite that far. Second, *Sweet v. Parsley* uses the language of "public welfare offenses" (also used in *Morissette*) to describe strict liability. This phrase seems to capture the idea that strict liability for quite minor offenses may promote greater overall benefit for society and facilitates proof of violation in the courts. The reader might ask, "Can you imagine having a full criminal trial for every strict liability offense with proof of specific *mens rea*?" Of course, on the other side of strict liability offenses is the concern that if strict liability becomes too widely used, it undermines important protections for defendants in the criminal law as *Morissette* points out.

In the next chapter, we see how the different essential elements of a criminal offense function to hold individuals accountable (or not, as the case may be) for acting with different culpable states of mind. And toward the end of that chapter, we will begin to understand why some of those components are so important, given the sanction of the criminal law.

CHAPTER 2

Criminal Homicide

Introduction

In Chapter 1, we considered several of the main components of a criminal offense—to be convicted of a crime, a person must act voluntarily, violate a legal duty typically created to prevent harm to others (or perhaps institutions), must be sane at the time of committing the crime and not have the mental age of a child (have general *mens rea*), and exhibit the state of mind that defines the crime in question (or have *specific mens rea*).

These components are nicely illustrated with respect to criminal homicide. Under homicide law, the victim of any alleged homicide is dead. That death may have occurred intentionally, knowingly, recklessly, negligently, accidentally or justifiably (in the case of justifiable homicide).

However, the different kinds of homicide for which an alleged defendant might be convicted are typically specified by different mental states exhibited by the defendant at the time of acting, pointing to different degrees of culpability depending upon the state of mind. A major question to ask of a person charged with a homicide is, "At the time of causing the death of another, did the actor satisfy the background conditions required of a crime in general (i.e., did he or she act voluntarily, violate a legal duty, and have a sound mind?), and most importantly, did he or she exhibit the states of mind required of the particular crime (have *specific mens rea*)?

Specific mens rea is especially important in the criminal law for a couple of reasons. Common-law crimes that have come to us as a result of legal decisions are typically defined by mental state terms, using what some courts specify as "infamous crimes." Criminal offense definitions typically contain numerous mental state terms, and criminal liability is established by matching an alleged offender's conduct to the definition of an offense.

The criminal law distinguishes between the seriousness of killings. With homicides the victim is dead in any case, but killing with some states of mind are socially and legally much more serious wrongs than others because they exhibit a greater degree of culpable behavior on the part of the defendant in some instances compared with others. It is a much greater legal wrong (a more legally culpable act) to *purposely* kill another human being than it is to negligently kill.

At the same time *specific mens rea* concomitantly identifies degrees of criminal punishment for the death of another, which is also significantly based on the degree of culpability exhibited by the actor; i.e., purposeful or intentional killing merits much greater punishment than negligent or grossly negligent killing based on several different theories of punishment. Whether one views punishment of offenders based on seeking to discourage others from committing similar crimes (so-called deterrence by example) or reinforcing the general aim of the criminal law (to discourage the committing of crimes), or punishment that seeks to recognize the moral or social seriousness of the offense (called a "retributive" account of punishment), the more culpable offense would typically receive a greater punishment.

Even though the homicide victim is dead, how seriously an agent violated legal (or underlying moral) norms (if at all) can be quite different and is treated differently in grading the different offenses and reserving penal sanctions for them. The difference between these has to do, other things being equal, with the degree of culpability that is exhibited by the agent who brought about the death of another. In general, the grading of offenses and their specified punishments for defendants are determined by the culpability conditions exhibited by a defendant that are defined by the crime in question and the context of a homicide.

Common Law Homicides

The legal cases that follow below exhibit some of the main categories of homicide in the US legal system, although as you will see there can be some differences; e.g., compare common-law categories of homicide as discussed in *Malone*, *Maher*, and *Barnett* with California's as exhibited in *People v. Wolff* and *People v. Conley*. It should be noted that *all* the legal opinions we read are from appellate courts. These courts generally take the facts as established at the trial court and then address whether or not the law applied to those facts was correct law. Did the trial judge instruct the jury properly on what the law was and how it was to be applied? Was the law itself a defensible law of the legal system? Typically, the appellate court that reviews the outcome of trial courts summarizes the facts that were established at trial (if they can be—the case of *Jones v. U.S.* was particularly difficult on this issue), and then proceeds to discuss issues of law that are pertinent to the outcome of the case.

The first case presented, *Commonwealth v. Malone*, while specifically discussing murder in the second degree, also contrasts it with murder in the first degree, distinctions followed by many jurisdictions.

Mr. Malone went to the movie with his friend, William Long. Before going to the movie, Malone had taken a revolver from where he was staying plus one cartridge for it. After the movie, the two teenagers went to a drugstore where they ordered milk shakes. While sitting there, Malone asked Long if he would like to play Russian roulette, to which Long seemed to agree, although perhaps not enthusiastically. Malone inserted the cartridge into the first slot of the cylinder to the right of the hammer of a six-shooter pistol, seemingly expecting that he could pull the trigger up to five times rotating the cylinder clockwise before the hammer would fall on the cartridge, causing the gun to shoot. He put the gun to Long's head and pulled the trigger three times, but on the third occasion the gun went off and Long died because of a wound to his head.

Malone immediately expressed sorrow and regret concerning the harm to and death of his friend, as he cried out, "'Oh! Oh! Oh!' and ... said: 'Did I hit you, Billy? Gee, Kid, I'm sorry.'" The court says there appeared to be no ill feelings between them.

The issue before the trial court was what was the appropriate charge for Malone, given the facts of the case—murder in the first degree, murder in the second degree, or some other category of homicide—and at the appellate court level whether the trial court's interpretation of the homicide laws given the facts of the case was appropriate. The overall discussion in the case and its strength is that it lays out what one might call the common-law categories for and distinctions between first- and second-degree murder as developed by courts over time. (Other jurisdictions, such as California in particular, endorse somewhat different definitions of homicides. And the Model Penal Code adopts a somewhat different approach.)

Malone was charged with murder in the first degree, tried before a jury, and found guilty of second-degree murder. He appealed the jury decision to the Supreme Court of Pennsylvania, whose legal opinion of the facts and the law pertinent to the issues follow below.

Claiming his killing of Long was an accident, Malone urged that he should not have been found guilty of either first- or second-degree murder. What do you think? What did the Supreme Court of Pennsylvania find?

In its opinion, the supreme court discussed differences between first-degree and second-degree murder. What are the definitions of each, and how do they differ from each other? What is the Court's final conclusion about the degree of homicide Malone committed, and why?

What reasons are there for thinking that second-degree murder, while quite serious, shows a defendant as less legally culpable than first-degree murder? Should the culpability differences between two degrees of murder be important for how we assess the wrongness of one compared with the other? Given the court's definition of each one, if someone were convicted for first-degree murder rather than second-degree murder, would one think first-degree murder or murder 1 is legally or morally worse than second-degree murder or murder 2? Why?

Since Malone intentionally put the revolver to Long's head and deliberately pulled the trigger, do his actions show that Long's death was an accident? Were there nonaccidental features to Malone's actions that were important in the court's decision?

Commonwealth v. Malone

Supreme Court of Pennsylvania

354 Pa. 180 (1946)

Opinion: MAXEY, Chief Justice

This is an appeal from the judgment and sentence under a conviction of murder in the second degree. William H. Long, age 13 years, was killed by a shot from a 32-caliber revolver held against his right side by the defendant, then aged 17 years. These youths were on friendly terms at the time of the homicide. The defendant and his mother while his father and brother were in the U. S. Armed Forces, were residing in Lancaster, Pa., with the family of William H. Long, whose son was the victim of the shooting.

On the evening of February 26th, 1945, when the defendant went to a moving picture theater, he carried in the pocket of his raincoat a revolver which he had obtained at the home of his uncle on the preceding day. In the afternoon preceding the shooting, the decedent procured a cartridge from his father's room and he and the defendant placed it in the revolver.

After leaving the theater, the defendant went to a dairy store and there met the decedent. Both youths sat in the rear of the store ten minutes, during which period the defendant took the gun out of his pocket and loaded the chamber to the right of the firing pin and then closed the gun. A few minutes later, both youths sat on stools in front of the lunch counter and ate some food. The defendant suggested to the decedent that they play "Russian Poker."[1] Long replied; "I don't care; go ahead." The defendant then placed the revolver against the right side of Long and pulled the trigger three times. The third pull resulted in a fatal wound to Long. The latter jumped off the stool and cried: "Oh! Oh! Oh!" and Malone said: "Did I hit you, Billy? Gee, Kid, I'm sorry." Long died from the wounds two days later.

The defendant testified that the gun chamber he loaded was the first one to the right of the firing chamber and that when he pulled the trigger he did not "expect to have the gun go off." He declared he had no intention of harming Long, who was his friend and companion. The defendant was indicted for murder, tried and found guilty of murder in the second degree and sentenced to a term in the penitentiary for a period not less than five years and not exceeding ten years. A new trial was refused and after sentence was imposed, an appeal was taken.

Appellant alleges certain errors in the charge of the court and also contends that the facts did not justify a conviction for any form of homicide except involuntary manslaughter. This contention we over-rule. A specific intent to take life is, under our law, an essential ingredient of murder in the first degree. At common law, the "grand criterion" which "distinguished murder from other killing" was malice on the part of the killer and this malice was not necessarily "malevolent to the deceased particularly" but "any evil design in general; the dictate of a wicked, depraved and malignant heart"; 4 Blackstone 199. Among the examples that Blackstone cites of murder is "coolly discharging a gun among a multitude of people," causing the death of someone of the multitude.

In Pennsylvania, the common law crime of murder is divided into two degrees, and murder of the second degree includes every element which enters into first degree murder except the intention to kill ... When an individual commits an act of gross recklessness for which he must reasonably anticipate that death to another is likely to result, he exhibits that "wickedness of disposition, hardness of heart, cruelty, recklessness of consequences, and a mind regardless of social duty" which proved that there was at that time in him "the state or frame of mind termed malice."[2] This court has declared that if a driver "wantonly, recklessly, and in disregard of consequences" hurls "his car against another, or into a crowd" and death results from that act "he ought *** to face the same consequences that would be meted out to him if he had accomplished death by wantonly and wickedly firing a gun." ...

In Com v. Hillman, the charge of the court below was approved by this court. In that charge appears this statement: "Malice in law means a depraved and wicked heart that is reckless and disregards the rights of others. Reckless conduct that results in the death of another is malice. To illustrate that: If a man fires a gun into a crowd and kills another it is murder, because the fact of the reckless shooting of a gun into a crowd is malice in law. That wicked and depraved disposition and that recklessness and disregard of human life is malice."

In Com. v. Knox, the following instructions by the trial judge in a murder case was held by this court not to be error: "When a man uses a gun loaded with powder and shot and aimed at a vital part of the body of another and discharges it, he must be presumed to know that death is likely to follow." In Com. v. Arnold, this court said: "Malice will be implied from conduct, recklessness of consequences, or the cruelty of the crime."

Appellant has assigned for error certain excerpts from the charge of the court. The charge in its entirety affords no grounds for the reversal of the judgment and sentence. Certain excerpts if they stood alone might have misled the jury to the defendant's prejudice. For example, the trial judge said: "All felonious homicide or illegal or unlawful homicide is presumed to be malicious, that is, murder of some degree, until the contrary appears in the evidence." The second sentence after this one reads as follows: "Accordingly, when a felonious or unlawful homicide is proved, malice is presumed to have existed * * * as a presumption of fact." A homicide may be unlawful without being presumably malicious. The homicide known as involuntary manslaughter occurs when death is caused by an unlawful act or by a lawful act done in an unlawful manner. While there do appear statements in some of the reports that "all unlawful homicide is presumed to be malicious and, therefore, murder," careful trial judges always qualify that statement, as Chief Justice Agnew did in Com. V. Drum, where he said: "All murder * * * includes all unlawful killing under circumstances of depravity of heart, and a disposition of mind regardless of social duty." Trial judges should make it clear to the jury that an unlawful killing in order to constitute murder must result from an intentional, felonious act and not merely from an inadvertent or negligent act. "[A] presumption of malice does not rise, however, until the Commonwealth has made out a prima facie case of felonious homicide." [...]

However, the charge was in several respects prejudicial to the Commonwealth. For example, the trial judge said: "It is the duty of the Commonwealth to prove that the killing was unlawful and intentional, and if the evidence taken as a whole raises reasonable doubt in the minds of the jury as to whether the killing was accidental or intentional, you must acquit the accused, for the reason that the Commonwealth has failed to sustain its case." This instruction was tantamount to saying that the Commonwealth in order to obtain the conviction of the defendant of any crime included in the indictment had to prove him guilty of murder in the first degree, for if the killing was intentional, it would have been murder in the first degree. The alternative presented to the jury by the instructions was limited to an intentional killing or to an accidental killing. The jury found that the killing was neither intentional nor accidental but that it was a malicious killing though without a specific intent in the killer to take life, and that, therefore, it was murder in the second degree.

The trial judge also erred in charging that "A person on trial for murder cannot be convicted of any offense if the testimony shows that the death was accidental". Death may be accidental though it resulted from a malicious act intentionally committed. In such a case the means were not accidental; the result was.[3] In the instant case if the defendant had by some negligent, unintentional act, caused Long to fall off the stool at which he was sitting in the store and if, as a result of that fall, Long had sustained a fatal injury, both the initial act and the death might be correctly characterized as accidental. But when the defendant knowing that a revolver had at least one loaded cartridge in it, pressed the muzzle of that revolver to the side of Long and pulled the trigger three times, his act cannot be characterized as accidental, even if his statement that he had no intention to kill Long is accepted (as the jury accepted it). The way the trial judge used the word "accidental" throughout the charge must have been confusing to the jury and might easily have misled it into acquitting the accused on the theory that since the death of Long was accidental, "the defendant cannot be convicted of any offense" (as the trial judge said). The latter should have made it clear to the jury that even though Long's death might have been unintended and, therefore, accidental, the evidence showed that the act which caused the victim's death was not accidental. This was the view the jury took of the case despite the court's instructions.

In another portion of the charge, the trial judge said to the jury: "If you believe the testimony of the defendant, that the shot was accidental and without intention on his part, and that the shot accidentally and without intention on his part struck the body of William H. Long, from the effects of which he afterwards died, then you should acquit the defendant". There was not in this record any evidence which would warrant a finding that "the shot was accidental". Later the judge instructed the jury that "If the killing was accidental, although done with a deadly weapon, it could not be said to be intentional or wilful; and, if neither intentional nor wilful, the crime of murder is not made out". What we have already said on this phase of the case sufficiently reveals the error in these instructions. Of such and similar errors, the appellant cannot complain; they were prejudicial only to the Commonwealth.

[....]

The killing of William H. Long by this defendant resulted from an act intentionally done by the latter, in reckless and wanton disregard of the consequences which were at least sixty per cent certain from his thrice attempted discharge of a gun known to contain one bullet and aimed at a vital part of Long's body. This killing was, therefore, murder, for malice in the sense of a wicked disposition is evidenced by the intentional doing of an uncalled-for act in callous disregard of its likely harmful effects on others. The fact that there was no motive for this homicide does not exculpate the accused. In a trial for murder proof of motive is always relevant but never necessary.

All the assignments of error are overruled and the judgment is affirmed. The record is remitted to the court below so that the sentence imposed may be carried out. (Citations omitted)

Note

1 It has been explained that "Russian poker" is a game in which the participants, in turn, place a single cartridge in one of the five chambers of a revolver cylinder, give the latter a quick twirl, place the muzzle of the gun against the temple and pull the trigger.

The *Malone* case introduced traditional differences between first-degree and second-degree murder. *Maher v. the People* develops the discussion of degrees of homicide, with an extended consideration of voluntary manslaughter inside the main issue of the case.

Voluntary manslaughter is distinguished from both murder 1 and murder 2. What are the important differences between the two kinds of murder and voluntary manslaughter? How is voluntary manslaughter defined in this case? It's a fairly standard account. What is the role of "provocation" in voluntary manslaughter? And more subtly, what is the major presupposition about why provocation should modify the culpability of an actor who might otherwise be found accountable for first-degree murder? You should note that the case *does not* involve the death of Mr. Patrick Hunt, so this does not become an actual case of voluntary manslaughter, but the discussion of manslaughter is present to set up discussion of the what the ultimate charge against Mr. Maher can be.

As you will read, Mr. Maher intentionally put a loaded pistol to the head of Patrick Hunt and then pulled the trigger, resulting in injury to Hunt. This case is somewhat different from *Malone*, although both involve a defendant deliberately putting a gun to the head of a person who becomes a victim and shooting him. What are important differences between the actions of Maher and those of Malone, and how does this affect the culpability of each?

If Maher had killed Mr. Hunt, would this be considered a homicide less culpable than murder 1 and murder 2? What differences are important between both kinds of murder and voluntary manslaughter? Should voluntary manslaughter be considered a serious crime, which it is, but not as culpably serious as one of the two kinds of murder? What is the key exonerating condition of voluntary manslaughter? Do you think it in fact constitutes exonerations?

Read *Maher* for the extensive discussion of voluntary manslaughter. However, despite this discussion of voluntary manslaughter and how that is typically distinguished from murder in the first degree in the common law (be able to explain the differences), Maher could not be convicted of voluntary manslaughter. Why not? What kind of crime can he be convicted of, and why? (In contrast to the common-law distinctions between murder and manslaughter, the Model Penal Code, seeking to provide improved guidance for distinguishing murder from voluntary manslaughter considers "Murder" to be the purposefully or knowingly killing of another person, while manslaughter is a killing "committed recklessly" or "under the influence of extreme mental or emotional disturbance for which there is a reasonable explanation or excuse.") (The terms *purposefully*, *knowingly*, and *recklessly* reference the MPC definitions.)[1]

Maher v. The People

Supreme Court of Michigan

10 Mich. 212 (1862)

CHRISTIANCY J.:

The prisoner was charged with an assault with intent to kill and murder one Patrick Hunt. The evidence on the part of the prosecution was, that the prisoner entered the saloon of one Michael Foley, in the village of Houghton, where said Hunt was standing with several other persons; that prisoner entered through a back door and by a back way leading to it, in his shirt sleeves, in a state of great perspiration, and appearing

1 American Law Institute Model Penal Code. In Kadish & Schulhofer, *Criminal law and its processes: Cases and materials*, pp. 1225–1226.

to be excited; and on being asked if he had been at work, said he had been across the lake; that, on entering the saloon, he immediately passed nearly through it to where said Hunt was standing, and, on his way towards Hunt, said something, but it did not appear what, or to whom; that as soon as the prisoner came up to where Hunt was standing, he fired a pistol at Hunt, the charge of which took effect upon the head of Hunt, in and through the left ear, causing a severe wound thereon; by reason of which Hunt in a few moments fell to the floor, was partially deprived of his sense of hearing in that ear, and received a severe shock to his system which caused him to be confined to his bed for about a week, under the care of a physician; that immediately after the firing of the pistol prisoner left the saloon, nothing being said by Hunt or the prisoner. It did not appear how, or with what, the pistol was loaded. **The prisoner offered evidence tending to show an adulterous intercourse between his wife and Hunt** on the morning of the assault, and within less than half an hour previous; that the prisoner saw them going into the woods together about half an hour before the assault; that on their coming out of the woods the prisoner followed them immediately (evidence having already been given that the prisoner had followed them to the woods); that, on their coming out of the woods, the prisoner followed them and went after said Hunt into the saloon, where, on his arrival, the assault was committed; that the prisoner on his way to the saloon, a few minutes before entering it, was met by a friend who informed him that Hunt and the prisoner's wife had had sexual intercourse the day before in the woods. **This evidence was rejected by the court, and the prisoner excepted. Was the evidence properly rejected?** This is the main question in the case, and its decision must depend upon the question whether the proposed evidence would have tended to reduce the killing—had death ensued—from murder to manslaughter, or rather, to have given it the character of manslaughter instead of murder? If the homicide—in case death had ensued—would have been but manslaughter, then defendant could not be guilty of the assault with intent to murder, but only of a simple assault and battery. The question therefore involves essentially the same principles as where evidence is offered for a similar purpose in a prosecution for murder; except that, in some cases of murder, an actual intention to kill need not exist; but in a prosecution for an assault with intent to murder, the actual intention to kill must be found, and that under circumstances which would make the killing murder.

Homicide, or the mere killing of one person by another, does not, of itself, constitute murder; it may *be* murder, or manslaughter, or excusable, or justifiable homicide, and therefore entirely innocent, according to the circumstances, or the disposition or state of mind or purpose, which induced the act. It is not, therefore, the act which constitutes the offense, or determines its character; but the quo animo, the disposition, or state of mind, with which it is done. Actus non facit reum nisi mens sit rea."

To give the homicide the legal character of murder, all the authorities agree that it must have been perpetrated with malice prepense or aforethought. This malice is just as essential an ingredient of the offense as the act which causes the death; without the concurrence of both, the crime cannot exist; and, as every man is presumed innocent of the offense with which he is charged till he is proved to be guilty, this presumption must apply equally to both ingredients of the offense—to the malice as well as to the killing. Hence, though the principle seems to have been sometimes overlooked, the burden of proof, as to each, rests equally upon the prosecution, though the one may admit and require more direct proof than the other; malice, in most cases, not being susceptible of direct proof, but to be established by inferences more or less strong, to be drawn from the facts and circumstances connected with the killing, and which indicate the disposition or state of mind with which it was done. It is for the court to define the legal import of the term, malice aforethought, or, in other words, that state or disposition of mind which constitutes it; but the question whether it existed or not, in the particular instance, would, upon principle, seem to be as clearly a question of fact for the jury, as any other fact in the cause, and that they must give such weight to the various facts and circumstances accompanying the act, or in any way bearing upon the question, as in their judgment, they deserve: and that the court have no right to withdraw the question from the jury by assuming to draw the proper inferences from the whole, or any part of, the facts proved, as presumption of law. If courts could do this, juries might be required to find the fact of malice where they were satisfied from the whole evidence it did not exist. I do not here speak of those cases in which the death is caused in the attempt to commit some other offense, or in illegal resistance to public officers, or other classes of cases which may rest upon peculiar grounds of public policy, and which may or may not form an exception; but of ordinary cases, such as this would have been had death ensued. It is not necessary here to enumerate all the elements which enter into the legal definition of malice aforethought. It is sufficient to say that, within the principle of all the recognized definitions, the homicide must, in all ordinary cases, have been committed with some degree of coolness and deliberation, or, at least, under circumstances in which ordinary men, or the average of men recognized as peaceable citizens, would not be liable to have their reason clouded or obscured by passion; and the act must be prompted by, or the circumstances indicate that it sprung from, a wicked, depraved or malignant mind—a mind which, even in its habitual condition, and when excited by no provocation which would be liable to give undue control to passion in ordinary men, is cruel, wanton or malignant, reckless of human life, or regardless of social duty.

But if the act of killing, though intentional, be committed under the influence of passion or in heat of blood, produced by an adequate or reasonable provocation, and before a reasonable time has elapsed for the blood to cool and reason to resume its habitual control, and is the result of the temporary excitement, by which the control of reason was disturbed, rather than of any wickedness of heart or cruelty or recklessness of disposition; then the law, out of indulgence to the frailty of human nature, or rather, in recognition of the laws upon which human nature is constituted, very properly regards the offense as of a less heinous character than murder, and gives it the designation of manslaughter.

To what extent the passions must be aroused and the dominion of reason disturbed to reduce the offense from murder to manslaughter, the cases are by no means agreed; and any rule which should embrace all the cases that have been decided in reference to this point, would come very near obliterating, if it did not entirely obliterate, all distinction between murder and manslaughter in such cases. We must, therefore, endeavor to discover the principle upon which the question is to be determined. It will not do to hold that reason should be entirely dethroned, or overpowered by passion so as to destroy intelligent volition: State v. Hill; Haile v. State; Young v. State. Such a degree of mental disturbance would be equivalent to utter insanity, and, if the result of adequate provocation, would render the perpetrator morally innocent. But the law regards manslaughter as a high grade of offense; as a felony. On principle, therefore, the extent to which the passions are required to be aroused and reason obscured must be considerably short of this, and never beyond that degree within which ordinary men have the power, and are, therefore, morally as well as legally bound to restrain their passions. It is only on the idea of a violation of this clear duty, that the act can be held criminal. There are many cases to be found in the books in which this consideration, plain as it would seem to be in principle, appears to have been, in a great measure, overlooked, and a course of reasoning adopted which could only be justified on the supposition that the question was between murder and excusable homicide.

The principle involved in the question, and which I think clearly deducible from the majority of well considered cases, would seem to suggest as the true general rule, that **reason should, at the time of the act, be disturbed or obscured by passion to an extent which might render ordinary men, of fair average disposition, liable to act rashly or without due deliberation or reflection, and from passion, rather than judgment**.

To the question, what shall be considered in law a reasonable or adequate provocation for such state of mind, so as to give to a homicide, committed under its influence, the character of manslaughter? On principle, the answer, as a general rule, must be, anything the natural tendency of which would be to produce such a state of mind in ordinary men, and which the jury are satisfied did produce it in the case before them—not such a provocation as must, by the laws of the human mind, produce such an effect with the certainty that physical effects follow from physical causes; for then the individual could hardly be held morally accountable. Nor, on the other hand, must the provocation, in every case, be held sufficient or reasonable, because such a state of excitement has followed from it; for then, by habitual and long continued indulgence of evil passions, a bad man might acquire a claim to mitigation which would not be available to better men, and on account of that very wickedness of heart which, in itself, constitutes an aggravation both in morals and in law.

In determining whether the provocation is sufficient or reasonable, ordinary human nature, or the average of men recognized as men of fair average mind and disposition, should be taken as the standard—unless, indeed, the person whose guilt is in question be shown to have some peculiar weakness of mind or infirmity of temper, not arising from wickedness of heart or cruelty of disposition.

It is, doubtless, in one sense, the province of the court to define what, in law, will constitute a reasonable or adequate provocation, but not, I think, in ordinary cases, to determine whether the provocation proved in the particular case is sufficient or reasonable. This is essentially a question of fact, and to be decided with reference to the peculiar facts of each particular case. As a general rule, the court, after informing the jury to what extent the passions must be aroused and reason obscured to render the homicide manslaughter, should inform them that the provocation must be one, the tendency of which would be to produce such a degree of excitement and disturbance in the minds of ordinary men; and if they should find such provocation from the facts proved, and should further find that it did produce that effect in the particular instance, and that the homicide was the result of such provocation, it would give it the character of manslaughter. Besides the consideration that the question is essentially one of fact, jurors, from the mode of their selection, coming from the various classes and occupations of society, and conversant with the practical affairs of life, are, in my opinion, much better qualified to judge of the sufficiency and tendency of a given provocation, and much more likely to fix, with some degree of accuracy, the standard of what constitutes the average of ordinary human nature, than the judge whose habits and course of life give him much less experience of the workings of passion in the actual conflicts of life.

The judge, it is true, must, to some extent, assume to decide upon the sufficiency of the alleged provocation, when the question arises upon the admission of testimony; and when it is so clear as to admit of no reasonable doubt upon any theory, that the alleged provocation could not have had any tendency to produce such state of mind, in ordinary men, he may properly exclude the evidence; but, if the alleged provocation be such as to admit of any reasonable doubt, whether it might not have had such tendency, it is much safer, I think, and more in accordance with principle, to let the evidence go to the jury under the proper instructions. As already intimated, the question of the reasonableness or adequacy of the provocation must depend upon the facts of each particular case. That can, with no propriety, be called a rule (or a question) of law which must vary with, and depend upon the almost infinite variety of facts presented by the various cases as they arise. … The law can not with justice assume, by the light of past decisions, to catalogue all the various facts and combinations of facts which shall be held to constitute reasonable or adequate provocation. Scarcely two past cases can be found which are identical in all their circumstances; and there is no reason to hope for greater uniformity in future. Provocations will be given without reference to any previous model, and the passions they excite will not consult the precedents.

The same principles which govern, as to the extent to which the passions must be excited and reason disturbed, apply with equal force to the time during which its continuance may be recognized as a ground for mitigating the homicide to the degree of manslaughter, or, in other words, to the question of cooling time. This, like the provocation itself, must depend upon the nature of man and the laws of the human mind, as well as upon the nature and circumstances of the provocation, the extent to which the passions have been aroused, and the fact, whether the injury inflicted by the provocation is more or less permanent or irreparable. The passion excited by a blow received in a sudden quarrel, though perhaps equally violent for the moment, would be likely much sooner to subside than if aroused by a rape committed upon a sister or a daughter, or the discovery of an adulterous intercourse with a wife; and no two cases of the latter kind would be likely to be identical in all their circumstances of provocation. No precise time, therefore, in hours or minutes, can be laid down by the court, as a rule of law, within which the passions must be held to have subsided and reason to have resumed its control, without setting at defiance the laws of man's nature, and ignoring the very principle on which provocation and passion are allowed to be shown, at all, in mitigation of the offense. The question is one of reasonable time, depending upon all the circumstances of the particular case; and where the law has not defined, and can not without gross injustice define the precise time which shall be deemed reasonable, as it has with respect to notice of the dishonor of commercial paper. In such case, where the law has defined what shall *be* reasonable time, the question of such reasonable time, the facts being found by the jury, is one of law for the court; but in all other cases it is a question of fact for the jury; and the court can not take it from the jury by assuming to decide it as a question of law, without confounding the respective provinces of the court and jury: … this question of reasonable cooling time was expressly held to be a question of fact for the jury. … I am aware there are many cases in which it has been held a question of law; but I can see no principle on which such a rule can rest. The court should, I think, define to the jury the principles upon which the question is to be decided, and leave them to determine whether the time was reasonable under all the circumstances of the particular case. I do not mean to say that the time may not be so great as to enable the court to determine that it is sufficient for the passion to have cooled, or so to instruct the jury, without error; but the case should be very clear. And in cases of applications for a new trial, depending upon the discretion of the court, the question may very properly be considered by the court.

It remains only to apply these principles to the present case. The proposed evidence, in connection with what had already been given, would have tended strongly to show the commission of adultery by Hunt with the prisoner's wife, within half an hour before the assault; that the prisoner saw them going to the woods together, under circumstances calculated strongly to impress upon his mind the belief of the adulterous purpose; that he followed after them to the woods; that Hunt and the prisoner's wife were, not long after, seen coming from the woods, and that the prisoner followed them, and went in hot pursuit after Hunt to the saloon, and was informed by a friend on the way that they had committed adultery the day before in the woods. I can not resist the conviction that this would have been sufficient evidence of provocation to go to the jury, and from which, when taken in connection with the excitement and "great perspiration" exhibited on entering the saloon, the hasty manner in which he approached and fired the pistol at Hunt, it would have been competent for the jury to find that the act was committed in consequence of the passion excited by the provocation, and in a state of mind which, within the principle already explained, would have given to the homicide, had death ensued, the character of manslaughter only. In holding otherwise the court below was doubtless guided by those cases in which courts have arbitrarily assumed to take the question from the jury, and to decide upon the facts or some particular fact of the case, whether a sufficient provocation had been shown, and what was a reasonable time for cooling.

But there is still a further reason why the evidence should have been admitted. No other cause being shown for the assault, the proposed evidence, if given, could have left no reasonable doubt that it was, in fact, committed in consequence of the alleged provocation, whether sufficient or not; and all the facts constituting the provocation, or which led to the assault, being thus closely connected, and following each other in quick succession, and the assault itself in which they resulted, constituted together but one entire transaction. The circumstances which, in fact, led to the assault were a part of the res gestae, which the jury were entitled to have before them, to show what was the real nature of the act, the quo animo, state of mind and intention, with which it was done. The object of the trial should be to show the real nature of the whole transaction, whether its tendency may be to establish guilt or innocence; but, until the whole is shown which might have any bearing one way or the other, its tendency to establish the one or the other can not be known. Any inference drawn from a detached part of one entire transaction may be entirely false. And, for myself, I am inclined to the opinion, that all the facts constituting the res gestae, so far as the prosecuting counsel is informed of, and has the means of proving them, should, on principle and in fairness to the prisoner, be laid before the jury by the prosecution. They naturally constitute the prosecutor's case. And whenever it may appear evident to the court, that but a part of the facts, or a single fact, has been designedly selected by the prosecution from the series constituting the res gestæ, or entire transaction, and that the evidence of the others is within the power of the prosecutor, it would, I think, be the duty of the court to require the prosecutor to show the transaction as a whole. [...] Until this should be done it is difficult to see how any legitimate inference of guilt, or of the degree of the offense, can be drawn; as every reasonable hypothesis of innocence, or a lower degree of guilt, is not, it seems to me, excluded. Criminal prosecutions do not stand on the same ground, in this respect, as civil cases. In the latter no such presumption is to be overcome; nor is it necessary to exclude every other hypothesis than the one sought to be established. ... But however this may be, it was clearly competent for the defendant to show the rest of the transaction, whether known to the prosecution or not. I think, therefore, for the several reasons stated, the evidence offered was erroneously rejected.

After the evidence was closed, the prisoner was called by his counsel to make a statement under the statute. This statement went strongly to corroborate the facts offered to be shown by the evidence rejected. The prisoner's counsel requested the court to charge, that the prisoner's statement was for the consideration of the jury; that they should receive it as evidence in the cause, and give it such credit as, under the circumstances, they believed it entitled to; which the court refused, and the prisoner's counsel excepted. But the court in this connection did charge, that the statement could not be received in relation to matters of defense excluded by the court, the conduct of Hunt and the prisoner's wife; but that where there were facts and circumstances in relation to the commission of the offense, the jury might consider the prisoner's statement in considering the evidence, and give it such weight as they thought proper.

The only substantial error of the court in relation to this "statement," is that which grew out of the exclusion of the evidence, and was the natural consequence of that error. All he intended to say was, that the statement might be considered by the jury so far only as it had any bearing upon the case; but that, so far as it related to the conduct of Hunt and the prisoner's wife, it had no such bearing. It was, thus far, erroneous; but in other respects substantially correct. It is of little consequence whether the statement be called evidence, or by some other name. It is not evidence within the ordinary acceptation of that term; because not given under the sanction of an oath, nor is the prisoner liable for perjury or to any other penalty, if it be false; nor can a full cross-examination be enforced. Yet it is clear the jury have a right to give it such credit, in whole or in part, as under all the circumstances they may think it entitled to.

The judgment should be reversed and a new trial granted.

MARTIN CH. J. and CAMPBELL J. concurred.

MANNING J.

I differ from my brethren in this case. I think the evidence was properly excluded. To make that manslaughter which would otherwise be murder, the provocation—I am not speaking of its sufficiency, but of the provocation itself—must be given in the presence of the person committing the homicide. The cause of the provocation must occur in his presence. PARK J., in Regina v. Fisher, in speaking of the cause of provocation, says, "In all cases the party must see the act done." Any other rule in an offense so grave as taking the life of a fellow-being, in the heat of passion, I fear would be more humane to the perpetrator than wise in its effects on society. More especially since the abolition of the death penalty for murder, and the division of the crime into murder in the first and second degree. There is not now the same reason, namely, the severity of the punishment, for relaxing the rules of law in favor of a party committing homicide as before. It would, it seems to me, be extremely mischievous to let passion engendered by suspicion, or by something one has heard, enter into and determine the nature of a crime committed while under its influence. The innocent as well as the guilty, or those who had not as well as those who had given provocation, might be the sufferers. If it be said that in such cases the giving of the provocation must be proved or it would go for nothing; the answer is, that the law will not, and should not permit the lives of the innocent to be exposed with the guilty in this way, as it would do did it not require the cause of the provocation to occur in the presence of the person committing the homicide. …

I think the judgment should be affirmed.

Judgment reversed, and new trial ordered.

(Citations omitted)

Since there is a dissenting judge in *Maher*, what are his objections to the majority decision? Are you persuaded by his reasons? Was Maher's "provocation" too remote from the time he shot Mr. Hunt to reduce the seriousness of his charge (had he actually killed Hunt), or to use a technical term we discuss later, to be "a mitigating factor" in his choice to shoot the victim?

State v. Barnett continues discussion of standard instances of criminal homicide, but as with several of the cases we have read, with something of a twist. While Mr. Barnett was driving his car, he hit someone (whom we don't know nor any of the circumstances from the case) and killed him. Barnett was charged and found guilty of criminal negligence for killing the victim with his car. Recall the differences between negligence and gross negligence from Chapter 1.

According to the Model Penal Code, a person acts negligently with respect to a material element of an offense when he *should be aware* of a substantial and unjustifiable risk that the material element exists or will result from his conduct. In Barnett's circumstances, this would be a failure to be aware of a substantial and unjustifiable risk to others based on how he was driving his car or a failure to be aware of others who were nearby who might be hit by his car. The risk must be of such a nature and degree that the actor's failure to perceive it, considering the nature and purpose of his conduct and the circumstances known to him, involves a deviation from the standard of care that would be exercised by a reasonable person in his situation.

A person acts grossly negligently with respect to a material element of an offense when he *should be aware* of a substantial and unjustifiable risk that the material element exists; e.g., risks to others from how a car is driven, or will result from his conduct. Gross negligence involves a *gross deviation* from the standard of care that would be exercised by a reasonable person in his situation. Sometimes, negligence is called "mere negligence," or "simple negligence" (as the Court says in this case) and is distinguished from gross negligence. The difference between simple and gross negligence is typically indicated by the somewhat vague idea of whether or not an actor *merely deviated* from the standard of care one should exercise toward those around one in a community (constituting simple negligence) or whether an actor *grossly deviated* from the reasonable care one should exercise toward others (constituting gross negligence).

If these differences were important in a particular legal case, a judge would typically provide some guidance on the difference between simple and gross negligence, but leave to a jury to decide how much a defendant, such as Barnett, had merely deviated or grossly deviated from the standard of care a reasonable person in the community would have exhibited in similar circumstances.

As you will read, Barnett was convicted in simple negligence for how he drove his car that killed the victim. Simple negligence is controversial in the criminal law because a background consideration of a criminal conviction in the vast majority of cases is that an actor, at the time of an action which violates the law, must be *aware* of what he or she is doing or at least be aware that he or she is creating a substantial risk of harm to another person. A common assumption is that an agent must have some degree of consciousness or awareness of causing harm to another (acting purposefully according to the MPC), or practically certain of causing harm to another (acting "knowingly" according to the MPC), or at a minimum, of *being aware* of posing a substantial and unjustifiable risk to harm to another. We can glean that for a large number of cases of criminal liability, persons charged with crimes must *have in their heads at the time of acting* an awareness of risking harm to others (or purposely or knowingly causing them harm).

The deficiency of negligence and even gross negligence is that they specify that an actor *should have been aware* (but was not) of the possibility of risks of harm to others, and that his or her failure to be aware violates an *objective standard of behavior*—reasonable care that others in the community would exhibit. Thus, when acting with either kind of negligence, a person is held accountable for failing to measure up to an objective community standard, not for having a state of mind to inflict harm on others or at least risk inflicting such harm, as the other standards of culpability require.

The Court's discussion in *Barnett* focuses on whether the defendant when driving his car should have been held accountable in negligence, gross negligence, or perhaps recklessness. Barnett's concern is that this standard of culpability—namely, that he just wasn't taking sufficient care about how his driving would affect others—is an onerous standard of culpability that can lead to a conviction for involuntary manslaughter and likely some degree of condemnation of his behavior from the name of the offense, but negligence does not seem to be such a serious culpable state of mind. Simple negligence is the standard of care that is quite common in the tort law, which has much different sanctions and consequences for individuals found liable, so it seems to make it too easy to hold someone accountable in the criminal law for how they drive.

To have a sense of this, imagine that you drive from Washington, DC, to Boston. During this time, you might be negligent on about 150 different occasions because it's so easy to be negligent. You may look off; you may merely get distracted; the kids may yell in the backseat; you may try to change the radio. In these examples, you're not taking sufficient care about how you drive that car. Yet had your momentary distraction led to your driving so that someone was killed, according to the *Barnett* decision, you could be found guilty of involuntary manslaughter.

The South Carolina Supreme Court is aware of these implications of a negligent standard of conduct, yet they held Barnett may be properly held for a failure in simple negligence. Why is that? To what extent does Barnett's handling a "dangerous instrumentality" contribute to their decision? What argument do they give for what seems to be departure from holding one criminally accountable, even though it is "merely" involuntary manslaughter?

The Court also importantly discusses general categories of involuntary manslaughter with examples, which help fill out some of the categories of homicide.

State v. Barnett

Supreme Court of South Carolina

218 S.C. 415 (1951)

Opinion: OXNER, Justice. Appellant was convicted of involuntary manslaughter.

[...] It was alleged in the indictment that the homicide resulted from criminal negligence in the operation of an automobile. The exceptions on this appeal relate solely to the charge.

[...]

After defining involuntary manslaughter and distinguishing that offense from voluntary manslaughter, the Court stated that involuntary manslaughter may consist in the "killing of another without malice and unintentionally, but while one is engaged in the commission of some unlawful act not amounting to a felony and not naturally tending to cause death or great bodily harm", or in "the killing of another without malice and unintentionally but while one is negligently engaged in doing a lawful act." The jury was given the usual definition of negligence but was not instructed as to gross negligence, recklessness or wantonness. The testimony is not incorporated in the record but we assume from the charge that the State relied on the violation of certain statutes in this State regulating the operation of automobiles, and the jury was instructed that a violation of a statute of this kind constitutes negligence per se.

The charge of the trial Judge is in accord with the rule laid down by this Court in [several previous cases]. ... [where it] was held in these cases that simple negligence in the operation of an automobile is sufficient to support a conviction of involuntary manslaughter.

We ordered a reargument of this case on the question of whether we should adhere to the rule established by the foregoing decisions ... [which has] been of much aid in our reexamination of the question.

The degree of negligence necessary to establish criminal liability has perplexed the courts of England and America for centuries. The subject has at times been the source of much confusion. In the early development of the criminal law in England it was held that ordinary negligence, that is, the failure to exercise due care, was sufficient. Later it was found that this rule was too harsh. A noted English authority observed that an accident brought about by an act of ordinary negligence "may be the lot of even the wisest and best of mankind." The English courts finally concluded that more carelessness was required to create criminal liability than civil but they found it difficult to determine "how much more". They use such words as "gross", "reckless" and "culpable", and hold that it is for the jury to decide, in view of all the circumstances, whether the act was of such character as to be worthy of punishment. ... It seems to be the rule in Canada that there is no criminal liability unless there is gross negligence or wanton misconduct and that "to constitute crime, there must be a certain moral quality carried into the act before it becomes culpable." ... There was a tendency in the early American decisions to follow the rule first adopted in England to the effect that ordinary negligence was sufficient. That standard was soon repudiated, however, by the great majority of the courts in this country and it is now generally held that the negligence of the accused must be "culpable", "gross", or "reckless", that is, the conduct of the accused must be such a departure from what would be the conduct of an ordinarily prudent or careful man under the same circumstances as to be incompatible with a proper regard for human life, or conduct amounting to an indifference to consequences. … Of course, under all the authorities the conduct of the accused must be judged in the light of the potential danger involved in the lawful act being performed. In perhaps a majority of the states, the offense of involuntary manslaughter is now defined by statute. Although variously worded, these statutes, with a few exceptions, have been construed as requiring gross negligence or recklessness.

Adverting now to homicides resulting from the operation of automobiles, in almost all jurisdictions, either by statute or by application of the rule governing involuntary manslaughter at common law, the rule is that the negligence necessary to convict a motorist of involuntary manslaughter must be of a higher degree than is required to establish negligent default on a mere civil issue and that the proof must show recklessness or such carelessness as is incompatible with proper regard for human life. … Most courts have refused to consider an automobile as an inherently dangerous instrumentality so as to warrant the application of the "deadly weapon" rule. …

In the light of the foregoing general background, we shall now consider and review the decisions of this Court relating to involuntary manslaughter resulting from negligence. The legislature of this State has never undertaken to define involuntary manslaughter. The general statutory definition, Section 1107 of the 1942 Code, that manslaughter is "the unlawful killing of another without malice, express or implied", includes both voluntary and involuntary manslaughter. For a long number of years the punishment for both offenses was the same, namely, imprisonment for not less than two years nor more than thirty years. […]

There being no statutory definition of involuntary manslaughter, the courts of this State necessarily followed the common law definition. In doing so, as might have been expected from the experience of other courts, there has been some difficulty, and at times confusion, in determining the degree of negligence necessary to establish the offense.

We shall first review the cases in this State involving the use of firearms. Passing over the earlier decisions, it was held in State v. Gilliam, that one who causes the death of another by the negligent use of a pistol or gun is guilty of involuntary manslaughter, unless the negligence is so wanton as to make the killing murder. In State v. Clardy, the Court indicated that gross carelessness in the handling of a deadly weapon was necessary to support a verdict of involuntary manslaughter, and quoted with approval the following: "And undoubtedly the common-law rule is that criminality may be affirmed of a lawful act carelessly or negligently done. The negligence, however, must be aggravated, culpable, gross. That is, it must be such a departure from what would be the conduct of an ordinarily prudent or careful man under the same circumstances as evidences a disregard of human life or indifference to consequences." In the following subsequent cases, the Court, without referring to State v. Clardy, supra, held that simple negligence in the handling of a pistol or gun was sufficient to support a conviction of involuntary manslaughter. … In State v. McCalla, the Court was asked to review the simple negligence rule laid down in State v. Gilliam and concluded that it was sound and should stand. Mr. Justice Watts dissented upon the ground that the State should be required to show gross negligence. The rule announced in State v. Gilliam has been consistently followed and may now be regarded as well settled in this jurisdiction. […]

The question of the degree of negligence necessary to convict the driver of a motor vehicle of involuntary manslaughter came before this Court for the first time in 1918 … On the analogy of the cases involving the use of a deadly weapon, it was held that simple negligence was sufficient. The rule there laid down was distinctly recognized, although not discussed, … In State v. Sussewell, the defendant was convicted of assault and battery of a high and aggravated nature growing out of the operation of an automobile. The trial Judge charged the jury that the State was required to prove "gross carelessness or recklessness on the part of the defendant." Of course, there was no complaint by the defendant as to this phase of the charge and the question under consideration was not discussed in the majority opinion of the Court. In State v. Dickerson, a case of involuntary manslaughter growing out of the operation of a truck, the trial Judge charged the jury that the burden was upon the State to prove that the death of the deceased "was caused not from mere carelessness, but through criminal carelessness, which includes recklessness." There was no comment in the leading opinion on the correctness of this instruction. In a concurring opinion, however, Mr. Chief Justice Stabler referred to the case of State v. Hanahan, supra, and stated that the foregoing instruction was "more favorable to the defendant than he was entitled to."

The question now under consideration was squarely presented to the Court in State v. Dixon, supra, 181 S.C. 1, 186 S.E. 531. In that case the trial Judge refused a request by defendant to the effect "that before he could be convicted of involuntary manslaughter, the State must prove him guilty of gross negligence." After reviewing the line of cases in this State holding that a person causing the death of another by the negligent use of a deadly weapon is guilty of involuntary manslaughter, and the case of State v. Hanahan, supra, holding that the "deadly weapon" rule should be applied to an automobile, the Court held that defendant's request was properly refused. In that case the trial Judge permitted the jury to determine whether an automobile was a dangerous instrumentality and the Court observed that "the charge in this respect was more favorable to appellant and he has no ground of complaint thereabout." The Dixon case was followed in State v. Staggs, and in State v. Brown, … In the last mentioned case, the Court said: "It is the established rule in this jurisdiction that one who causes the death of another by the negligent use of a deadly weapon or instrumentality may be convicted of involuntary manslaughter. And it is further declared that one who uses an automobile on the highways without due care and caution (which is but negligence), and in violation of the statutes of the State, or the ordinances of a town or city, and thereby causes the death of a person, is guilty of manslaughter."

It is clear from the foregoing decisions that in respect to the degree of negligence necessary to establish involuntary manslaughter at common law, we have classified motor vehicles as dangerous instrumentalities and have applied the "deadly weapon" rule, which requires only simple negligence. We have refused, however, to apply this rule to instrumentalities not inherently dangerous. In State v. Davis, the defendant claimed that the injury resulting in the death of his wife was caused by his stumbling over a chair as he attempted to carry her to bed after she had fallen in an epileptic seizure. The trial Judge charged the jury that simple negligence on the part of the defendant would be sufficient to support a conviction of involuntary manslaughter. The Court held that this was error and that more than ordinary negligence was required. It was there stated: "There may be circumstances connected with the homicide, such as the situation of the parties, the character of the instrumentality carelessly handled, and others, which may convert an act, otherwise one of simple negligence into gross or reckless negligence, and justify a conviction of manslaughter or even murder; but it was manifest error to charge that in every instance, regardless of the circumstances, an act of ordinary negligence will constitute manslaughter."

It seems to be thoroughly settled by the foregoing decisions that where the instrument involved is not inherently dangerous, we follow the general rule requiring more than ordinary negligence to support a conviction for involuntary manslaughter, but hold that simple negligence causing the death of another is sufficient if the instrumentality is of such character that its negligent use under the surrounding circumstances is necessarily dangerous to human life or limb. This Court is also committed to the view that firearms and motor vehicles fall within the latter category. We shall not now undertake to develop the rationale of this distinction. It may perhaps be explained upon the theory that want of ordinary care in the handling of a dangerous instrumentality is the equivalent of culpable or gross negligence. This seems to be the conclusion reached by the Court of Appeals of Kentucky in Held v. Commonwealth.

We shall next consider the effect of the statutory offense of reckless homicide which was enacted in 1937. … It is as follows: "When the death of any person ensues within one year as a proximate result of injury received by the driving of any vehicle in reckless disregard of the safety of others, the person so operating such vehicle shall be guilty of reckless homicide." Under the terms of Section 33 of the above Act, the punishment for this offense is "by a fine of not less than One Thousand ($1,000.00) Dollars nor more than Five Thousand ($5,000.00) Dollars, or imprisonment for not more than five (5) years, or both."

The foregoing statute is now incorporated in the 1942 Code as Section 1616. The above mentioned offense of reckless homicide in identical form was reenacted when the Uniform Act Regulating Traffic on Highways was adopted in 1949.

It was distinctly held in State v. Rachels, that the foregoing statute means "something more than the mere failure to exercise due care" and that "the offense denotes operation of a vehicle under such circumstances, and in such manner, as to show a wilful or reckless disregard of consequences." It will be noted that this is a greater degree of negligence than we have held necessary to support the common law offense of involuntary manslaughter where a dangerous instrumentality is involved. Ordinarily, it might be argued that the reckless homicide statute was designed as a substitute for, and has the effect of superseding, the common law offense of involuntary manslaughter in cases of death resulting from the operation of a motor vehicle. … But the statute discloses a contrary intention. It provides that the section creating the offense of reckless homicide "shall not affect, impair or repeal" the statute fixing the punishment for involuntary manslaughter. … This provision was inserted with knowledge of the fact that we had held that simple negligence in the operation of an automobile was sufficient to support a conviction of involuntary manslaughter. The only reasonable construction of the statute is that the Legislature did not intend to repeal the common law offense of involuntary manslaughter where death resulted from the operation of an automobile but, on the contrary, desired to preserve that offense as defined by this Court. The incentive for this action may have been knowledge on the part of the law-making body of the practical difficulties of obtaining convictions in automobile homicide cases.

It is apparent from the foregoing that we have a rather anomalous situation in this State. In automobile homicide cases, not involving the elements of murder, the solicitor may prosecute the accused for reckless homicide, in which event the State must show recklessness, or he may seek a conviction for involuntary manslaughter, in which event the State is only required to show simple negligence. Any remedy for this condition, however, must come from the Legislature.

We have reviewed at great length, perhaps too much so, the decisions in this State, as well as the authorities elsewhere, relating to involuntary manslaughter. This has been deemed necessary in deciding whether we should adhere to the rule that an automobile is an instrumentality of such character that simple negligence in its operation is sufficient to support the common law offense of involuntary manslaughter. It must be conceded that only scant support can be found for this rule in other jurisdictions. But public policy requires that due consideration should be given to the principle of stare decisis. The Hanahan case has withstood attack for over a quarter of a century. The rule there announced and followed in a long line of cases was sanctioned, impliedly at least, by the Legislature, when it enacted the offense of reckless homicide. Under all the circumstances mentioned, we think the wisest policy is to adhere to the simple negligence rule in automobile homicide cases. If a change or modification is desirable, it should come from the law-making body.

Mr. Justice Taylor and the writer desire to say that they regard the simple negligence rule in automobile homicide cases as too harsh and if the question were one of original impression, they would not be in favor of adopting it.

All exceptions are overruled and the judgment affirmed.

FISHBURNE, STUKES and TAYLOR, JJ., concur.

BAKER, C. J., not participating.

(Citations omitted)

Some California Homicide Cases

The next two cases diverge to some extent from the standard common-law categories of homicide. California has some slightly more complex statements of first-degree murder and second-degree murder, which we see in *People v. Wolff*, and a somewhat broader notion of voluntary manslaughter in *People v. Conley*, the following case. While the holding in *Conley* has been modified by the California legislature because of an instance of voluntary manslaughter in *People v. White*, the *Wolff* and *Conley* cases together illustrate the Supreme Court of California exploring and modifying liability for both second-degree murder and voluntary manslaughter, roughly as a result of developments in the psychological understanding of less than full responsibility of an actor for his or her actions. I do not add these cases because they or their residuum necessarily remain the law of California, but to illustrate a court developing and modifying traditional understandings of criminal responsibility based on analogies with existing crimes and some of their implications for citizens.

In a series of cases following *People v. Wells*, 33 Cal.2d 330, 202 P.2d 53, the California Supreme Court held, "evidence of *diminished mental capacity*, whether caused by intoxication, trauma, or disease, can be used to show that a defendant did not have a specific mental state essential to an offense, ... [thus] evidence must be admitted that shows that at the time a defendant committed an overt act he did or did not have a specific mental state such as malice aforethought [emphasis added]." This doctrine was developed in a number of cases in which diminished mental states might be exhibited by defendants that should be considered and taken into account in adjudicating both murder and voluntary manslaughter. In *Wolff* and *Conley,* the California Supreme Court noticed that it was possible for a defendant to exhibit some degree of diminished mental capacity, but not so diminished that a defendant could be judged insane, and in appropriate circumstances, a defendant's diminished mental capacities might be judged as a formal mitigating condition in criminal homicide law.

In effect, the California Supreme Court noticed an important conceptual point about sanity and insanity. These states of mind are not dichotomous alternatives, such as pregnancy; a woman is either pregnant or not, there is no in-between. Instead, sanity and insanity are matters of degree, or are graduated concepts, admitting judgments of more or less realized states of mind. Recall from Chapter 1 that all adults are presumed to be sane. However, a person can be judged to be sane but have some diminished mental capacity as the jury and the California Supreme Court found in *Wolff*. Yet Mr. Wolff was not insane; he had considerable knowledge of the nature of his action and its degree of wrongness. The supreme court reasoned that he had sufficient mental capacities to be properly held accountable, despite whatever diminishment of his capacities had been revealed.

In *Wolff*, a 15-year-old teenager with a history of mental disease was found to be sane by a jury at trial court. He appealed a conviction of first-degree murder for killing his mother, even though it involved a reasonable amount of planning.

In California, murder in the first degree as used in these cases was defined as any kind of "wilful, deliberate, and premeditated killing of another human being with malice aforethought" (*People v. Conley*). Second-degree murder was the "unlawful killing of a human being … with malice aforethought, but without deliberation and premeditation, that is, without the wilful, deliberate and premeditated intent to take life that is an essential element of first-degree murder …" (*People v. Conley*).

The court recognized in *Wolff* that because of the characterization of murder in the first degree, it required that the actor kill with deliberation and with premeditation, but given Mr. Wolff's age (15), history of mental disorders, and perhaps the behavior he exhibited in killing his mother, he did not satisfy the conditions required of first-degree murder. It found that Mr. Wolff was not and is not a fully normal or mature, mentally well person. "He knew the difference between right and wrong [he was not legally insane as the jury found]; he knew that the intended act was wrong and nevertheless carried it out. But the extent of his understanding, reflection upon it and its consequences, with realization of the enormity of the evil, appears to have been materially as relevant to appraising the quantum of his moral turpitude and depravity vague and detached."

The legislature had required "as an essential element of first-degree murder … substantially more reflection; i. e., more understanding and comprehension of the character of the act than the mere amount of thought necessary to form the intention to kill." Thus, "dividing the offense of murder into two degrees is a … recognition of [the] infirmity [of human nature] and of difference in the quantum of personal turpitude of the offenders." In these phrases, the court recognizes that there may be limits to humans' abilities to either control their behaviors (referencing "infirmities of human nature") and that there can be differences in the extent to which offenders exhibit the needed degree of a guilty mind (referencing "moral turpitude") to be held accountable for a particular category of homicide.

Wolff might be seen opening new legal ground compared with common-law accounts of second-degree murder (recall *Malone*) because more traditional understandings limit second-degree murder to recklessness toward human life, which recognizes lesser culpability in acting, while the California Supreme

Court, continuing to recognize reckless killing as second-degree murder, also held that a lesser degree of moral turpitude or culpability could be indicated by sufficiently diminished mental capacity. In *Malone*, one might say the defendant exhibited lesser moral turpitude because the defendant was only reckless toward taking Long's life, whereas *Wolff* revealed lesser culpability because of his diminished mental capacity to exhibit the needed understanding of the enormity of the consequences of his action.

People v. Wolff

Supreme Court of California

61 Cal. 2d 795 (1964)

Opinion: SCHAUER, Justice.

Defendant appeals from a judgment imposing a sentence of life imprisonment (with recommendation that he be placed in a hospital for the criminally insane) after he pleaded not guilty by reason of insanity to a charge of murder, the jury found that he was legally sane at the time of the commission of the offense, and the court determined the killing to be murder in the first degree.

Defendant contends that the evidence is insufficient to support the verdict of sanity, that the court gave conflicting instructions on the presumptions of sanity and of the continuance of prior "permanent" insanity, and that his crime should have been determined to be second degree rather than first degree murder. Upon a comprehensive view of all the evidence we have concluded that the first two of these contentions are without merit, but that the judgment should be reduced to murder of the second degree.

Defendant, a 15-year-old boy at the time of the crime, was charged with the murder of his mother. The juvenile court found him to be "not a fit subject for consideration" under the Juvenile Court Law, and remanded him to the superior court for further proceedings in the criminal action. To the information accusing him of murder defendant entered the single plea of "not guilty by reason of insanity," thereby admitting commission of the basic act which, if not qualified under the special plea, constitutes the offense charged. … After considering reports of three alienists appointed to examine defendant … the court declared a doubt as to his mental capacity to stand trial. … At a hearing on that issue, however, the court found defendant to be "mentally ill but not to the degree that would preclude him from cooperation with his counsel in the preparation and presentation of his defense." The plea of not guilty by reason of insanity was then tried to a jury and resulted in a verdict that defendant was legally sane at the time of the commission of the jurisdictional act of killing. Defendant's motion for new trial on the ground of insufficiency of the evidence was heard and denied, and by stipulation the question of the degree of the crime was submitted to the court on the basis of the evidence introduced at the trial and the report of the probation officer. The court determined the crime to be murder in the first degree; sentenced defendant to life imprisonment; and to the judgment added, "Placement in hospital for criminally insane recommended."

[Detailed discussions of sanity evidence deleted] …

[Detailed discussion of jury instructions deleted] …

The Degree of the Murder

From what has been said it follows that there was no substantial error in the trial on the issue raised by the plea of not guilty by reason of insanity and that the evidence adequately supports the jury's verdict. But another and more substantial problem remains to be considered: the contention that the evidence is insufficient to support the trial court's finding that the murder was of the first, rather than the second, degree. This problem, however, is by no means new to us. In dealing with it we recognize that every relevant and tenable presumption is to be indulged in favor of sustaining the judgment of the trial court; but when a proper case appears … we do not hesitate to modify the judgment to murder of the second degree and affirm it as modified.

As hereinabove mentioned, by stipulation of the parties the question of the degree of the crime was submitted to the court on the basis of the evidence introduced at the trial on the plea of not guilty by reason of insanity, as augmented by the report of the probation officer. To confidently resolve the issue it is essential that we identify the elements which (insofar as relevant to the facts of this case) should as a matter of law be given weight as characterizing, distinguishing, or differentiating, the two degrees of murder. In *People* v. Holt (1944) supra, 25 *Cal.*2d 59, we said "Murder, and this, of course, includes murder of the second degree as well as murder of the first degree, is defined as 'the unlawful killing of a human being, with malice aforethought.'" … * * *

"The legislative definition of the degrees of murder leaves much to the discretion of the jury in many cases. That discretion, however, must have a sound factual basis for its exercise, as hereinafter is more particularly discussed. The Penal Code (section 189) declares that 'All murder which is perpetrated by means of poison, or lying in wait, torture, or by any other kind of willful, deliberate, and premeditated killing, or which is committed in the perpetration or attempt to perpetrate arson, rape, robbery, burglary, or mayhem, is murder of the first degree; and all other kinds of murders are of the second degree.'"

… "Obviously the homicide in this case was not perpetrated by means of poison, or lying in wait, or torture, nor was it committed in the perpetration of or attempt to perpetrate any of the enumerated felonies. Hence, if it is first degree murder it must come within the classification of 'any other kind of willful, deliberate, and premeditated killing.' But homicide to amount to even second degree murder must be 'the unlawful killing of a human being, with malice aforethought.' The malice which is one of the two essential elements of the offense whether of the first or of the second degree is defined by section 188 of the Penal Code. 'Such malice may be express or implied. It is express when there is manifested a deliberate intention unlawfully to take away the life of a fellow creature. It is implied, when no considerable provocation appears, or when the circumstances attending the killing show an abandoned and malignant heart.'"

As noted in Holt … there has sometimes appeared to be a tendency to emasculate the distinction between the two degrees of murder. In Holt we declared firmly against any such emasculation: … "Regardless of imperfection of academic concept either in the statutory law as enacted or in some of the decisions interpreting it, we are faced with the task of making practical application of that law to actual facts. In such application certain principles are entitled to recognition. Dividing intentional homicides into murder and voluntary manslaughter was a recognition of the infirmity of human nature. Again dividing the offense of murder into two degrees is a further recognition of that infirmity and of difference in the quantum of personal turpitude of the offenders. * * * The victim of manslaughter or second degree murder is just as dead as is the victim of first degree murder. The law has fixed standards by which such personal depravity of the offender; i. e., the character of the particular homicide, is to be measured. When the homicide is perpetrated by means of poison, or lying in wait, or torture, or in the perpetration of or attempt to perpetrate the enumerated felonies the standard is definite and no difficulty in fixing the degree ensues. But when it is claimed that the homicide is by 'any other kind of willful, deliberate, and premeditated killing' there is necessity for an appraisal which involves something more than the ascertainment of objective facts. This appraisal is primarily a jury (or trial court) function and within a wide field of discretion its determination is final. But as is true as to all factual issues resolved by a jury (or trial court), the evidence upon which the determination is made is subject to review on the question of its legal sufficiency to support the verdict. To the extent that the character of a particular homicide is established by the facts in evidence the jury is bound, as are we, to apply the standards fixed by law."

Holt had been convicted of first degree murder and sentenced to death. After reviewing the governing law as above set forth we scrutinized the evidence and pointed out that, as analyzed, it demonstrated that the defendant at the time of the shooting did not have a premeditated specific intent to kill. Accordingly, we modified the judgment to murder of the second degree and affirmed as modified. In the case at bench there is no question that the defendant had the intent to kill; but the mental infirmity of this defendant presents a very serious factual problem as to the quantum of his personal turpitude and depravity as inherently related to the degree of the murder.

[...] Hence, the more general words "or any other kind of willful, deliberate, and premeditated killing," following the specifically enumerated instances of killing which are expressly declared to constitute murder of the first degree, must be construed in the light of such specifically listed types and be held to include only killings of the same general kind or character as those specifically mentioned. By conjoining the words "willful, deliberate, and premeditated" in its definition and limitation of the character of killings falling within murder of the first degree the Legislature apparently emphasized its intention to require as an element of such crime substantially more reflection than may be involved in the mere formation of a specific intent to kill. ...

"... Neither the statute nor the court undertakes to measure in units of time the length of the period during which the thought must be pondered before it can ripen into an intent which is truly deliberate and premeditated. The time would vary with different individuals and under differing circumstances. The true test is not the duration of time as much as it is the extent of the reflection." In the case now at bench, in the light of defendant's youth and undisputed mental illness, all as shown under the California M'Naughton rule on the trial of the plea of not guilty by reason of insanity, and properly considered by the trial judge in the proceeding to determine the degree of the offense, the true test must include consideration of the somewhat limited extent to which this defendant could maturely and meaningfully reflect upon the gravity of his contemplated act. [....]

In People v. Bender (1945), we ... considered the elements of proof essential to sustain a finding (on the theory of premeditation and deliberation) that a murder was of the first, rather than the second degree. We reiterated that in the circumstances of that case ..., "The true test is not the duration of time as much as it is the extent of the reflection." We held that the evidence was insufficient to sustain a finding of first degree murder, modified the judgment by reducing it to murder of the second degree, and affirmed it as modified.

Certainly in the case now at bench the defendant had ample time for any normal person to maturely and appreciatively reflect upon his contemplated act and to arrive at a cold, deliberated and premeditated conclusion. He did this in a sense and apparently to the full extent of which he was capable. But, indisputably on the record, this defendant was not and is not a fully normal or mature, mentally well person. He knew the difference between right and wrong; he knew that the intended act was wrong and nevertheless carried it out. But the extent of his understanding, reflection upon it and its consequences, with realization of the enormity of the evil, appears to have been materially as relevant to appraising the quantum of his moral turpitude and depravity vague and detached. We think that our analysis in Holt of the minimum essential elements of first degree murder, especially in respect to the quantum of reflection, comprehension, and turpitude of the offender, fits precisely this case: that the use by the Legislature of "wilful, deliberate, and premeditated" in conjunction indicates its intent to require as an essential element of first degree murder (of that category) substantially more reflection; i. e., more understanding and comprehension of the character of the act than the mere amount of thought necessary to form the intention to kill. It bears repeating … that "Dividing intentional homicides into murder and voluntary manslaughter was a recognition of the infirmity of human nature. Again dividing the offense of murder into two degrees is a further recognition of that infirmity and of difference in the quantum of personal turpitude of the offenders. The difference is basically in the offenders. * * *"

The foregoing discussion disposes of any basis for urging that defendant's preparations and procedures might be deemed to constitute a form of "lying in wait" … and that therefore he is necessarily guilty of first degree murder. It must be remembered that "lying in wait" is simply evidence which, if unexplained and unqualified by other evidence, would ordinarily establish that the perpetrator was guilty of a "wilful, deliberate, and premeditated killing". But here, as emphasized above, the controlling issue as to degree depends not alone on the character of the killing but also on the quantum of personal turpitude of the actor. And in this case, as in Holt, the difference is basically in the offender.

Upon the facts, upon the law, and for all of the reasons hereinabove stated we are satisfied that the evidence fails to support the finding that the murder by this defendant, in the circumstances of his undisputed mental illness, was of the first degree, but that it amply sustains conviction of second degree murder.

The fact that we reduce the degree of the penal judgment from first to second degree murder is not to be understood as suggesting that this defendant's confinement should be in an institution maintaining any lower degree of security than for persons convicted of murder of the first degree. To the contrary, we approve of the trial court's recommendation that defendant be placed in a hospital for the criminally insane of a high security character, such as the California Medical Facility at Vacaville where he is presently confined.

For all of the reasons above stated, the judgment is modified by reducing the degree of the crime to murder of the second degree and, as so modified, is affirmed. The cause is remanded to the trial court with directions to arraign and pronounce judgment on defendant in accordance with the foregoing ruling.

GIBSON, C. J., and TRAYNOR, McCOMB, PETERS, TOBRINER and PEEK, JJ., concur.

Following *Wolff*, the California Supreme Court extended its doctrine of diminished mental capacity that could modify specific *mens rea* for different kinds of homicide. The factually complex case of *People v. Conley*, *inter alia*, addresses the reduction of first-degree murder to voluntary manslaughter. In many jurisdictions, while both murder 1 and voluntary manslaughter require that an alleged defendant *intentionally* kill another human being, murder 1 requires that the defendant exhibit malice aforethought, but voluntary manslaughter specifically does not require this state of mind. Instead, as we saw in the court's discussion in *Maher v. the People*, if a defendant has been sufficiently "provoked" so as to have his or her "reason clouded or obscured by passion," that is, his or her rational faculties sufficiently disturbed as to preclude that the defendant acted with malice. Thus, in many jurisdictions, including California's, the state of mind of malice required of murder may be undermined by a defendant being sufficiently "provoked" as to reduce murder in the first degree to voluntary manslaughter. (As noted earlier, the Model Penal Code introduced a different approach, avoiding the use of "malice" in its accounts of voluntary manslaughter and emphasizing that for voluntary manslaughter, offenders must act "under the influence of extreme mental or emotional disturbance for which there is a reasonable explanation or excuse."[2])

The California Supreme Court noticed that a person's rational faculties can be sufficiently rendered less than fully functioning by something other than provocation; these faculties may be interfered with by diminished mental capacities, which can be sufficient to undermine the malice required of murder in the first degree. Thus, the California Supreme Court extends the kinds of mental states that, if sufficiently present, can undermine a finding of first-degree murder.

In reading this case, you should also pay attention to the legal role of unconsciousness and intoxication.

People v. Conley

Supreme Court of California

64 Cal.2d 310 (1966)

Opinion: TRAYNOR, Chief Justice.

Defendant appeals from a judgment of conviction entered on jury verdicts finding him guilty on two counts of first degree murder, finding him sane at the time of the commission of the crimes, and fixing the penalty on each count at life imprisonment. He contends that the court erred in instructing the jury on the elements of murder, in refusing to give requested instructions on manslaughter, and in admitting into evidence photographs of the victims.

Defendant shot and killed Clifton and Elaine McCool on Sunday, July 19, 1964, in Ukiah. The victims, who were married and the parents of three children, had recently reconciled after a period of separation and were preparing to move to the State of Washington. They occupied cabin No. 7 of a bungalow court near the home of defendant's sister, Goldie Haley, with whom defendant was living at the time of the killings. While the McCools were separated, Elaine became romantically involved with defendant

2 American Law Institute Model Penal Code. In Kadish & Schulhofer, *Criminal law and its processes: Cases and materials*, pp. 1225–1226.

and told him that she would get a divorce and marry him.

Defendant injured his back in an industrial accident several months before the killings and had no regular employment since that accident. On July 15, the Wednesday before the shooting, he received two compensation checks and, as was his habit when he had funds, began a prolonged period of steady drinking. He and several other witnesses testified that he drank whiskey, vodka, and finally wine continually for over three days before the homicides. Defendant also testified that he had been taking medication to relieve the pain of his back injury and an ulcer. A medical expert testified that some of the medication prescribed for defendant could have increased the effect of alcohol.

On Thursday, July 16, the defendant took Elaine and the McCool children on an outing and apparently engaged in intimate relations with Elaine. When he brought her and the children back to their cabin, she told him that she had decided to return to her husband.

On Sunday, July 19, defendant purchased a .30-.30 rifle and early that evening tried it out with two friends at a nearby dump. His friends testified that on their way back defendant said that he ought to kill the McCools, but they dismissed the remark as "just the booze talking" and changed the subject. Thereafter, defendant went to his sister's home and drank wine until about 9:00 p. m. He then went to cabin No. 3 of the bungalow court and told other friends who lived there that he was going to kill the McCools because, "I have been hurt by three different woman before. I can't take any more. She promised to marry me." They attempted to dissuade him, but he said he had made up his mind. Once again, however, he was not taken seriously and his friends allowed him to leave with his rifle.

A few minutes later, four shots rang out. Upon hearing the first shots, the occupants of cabin No. 1 went to their front porch and saw defendant shoot Elaine as she was running from him. Defendant walked back to cabin No. 3, told his friends that he had killed the McCools, and then went to his sister's house and told her what he had done. He left and was found two hours later in a nearby field.

Defendant testified that he did not intend to kill the McCools and remembered nothing from the time he was drinking at his sister's house until his arrest. The results of a blood alcohol test given about three hours after the shooting showed that his blood then contained .21 per cent alcohol. A medical expert testified that this alcohol level would be sufficient to impair fine muscular coordination and judgment in the average individual and that if defendant had consumed no food or alcohol between 9:00 p. m. and midnight, the blood alcohol level at 9:00 p. m. could have been .27 per cent, but that it might have been even less than .21 per cent.

A defense psychologist testified that in his opinion defendant was in a dissociative state at the time of the killings and because of personality fragmentation did not function with his normal personality.

Both sides requested manslaughter instructions. The court ruled that even if initially there had been adequate provocation to reduce the killing from murder to manslaughter, a sufficient cooling period had elapsed as a matter of law to preclude consideration of the crime as having been committed in the heat of passion. The court suggested that if either party could present an evidentiary theory upon which a manslaughter instruction could be based it would be given but ultimately refused any such instruction, although diminished capacity and intoxication were both suggested as theories upon which instructions on manslaughter were required. This refusal was prejudicial error.

It has long been settled that evidence of diminished mental capacity, whether caused by intoxication, trauma, or disease, can be used to show that a defendant did not have a specific mental state essential to an offense. Seventeen years ago, in People v. Wells, we held that evidence must be admitted that shows that at the time a defendant committed an overt act he did or did not have a specific mental state such as malice aforethought. By way of examples of the classes of crimes that require proof of a specific mental state we mentioned "the homicides, wherein, if a charge of murder in either degree is to be supported, there must be proof of malice aforethought; lacking proof of malice aforethought the homicide can be no higher offense than manslaughter. …" Section 22 of the Penal Code provided then, as it does now, that intoxication may be shown to negate an essential state of mind. We pointed out that in providing for the admissibility of such evidence in certain circumstances the statute "is but declaratory of what would be the rule were there no statute on the subject. * * * Thus the Legislature was at pains to insure that the (rule declaring no act less criminal because of voluntary intoxication) should not affect the general rule as to admissibility of evidence and necessity for proof relative to an essential specific state of mind." (Id. at p. 357.) We concluded, therefore, that evidence of an accused's abnormal mental condition that was relevant to malice aforethought was admissible, for malice aforethought was a "particular purpose, motive, or intent" essential to the crime charged. "Here, the offer was to show not insanity, not a lack of mental capacity to have malice aforethought, but, rather, the fact of nervous tension and that the particular tension was directly relevant to the issue of 'purpose, motive, or intent'; i. e., to the critical question as to whether defendant's overt act was done with 'malice aforethought' * * *." (Id. at p. 356)

We thus clearly recognized that malice aforethought is a specific mental state and that a defendant may show that he lacked that mental state when it is an essential element of the offense of which he stands accused. Since Wells had not committed a homicide, however, it remained for later cases to demonstrate the applicability of the general rule to the manslaughter-murder distinction. It is now urged by amicus curiae that evidence of diminished capacity can serve to reduce murder from first degree to second degree, but not to reduce murder to manslaughter, on the ground that the latter class of offenses is restricted to homicides having the specific statutory elements prescribed by Penal Code, section 192. This misunderstanding may have arisen from the statement in … decided at the time of the Wells case; that "To reduce a homicide from the class of murder to that of manslaughter the evidence must be such as to reasonably lead the jury 'to believe that the defendant did, or to create a reasonable doubt in their minds as to whether or not he did, commit his offense under a heat of passion' * * *." … This statement, made in reference to evidence that the court found insufficient to establish "heat of passion," has been interpreted as limiting the rule of the Wells case to allow a showing only of impairment of a defendant's ability to premeditate or deliberate and thus reduce an offense from first degree to second degree murder. … Read in its proper context the statement implies no such limitation, as People v. Gorshen, demonstrates.

In the Gorshen case we considered the specific question: can "evidence of defendant's abnormal mental or physical condition (whether caused by intoxication, by trauma, or by disease, but not amounting to legal insanity or unconsciousness) * * * be considered to rebut malice aforethought and intent to kill in a case * * * where the prosecution evidence shows infliction of a mortal wound for the purpose of killing and the evidence does not show provocation which would meet the law's definition of voluntary manslaughter, * * *." In resolving this question in the affirmative we overruled earlier cases that held that the question whether the defendant was guilty of murder or manslaughter is to be decided solely on the basis of the reasonable man objective standard of provocation and also overruled those cases that held that voluntary intoxication could not be considered on the question whether the defendant is guilty of murder or manslaughter. We thus gave effect to the statutory requirements for the offense of manslaughter, "the unlawful killing of a human being without malice," and recognized that since the statute had been enacted before the concept of diminished capacity had been developed, its enumeration of nonmalicious criminal homicides did not include those in which the lack of malice results from diminished capacity. That enumeration could not be exclusive, for in the absence of malice a homicide cannot be an offense higher than manslaughter. … Accordingly, a finding of provocation sufficient to reduce murder to manslaughter is not the sole means by which malice can be negated and voluntary manslaughter established. A person who intentionally kills may be incapable of harboring malice aforethought because of a mental disease, defect, or intoxication, and in such case his killing, unless justified or excused, is voluntary manslaughter. [...]

In the present case the jury was instructed that "You should find Mr. Conley guilty of first degree murder if you are convinced beyond a reasonable doubt that any shooting of either of the McCools was deliberate and premeditated as (the court has) defined those terms and that Mr. Conley was conscious of the shooting at the time." The jury was not advised that malice was also an essential element of murder. Defendant's plea of "not guilty" to the charge of first degree murder put in issue the existence of the mental states that are elements of that offense, namely, intent, deliberation, wilfulness, premeditation, and malice aforethought.[2] … Accordingly, the introduction of any evidence deserving of consideration that defendant lacked any one of these mental states entitled him to an instruction as to the effect of this lack. … "The defense of mental illness not amounting to legal insanity is a 'significant issue' in any case in which it is raised by substantial evidence. Its purpose and effect are to ameliorate the law governing criminal responsibility prescribed by the M'Naghton rule. * * * Under the Wells-Gorshen rule of diminished responsibility even though a defendant be legally sane according to the M'Naghton test, if he was suffering from a mental illness that prevented his acting with malice aforethought or with premeditation and deliberation, he cannot be convicted of murder of the first degree * * * and where * * * substantial evidence sufficient to inform the court that defendant is relying upon the defense of diminished responsibility is received, it must on its own motion instruct the jury as to the legal significance of such evidence, for such an instruction is 'necessary for the jury to be fully and fairly charged upon the relevant law." […]

Hoping to gain complete exculpation, defendant based his defense in part on a theory of unconsciousness. In support of that defense he introduced evidence of intoxication and mental illness and testified that he had no recollection of the shootings and did not intend to kill the McCools. Implicit in such a defense is also the defense of diminished capacity. The jury could well reject the claim of complete unconsciousness and yet believe that the evidence introduced to establish unconsciousness was sufficient to indicate that defendant's mental capacity was substantially reduced. Counsel for both sides made known to the court defendant's reliance on the defense of diminished capacity. Since the jury was not advised that diminished capacity could negate the existence of malice and that if malice were absent the offense could not be murder, a material issue was withheld from its consideration. The denial of the right to have a significant issue determined by the jury is in itself a miscarriage of justice within the meaning of article VI, section 4 1/2, of the Constitution and requires reversal.

The Attorney General contends, however, that the jury necessarily determined this issue under the instructions given by finding defendant guilty of first rather than second degree murder. There is no merit in this contention, for the issue of malice aforethought was not presented to the jury. In the Gorshen case we emphasized that malice is a necessary element of both degrees existing when a defendant has a specific intent to kill is not a necessary element of second degree murder, it is of both first degree murder and voluntary manslaughter. We thus made it clear that the mental state existing when a defendant has a specific intent to kill is not necessarily the mental state known as malice aforethought. We also pointed out that when used in the statute defining murder that term imports something more than malice as defined in Penal Code section 7, subdivision 4, as "a wish to vex, annoy, or injure another person, or an intent to do a wrongful act, * * *." … In returning a verdict of first degree murder, the jury found that defendant's act was intentional, voluntary, deliberate, and premeditated. They did not necessarily find, however, that defendant acted with malice aforethought.

We have previously noted the difficulty of formulating a comprehensive definition of malice aforethought that will serve to distinguish murder and manslaughter. Penal Code, section 188 provides that malice "may be express or implied. It is express when there is manifested a deliberate intention unlawfully to take away the life of a fellow creature. It is implied, when no considerable provocation appears, or when the circumstances attending the killing show an abandoned and malignant heart." These provisions create a presumption of malice when the commission of a homicide by the defendant has been proved and place the burden on him to raise a reasonable doubt in the minds of the jurors that malice was present. … The "conclusive presumption" of a malicious and guilty intent set forth in section 1962 of the Code of Civil Procedure offers no help to the jury. To bring it into operation the jury must find "the deliberate commission of an unlawful act for the purpose of injuring another," which involves subjective factors on which evidence of diminished capacity is also relevant. … As noted above, the term imports something more than the definition given in section 7 of the Penal Code when used in statutes relating specifically to homicides. Indeed, section 7's definition of malice should not be read to a jury in a murder case. […]

The instructions given to the jury in the present case were phrased in language more meaningful to the average layman than the standard jury instructions in CALJIC. In attempting to adapt the CALJIC instructions to the facts of this case and to simplify the language, however, the court failed to define malice or instruct the jury that a finding of malice was essential to a verdict convicting the defendant of murder in either degree. "Malice aforethought is a term ordinarily used in connection with the felonious killing which is murder to designate it from manslaughter. The words do not imply deliberation or the lapse of considerable time between the malicious intent to take life and its actual execution, but rather denote purpose and design in contra-distinction to accident and mischance. * * * But this is not a sufficiently complete definition or test, for (a) voluntary and some kinds of involuntary manslaughter may in fact be committed with purpose and design, yet the law removes malice aforethought from all forms of manslaughter * * *. 'Malicious intent' is not synonymous with 'willful, deliberate, and premeditated' intent." [...]

The mental state constituting malice aforethought does not presuppose or require any ill will or hatred of the particular victim. ... When a defendant "with wanton disregard for human life, does an act that involves a high degree of probability that it will result in death," he acts with malice aforethought. ... This mental state must be distinguished from that state of mind described as "wilful, deliberate, and premeditated," however. The latter phrase encompasses the mental state of one who carefully weighs the course of action he is about to take and chooses to kill his victim after considering the reasons for and against it. ... A person capable of achieving such a mental state is normally capable also of comprehending the duty society places on all persons to act within the law. If, despite such awareness, he does an act that is likely to cause serious injury or death to another, he exhibits that wanton disregard for human life or antisocial motivation that constitutes malice aforethought. An intentional act that is highly dangerous to human life, done in disregard of the actor's awareness that society requires him to conform his conduct to the law is done with malice regardless of the fact that the actor acts without ill will toward his victim or believes that his conduct is justified. In this respect it is immaterial that he does not know that his specific conduct is unlawful, for all persons are presumed to know the law including that which prohibits causing injury or death to another. An awareness of the obligation to act within the general body of laws regulating society, however, is included in the statutory definition of implied malice in terms of an abandoned and malignant heart and in the definition of express malice as the deliberate intention unlawfully to take life.

Thus, one who commits euthanasia bears no ill will toward his victim and believes his act is morally justified, but he nonetheless acts with malice if he is able to comprehend that society prohibits his act regardless of his personal belief. If because of mental defect, disease, or intoxication, however, the defendant is unable to comprehend his duty to govern his actions in accord with the duty imposed by law, he does not act with malice aforethought and cannot be guilty of murder in the first degree. The situation of an individual who kills with intent, deliberation, and premeditation, but without malice aforethought is illustrated by the evidence in the Gorshen case. Had the trial court in that case believed the defendant's testimony, it might have concluded that he acted without malice when, after an altercation with his foreman and after consuming a large quantity of alcohol, he went to his home, got his pistol, fired a shot in his living room, drove back to his place of employment, and then after being searched by two police officers (who did not find his gun) and while still in their company shot the foreman. The psychiatric expert urged that because of personality disintegration and paranoic schizophrenia the defendant believed the act necessary to prevent his own insanity and that the defendant was incapable of having the "mental state which is required for malice aforethought, or premeditation or anything which implies intention, deliberation, or premeditation." ... The defendant had testified that he had forgotten about "God's laws and human's laws and everything else." (Id.) Confronted with this evidence, the court or a jury could conclude that the defendant killed intentionally, with premeditation and deliberation, but did not do so with malice aforethought. Although legally sane according to the M'Naughton test, such a defendant could not be convicted of murder if mental illness prevented his acting with malice aforethought. … Similarly in the present case, the jury could have found that although defendant deliberated and premeditated the killings, his intoxication and mental disorder precluded malice aforethought. In finding him guilty of first degree murder under the instructions given it therefore did not necessarily determine that he acted with malice aforethought.

Inasmuch as reversal is required and similar issues will undoubtedly be raised on retrial we deem it advisable to comment on the defendant's theory that unconsciousness would be a complete defense to the murder charge. The court instructed the jury in accord with this theory that "If you are convinced that William Conley shot either of the McCools, you will then have to decide whether such shooting occurred without the defendant William Conley, being conscious of the shooting. If he shot either of said persons without being conscious of the shooting, he would not be guilty of a crime, and your verdict as to any such shooting would be not guilty."

Defendant offered evidence of intoxication caused by alcohol and drugs to support his defense of unconsciousness. Unconsciousness is ordinarily a complete defense to a criminal charge. … If the state of unconsciousness is caused by voluntary intoxication, however, it is not a complete defense. Intoxication can so diminish a person's mental capacity that he is unable to achieve a specific state of mind requisite to a crime, but, even if it is sufficient to destory volition, it cannot excuse homicide. Unconsciousness caused by voluntary intoxication is governed by Penal Code, section 22,[3] rather than section 26, and it is not a defense when a crime requires only a general criminal intent. (The union or joint operation of act and intent or criminal negligence must exist in every crime, including manslaughter…, and is deemed to exist irrespective of unconsciousness arising from voluntary intoxication. An instruction that does not distinguish unconsciousness caused by voluntary intoxication from that induced by other causes is erroneous.

It is urged that no instruction on manslaughter need be given when a defense of unconsciousness caused by voluntary intoxication is presented unless the defense is supported by expert testimony regarding diminished capacity. Although expert testimony with regard to a defendant's inability to achieve a specific state of mind may be necessary when the defense of diminished capacity is based upon mental disease or defect, such testimony is not essential to a determination by a jury that a defendant has diminished capacity to achieve a specific state of mind because of intoxication. Nonexpert witnesses may offer opinion testimony based on their observations as to a person's intoxication … and the jury may infer the presence and extent of a defendant's intoxication from evidence of his behavior and the amount of his drinking. […]

Defendant contends also that the trial court erred in admitting photographs of the bodies of Clifton and Elaine McCool on the ground that the prejudicial effect of the photographs outweighed any probative value they might have. The photographs are not inflammatory and are relevant to show the physical surroundings of the crime and the means by which the wounds were inflicted. The trial court did not abuse its discretion in determining that their probative value outweighed any possible prejudicial effect. […]

The judgment is reversed.

PETERS, TOBRINER, PEEK, and BURKE, JJ., concur.

MOSK, Justice (concurring).

I concur under compulsion of the first Modesto decision. (People v. Modesto (1963).

McCOMB, Justice (dissenting).

I dissent. In my opinion there was no prejudicial error. Therefore, pursuant to the mandate of article VI, section 4 1/2, of the Constitution of the State of California, the alleged error should be disregarded and the judgment affirmed.

Rehearing denied. McCOMB, MOSK and BURKE, JJ., dissenting.

Major footnote from this case: [This footnote is important because it identifies the main kinds of homicide in California, thus providing an outline of homicide laws in California at the time.] In adapting its instructions to a case such as this in which diminished capacity and unconsciousness because of voluntary intoxication are relied on by the defense, the felony murder doctrine is not involved, and there is no evidence of poisoning, torture, or lying in wait, the court might advise the jury:

"**Murder** is the unlawful killing of a human being with malice aforethought.

Such malice may be express or implied. It is express when there is manifested a deliberate intention unlawfully to take away the life of a fellow creature. It is implied when no considerable provocation appears, or when the circumstances attending the killing show an abandoned and malignant heart.

The law prohibits acts highly dangerous to human life that cause serious injury or death unless legal cause or excuse is shown. Malice aforethought, either express or implied, is manifested by the doing of such an act by a person who is able to comprehend this prohibition and his obligation to conform his conduct to it. There is a presumption that the defendant was able to understand this prohibition but he may rebut the presumption by evidence of diminished capacity on which I shall instruct you shortly. Malice does not require a pre-existing hatred or enmity toward the person injured.

All murder perpetrated by any kind of **wilful, deliberate, and premeditated killing is murder of the first degree**. (To be followed here by definitions of deliberation and premeditation as in customary instructions.)

Murder of the second degree must be distinguished not only from murder of the first degree, but also from manslaughter. Manslaughter shortly will be defined for you, and you will note that an essential feature of that offense, which distinguishes it from murder, is that the killing be done without malice.

If the unlawful killing of a human being is done with malice aforethought but without deliberation and premeditation, that is, without the wilful, deliberate and premeditated intent to take life that is an essential element of first degree murder, then the offense is **murder in the second degree**.

The defendant has offered evidence that because of mental illness and intoxication he was unconscious. If you find that he was conscious of the shootings, but had substantially reduced mental capacity because of mental illness or intoxication, you must consider what effect, if any, this diminished capacity had on the defendant's ability to form any of the specific mental states that are essential elements of murder, which I have defined for you, or of manslaughter, which I will define shortly.

Thus, if you find that the defendant killed Mr. or Mrs. McCool while conscious and with malice, you will return a verdict of murder. If you find that this murder was committed wilfully, deliberately, and with premeditation, you will find the murder to be of the first degree. If you find, however, that the defendant's mental capacity was so diminished that he did not, or you have a reasonable doubt whether he did, premeditate, deliberate, or form an intent to kill, you will find the murder to be of the second degree.

Premeditation, deliberation, an intent to kill, and malice must be present for the killing to be first degree murder.

Malice is an essential element of either degree of murder. Therefore, if you find that the defendant did not harbor malice because of his diminished capacity, or have a reasonable doubt whether he harbored malice, you cannot find him guilty of a higher offense than manslaughter.

Manslaughter is the unlawful killing of a human being **without malice**. Two kinds of manslaughter, the definitions of which are pertinent here, are:

1. **Voluntary manslaughter**, an intentional killing in which the law, recognizing human frailty, permits the defendant to establish the lack of malice either by
   a. **Showing provocation** such as to rouse the **reasonable man to heat of passion or sudden quarrel**. When such provocation is shown, **the law will presume that the defendant who acts in the heat of passion or on sudden quarrel, acts without malice**. I instruct you that as a matter of law no such provocation was shown to exist at the time of the killing of Mr. and Mrs. McCool. Or by
   b. Showing that **due to diminished capacity caused by mental illness, mental defect, or intoxication, the defendant did not attain the mental state constituting malice**.
2. **Involuntary manslaughter** is a killing in the commission of an unlawful act not amounting to a felony, or in the commission of a lawful act which might produce death, in an unlawful manner, or without due caution and circumspection.

Thus, if you find that the defendant killed while unconscious as a result of voluntary intoxication and was therefore unable to formulate a specific intent to kill or to harbor malice, his killing is involuntary manslaughter. **The law does not permit him to use his own vice as a shelter against the normal legal consequences of his act**. An ordinary and prudent man would not, while in possession of a dangerous weapon, permit himself to reach such a state of intoxication as to be unconscious of his action."

Causation in Homicides

An obvious component that must be shown in every murder is a casual relationship between a defendant's actions and the death of a victim. (Recall that we briefly considered one case, *Stamp,* which concerned felony murder. In that case, the excitement and fear produced in the victim by the robbery led to the victim's death for which the robber was held accountable, even though the robber did not intentionally, knowingly, or recklessly actually kill the victim. He died in part because of biologically vulnerable emotions generated by the robbery.) Recall also that not all crimes have a causal component as we considered in the essential elements of a criminal offense. However, many homicides have such sufficiently obvious causal antecedents that they may not raise legally, conceptually, or philosophically issues. Yet some may do so, as the next two cases illustrate.

In the first case, *Wilson v. State*, two brothers attacked a fiddler, Bagley, at a dance in Texas after which he died. Sam Wilson attacked Bagley with a knife; his brother Reeves struck Bagley with a rock. Because two Wilson brothers attacked Bagley, who should be held accountable for his death—both brothers, or only one of them? The Court of Appeals sorts this out. Did each Wilson brother act independently in the attack, or did they jointly agree to attack Bagley? The trial judge did not permit Reeves Wilson to present evidence that his blow did not kill Bagley. However, this is a substantial matter, depending upon further facts about the attack.

Did each act independently of the other? Even if this were the case, if each made some contribution to Bagley's death, both could have been held accountable. In this instance, however, the contribution of each would matter; did one contribute the fatal blow, did both aid and abet the other regardless of any fatal strike?

If the brothers conspired to attack Bagley—that is, had an agreement that they would jointly attack him—then each would have been accountable for the actions of the other. Roughly speaking, a conspiracy is an agreement between two or more people to commit a crime with some steps taken in furtherance of the conspiracy. Should the trial judge have permitted Reeves to present evidence to the jury about his role in Bagley's death? What testimony to the jury would help settle this issue? It is also important to note that if the brothers conspired to attack Bagley, there would be no issue of each of their individual causal contributions because each is held accountable for the actions of the other, even if one brother did not cause the fatal blow.

Wilson v. State

Court of Criminal Appeals of Texas

24 S.W. 409 (1893)

Opinion: HURT, P. J.

There was a dance at the house on S. Winkfield's farm in Gonzales county on the night of the 26th of November, 1892. The deceased, Bagley, was the "fiddler;" and while "playing the fiddle," there being quite a number of ladies present, Steve Wilson (brother of appellant) came into the room, and began cursing and using vulgar language. Bagley requested him to stop using such language in presence of the ladies, whereupon Steve said, "If you think you can make me stop, you had better try it." Bagley got up, fiddle in hand, and placed one hand on Steve, and said, "You ought not to do that way." They then struck one or two blows, when defendant and his brother Sam came up, defendant striking Bagley on the head with a large rock, and some one stabbing him with a knife, inflicting a mortal wound. Some of the witnesses saw the knife before Sam struck deceased, and some did not. No witness swears that appellant saw the knife.

There is no proof beyond the mere fact that they acted together as above that Sam and appellant had conspired to make the assault and battery upon deceased. Now, if they had conspired—agreed together to commit the battery,—appellant to use the rock and Sam the knife,—Bagley being killed by either one, the homicide being culpable, both would be guilty to the same extent, without reference to who inflicted the mortal wound.

On the other hand, if the act of appellant was not in prosecution of an assault,—conspiracy between Sam and himself,—but was independent of it, he acting upon his own motion, Sam, having inflicted the mortal wound, would be responsible for the homicide. Again, if two or more persons conceive the intention at the same time to strike B. without previous concert, and do strike him without knowing the intention of the other, each would be responsible for his own acts, but would not be an aider or abettor of the other.

To apply this rule to this case, if appellant, without concert with Sam, and without knowledge of his intentions, conceived the intention to and did strike Bagley with a rock about the time that Sam stabbed him, he would not be responsible for said act; nor would he, in striking Bagley, be aiding or abetting Sam in his acts. But, notwithstanding this, if appellant assaulted deceased with the rock he would be responsible for the homicide; or, if the blow with the rock contributed materially to the death of Bagley, he also would be responsible. This being so, appellant had the right to prove the extent of the wound caused by the rock. He had the right to go into this subject fully. And if he could have shown that the wound inflicted by him did not materially contribute to the death of deceased, and that there was no concert between Sam and himself, nor that he had knowledge of Sam's intentions, then he would not have been responsible for the homicide.

The court erred in rejecting the proposed evidence regarding the extent of the wound made by the rock, and, in line with this theory of the case, the special instructions requested by counsel for appellant. Though but slightly correct, they very pertinently called the attention of the court to the proper charge which should have been prepared and given to the jury. Judgment reversed, and cause remanded.

In this second case, *State v. Newberg, et al.*, two friends, Newberg and Black, went to hunt deer and camped the night before the season opened. Hearing sounds in the brush, they decided they would try to kill their game early. In doing so, they violated at least three laws—they were hunting out of season once they began shooting at what they thought was a deer; they were shooting near a road; and they were shooting at night when they could not see their target clearly. One hunter suggested he shoot the "deer" while the other held a light so that the first could see the target. After several shots, he missed. The second hunter urged that he be given the gun while the first hunter held the light. After a few shots, they heard a thump as if something hit the ground. Going to investigate they found a dead horse and a dead man who had been riding the horse through the woods.

They had committed a homicide. Should it be considered murder or some form of manslaughter? Should both be held accountable or, perhaps only the second shooter who may have caused the fatal blow? Should it matter who actually pulled the trigger that delivered the bullet of death? What does the Supreme Court of Oregon hold? Who should be held accountable? What principles guide their deliberations, or what is their rationale?

State v. Newberg

Supreme Court of Oregon.

129 Or. 564 (1929)

Defendant was indicted for second degree murder. He was found guilty of manslaughter and appeals from judgment entered on the jury's verdict.

The appellant and his codefendant, Fred N. Black, were indicted by the grand jury of the county of Wallowa for the crime of second degree murder. The indictment charged that the two defendants, on the 25th day of September, 1928, in that county, without due caution and circumspection, involuntarily killed one Leonard Olsen. … Upon the trial of the appellant it developed that the deceased was shot to death at approximately 9:20 p. m. September 25, 1928, by a bullet fired by one of the two defendants, when they mistook the horse upon which he was riding for a deer. At the close of all the evidence the court withdrew from the jury's consideration the charge of second degree murder, and submitted only the lesser charge of manslaughter. From a verdict of guilty a judgment to that effect was entered, from which the appellant has appealed. He presents for our consideration five assignments of error, one of which is based upon the denial of the motion for a change of venue. The second is premised upon an objection to a portion of the argument of the special prosecutor; a third arises out of the refusal of the court to give three instructions requested by the defendant; a fourth contends that error was committed when the state was permitted to offer some evidence in rebuttal, which the defendant contends constituted part of its case in chief; and the fifth assignment predicates error upon the denial of a motion for a directed verdict.

Opinion: ROSSMAN, J. (after *stating* the facts as above).

[The court rejected appeals based on the first, second, fourth, and fifth appeals. The court largely addresses the third basis of appeal concerning jury instructions both given and denied by the trial judge.]

[…]

The court instructed the jury:

"I instruct you that, if you find from the evidence in this case beyond a reasonable doubt that the defendant, Newberg, at or about the time alleged in the indictment in this county and state, fired his rifle at an object which he thought to be a deer, he failed to use due caution and circumspection and involuntarily killed Leonard Olsen, then the defendant would be guilty of involuntary manslaughter. Upon the other hand, if the state has failed to establish beyond a reasonable doubt, the guilt of the defendant of the crime of involuntary manslaughter, you should find him not guilty. * * * And I further instruct you that it is your duty to consider this case alone, without any reference to the indictment against Fred M. Black. In order to convict the defendant Harry Newberg of the charge made against him in this indictment, there must be evidence against him which convinces you beyond a reasonable doubt of his guilt. While these defendants are indicted together, and are charged with a joint offense, it is necessary that evidence should be given against each one of them, and it is within the power of the jury, and it is the duty of the jury, to consider the case of each defendant separately, and if the evidence is not sufficient to convict this defendant, Harry Newberg, under the instructions of the court, no matter whether sufficient to convict the other defendant or not, you should consider the case of Harry Newberg alone, and if the state has not satisfied you of his guilt beyond a reasonable doubt you should acquit him."

The defendant does not criticize the foregoing, but complains because the court did not give three of his requested instructions, the trend of which is suggested by the following excerpts:

"Each of the defendants in this case cannot be guilty of the crime of involuntary manslaughter. * * * If there is a reasonable doubt in your minds as to whether or not the deceased met his death as a result of a bullet from the gun when fired by Harry Newberg, it is your duty to find him not guilty of involuntary manslaughter. * * * The party who fired the gun, whose bullet struck Leonard Olsen, could be guilty of involuntary manslaughter. In this connection I therefore instruct you that, even though you may believe from all of the evidence in the case that Harry Newberg was negligent under all the surrounding circumstances, or that he failed to use due caution and circumspection, you cannot find him guilty of involuntary manslaughter in this case, if you believe from the evidence that Leonard Olsen met his death at the result of a bullet fired from the gun when held by Fred M. Black."

The refusal of the court to give the latter instructions is assigned as error. It seems desirable to briefly state some of the facts. The appellant and his companion, Crews, who were upon a deer-hunting expedition, were camped for the night at the edge of a clearing immediately adjacent to a roadway, which apparently bore a fair amount of travel. Less than 200 feet from this road, and running in a course generally parallel to it, was another road, which bore occasional travel. The area between the two roads, at the place with which we are concerned, was cleared of timber and of all underbrush, except such as would generally be called weeds. With the two men at the time in question was the codefendant, Black, who was anxious to participate in the hunt, but could not do so until a day or two later. The three hunters did not expect to find deer at that precise place, but testified, nevertheless, that they had heard that deer had been seen in that vicinity. The land upon which they were camped was in private ownership, but was frequently used for camping. In fact, it was equipped with some crude tables and benches. At approximately 9:20 p. m., when the full moon was shining, Leonard Olsen, the deceased, who was upon horseback, left the upper roadway with the intention, apparently, of cutting across the clearing and entering upon the road which we have described as bearing the greater travel. At that time the hunters were about their camp fire. Crews heard the noise made by the hoofs of the horse and called it to the attention of the other two. Thereupon Black reached for a spot light and remarking, "Maybe it is a buck," directed its rays to the vicinity of the noise. In a moment he exclaimed: "It is a buck. Harry, get your gun." At that time the object was 125 feet away. The appellant had his gun at hand, and, although he testified he could not distinguish the nature of the object, fired three shots at it. During all of this time Black directed the rays of his spot light at the object. When the third shot had been fired, Black said: "Hell, you never hit him; give me that gun." Thereupon, the appellant handed his gun to Black, and took the latter's spot light, directing its rays at the object while Black fired one shot. About that time a thump was heard, as though a heavy object had fallen to the ground, and this in turn was followed by groans. Black approached the object, and discovered that it was a man gasping for breath and unable to speak. Shortly thereafter the man, Leonard Olsen, died.

We need not recount the further details, except to say that shortly after midnight the public officers arrived and the three men denied that they had caused the death. The next morning, at a distance of 200 or 300 feet from Olsen's body, the dead horse, light gray in color, was discovered. It was the horse upon which Olsen was riding when the shots were fired; two had entered its body. About that time the three men withdrew their previous denials and said that Olsen was shot when his horse was mistaken by them for a deer.

The above, we believe, warrants the conclusion that appellant and Black both desired to kill the object at which they were firing they supposing it to be a deer. Their plan and purpose was a joint one, which the one entertained to the same extent as the other. To provide for its execution they proceeded together; Black got his spot light while the appellant reached for his rifle; then Black directed the rays of his light upon the object, while the appellant fired three bullets. After these shots were fired, the appellant gave the gun to Black, who fired at the object while appellant directed the rays of the spot light.

The court's instructions were manifestly based upon the theory that the appellant could not be guilty of manslaughter, unless one of his shots killed Olsen. Appellant's requested instructions were to the same effect, but were perhaps more pointed. If appellant's theory is correct and applicable to this case, the court below for the sake of clearness of instruction should have given these requested instructions. The precise problem presented by this situation—that is, whether a party is guilty of manslaughter when a death is the proximate result of the joint culpable negligence of himself and another—has never been determined by this court, but we believe that two of our decisions foreshadow the result.

Our statute defining manslaughter (section 1898, Or. L.) provides: "If any person shall, in the commission of an unlawful act, or a lawful act without due caution or circumspection, involuntarily kill another, such person shall be deemed guilty of manslaughter." ...

In State v. Miller, the defendant was charged with manslaughter, predicated upon the operation of his automobile in such a negligent manner that it caused a death. In holding proper the rejection of an instruction, requested by the defendant, upon the subject of contributory negligence, this court said: "The instruction requested was sound, but was apt to be misleading, in view of the fact that contributory negligence in an action of this kind is no defense." The rule that contributory negligence is no defense in prosecutions for manslaughter has been many times reiterated by the courts. Since a negligent act of the deceased, which contributed as a cause in bring about the ultimate result, does not defeat the prosecution, we fail to understand why a similar act, performed by a third party, should demand a judgment of innocence.

The authorities recognize no difference between the effect of the contributory negligence of the deceased and the concurring negligence of a third party. In fact, the authorities apply to a situation, such as is presented by this assignment of error, substantially the same principles of law as are applied in a civil action based upon negligence, except that they demand a higher degree of carelessness than constitutes negligence, and require that the evidence must establish, between that culpable negligence and the death, the relationship of an efficient proximate cause.

We shall now refer to some of the authorities. In Brill's Cyclopedia of Criminal Law, § 221, we find: "There may be principals in the second degree, aiders and abettors, and accessaries before the fact in involuntary manslaughter. * * * There may be accessaries after the fact to both voluntary and involuntary manslaughter." From Clark's Criminal Law...: "Where the culpably negligent acts of two or more persons concur in causing another's death, all of them are guilty." ... [F]rom Clark & Marshall, Crimes (3d Ed.) § 164:

"There may be principals in the second degree and accessories before the fact to involuntary manslaughter. Thus, if two men drive separate vehicles at a furious and dangerous speed along the highway, each inciting and abetting the other, and one of them drives over and kills a person, the one thus causing the death is guilty of manslaughter as principal in the first degree, and the other is guilty as principal in the second degree. And the same would be true of two persons in the same vehicle, one driving and the other inciting and abetting him."

We have read substantially all of the cases cited by the writers, and find that they fully support the text. ...

We deduce the rule from the above that, where the act of a defendant is of the required degree of culpability and it operates as an efficient proximate cause of the death, the defendant is guilty of the crime of involuntary manslaughter, even though some one else's negligence may have concurred. Such being our conclusion, we find no error in the refusal of the court to give the requested instructions.

There remains undisposed of only the assignment of error predicated upon the refusal of the court to direct a judgment in the appellant's favor. …

Under the foregoing [review] we cannot say that the jury erred in concluding that appellant's act was accompanied with the degree of culpability which our statute defines as manslaughter. …

It follows from the foregoing that the judgment of the circuit court is affirmed.

BEAN, McBRIDE, and RAND, JJ., concur

(Citations omitted)

You will want to recall this case when we consider some of the cases concerning causation in the tort law, especially *Summers v. Tice*. What are some similarities between that case and this one? Are defendants treated similarly by the two areas of the law or differently? Should they be treated similarly or not? Be prepared to discuss these issues.

Excuses, Justifications, and Mitigations

To this point we have considered elements of a crime that must be established in order to find a person guilty, and examples that illustrate different kinds of homicide that may be committed, together with various homicides. However, there are some factual conditions that might *excuse* one's conduct, *justify* it, or *mitigate* it for convicting or sentencing purposes. A brief review of these terms follows to provide some context for discussions of insanity and to illustrate some features of legal decisions we have already read.

Sometimes a person accused of a crime, or even a moral failure, will offer an *excuse*. With an excuse, defendants are asserting that what they did was wrong (e.g., "I dropped your valuable vase), but at the same time asserts that they are not properly to blame for what occurred, (e.g., "Bobby hit me with his bicycle and I did not see him coming, causing me to drop it"). In the law, typical instances of excuses might be that the defendant was not properly responsible for acting unlawfully because of *ignorance or mistake of facts* about the circumstances ("I did not see Johnny sneak behind the target at which I was shooting even though I carefully checked"), or perhaps of an *accident*, such as "I stumbled and dropped my sick child, injuring her." Excuses arise from particular facts about the defendants or circumstances in which the defendants find themselves.

There are two excuses that have prominent roles in homicide cases, including two of which we have already seen—insanity and infancy (absence of general *mens rea*). These excuses point to something about the condition or state of the person, not particular facts about the circumstances in which a violation occurred. A defendant who claims she lacked general *mens rea* is asserting that at the time she acted and killed a victim, she lacked the substantial capacity to understand what she was doing or lacked substantial capacity to control her conduct to abide by the law. In both *Wolff* and *Conley,* the defendants presented claims that each was insane, but the jury was not persuaded, so neither was successful.

Excuses are distinguished from *justifications*. By offering a justification, defendants implicitly recognize that the act would typically be unlawful, but they claim the law should not see their action as unlawful and hence punishable given the circumstances (e.g., necessity, self-defense). These reasons might rest on the claims that what they did was justifiable or at least not legally wrong in the circumstances. A notable example of a justification occurs when a defendant claims that indeed he hit and injured Smith who was attacking him, but in the circumstances, it was justifiable or at least not wrong for him to protect himself because he was in serious danger, could not escape without fighting back, and no policeman was nearby to whom he might appeal for protection. A defendant might also assert that he assaulted someone who was attacking others, invoking the justification of *defense of others*. A more ambiguous defense is duress, sometimes called "coercion" or "compulsion" (*U.S. v. Logan*, 49 F.3d 352 (8th Cir. 1995).[3] In this instance, Sally may assert that she was held at gunpoint and threatened with obvious and believable harm if she did not break the law; e.g., by helping to rob a bank, unless she did as she was told.

Finally, *mitigations* may be of two kinds: formal and informal. *Formal mitigations* are part of the rules of the law that permit a reduction of a more serious crime to a less serious crime, if appropriate facts are established (e.g., *provocation* reduces murder in the first degree to voluntary manslaughter). The discussion in *Maher v. the People* considers the formal mitigation of murder in the first degree to voluntary manslaughter provided a defendant could establish facts showing that the defendant was sufficiently *provoked*, thus undermining his rational ability to control himself, causing him to act in the heat of passion (or upon a sudden quarrel). Recall, in addition, that in *People v. Conley,* the California Supreme Court held that if a defendant, such as Conley, had diminished mental capacity but was not found insane, and intentionally killed the McCools, he would be permitted to argue that this defense mitigated a charge of first-degree murder to voluntary manslaughter, provided appropriate facts on his behalf could be established.

Informal mitigations are considerations that are typically addressed at the time of sentencing a person already found guilty; they are based on information about the person, perhaps his or her life, and even his or her legal record. Was the person a first-time offender or a repeat offender? Was the manner of committing the crime particularly vicious, revealing a person who may deserve a longer punishment? And so on.

Next, we consider a well-known but rarely used excuse to a charge of murder—namely that at the time of killing another person, the defendant was insane.

A Note on Insanity in the Criminal Law

To be justly held accountable under the criminal law, subject to the harsh treatment of punishment and its condemnatory aspect that typically accompanies a finding of guilt, a person must exhibit the minimal capacities needed to be judged a responsible person versus a person lacking in the capacity to be a responsible person under the law. As discussed in Chapter 1, a person may fail to have these capacities if he or she has the mental development of a child, that is, judged to be like an infant. A second reason

---

3 American Law Institute Model Penal Code Official Draft, 1962: Section 2.09 for duress and sections 301 and 302 for justification. In Sanford H. Kadish & Stephen J. Schulhofer (1989). *Criminal law and its processes: Cases and materials* (5th ed.), p. 1190. Little, Brown.

a person may not be judged to be a responsible person is that one lacks sufficient mental capacities that a normal adult would have to understand the law and abide by it. This second condition occurs if an alleged defendant is judged to be insane. If one is found to be insane, the person is judged to have an *excuse* for actions at the time of committing a crime; he or she is sufficiently unlike normal adults that he or she may not be justly held accountable and punished. This does not mean a person goes free from legal confinement, just that they are sent to a different institution, typically to an institution for the criminally insane. A person may spend many years in such confinement, but it is not a legal "punishment," merely confinement away from normal society.

A legal assessment of insanity may enter into legal charges in three different ways: 1) At the time of acting, was the alleged defendant a sufficiently sane, responsible person to be justly punished and held accountable? 2) Is the alleged defendant sufficiently sane to participate in his or her own defense? 3) If a person is convicted and required to be punished, is the convicted defendant sufficiently sane to appreciate the punishment? We are only concerned with issue 1).

One of the earliest and most influential legal cases characterizing insanity is Daniel M'Naghten's Case decided in 1843 in England. M'Naghten was indicted for murder for killing the "secretary to the British Prime minister, believing that the Prime Minister was conspiring against him."[4] As you will read, M'Naghten was found not guilty by reason of insanity at a jury trial, which was reaffirmed by the top appellate court in England, the House of Lords.

Jury instructions to guide whether or not an actor was insane at the time of acting is the following:

> Jurors ought to be told in all cases that every man is to be presumed to be sane, and to possess a sufficient degree of reason to be responsible for his crimes, until the contrary be proved to their satisfaction; and that to establish a defence on the ground of insanity, it must be clearly proved that, at the time of the committing of the act, the party accused was labouring under such a defect of reason, from disease of the mind, as not to know the nature and quality of the act he was doing; or, if he did know it, that he did not know he was doing what was wrong.

Notably this court strongly emphasizes that a person must be found to be acting with a "defect of reason" so "as not to know the nature and quality of his act" or "if he did know it, he did not know he was doing what is wrong." The emphasis here is that insanity is characterized as a deficiency of knowledge, which became the test for insanity for decades. Ultimately, influenced by developments in psychology and psychiatry, courts endorsed broader conceptions of insanity. I introduce some of these after the M'Naghten case.

4 Cornell Law School, Legal Information Institute. The insanity defense: The M'Naghten case. Located at https://www.law.cornell.edu/wex/insanity_defense.

Daniel M'Naghten's Case

House of Lords, 1843

10 Cl. & F. 200, S Eng, Rep. 718

The prisoner had been indicted for that he, on the 20th day of January 1843, at the parish of Saint Martin in the Fields, in the county of Middlesex, and within the jurisdiction of the Central Criminal Court, in and upon one Edward Drummond, feloniously, wilfully, and of his malice aforethought, did make an assault; and that the said Daniel M'Naghten, a certain pistol of the value of 20s, loaded and charged with gunpowder and a leaden bullet (which pistol he in his right hand had and held), to, against and upon the said Edward Drummond, feloniously, wilfully, and of his malice aforethought, did shoot and discharge; and that the said Daniel M'Naghten, with the leaden bullet aforesaid, out of the pistol aforesaid, by force of the gunpowder, etc., the said Edward Drummond, in and upon the back of him the said Edward Drummond, feloniously, etc. did strike penetrate and wound, giving to the said Edward Drummond, in and upon the back of the said Edward Drummond, one mortal wound, etc., of which mortal wound the said E. Drummond languished until the 25th of April and then died; and that by the means aforesaid, he the prisoner did kill and murder the said Edward Drummond. The prisoner pleaded not guilty.

Evidence having been given of the fact of the shooting of Mr. Drummond, and of his death in consequence thereof, witnesses were called on the part of the prisoner, to prove that he was not, at the time of committing the act, in a sound state of mind. The medical evidence was in substance this: That persons of otherwise sound mind, might be affected by morbid delusions: that the prisoner was in that condition: that a person so labouring under a morbid delusion, might have a morbid perception of right and wrong, but that in the case of the prisoner it was a delusion which carried him away beyond the power of his own control, and left him no such perception; and that he was not capable of exercising any control over acts which had connexion with his delusion: that it was of the nature of the disease with which the prisoner was affected, to go on gradually until it had reached a climax, when it burst forth with irresistible intensity: that a man might go on for years quietly, though at the same time under its influence, but would all at once break out into the most extravagant and violent paroxysms.

Some of the witnesses who gave this evidence, had previously examined the prisoner. Others had never seen him till he appeared in Court, and they formed their opinions on hearing the evidence given by the other witnesses.

The presiding judge, Lord Chief Justice Tindal, in his charge to the jury stated: "The question to be determined is whether at the time the act in question was committed, the prisoner had or had not the use of his understanding, so as to know that he was doing a wrong or wicked act. If the jurors should be of opinion that the prisoner was not sensible, at the time he committed it, that he was violating the laws both of God and man, then he would be entitled to a verdict in his favour, but if, on the contrary, they were of opinion that when he committed the murder, he was in a sound state of mind, then their verdict must be against him."

The jury returned a verdict of "Not guilty" on the ground of insanity.

The case and the verdict attracted considerable attention, as well as the general problem of the defense of legal insanity, which was debated in the House of Lords. As a result, the English judiciary (there were some fifteen judges at the time) were invited to attend the House of Lords for the purpose of delivering answers to certain questions propounded to them. The famous "M'Naghten rule" is found in the answer to the second and third questions delivered by Lord Chief Justice Tindal.

> Your Lordships are pleased to inquire of us, secondly, "What are the proper questions to be submitted to the jury where a person alleged to be afflicted with insane delusion respecting one or more particular subjects or persons, is charged with the commission of a crime (murder, for example and insanity is set up as a defence?" And, thirdly, "In what terms ought the question to be left to the jury as to the prisoner's state of mind at the time when the act was committed?" And as these two questions appear to us to be more conveniently answered together, we have to submit our opinion to be, that the Jurors ought to be told in all cases that every man is to be presumed to be sane, and to possess a sufficient degree of reason to be responsible for his crimes, until the contrary be proved to their satisfaction; and that to establish a defence on the ground of insanity, it must be clearly proved that, at the time of the committing of the act, the party accused was labouring under such a defect of reason, from disease of the mind, as not to know the nature and quality of the act he was doing; or, if he did know it, that he did not know he was doing what was wrong. The mode of putting the latter part of the question to the jury on these occasions has generally been, whether the accused at the time of doing the act knew the difference between right and wrong: which mode, though rarely, if ever, leading to any mistake with the jury, is not, as we conceive, so accurate when put generally and in the abstract; as when put with reference to the party's knowledge of right and wrong in respect to the very act with which he is charged. If the question were to be put as to the knowledge of the accused solely and exclusively with reference to the law of the land, it might tend to confound the jury, by inducing them to believe that an act of knowledge of the law of the land was essential in order to lead to a conviction; whereas the law is administered upon the principle that every one must be taken conclusively to know it, without proof that he does know it. If the accused was conscious that the act was one which he ought not to do, and if the act was at the same time contrary to the law of the land, he is punishable; and the usual course therefore has been to leave the question to the jury, whether the party accused had a sufficient degree of reason to know that he was doing an act that was wrong: and this course we think is correct, accompanied with such observations and explanations as the circumstances of each particular case may require.

Influenced by developments in psychiatry and psychology, courts began to broaden the legal conception of insanity because a person may be judged to be a non-responsible person—to lack the minimal conditions to be held legally accountable—for reasons other than failing to know or understand the difference between right and wrong or a failure to understand that what one is doing is wrong.

Irresistible Impulse Defense: An early modification of the M'Naghten rule for judging that a person is not sufficiently responsible to be held accountable was the "irresistible impulse" defense (1929). This focuses on an actor's inability to exercise *volitional* control over one's actions because of a mental disease or defect and echoes one aspect of the M'Naghten opinion. Under this test,

> [A] jury may find a defendant not guilty by reason of insanity where the defendant was laboring under a mental disease or defect that compelled him to commit the object offense. This test is well-suited for persons suffering from manias and paraphilias [a condition in which a person's sexual arousal and gratification depend on fantasizing about and engaging in sexual behavior that is atypical and extreme].[5]

Model Penal Code Insanity Defense

The American Law Institute's Model Penal Code, in focusing on the insanity defense, learned from various shortcomings of previous formulations for legal insanity and presented a more comprehensive account: "a defendant is not responsible for criminal conduct where (s)he, as a result of mental disease or defect, did not possess a 'substantial capacity either to appreciate the criminality of his conduct or to conform his conduct to the requirements of the law.'"[6]

This account recognizes that a defendant must have a mental disease or defect (following the early M'Naghten rule), and it must manifest itself in an alleged defendant lacking a "substantial capacity to appreciate the criminality of his conduct" (a kind cognitive deficiency also using aspects of M'Naghten) or to "conform his conduct to the requirements of the law," an emphasis on the actor's volition, echoing aspects of M'Naghten and at least in part the irresistible impulse rule.

The Model Penal Code rule provides a less sharp distinction between insanity and sanity than M'Naghten and uses "substantial capacity" to conform to the law instead of being "compelled" to act as he or she did under the Irresistible Impulse Rule. One might say it endorses graduated concepts compared with more discrete concepts, which assist recognition of degrees of sanity or insanity (recall *Wolff* and *Conley* for approximate similarities). Importantly, how the insanity defense is treated in different jurisdictions can vary. Typically, a defendant must raise this possible excuse. After that, in some jurisdictions a prosecutor must show that defendants claiming insanity were sane beyond a reasonable doubt, or in other jurisdictions defendants must show they were insane by a preponderance of the evidence.

Can Corporations and Their Officers Be Held Accountable for Homicides?

One of the last cases we consider on homicide involves a corporation and its officers. One might think that organizations cannot be held accountable for homicides because they are organizations—aren't murders committed by people, not organizations? In addition, people can be sent to prison, but corporations cannot? This puts the questions a bit simply, but one might also suppose that because fine, upstanding people own and manage corporations, it's implausible that they could commit some form of homicide.

---

5 Cornell Law School, Legal Information Institute. The insanity defense. Located at https://www.law.cornell.edu/wex/insanity_defense.

6 American Law Institute Model Penal Code Official Draft, 1962: Section 4.01. In Sanford H. Kadish & Stephen J. Schulhofer (1989). *Criminal law and its processes: Cases and materials* (5th ed.), pp. 1204–1205. Little, Brown.

This is a mistake. In *People v. O'Neil and Film Recovery Systems*, except for an error by the trial judge, the law recognized individuals that were officers or managers of a corporation could be held for murder in Illinois, and the organization they ran—the corporation—could be held accountable for manslaughter. A judicial error prevented this case from being upheld by the Illinois Supreme Court, but both claims might have been true under the law had a trial judge not erred.

Mr. Golab worked for Film Recovery Systems, a company that was in the business of recovering silver from used photographic film. Silver chloride made photographic film function as it did. In taking a picture, if the film is exposed to light, in places it changes from dark to light or the reverse in black and white film (which few of you may know about because photographic film has been replaced by digital photography). However, even used silver chloride on previously exposed film was sufficiently valuable, so that money could be made reclaiming the silver, by separating it with a physical and chemical process and selling it to a reprocessing plant in Nevada.

In the processing the company used cyanide. They appeared to have used big vats of cyanide, but from time to time those needed to be cleaned out. One morning Mr. Golab was inside a cyanide vat, cleaning it out. He began to suffer convulsions. Other employees helped him out of the vat, brought him to safety on the plant floor, but his convulsions continued, leading to his death.

Because of his death and the circumstances surrounding it, the district attorney brought murder charges against the manager, the president, and the vice president of the company. These individuals were charged with murder because the conditions on the plant floor were too dangerous for employees and Mr. Golab died.

In addition, the company was charged with involuntary manslaughter because of the general risky, dangerous conditions in the plant leading to Mr. Golab's death.

Two major takeaways from this case are that individual corporate offices can be charged with homicides, including murder, and the company as a whole can be charged with lesser homicides, in this case involuntary manslaughter.

At trial the three officers were found guilty of murder under Illinois law and the corporation was found guilty of involuntary manslaughter. An intermediate appellate court upheld the trial court convictions. The Illinois Supreme Court overturned both lower court decisions, but for technical reasons, which the court suggests has little to do with the *mens rea* of the defendants.

To find a company guilty of a crime, a court must find an individual within the company whose state of mind is needed for the specific *mens rea* of the crime, so the courts had to identify individuals within the company with the appropriate state of mind. At trial, defendants O'Neil, Kirschbaum, and Rodriguez each received sentences of 25 years' imprisonment for murder and 14 concurrent 364–day imprisonment terms for reckless conduct toward their employees.

Thus, even if one is employed in a corporation, that person can still be found guilty of committing a crime, depending upon how one treats employees. Second, the trial court found the corporations represented by O'Neil, Kirschbaum, and Rodriguez and others guilty of involuntary manslaughter. To do this, the court had to identify an individual who represents the state of mind of a person making decisions that led to the corporate crime. Similarly, if a prosecutor charges a corporation with reckless homicide, she has to find individual decision-makers who exhibited recklessness leading to Mr. Golab's death.

What courts may not do according to this case is to attribute two incompatible states of mind to one person charged with two different crimes. One person may not be held accountable for knowingly causing the death of another and negligently causing the death of the same person.

People v. O'Neil, Film Recovery Systems, Inc.

Appellate Court of Illinois

194 Ill. App. 3d 79 (1990)

Opinion: Justice LORENZ delivered the opinion of the court:

Following a joint bench trial, individual defendants Steven O'Neil, Charles Kirschbaum, and Daniel Rodriguez, agents of Film Recovery Systems, Inc. (Film Recovery), were convicted of murder... in the death of Stefan Golab, a Film Recovery employee, from cyanide poisoning stemming from conditions in Film Recovery's plant in Elk Grove Village, Illinois. Corporate defendants Film Recovery and its sister corporation Metallic Marketing Systems, Inc. (Metallic Marketing), were convicted of involuntary manslaughter ...in the same death. O'Neil, Kirschbaum, Rodriguez, Film Recovery, and Metallic Marketing were also convicted of 14 counts of reckless conduct ... involving 14 other Film Recovery employees. [...]

Individual defendants O'Neil, Kirschbaum, and Rodriguez each received sentences of 25 years' imprisonment for murder and 14 concurrent 364–day imprisonment terms for reckless conduct. O'Neil and Kirschbaum were also each fined $10,000 with respect to the murder convictions and $14,000 with respect to the convictions for reckless conduct. Corporate defendants Film Recovery and Metallic Marketing were each fined $10,000 with respect to the convictions for involuntary manslaughter and $14,000 with respect to the convictions for reckless conduct.

On appeal, defendants urge that their convictions must be reversed and the cause remanded for retrial because the judgments rendered were inconsistent. Defendants also contend that the evidence presented at trial was insufficient to support the convictions.

We conclude that the judgments rendered are legally inconsistent. Therefore, we now reverse those convictions as to both the individual and corporate defendants and remand the matter for retrial. We summarize below those facts, as they appear in the record, which are pertinent to our disposition.

In 1982, Film Recovery ... was there engaged in the business of extracting, for resale, silver from used x-ray and photographic film. Metallic Marketing operated out of the same premises ... and owned 50% of the stock of Film Recovery. The recovery process was performed at Film Recovery's plant located at the 1855 address and involved "chipping" the film product and soaking the granulated pieces in large open bubbling vats containing a solution of water and sodium cyanide. The cyanide solution caused silver contained in the film to be released. ...

On the morning of February 10, 1983, shortly after he disconnected a pump on one of the tanks and began to stir the contents of the tank with a rake, Stefan Golab became dizzy and faint. He left the production area to go rest in the lunchroom area of the plant. Plant workers present on that day testified Golab's body had trembled and he had foamed at the mouth. Golab eventually lost consciousness and was taken outside of the plant. Paramedics summoned to the plant were unable to revive him. Golab was pronounced dead upon arrival at Alexian Brothers Hospital.

The Cook County medical examiner performed an autopsy on Golab the following day. ... After receiving the toxicological report, the medical examiner determined Golab died from acute cyanide poisoning through the inhalation of cyanide fumes in the plant air.

Defendants were subsequently indicted by a Cook County grand jury. The grand jury charged defendants O'Neil, Kirschbaum, Rodriguez, Pett, and Mackay with murder, stating that, as individuals and as officers and high managerial agents of Film Recovery, they had, on February 10, 1983, knowingly created a strong probability of Golab's death. Generally, the indictment stated the individual defendants failed to disclose to Golab that he was working with substances containing cyanide and failed to advise him about, train him to anticipate, and provide adequate equipment to protect him from, attendant dangers involved. The grand jury charged Film Recovery and Metallic Marketing with involuntary manslaughter stating that, through the reckless acts of their officers, directors, agents, and others, all acting within the scope of their employment, the corporate entities had, on February 10, 1983, unintentionally killed Golab. Finally, the grand jury charged both individual and corporate defendants with reckless conduct as to 20 other Film Recovery employees based on the same conduct alleged in the murder indictment, but expanding the time of that conduct to "on or about March 1982 through March 1983."

Proceedings commenced in the circuit court in January 1985 and continued through the conclusion of trial in June of that year. In the course of the 24–day trial, evidence from 59 witnesses was presented, either directly or through stipulation of the parties. That testimony is contained in over 2,300 pages of trial transcript. [...]

On June 14, 1985, the trial judge pronounced his judgment of defendants' guilt. The trial judge found that "**the mind and mental state of a corporation is the mind and mental state of the directors, officers and high managerial personnel because they act on behalf of the corporation** for both the benefit of the corporation and for themselves." Further, "if the corporation's officers, directors and high managerial personnel act within the scope of their corporate responsibilities and employment for their benefit and for the benefit of the profits of the corporation, the corporation must be held liable for what occurred in the work place."

Defendants filed timely notices of appeal, the matters were consolidated for review, and arguments were had before this court in July 1987. One of defendants' principal contentions was that the federal Occupational Safety and Health Act of 1970 (OSHA) preempted state criminal prosecutions against individual and corporate defendants for conditions in an industrial workplace. That identical issue was the subject of a then pending appeal before the Illinois Supreme Court in People v. Chicago Magnet Wire (1989). ... Accordingly, we postponed disposition in this case until the supreme court decided Chicago Magnet Wire. Following the determination in Chicago Magnet Wire that such prosecutions were not preempted under OSHA, we invited the parties to file new briefs and scheduled further oral argument on the remaining issues.

OPINION

Defendants raise two contentions with respect to the consistency of the judgments rendered at trial. Each contention rests, ultimately, on the observation that **the offense of murder requires a mental state different from that required for the offenses of involuntary manslaughter and reckless conduct.**

In their first contention, defendants argue that the judgments for murder and reckless conduct against individual defendants O'Neil, Kirschbaum, and Rodriguez are inconsistent because, while the offense of murder requires a knowing and intentional act ..., reckless conduct does not. ... Defendants argue both convictions, however, arose from the same acts of the individual defendants. Defendants reason

O'Neil, Kirschbaum, and Rodriguez could not be responsible for intentional and unintentional conduct at the same time and, therefore, the judgments for murder and reckless conduct against them are inconsistent.

Defendants rely on the same logic to support the contention that the murder convictions against individual defendants O'Neil, Kirschbaum, and Rodriguez are inconsistent with the convictions for involuntary manslaughter against the corporate defendants. To arrive at that conclusion, however, defendants first note that the corporate defendants could be culpable only through the acts and omissions of the individual defendants. Defendants observe that the mind and mental state of a corporation is the collective mind and mental state of its board of directors or high managerial agents. ... Further noting that involuntary manslaughter is based on unintended and reckless conduct ..., defendants reason the convictions against the corporate entities for that offense are inconsistent with the individual defendants' convictions for murder because both offenses were based on the same conduct: the acts of the individual defendants.

We find it helpful to set out the pertinent statutory language of the offenses for which the defendants were convicted. The Criminal Code of 1961 defines murder as follows:

> "A person who kills an individual without lawful justification commits murder if, in performing the acts which cause the death:
>
> * * *
>
> He **knows** that such acts create a strong probability of death or great bodily harm to that individual[.]" (Emphasis added.)

Involuntary manslaughter is defined as:

> "A person who **unintentionally** kills an individual without lawful justification commits involuntary manslaughter if his acts whether lawful or unlawful which cause the death are such as are likely to cause death or great bodily harm to some individual, and he performs them **recklessly** [.]" (Emphasis added.)

Reckless conduct is defined as:

> "A person who causes bodily harm to or endangers the bodily safety of an individual by any means, commits reckless conduct if he performs *recklessly* the acts which cause the harm or endanger safety, whether they otherwise are lawful or unlawful." (Emphasis added.) Ill.Rev.Stat 1981, ch. 38, par. 12–5(a).

The supreme court, in People v. Spears (1986), ... and People v. Hoffer (1985), ... has addressed issues with respect to consistency of verdicts rendered for the above offenses in light of the mental states required to sustain each.

In Hoffer, defendant Donald Hoffer was indicted on three counts of murder in the shooting death of Harold (Ed) Peters. In a trial before a jury, the State presented evidence that Hoffer shot Peters with a shotgun after a heated exchange of words outside Hoffer's home. Hoffer testified that he thought Peters was reaching for a gun at the time of the shooting. Hoffer stated the shotgun discharged as he lowered it with one hand and reached with his other hand to grab the gunstock.

Pursuant to Illinois Pattern Jury Instructions, the trial judge instructed the jury that the offense of murder included the offenses of voluntary and involuntary manslaughter. Definitional and issues instructions were tendered to the jury on murder, voluntary manslaughter (unreasonable belief that the killing was justified), and involuntary manslaughter. The jurors, however, were not informed that they could return a guilty verdict on only one of the offenses. (Hoffer. ...)

On appeal, the appellate court vacated all three convictions and remanded the case for a new trial.

The supreme court affirmed the reversal, rejecting the State's argument that the verdicts could be reconciled because the mental state required for murder " 'subsumed the lesser mental states required for voluntary manslaughter and involuntary manslaughter.' " ... After noting the three offenses differed only in the particular mental culpability required to sustain each, the court concluded the mental states involved are mutually inconsistent. ... Thus, "[w]here a determination is made that one [of the mental states] exists, the others, to be legally consistent, must be found not to exist."

[...]

Under the rule in Hoffer, the judgments rendered by the circuit court in the instant case appear inconsistent as based on mutually exclusive mental states. However, we must consider whether, under similar analysis used by the supreme court in Spears, the judgments are supported by separable acts occurring at different times against different victims by legally different defendants. We therefore begin with a review of the indictments, as they represent the State's prosecutorial intentions in charging defendants, and proceed to evaluate the record of evidence in light of those charges.

The murder indictment states that on February 10, 1983, defendants O'Neil, Kirschbaum, Rodriguez, Pett, and Mackay, acting as individuals and as officers and high managerial agents of Film Recovery, committed murder in that they knowingly created a strong probability of Stefan Golab's death. Specifically, the grand jury charged those individuals had "failed to disclose and make known to [Golab] that he was working with cyanide and substances containing cyanide and failed to instruct him as to matters involving safety procedures and proper handling of said chemicals[.]" Further, those individuals "failed to provide * * * Golab with appropriate and necessary safety and first-aid equipment and sundry health-monitoring systems for his protection while working with and handling cyanide and substances containing cyanide[.]" The murder indictment also states O'Neil, Kirschbaum, Rodriguez, Pett, and Mackay failed to "properly provide for the storage, detoxification and disposition of * * * cyanide and substances containing cyanide * * * [and] failed to advise * * * Golab of the dangerous nature of his work, and the conditions under which he engaged in it[.]"

The involuntary manslaughter indictment against Film Recovery and Metallic Marketing states that, on February 10, 1983, they "unintentionally killed Stefan Golab by authorizing, requesting, commanding and performing certain acts of commission and acts of omission[ ] by its [sic] officers, board of directors and high managerial agents, to wit: Steven J. O'Neil, Michael T. Mackay, Gerald Pett, Charles Kirschbaum, Daniel Rodriguez, and others, who acting within the scope of their employment * * * performed the said acts recklessly in such manner as was likely to cause death and great bodily harm to some individual and * * * caused the death of Stefan Golab [.]" The indictment did not otherwise specify the nature of the acts.

The indictments against all defendants for reckless conduct contain identical charges made in the murder indictment against the individual defendants as summarized above, save for stating that the conduct occurred "on or about March 1982 through March 1983."

[...]

None of the above testimony in any way substantially differs from that otherwise contained in the record regarding conditions in the plant, generally. Thus, we cannot conclude the record supports a determination that the individual defendants possessed different mental states on

February 10, 1983, as distinguished from the period of March 1982 to March 1983, such as might support separate offenses of murder and reckless conduct. While we do not believe it helpful to summarize the considerable amount of that testimony in detail here, those who testified as to working conditions in the plant established the following: workers were not told that they were working with cyanide or that the compound put into the vats could be harmful when inhaled; although ceiling fans existed above the vats, ventilation in the plant was poor; workers were not informed they were working with cyanide and were given no safety instruction; workers were given no goggles to protect their eyes; workers were given no protective clothing and, as a result, workers' clothing would become wet with the solution used in the vats; there were small puddles of that solution as well as film chips on the plant floor around the vats; the solution burned exposed skin; a strong and foul odor permeated the plant; the condition of air in the plant made breathing difficult and painful; and, finally, workers experienced dizziness, nausea, headaches, and bouts of vomiting.

Because the offenses of murder and reckless conduct require mutually exclusive mental states, and because we conclude the same evidence of the individual defendants' conduct is used to support both offenses and does not establish, separately, each of the requisite mental states, we conclude that the convictions are legally inconsistent.

[…]

To state it differently, in Illinois, a corporation is criminally responsible for offenses "authorized, requested, commanded, or performed by the board of directors or by a high managerial agent acting within the scope of his employment." (Emphasis added.) … A high managerial agent is defined as "an officer of the corporation, or any other agent who has a position of comparable authority for the formulation of corporate policy or the supervision of subordinate employees in a managerial capacity." … Thus, a corporation is criminally responsible whenever any of its high managerial agents possesses the requisite mental state and is responsible for a criminal offense while acting within the scope of his employment. To the extent the record discloses that a high managerial agent of Film Recovery or Metallic Marketing, other than individual defendants O'Neil, Kirschbaum, and Rodriguez, might provide foundation for the charge of involuntary manslaughter, that judgment would not be inconsistent with judgment for murder against the individual defendants.

[…]

After carefully considering the above testimony, we cannot conclude the record supports a basis upon which we might reconcile the individual defendants' convictions for murder with the convictions for involuntary manslaughter against Film Recovery and Metallic Marketing.

[…]

Therefore, we find no basis in the record upon which to conclude that the conduct of a high managerial agent, apart from that of the individual defendants found guilty of murder, could provide the basis for establishing criminal responsibility against the corporate defendants for Golab's death. And, because the same conduct is used to support offenses which have mutually exclusive mental states, we conclude the judgments rendered for both offenses are legally inconsistent.

In Hoffer, the supreme court affirmed its earlier pronouncement in People v. Frias (1983) and People v. Hairston (1970), that, where judgments are legally inconsistent, as they are when rendered for offenses requiring mutually exclusive mental states, reversal and retrial must follow. … We are mindful, however, the supreme court has also directed that, where, as in the instant case, defendants challenge the sufficiency of evidence at the first trial, it is necessary to address that issue to avoid the risk of subjecting defendants to double jeopardy. … **Our review of the record does not lead us to conclude that the evidence, as first adduced, was so insufficient as to bar retrial** (emphasis added).

Evidence at trial indicated Golab died after inhaling poisonous cyanide fumes while working in a plant operated by Film Recovery and its sister corporation Metallic Marketing where such fumes resulted from a process employed to remove silver from used X-ray and photographic film. The record contains substantial evidence regarding the nature of working conditions inside the plant. Testimony established that air inside the plant was foul smelling and made breathing difficult and painful. Plant workers experienced dizziness, nausea, headaches, and bouts of vomiting. There is evidence that plant workers were not informed they were working with cyanide. Nor were they informed of the presence of, or danger of breathing, cyanide gas. Ventilation in the plant was poor. Plant workers were given neither safety instruction nor adequate protective clothing. Finally, testimony established that defendants O'Neil, Kirschbaum, and Rodriguez were responsible for operating the plant under those conditions. For purposes of our disposition, we find further elaboration on the evidence unnecessary. Moreover, **although we have determined evidence in the record is not so insufficient as to bar retrial, our determination of the sufficiency of the evidence should not be in any way interpreted as a finding as to defendants' guilt that would be binding on the court on retrial**.

REVERSED AND REMANDED. (Citations omitted)

COCCIA, P.J., and MURRAY, J., concur.

The Criminal Sanction: Punishment

Punishment is the central sanction for violations of the criminal law. If a person is found to have violated the criminal law and convicted for it, he or she is typically punished for the crime in question. Several aspects of punishment illustrate its undesirability from the point of view of the person punished. First, punishment is no fun; when a person is punished, something bad, unfortunate, or undesirable happens to him or her.

Second, the central sanction of the criminal law involves deprivation of liberty, because of confinement to jail or prison for shorter or longer periods of time, depending upon the offense in question. And in some jurisdictions they might lose their lives under death penalty laws for committing certain kinds of homicides.

Third, as one might infer, punishment is seen as "hard treatment" of those who violate the law. Of course, aspects of hard treatment come from loss of liberty and confinement, but often, perhaps too often, those who are jailed or imprisoned may be subjected to additional unpleasant tasks. Some may be activities such as cleaning up highways (although this might sometimes be better than in lockup), tasks that are given to some in confinement. However, other instances, at least historically, have exhibited much more serious kinds of hard treatment (many of which I do not mention). However, when I was growing up in Colorado, we would sometimes drive from my hometown past one of the Colorado state prisons. It was surrounded by a fence through which one could see. Behind the prison was a cliff within prison boundaries, with prisoners working at the cliff base. It seemed that at this particular prison, one kind of hard treatment for some prisoners was to have them work each day with sledgehammers, shovels, and picks breaking up the cliff, and then, presumably, disposing of the broken rock somewhere else. I don't know how common this was, but we have certainly had other and more offensive examples of the hard treatment of criminal punishment.

Fourth, not only does something unpleasant occur to the person punished, but we have to exercise care in using the criminal sanction because of what it does to a person. This point has been nicely, if strongly, captured by Jeffrie Murphy:

> The core punishments of the criminal law (deprivation of liberty or life) represent gravely serious assaults on the fundamental rights of persons, stigmatize and humiliate [them], and typically cause [them] great personal unhappiness. Even when punishments are not actually inflicted on a particular individual, the possibility that they might be inflicted may be sufficient to generate enough fear in that individual to cause him to refrain from acting in ways he otherwise would have found desirable—[constituting] a coercive curtailment of his liberty.[7]

On this view, punishment and the threat of punishment is radically intrusive in a person's life. Because of this, a long-standing tradition in philosophy of law regards it as quite important to justify, not only having punishment as the sanction of the criminal law, but also to justify inflictions of punishments on particular persons. It is clear that losing one's liberty or in the extreme, one's life, without some moral justification are seriously wrongful conditions to inflict on another person. However, as Murphy characterizes it, when somebody goes to trial for a crime, their actions are assessed, and they are found guilty, followed by a punishment appropriate to the crime; these constitute grave assaults on that person.

Fifth, because of the gravity of intrusions represented by punishments, a community should be careful how this sanction is used. Even worse, if a community values rights and liberties comparatively free from interferences from others, this is an additional reason for using criminal sanctions with care. We will return to this point toward the end of the book, because it sheds light on issues of institutional design and what aspects of different areas of law one might seek to use to protect people from invasions of their borders. To foreshadow a bit of that discussion, different areas of the law may be utilized to try to protect and discourage others from crossing the borders of our persons and possessions, so the discussion of this book is organized to call attention to some of these issues.

Consequently, even though one of the main aims of the criminal law is to protect persons and institutions from harms that might result from crimes, the community also needs to understand the consequences of what punishments do to persons and to carefully use the criminal sanction in pursuit of the protective goal.

Sixth, Murphy notes that punishments also "stigmatize" those who are punished. This idea echoes a fellow legal philosopher, Joel Feinberg, who argues that punishment cannot be fully understood if one does not recognize its *expressive function*.[8] Among other things, punishment is a conventional device for expressing community attitudes of condemnation, resentment, indignation, and disapproval of what the criminal did. That is, punishment

---

7 Jeffrie Murphy & Jules Coleman (1984). The *philosophy of law: An introduction to jurisprudence*, p. 113. Roman and Allenheld.

8 Joel Feinberg. (1970). The expressive function of punishment. *Doing and deserving*, pp. 98–99. Princeton University Press.

> [E]xpresses the community's strong disapproval of what the criminal did. ... and ... that what the criminal did was wrong ... It has in short a symbolic significance largely missing from other kinds of penalties."[9]

A person might suffer greater loss of money from gambling or from a tort law judgment than from a fine for criminal behavior, but neither of these would typically carry with them the condemnatory aspect that punishment does. In sum, punishment expresses condemnation, disapproval, and authoritative disavowal of what the person has done in violating the law.[10] One who has committed a crime separates him- or herself from the rest of the community in violating the law. In principle, punishment helps to restore the person to the community or pay his or her debt, after which the person should be restored to good standing in the community.[11]

We should recognize the social condemnation of punishment; it has an important role in judging the institution, to those typically punished under it, and to the elements of a criminal offense.

The Relationship Between the Penal Sanction and the Essential Elements of a Crime

The criminal sanction—punishment with its harshness and social condemnation—assists in understanding the essential elements of a crime. It's not clear which came first, but I'm inclined to the view that punishment and the elements needed to establish a crime in a general sense "grew up together," and in some cases one or the other was modified because of features of the other. This generic point is suggested in *Morissette*[12] that we considered in Chapter 1. Each helps understand the other better. Consider the essential elements in order.

The voluntary act requirement ensures that a defendant's action is properly attributable to the person and the choices that he or she made. Without the voluntary act requirements inflicting punishment on a defendant would likely be seen as violating a defendant's rights—inflicting punishment for acts that the defendant did not choose to do, a point that is implicit in the *Morissette* discussion of basic ideas of the criminal law.

Second, defendant's act must be in violation of a legal duty. There is nothing special about this and punishment, but the major point is that to "get in trouble with the law," one must violate it. One must act illegally.

Third, a defendant must be a person who is judged sufficiently responsible to be held accountable in the criminal law; one must not have the mentality of a child or an insane person. That is, a defendant must have the normal capacities to understand the law and to conform his or her conduct to it. This ensures that a defendant's choice came from a legally responsible person with the mental capability to understand the requirements of the law and to abide by it. "Punishing" a person who was insane or had the mental state of a child would be completely inappropriate, given the hard treatment and condemnatory aspects of punishments. Inflicting hard treatment on such a person would simply seem to be cruel.

---

9 Joel Feinberg. The expressive function of punishment, pp. 98–99.

10 Joel Feinberg. The expressive function of punishment, pp. 98–99.

11 Herbert Morris. (1988). The decline of guilt. *Ethics*, p. 62.

12 *Morissette v. United States*, 342 U.S. 246 (1952), at 250.

Similarly, "socially condemning" one who is insane or who has a child's mentality would be totally off target; there is no wrongful or culpable behavior to be the object of proper condemnation.

Fourth, and finally, to be found properly guilty for a criminal offense, in addition to satisfying the previous three elements of a crime, a defendant must have exhibited the specific *mens rea* for the crime for which he or she is charged. The voluntary act requirement, violation of a legal duty, and the general *mens rea* requirement are something like background conditions such that if defendant does not have one of them, the defendant cannot be found guilty. However, the requirement for a specific *mens rea* identifies the degree of culpability for the crime along with the appropriate punishment, other things being equal.

If all the elements of a crime are established beyond a reasonable doubt, this ensures that the loss of liberty, hard treatment and social condemnation that are part of punishment is fairly attributable to a culpable person (considered apart from the justice of the law being applied). The hard treatment and social condemnation that are part of punishment would be unjust if the conditions contained in the essential elements had not been established beyond a reasonable doubt. Certainly, the social condemnation that is part of punishment must reflect the culpability specified by the specific *mens rea*; these go hand in hand. If an appropriate *mens rea* for the crime in question had not been established, then social condemnation that would otherwise be appropriate to it would be seen to be unjust.

Satisfying the essential elements of a particular crime provides assurances that the punishment leveled against a defendant is fairly or justly attributable to him or her for the law in question. (Of course, I should add that none of this speaks to the underlying justice of the law. It could be quite unjust, but that aspect is outside these issues of the elements of a crime and the proper punishment.) On the other hand, inflicting loss of liberty, harsh treatment, frustration of desires, and the social condemnation that constitute punishment without some of the essential elements of a crime being present strongly suggests that the punishment would be unjust. Punishment would have been inflicted on an actor who did not act voluntarily *or* did not violate an appropriate law *or* did not have the fundamental capacities to understand the law and conform behavior to it *or* did not have the specific *mens rea* for the offense in question. Missing any one of these conditions would render punishment under the criminal law unjust.

In sum, satisfying all the essential elements of a crime beyond a reasonable doubt ensures that punishment for the crime identified by the specific *mens rea* is just, or at least not unjust. Conversely, punishing a person without having satisfied one or more of the essential elements would likely be unjust. Thus, speaking roughly, one might say that the essential elements of an offense are something like jointly sufficient for proper criminal punishment (apart from the underlying justice or injustice of the law) and that punishment without satisfying one of the elements would likely be unjust. This strongly suggests that just punishment depends upon proper satisfaction of all the essential elements of a crime. Of course, another condition that is not mentioned is that the content of the law applied may be unjust. Imagine a law that permitted the punishment of a person for being gay, transgender, or simply for being a redhead (extreme examples, I know). The law itself would be unjust.

These points are represented in the diagram that follows, showing something of a decision tree indicating the need for each element of a criminal offense, at least in an approximate manner (the text above is more important than the diagram).

DIAGRAM: **Elements of a Criminal Offense and Its Punishment**

Legal Aim Sought		**Component of a Crime (in bold)**	
		Actus Reus	**Defendant must act voluntarily in violation of the law**
Defendant's behavior is properly attributable to his/her **choices**.	**Present**		**Rationale: Voluntary act** requirement ensures that what was done is properly attributable to the agent (no proper guilt without the right connection between the agent's choices and what was done). If this is absent, no offense.
Act by defendant is the result of a **sane person's choices**.		**General** *mens rea*	**Rationale:** All adults are presumed to have normal capacities to understand the law and conform to its requirements. When present, merely a necessary element for an offense.
	Present		When general *mens rea* is absent, there is *no proper guilt*, no offense.
Defendant satisfies the **definition of the crime**.		**Specific** *mens rea*	Part of the definition of the crime; **ensures culpability** for act committed when present.
	Present		When absent there is no guilt for that crime (but recall the small class of strict liability laws for which no specific *mens rea* is required).
Offenses properly **individuated** by specific *mens rea*.	**Appropriate for the offense**		No guilt for that offense, except where transference of *mens rea* is permitted—certain felony murder laws (but in that case we might have concerns about whether the person was properly found guilty for the consequent action).
D. held accountable	**D. found guilty** for offense, if established beyond reasonable doubt		Establishing voluntary act, violation of law, general *mens rea* beyond a reasonable doubt **jointly ensure** social condemnation and hard treatment of punishment is fairly attributable to culpable D (does not address the justice of the underlying law).
Punishment for offense properly attributable to D.	**D. is punished:**		*loses liberty, other rights *suffers hard treatment *receives social condemnation *frustrates desires and other interferences with life

If these conclusions are correct or close to it, they suggest that over time the criminal has developed or been constructed to ensure that the essential elements of a crime are consistent with the attribution of punishment with its hard/harsh treatment and social condemnation for the offense as it is defined.

Putting the above points in a slightly weaker manner, one might say that over time as the criminal law was constructed by legislatures and judicial decisions, decision-makers realized that, given the loss of liberty, harsh treatment, and social condemnation that constitutes criminal punishment, they needed to update the essential elements for each crime in order to treat violators justly. If a person were punished with one (or more) of the essential elements missing or in too crude a form, the punishment would be unjust. Put in another way, decision-makers, realizing the nature of punishment, had to develop general doctrines for the criminal law to better ensure the justice of punishments leveled against convicted defendants. There is thus a tight connection between the essential elements that must be satisfied for a crime and the just punishment for that crime.

For example, provocation as a mitigation of murder likely arose in response to the harshness of murder convictions in the 16th and 17th centuries, when the death penalty was applied to all murders, even those for which legitimate provocation might exist.[13] That is, modifications in the definitions of homicide helped to mitigate the harshness of death penalty punishments. We have considered a few legal cases in this volume in which the Court recognized that formal mitigation of first-degree murder to a lesser offense could be broadened by diminished mental capacities, likely in recognition of punishments that would be inflicted without the mitigation. In *Wolff,* the California Supreme Court authorized reduction of first-degree murder to second-degree murder based on the diminished mental capacities of Mr. Wolff. The same court recognized that mitigation of first-degree murder to voluntary manslaughter could be broadened *beyond* provocation, if a defendant could establish that he exhibited diminished mental capacity that undermined malice that is typically required of murder in the first degree. It would be difficult to justify that the court necessarily did this because of the harshness of the punishment because that would require extensive research into their rationales and motivations, but it seems plausible that the punishment for first-degree murder called for the possibility for a different degree of homicide not based on provocation (that the Court said explicitly did not apply), but on the diminished mental state of Mr. Conley (if it could be established to the satisfaction of a jury).

Thus, as one thesis of the criminal law, it seems plausible that there has been a long-term judicial and perhaps legislative interaction between the elements of crimes and their associated punishments as the consequences of each was more fully appreciated. Much more research would be needed to develop this idea, but the essential elements of a crime seemed to grow up together with associated punishments.

---

13 Lenny Roth & Lynsey Blayden. (2012). Provocation and self-defence in intimate partner and sexual advance homicides. NSW [New South Wales] Parliamentary Research Service, Briefing Paper No. 5/2012, August 2012. Located at https://web.archive.org/web/20140623052433/http://www.parliament.nsw.gov.au/Prod/parlment/publications.nsf/0/F2BA1BFEED-2D87EECA257A4800001BD7/%24File/briefing%20paper.provocation%20and%20self-defence.pdf.

■ CHAPTER 3

The Elements of A Tort Offense and an Overview

The law of crimes may seem more familiar to us for a couple of reasons. Reports of crimes commonly make the television or newspapers, often being quite dramatic, such as bank robberies, murders, and rapes. Less well known may be the law of personal injuries, or the tort law. This chapter discusses major aspects of the tort law, or torts, for short. It is also known as "personal injury law" because it seeks to provide redress for injuries that persons may have suffered at the hands of others.

Salient Properties of the Tort Law and Contrasts with the Criminal Law

Suppose someone, call him Jones, is driving recklessly on a city street. His actions put other drivers, pedestrians, and property at risk. In fact, if his reckless driving kills a pedestrian, he would likely be guilty of both the felony of reckless driving and manslaughter, even if he did not intend to harm or kill the victim. However, Jones's driving, depending upon the circumstances, might be a mere traffic offense, a misdemeanor (a minor criminal offense), or, if the wild driving is particularly egregious or causes property damage or kills someone, it may rise to a criminal felony.

Instead of killing a pedestrian, suppose Jones's wild driving causes his car to jump the curb in a residential neighborhood and damage Sally's kitchen and dining room, but not harm a person. Of course, as a consequence of these actions, Jones is in a heap of legal trouble. What happens to him legally depends upon the area of the law at issue.

As we discussed in Chapter 1, the criminal law aims to secure the rightful borders of our possessions and ourselves by penalizing those who cross our legally protected borders and spaces. In contrast, the tort law seeks to secure the rightful borders of our legally protected possessions and ourselves indicated by several different phrases: **by requiring the defendant who violated them "to set things right," "to put matters right," "repair the damage," or (sometimes it is said) "to make us whole**" when we have suffered damages from the border crossings. While the criminal law imposes a penalty or punishment on a defendant who has violated our legal borders, the tort law requires that a defendant who violated us must repair the damage by putting matters "right," preferably as they were before we were harmed by his or her behavior to the extent this is possible. Again, we are invited to imagine an imaginary space around our bodies and ourselves that are legally protected from invasions by others that cause us harm.

For a more formal definition of the tort law, we might follow Prosser and Keeton on torts. Historically, a tort is "conduct which is twisted or crooked, not straight" (from the French).[1] More officially, a "[T]ort is a civil wrong, other than breach of contract, for which the court will provide a remedy in the form of an action for damages," but injunctions and perhaps some other remedies might be possible.[2]

Both the tort law and criminal law set standards for behavior that **are public** in the sense that every adult is required to observe them toward others in the community. Reckless driving Jones has a duty to conduct himself so that he does not put other members of the community at risk. He must also not cause harm to someone like Sally whose kitchen and dining room are damaged by his car hitting them.

Differences between the areas of law are revealed as we inquire further. Whereas we noted in Chapter 1, a crime is commonly characterized as "defining offenses against the community at large,"[3] a tort is seen as "a private or civil wrong independent of contract for which a remedy may be obtained, usually in the form of damages."[4] These characterizations hide important differences.

As we considered, the criminal law is enforced by a public official called by various names, depending upon the jurisdiction she presents. She might be a public prosecutor, a state's attorney, an attorney general, or a US attorney (in federal jurisdictions). By contrast, the tort law must be enforced by the party who has been injured. That is, if an injured party, such as Sally in our example, seeks to set matters right because of injuries caused by another, such as Jones who damaged her kitchen and dining room, Sally must initiate legal action against Jones.

If Sally seeks compensation for her injured house, she would typically find a lawyer, the lawyer would investigate the factual and legal issues in the case, and then decide to file, or "bring a legal action" against Jones or not on Sally's behalf (depending what the investigation showed). (In small claims court, Sally could bring her action for compensation without a lawyer.) If Sally does nothing to have her house repaired from the car crash, nothing legal would occur in the *tort law*. In contrast, while Sally might be a witness to Jones's reckless, wild driving and its consequences, she has no decision-making role in whether *criminal proceedings* are brought against Jones; that typically would be up to the appropriate legal official of the criminal law.

The adversaries in a tort case are the private plaintiff; e.g., Sally, versus the defendant, e.g., Jones, while the adversaries in a criminal case are conceived of as the community or public as a whole represented by an appropriate public official versus the defendant, e.g., Jones.

---

1 *Prosser and Keeton on Torts* (5th ed.), p. 2. W. Page Keeton et al., Eds. West Publishing.

2 *Ibid.*, at 2.

3 *Black's Law Dictionary* (8th ed.) (2004), p. 493. Bryan A. Garner, Ed. West Publishing.

4 *Black's Law Dictionary*, (8th ed.) (2004), p. 493. Bryan A. Garner, Ed. West Publishing.

The typical legal remedy or sanction in a criminal case is typically some kind of punishment or fine, but differs in the tort law. Normally, in our hypothetical example, if Sally's tort action were successful, defendant Jones typically would be required to pay compensatory monetary damages to Sally. Monetary damages could be compensatory, punitive, or nominal damages. Compensatory damages would be provided to compensate the injured party of losses from the tort. Punitive damages might be sought and awarded, if the defendant's behavior were sufficiently outrageous; e.g., if a company deliberately dumped toxic substances on public land threatening others. Nominal damages might be awarded in recognition that a defendant acted unlawfully but resulted in no significant harm to the plaintiff. Monetary transfers are typically the coin of torts because it provides a universal value-baseline for the law to be capable of covering multiple kinds of injuries. The reason: in many cases, a plaintiff's injuries cannot literally be repaired. In this last instance, monetary damages serve as the best surrogate there is.

Sometimes, but less commonly, other remedies might be sought and awarded. Jackie Kennedy Onassis, having been stalked and photographed by Ron Galella during a 10-year period and selling his pictures to various publications, as part of a larger tort suit against Mr. Galella, sued him for his constant harassment. He had harassed her in public places, in front of her house, "in restaurants, theaters, churches, public parks, walkways, beaches, and her children's school."[5] He did not merely photograph her, but intruded upon her personal activities in various ways, including physical interferences. She sought a *permanent injunction*—that is, a court order to cease or restrict some behavior permanently—that "forbade Mr. Galella [from coming] within 75 yards of her children and within 50 yards of Mrs. Onassis."[6] The permanent injunction seems to have been awarded in place of monetary damages that she might have sought.

Next, the standard of typical tort liability differs from the criminal law. Intentional conduct that harms others can be culpable in torts, but ordinary or simple negligence, and the use of strict liability are also typical standards of liability. We will consider more about intentional torts and strict liability torts below.

Strict liability is not particularly controversial in torts as it clearly is in the criminal law. Strict liability is "liability that is imposed apart from any recovery on a theory that defendant knowingly or purposely interfered with a legally protected interest or was negligent."[7] As we have seen, simple negligence is failure to exercise the degree of care that a reasonable person in the community would exercise toward others. Negligence is controversial in the criminal law because it does not require that at the time of acting the defendant be aware of the possibility of harming another or aware that his or her conduct might be illegal. The objective community standard of negligence thus is grounds for a tort action, even if the defendant was not aware of posing a risk to others. One might regard negligence as the minimum standard of culpability for standard torts. Intentional torts aside, someone can still be sued in negligence if they caused an injury by acting recklessly (and perhaps knowingly as well), like Jones above. Strict liability is the basis of a tort action in certain areas of torts—an individual merely has to do the act that causes harm to others, even if the person does not intentionally, knowingly, recklessly, or negligently cause the harm. The simple act of making a Coke bottle that explodes and harms a waitress is sufficient for a tort action by the waitress, even if Coca Cola Bottling Company was not negligent in how it manufactured or refilled the bottle with a beverage (*Escola v. Coca Cola*).

---

5 Mrs. Onassis v. Mr. Galella, *Washington Post*. Located at https://www.washingtonpost.com/archive/politics/1981/12/25/mrs-onassis-v-mr-galella/27e9563d-a55f-4652-822b-97df1a392b2c/.

6 Mrs. Onassis v. Mr. Galella, *Washington Post*, *ibid*.

7 *Prosser and Keeton on Torts*, 554.

The vast majority of tort actions brought are based on negligence.

Final points of salience that distinguish the tort law from the criminal law are the "burden of proof," properly speaking, and the "standard of proof."

The **burden of proof**, properly so called, refers to *who* has to initiate legal action and change the legal status quo of the parties. In the tort law, for the injured party, the plaintiff, to recover for injuries she has suffered, must initiate the legal action; she has the burden of proof.

The **standard of proof** sets standards for *how difficult it is to change the legal status quo; that is, to change legal relationships between the parties*. This is the *specified degree of certainty or the kind and degree of proof that must be established* before Jones is civilly liable in the tort law for damaging Sally's garage.

If Sally brings a complaint that Jones damaged her kitchen and dining room, she must establish her case to the satisfaction of a trier of fact by a "preponderance of the quality and quantity of the evidence," or phrased differently, "by a balance of the probabilities of the quality and quantity of evidence," or "by 50% of the quality and quantity of evidence, plus a feather." In some cases, the standard of proof may be somewhat higher for special claims—if one accuses the other party of fraud, that claim must be established by "clear and convincing evidence." There is a lesser requirement for the standard of proof in torts because "a mistaken judgment for the plaintiff is [seen as] no worse than a mistaken judgment for the defendant."[8] The tort sanction is typically a transference of money from the defendant to the plaintiff if the plaintiff proves her case. This is contrasted with the criminal law, where the defendant has an interest at stake of *transcendent value*—life, liberty, and good name, and the fact finder—the jury—must be persuaded of guilt beyond a reasonable doubt.[9] As we considered in Chapter 1, prosecutors have this more burdensome evidentiary standard of proof precisely because of potential losses to a defendant: losing his liberty by going to jail or prison, possibly losing his life as a result of a death penalty, and suffering social condemnation for one's act.

Some History of the Tort Law

Before we consider tort cases that illustrate some main elements of a tort offense, consider briefly some aspects of the tort law that developed comparatively recently, that is, in the last 150 years. Lawrence Friedman's chapter on the 19th-century development of the tort law provides important insights into the beginnings of modern American tort law and some current doctrines we will consider. Aspects of the tort law had been part of the legal systems for years, some for centuries. However, beginning in the 19th century, torts developed rapidly, largely brought on by steam generation that powered locomotives and factories, substantially increasing the forces to which objects and people might be subjected. The Industrial Revolution added to the injuries caused by one party to others.

> The industrial revolution,
>
> manufactured injury and sudden death, along with profits and the products of machines. The profits were a tempting and logical fund out of which the costs of the dead and the

8 *McCormick on Evidence* (1992). (4th ed.), pp. 957, 962. J. W. Strong, Ed. West Publishing.

9 *Ibid.*, 957, 962.

> injured might he paid. Moreover, the industrial relationship was impersonal. No ties of blood or love prevented one cog in the machine from suing the machine and its owners. But precisely here (to the 19th-century mind) lay the danger. Lawsuits and damages might injure the heath of precarious enterprise. The machines were the basis for economic growth, for national wealth, for the greater good of society.[10]

A variety of legal doctrines were influenced by this historical context. Liability in torts was based on "fault," simple negligence in particular. To hold one accountable, an injured party had to show that the defendant failed to exercise "reasonable care toward others," a notably vague notion. A much later idea that reigned in some areas of torts, strict liability, was not even considered by the judges; it was thought too dangerous, because of some concern by courts and the business community that a legal cause of action that was too easy to establish could impose costs on the burgeoning Industrial Revolution and could "strangle the economy."[11]

When a fire began in a roundhouse for train engines, it quickly spread to a nearby house and ultimately to much of a town. The negligently caused roundhouse fire was pretty clearly the direct cause of burning the local house and the general conflagration; in legal terms, it was the proximate cause of the additional fires. (We return to this technical legal idea later.) Yet, the court hearing this case "shrank in horror" from imposing liability on the railroad: "[To] hold that the owner … must guarantee the security of his neighbors on both sides, and to an unlimited extent … would be the destruction of all civilized society …"[12] Because of its hyperbolic view of legal consequences, the court endorsed only an extremely very narrow view of causes for which defendants could be held accountable.

When it came to protecting employees in factories, similar views protecting companies were adopted. If an employee made the slightest contribution to his (and it very likely was a "him") own injuries in a factory accident, his contribution negated any negligence or tort liability on the part of factory owners or practices. His actions had to be faultless where his injuries resulted. And similar doctrines applied to accidents at train crossings; if a train hit a wagon, in order to recover, the wagon owner had to show the railroad's negligence, but also his own faultless conduct.[13] If a fellow employee contributed to an employee's injuries that were otherwise the result of factory negligence, the outcome was the same—compensation for the injured partly would likely be blocked.

This early conception of contributory negligence is quite draconian. If a party injured by another made even a slight contribution to their own harm, this totally exonerated the party that initiated the harm, preventing plaintiffs' recovery of compensation for their injuries. Judges at the time sought to protect companies from what they saw as potentially harsh consequences of contributory negligence.[14] We will

---

10 Friedman, Tort law, 468.

11 *Ibid.*

12 *Ibid.*, 469.

13 *Ibid.*, 470–472.

14 Contributory negligence eventually gave way to comparative negligence doctrines Under comparative negligence, if two people make a negligent contribution to an accident that causes harm, each would be held responsible for the extent to which his or her negligence contributed to the harm; e.g., 55% negligence for one and 45% negligence for the other, or 35% for one and 65% for the other, and so on.

meet contributory negligence later in this chapter, concerning the tort responsibility of children, as it continued to influence the law for a number of decades, being invoked and seeking to preclude defendants from having to contribute to plaintiffs' injuries.

Ultimately, even more extreme rules were developed that blocked compensation for factory injuries; individuals that worked in risky or dangerous conditions were assumed to have taken on the risk ("willingly [put themselves] in a position of danger") and thus could not be compensated.[15]

If a person died as a result of an industrial injury, his or her family could recover nothing because all legal claims of the injured party went to the grave with him.[16] This doctrine followed passengers onto trains equipped with the newfangled Pullman cars.

During the time George Mortimer Pullman was designing the early sleeper cars, a standard story from tort law courses (that William Prosser calls a "lawyer's legend quite unfounded) suggests that he or the railroad thought that they should check with railroad lawyers to see if any legal doctrines might be applicable to the sleeper car's design. Indeed, so the story goes, the lawyers had input. If beds were placed so that a passenger slept feet-first toward the front of the train, it was more likely that the passenger might be merely injured in case of a crash or collision. However, if passengers slept head-first toward the front of the train and a crash occurred, they were more likely to be killed, thus taking any legal claims against the railroad to the grave.[17] This doctrine led one commentator to note that it was "more profitable for the defendant to kill the plaintiff than to scratch him."[18] This doctrine was ultimately replaced so widows and orphans were not left bereft in case a breadwinner died in an accident.

Eventually, these early doctrines came to be seen as too harsh and were ameliorated. An early one regarding railroads was the "last clear chance" applied to railroad train crossings. The party at a railroad crossing who had the last clear chance to avoid a crash—a wagoner or engineer—had a legal duty to avoid the collision. This gave railroads somewhat more responsibility for avoiding crashes at crossings.[19]

An 1863 case was decided in England, *Byrne v. Boadle,* with far-reaching consequences, that eased some of the difficulties plaintiffs faced in bringing a tort case for injuries. This was the doctrine of *res ipsa loquitur,* or the thing, the events, speak for themselves, in making a *prima facie* case that a defendant had been negligent. The plaintiff in *Byrne v. Boadle* was walking past a warehouse when he was hit on the head and shoulders by a barrel of flour. He was knocked out, did not see this coming, and did not know how it occurred. He could not identify a party who caused him harm, other than some evidence that people at the warehouse were loading barrels of flour onto a wagon and two witnesses saw him being hit with the barrel, but nothing other than these observations. A court, adjudicating this case, ruled,

> I think it would be wrong to lay down as a rule that in no case can a presumption of negligence arise from the fact of an accident. ... The present case upon the evidence comes to this, a man is passing in front of the premises of a dealer in flour, and there falls down upon

15 Friedman, Tort law, 472.

16 *Ibid.*, 470–472.

16 *Ibid.*, 473, 481.

17 Lectures in Tort Law, Yale Law School, 1980; *Prosser and Keeton on torts*, 942.

18 Friedman, Tort law, 474.

19 *Ibid.*, 477.

> him a barrel of flour. I think it apparent that the barrel was in the custody of the defendant who occupied the premises, and who is responsible for the acts of his servants who had the control of it; and in my opinion the fact of its falling is prima facie evidence of negligence, and the plaintiff who was injured by it is not bound to show that it could not fall without negligence, but if there are any facts inconsistent with negligence it is for the defendant to prove them.[20]

Bryne v. Boadle, despite its date of decision, has echoed through the years, justifying 20th-century modifications of tort rules for exploding boilers, wrecks, crashes, explosions, and various injuries caused by falling and flying objects,[21] and ultimately for injuries caused by some medical malpractice.

Other developments eased the harshness of the early tort law rules. Eventually, strict liability managed to replace some negligence standards but received little attention in the 19th century as the standard of behavior.[22] Safety legislation made interactions with railroads somewhat safer, with engine warnings on approaching crossings, warning signs, and broadened those who could receive compensation. The development of unions helped to make workplaces somewhat safer, ultimately replacing tort actions for workplace injuries with workers' compensation insurance policies (we consider one such case later in the book).

Friedman captures some of the modifications in the tort law while revealing the unfortunate origins of it: "Big corporations, particularly the railroads, spoiled children of land grants and subsidies, felt some blows of the rod of regulation."[23] These spoiled children—companies and other beneficiaries of wealth—despite some inroads in the mid-20th century, often still lament their treatment in the law, pushing back against tort law modifications and regulatory actions seeking to make the world safer for those they interact with.

Essential Elements of a Tort Law Violation

For contrasts with the criminal law, we consider the analogous "essential elements" for a tort offense. This comparison is particularly informative because of conditions that are present in one but not the other, or conversely.

Essential Elements of a Criminal Offense
To be held accountable under the criminal law, an alleged defendant must a) **breach** (violate) a legal duty b) **act voluntarily in violating the law**, and c) perform the illegal act(s) with the appropriate guilty mind (***mens rea***), which includes **general *mens rea*** (insanity or infancy excuse criminal acts) and **specific *mens rea***.

Essential Elements of a Tort Offense

20 *Byrne v. Boadle* (2 Hurl. & Colt. 722, 159 Eng. Rep. 299, 1863).

21 Friedman, Tort law, 478.

22 *Ibid.*, 485–486.

23 *Ibid.*, 479.

To be held accountable under the tort law, an alleged defendant must
a) **breach** (violate) a legal duty
b) voluntarily inflict a **legally compensable injury,**
c) **cause** plaintiff's harm, and
d) be the **proximate cause** of plaintiff's harm.

A superficial reading of elements of a criminal offense and of a tort offense reveal a few similarities and some differences. Both require a breach or violation of an applicable law. The reason is simple: one does not and should not get in trouble with the law without violating a particular law or a requirement of it.

Beyond this similarity, differences appear. The criminal law has an *explicit* voluntary act requirement that is often not explicitly stated about the tort law. As we will see from *Williams v. Hays I*, this early case asserts that a defendant need not act voluntarily to be held accountable for a tort. A much more recent case requires a voluntary act (or as it is stated, a person who causes injuries to another as a result of an unexpected convulsion may not be held liable for a tort (*Hammontree v. Jenner*)). We will discuss this further when we consider *Williams v. Hays I* in conjunction with *Hammontree v. Jenner.*

Prosser and Keeton on Torts endorses the need for a voluntary act requirement for torts. First, a prerequisite of liability is that "the defendant act or fail to act when there is a legal duty to act."[24] In addition, the act requirement is that a person must exhibit volition "in relation to muscular contractions" that violate the law. Thus, a person experiencing an unexpected convulsion would lack the "volition" and could not be held accountable.[25]

At the same time, the tort law requires that some party or parties be *harmed* in a manner that *is legally recognized as compensable* in the tort law, and that the *defendant cause* and be *the proximate cause of the harm*. This contrasts with the criminal law. Even though one might think that the criminal law requires that to commit a crime a defendant must harm someone or something, as we considered in Chapter 1, this is not universally true. One can violate the criminal law by *attempting* to commit a criminal offense; e.g., murder or burglary, by *conspiring* to commit a crime, e.g., bank robbery or burglary, by *preparing* to commit a crime, e.g., arson, and so on. For instance, imagine that Ranger, an expert marksman, seeks to shoot James. If Ranger clearly has James in her sights, pulls the trigger, and shoots, but hits a wayward seagull instead of James, the intended target, Ranger has still attempted murder. If a vigilant policeman witnesses this, he could arrest Ranger for the attempted crime, even though James and no one else was harmed or even aware of the attempt. The seagull is the only loser.

In the tort law, the category of legally recognized harms has undergone some modification over time. At one time it might have been the case that mainly physical injuries to persons were legally recognized. However, beginning in the mid-1960s, the law began to recognize that certain kinds of emotional harms should be compensated by a person who caused them. For example, a family was riding on a chair lift during ski season and the lift stopped partway up the mountain as a result of broken cables. Some members of the family fell off and died, but other members watched a related loved one fall and die. Of course, anyone *physically* injured by the malfunctioning ski lift would likely be entitled to compensation.

24 *Prosser and Keeton on torts*, 34.

25 *Ibid.*, 35.

However, what about the emotional harm of watching a family member fall to her death? Or consider a mother who was about to cross a street with her child. Suppose the young boy impulsively rushed into the street, was hit by a car, and died. The mother would be entitled to compensation from the injuries to and the death of him because she suffered those losses. However, should she be entitled to compensation for emotional damages she experienced *watching* her child die as he was hit by a car? Emotional injuries such as these (and others) began to make their way into the tort law and be a legally recognized harm meriting compensation. The point is that the category of legally recognized injuries may change over time as the law gains experience with different kinds of harms and begins to understand their significance.

Overview of Tort Law Requirements for Causation and Proximate Causation

Next, notice that the tort law has two requirements that on the face of it are not obviously present in the criminal law. To be found liable in the tort law, a defendant must both *cause* harm to the plaintiff(s) and the defendant's violation must be the *proximate cause* of plaintiff's harm.

For a tort offense, a defendant must be the *cause* or the *material cause* of plaintiff's harm. An actual causal relationship between a defendant's action and plaintiff's harm connects the defendant to plaintiff's harm. While causation can be a requirement for particular crimes, such as homicides, rapes, assaults and battery, not every crime must cause harm; this is an important difference between the tort law and criminal law.

Next, to be found liable for a tort, the defendant must not only cause plaintiff's harm but be the *proximate cause* of it. Thus, causation in torts has two components—the defendant must *cause* plaintiff's harm, but this causal connection must be judged sufficiently legally *proximate* that defendant can be held accountable for it. The early idea of proximate causation is the following. If I act and causally modify other events in the world, I set in motion a variety of causal events that at least theoretically could go on influencing further events forever. In the law, if I set in motion a variety of causal events, some of which harm others, and for some of which I might be held accountable, is the causal sequence legally judged to be sufficiently connected or "proximate" to what I did for me to be held accountable to compensate someone who has been harmed by my action? One might think that the idea of proximate causation refers to events following a tortious activity that are close or proximate in time and space to the initiating act. While early cases likely resembled this idea, sometimes they can certainly be separated in miles from the initiating cause. We will also see cases in which a causal chain triggered by an actor almost immediately injures another person, but it was not judged to be an instance of proximate causation (*Palsgraf v. Long Island Railroad*). Over time, proximate causation has taken on technical meanings developed in legal cases, losing any strong connection it might have had to spatial and temporal proximity.

We will read an unusual case, *Lynch v. Fisher*, in which a driver negligently parks his vehicle on a turn in the road and it's negligently hit by a second driver, followed by the second driver shooting a Good Samaritan. Can the first driver be held liable for the second driver's shooting the Good Samaritan who came to assist victims of the vehicular accident? This seems quite implausible, but sometimes courts face factual issues that challenge previously created legal rules concerning causation and force them to reassess doctrines. We will consider a number of causation and some proximate causation cases because of their centrality to the tort law.

The tort law tends not to have specific states of mind needed for a tort offense that the criminal law requires for offenses. Thus, there is nothing resembling a specific *mens rea* requirement for all torts as an essential condition of a *tort cause of action* that resembles how crimes are typically defined by requiring specific states of mind. There are, however, three general categories of torts: intentional, negligent, and strict liability torts.

Intentional torts—an area of the law that has a specific *mens rea* requirement resembling in the criminal law—require that a tortfeasor purposely or knowingly cause harm to someone and include, *inter alia*, "battery, assault, false imprisonment, trespass to land, trespass to chattels, and intentional infliction of emotional distress."[26] The vast majority of torts requires that a tortfeasor *negligently* inflict harm on another person, where this is similar to simple negligence discussed in Chapter 2 in *Barnett*. And finally, there are *strict liability* torts, some of which we will consider. These include escaping wild or dangerous animals, livestock that harms others; engaging in ultrahazardous activities that harm others, such as transporting dangerous chemicals, blasting, using explosives; and liability for consumer products that harm others.[27] The law has evolved to endorse different categories of tort wrongs, but there are few torts that require a highly specific *mens rea* as does the criminal law. *Culpability conditions* for tort offenses are simply not as carefully specified for the tort law as they are in the criminal law. The reason for this is that specific *mens rea* in the criminal law is required to identify the particular degree of culpability of the crime and the appropriate amount of punishment.

Finally, you might infer that there is no *general mens rea*, because like *specific mens rea*, it is not mentioned. That has some plausibility, but it has some subtlety. Unlike the criminal law, insanity is not an excuse for every tort as is for every crime. However, it may be an excuse for some intentional torts. According to the Restatement of Torts, 2d (analogous to the Model Penal Code), if the "defendant is extremely mentally impaired or very young, she may not actually possess the requisite intent" for a particular intentional tort. In addition, while children can be held more accountable in torts compared with the criminal law, they are not automatically excused from legal charges as they would be for certain crimes. Yet there are "pockets" of offenses for which children may not be held accountable, and we will consider several legal cases concerning children. Thus, as a generalization, one might say there is no general *mens rea* requirement for every tort (as there is for every crime), but there are pockets of general excusing conditions because of the state of mind or absence of maturity of the actor.

Responsibility of the Insane for Harm

We begin detailed presentation of tort cases about where we left off in the criminal law, with what in the criminal law would be called general *mens rea*. The rationale for this is that these issues present a sharp difference from the criminal law and call attention to its different rationales.

We consider two cases arising from the same events concerning the loss of a ship during a storm. A central issue in this case concerns the "insanity" of the captain of the ship. The first of these two cases addresses whether or not the captain of a ship, who is insane (or may be better described as "deranged" as a result of the events and perhaps his medication) may be held accountable in the tort law for harm done to the ship and its owners.

26 Cornell Law School, Intentional tort, Located at https://www.law.cornell.edu/wex/intentional_tort .

27 *Legal Dictionary*, Strict Liability, March 13, 2016. Located at https://legaldictionary.net/strict-liability/.

There is a nice discussion in this case about the responsibility of insane individuals under the tort law (and also some discussion of the responsibility for children), and why they should be held liable even though under the criminal law, if there were analogous circumstances, e.g., assault of a person, the defendant would be excused on grounds of insanity. One should note important language in this case, drawing attention to the different sanctions and purposes of the criminal law and torts, and how this functions to modify the basis of liability in torts compared with the criminal law.

> The general rule is that an insane person is just as responsible for his torts as a sane person, and the rule applies to all torts, except, perhaps, those in which malice, and therefore intention, actual or imputed, is a necessary ingredient, like libel, slander, and malicious prosecution. In all other torts, intention is not an ingredient, and the actor is responsible, although he acted with a good and even laudable purpose, without any malice. [Importantly, the court adds:] The law looks to the person damaged by another, and seeks to make him whole, without reference to the purpose or the condition, mental or physical, of the person causing the damage.[28]

In this short passage, the court provides an overview of why insanity is not a defense in torts, but also when it could be for certain kinds of intentional torts. This court's view of insanity has been more or less followed in legal cases and treatises. For example, insane persons have been found liable for assault and battery, false imprisonment, trespass on land, conversion, alienation of affection, and injuries caused by defective condition of one's property, *inter alia.* The textbook *Prosser and Keeton* notes that an insane person may be "incapable of entertaining the specific intent necessary for particular torts, [such as] ..." "deceit, malicious prosecution, defamation, or even battery, and so should not be liable simply because he has not committed the tort."[29]

Moreover, the focus of the tort law is on the person harmed or damaged by another and not the mental or physical condition of the actor causing the harm. In the *Williams v. Hays* I opinion, the court provides several underlying rationales for holding insane (or deranged) tortious defendants accountable for their actions. *Prosser and Keeton* adds to the rationales supporting holding the insane accountable: "it represents a conclusion that it is better that the estate of the lunatic should be taken to give compensation for the damage he has done than that it should remain to be administered by guardians for his own incompetent benefit."[30] Which of these reasons, and it could be more than one, do you find most plausible? Later in the *Hays* I opinion, the court gives a variety of examples in which insane persons have been found liable in the tort law for injuries caused to others. These provide a range of circumstances in which the rule about insanity for negligent torts applies.

---

28 *Williams v. Hays*, 98 Sickels 443 at 446–447.

29 *Prosser and Keeton on torts*, 1072–1073.

30 *Ibid.*

Williams v. Hays (I)

Court of Appeals of New York

98 Sickels 442 (1894)

Opinion: EARL, J.

The defendant and others, among whom were Parsons and Loud, were joint owners of the brig "Sheldon." By an arrangement between the defendant and the other owners, he took the vessel to sail on shares. He was to man the vessel, to pay the crew, and to furnish the supplies; and he was to have one-half of her earnings, after certain deductions, for his share, and the other owners were to have from him the other half, after certain deductions, for their share. He was to have the absolute control and management of the vessel, and became her owner pro hac vice. … The defendant, under the arrangement between him and the other owners, in no sense became their agent or servant. In Webb v. Pierce, it was held that where a master hires a vessel on shares under an agreement to victual and man her, and employ her on such voyages as he thinks best, having thereby the entire possession, command, and navigation of her, he thereby becomes her owner pro hac vice, and the relation of principal and agent does not exist between him and the owners. The other cases are to the same effect. […]

The Sheldon was loaded with ice, and started from the coast of Maine for a southern port. She soon encountered storms, and the defendant, for more than two days, was constantly on duty; and then, becoming exhausted, he went to his cabin, leaving the vessel in charge of the mate and crew. He took a large dose of quinine, and laid down. The mate found that the rudder was broken and useless, and that the vessel could not be steered. He caused the captain to come on deck. He refused to believe that the vessel was in any trouble, and refused the help of two tugs, the masters of which saw the difficulty under which his vessel was laboring, and successively offered to take her in tow. They cautioned him that his vessel was gradually and certainly drifting upon the shore, and in broad daylight she did drift upon the shore, without any effort upon the part of the defendant or any of his crew to save her, and she became a total wreck. […]

The defendant claims that from the time he went to his cabin, leaving the vessel in charge of his mate and crew, to the time the vessel was wrecked, and he found himself in the life-saving station, he was unconscious, and knew nothing of what occurred, that in fact he was, from some cause, insane, and therefore not responsible for the loss of the vessel. The case was submitted to the jury on the theory that the defendant, if sane, was guilty of negligence causing the destruction of the vessel, but, if insane, was not responsible for her loss through any conduct on his part which, in a sane person, would have constituted such negligence as would have imposed responsibility.

The important question for us to determine, then, is whether the insanity of the defendant furnishes a defense to the plaintiff's claim, and I think it does not. The general rule is that an insane person is just as responsible for his torts as a sane person, and the rule applies to all torts, except, perhaps, those in which malice, and therefore intention, actual or imputed, is a necessary ingredient, like libel, slander, and malicious prosecution. In all other torts, intention is not an ingredient, and the actor is responsible, although he acted with a good and even laudable purpose, without any malice. The law looks to the person damaged by another, and seeks to make him whole, without reference to the purpose or the condition, mental or physical, of the person causing the damage. The liability of a lunatic for his torts, in the opinions of judges, has been placed upon several grounds. The rule has been invoked that, where one of two innocent persons must bear a loss, he must bear it whose act caused it. It is said that public policy requires the enforcement of the liability, that the relatives of a lunatic may be under inducement to restrain him, and that tort feasors may not simulate or pretend insanity to defend their wrongful acts, causing damage to others. The lunatic must bear the loss occasioned by his torts, as he bears his other misfortunes, and the burden of such loss may not be put upon others.

In Buswell on Insanity (section 355) it is said: "Since, in a civil action for a tort, it is not necessary to aver or prove any wrongful intent on the part of the defendant, it is a rule of the common law that, although a lunatic may not be punishable criminally, he is liable in a civil action for any tort he may commit."

In Cooley on Torts … the learned author says: "A wrong is an invasion of right, to the damage of the party who suffers it. It consists in the injury done, and not commonly in the purpose or mental or physical capacity of the person or agent doing it. It may or may not have been done with bad motive. The question of motive is usually a question of aggravation only. Therefore, the law, in giving redress, has in view the case of the party injured, and the extent of his injury, and makes what he suffers the measure of compensation. * * * There is consequently no anomaly in compelling one who is not chargeable with wrong intent to make compensation for an injury committed by him, for, as is said in an early case, 'the reason is because he that is damaged ought to be recompensed." And at page 100 he says: "Undoubtedly, there is some appearance of hardship, even of injustice, in compelling one to respond for that which, for want of the control of reason, he was unable to avoid; that it is imposing upon a person already visited with the inexpressible calamity of mental obscurity an obligation to observe the same care and precaution respecting the rights of others that the law demands of one in the full possession of his faculties. But the question of liability in these cases, as well as in others, is a question of policy; and it is to be disposed of as would be the question whether the incompetent person should be supported at the expense of the public, or of his neighbors, or at the expense of his own estate. If his mental disorder makes him dependent, and at the same time prompts him to commit injuries, there seems to be no greater reason for imposing upon the neighbors or the public one set of these consequences, rather than the other; no more propriety or justice in making others bear the losses resulting from his unreasoning fury, when it is spent upon them or their property, than there would be in calling upon them to pay the expense of his confinement in an asylum, when his own estate is ample for the purpose."

In Shearman and Redfield on Negligence (section 57), it is said: "Infants and persons of unsound mind are liable for injuries caused by their tortious negligence; and, so far as their responsibility is concerned, they are held to the same degree of care and diligence as persons of sound mind and full age. This is necessary, because otherwise there would be no redress for injuries committed by such persons; and the anomaly might be witnessed of a child, having abundant wealth, depriving another of his property without compensation."

In Reeves' Domestic Relations (page 386), it is said: "Where the minor has committed a tort with force, he is liable at any age; for in case of civil injuries, with force, the intention is not regarded, for in such case a lunatic is as liable to compensate in damages as a man in his right mind."

The doctrine of these authorities is illustrated in many interesting cases. [...]

In Bullock v. Babcock, Judge Marcy, writing in a case where an infant 12 years old was held liable for putting out one of the eyes of another infant, said: "The liability to answer in damages for trespass does not depend upon the mind or capacity of the actor, for idiots and lunatics are responsible, in the action of trespass, for injuries inflicted by them."

In Krom v. Schoonmaker, it was held that a lunatic may be sued for an injury done to another, because the intent with which the act was done is not material. There the action was against a justice of the peace for false imprisonment for issuing a warrant without any complaint, by virtue of which the plaintiff was arrested.

In Cross v. Kent, it was held that a lunatic or insane person, though not punishable criminally, is liable to a civil action for any tort he may commit; that, in an action against a party for setting fire to and burning a barn, neither evidence of his lunacy, nor that the burning was the result of accident, is admissible in mitigation of compensatory damages.

In Neal v. Gillett, in an action on the case for damages caused by the negligence of the defendants, who were severally of the ages of 13 and 16 at the time of the injury, it was held that, where the plaintiff claims only actual damages, the youth of the defendants is not to be taken into consideration in determining the question of their negligence.

In Huchting v. Engel, it was held that an infant, though under seven years of age, was liable in an action of trespass for breaking and entering the plaintiff's premises, and breaking down and destroying his shrubbery and flowers.

In Karow v. Insurance Co. (Wis.), it is said in the opinion: "While the burning of his own property by an assured under no restraint of duty, and incapable of care, and without any intent or design, does not relieve the company from liability, yet the same act of burning another's property might subject such person to damages therefor, not on the ground of 'negligence,' as that word is usually understood, but, in the language of Chief Justice Gibson, 'on the principle that, where a loss must be borne by one of two innocent persons, it should be borne by him who occasioned it.'"

In Brown v. Howe, an insane person carelessly set fire to the dwelling house of his guardian, and while it was held that the guardian could not be allowed the amount of his damages in his probate account, it was held that his only course was to sue the administrator of the lunatic, who had died, in a court of law, and have a judgment fixing his damages, and collect it from the assets, if the estate was solvent; if not, to share with the other creditors.

In Morain v. Devlin, it was held that a lunatic was civilly liable for an injury caused by the defective condition of a place, not in the exclusive occupancy and control of a tenant, upon real estate of which he is the owner, and of which his guardian has the care and management.

In Beals v. See, it was said by Gibson, C. J.: "As an insane man is civilly liable for his torts, he is liable to bear the consequences of his infirmity, as he is liable to bear his misfortunes, on the principle that, where a loss must be borne by one of two innocent persons, it shall be borne by him who occasioned it."

In Morse v. Crawford, in an action for tort, it was held that the fact that the defendant was insane at the time of committing the injury was no defense to the action, and that, if the action be for destroying property intrusted to the defendant, it is no defense that the plaintiff, at the time of delivering the property to the defendant, knew that he was insane. In the opinion of the court, it is said: "It is a common principle that a lunatic is liable for any tort which he may commit, though he is not punishable criminally. When one receives an injury from the act of another, this is a trespass, though done by mistake or without design. Consequently, no reason can be assigned why a lunatic should not be held liable."

In Jennings v. Rundall, Lord Chief Justice Kenyon said, "If an infant commit an assault, or utter slander, God forbid that he should not be answerable for it in a court of justice." Lawrence, J., also writing in that case, mentioned the distinction between negligence and an act done by an infant; and he held that the same rule would have to be applied if an action was brought against an infant for negligently keeping the plaintiff's cattle, by which they died, as would be applied if the declaration charged the infant with having given the cattle bad food, by which they died.

There can be no distinction as to the liability of infants and lunatics, between torts of nonfeasance and of misfeasance,—between acts of pure negligence and acts of trespass. The ground of the liability is the damage caused by the tort. That is just as great, whether caused by negligence or trespass; the injured party is just as much entitled to compensation in the one case as in the other; and the incompetent person must, upon principles of right and justice and of public policy, be just as much bound to make good the loss in the one case as the other; and I have found no case which makes the distinction. That infants and lunatics are liable for damage to property caused by their negligent acts was asserted in several of the authorities above cited; and it has never been doubted that at common law an action of trover would lie against one intrusted with the personal property of another, who destroys it, whether the destruction be by a negligent act or a willful tort.

I sum up the result of my examination of the authorities as follows: This vessel was intrusted to the defendant, not as agent, but, as to the other owners, as charterer, lessee, or bailee; and if he caused her destruction by what, in some persons, would be called willful or negligent conduct, the law holds him responsible. The misfortune must fall upon him, and not upon the other owners of the vessel.

If the defendant had become insane solely in consequence of his efforts to save the vessel during the storm, we would have had a different case to deal with. He was not responsible for the storm, and while it was raging his efforts to save the vessel were tireless and unceasing; and, if he thus became mentally and physically incompetent to give the vessel any further care, it might be claimed that his want of care ought not to be attributed to him as a fault. In reference to such a case, we do not now express any opinion.

If it could be held that the obligation of the defendant to take due care of the vessel while she was in his possession, under his contract with the other owners, was an obligation springing out of his contract, and thus a contract obligation, such a view of the case would not aid him. He was sane when he entered into the contract, and his subsequent insanity would furnish no defense to an action for a breach of the contract. [...]

If it should be found, upon the new trial of this action, that the defendant's mental condition was produced wholly by his efforts to save the vessel during the storm, and it should therefore be held that no fault could be attributed to him on account of what he personally did or omitted to do, then the question would still remain whether the carelessness of his mate and crew, who were his servants, could not be attributed to him, and his liability be thus based upon their carelessness. They did nothing whatever to save the vessel. They did not even expostulate with him, or tender him any advice, or a word of caution; and yet the mate saw what the captains of the tugs saw at a distance,—that something was the matter with him. It is difficult to perceive how they could have failed to see that he was either incompetent to manage the vessel, or that he was willfully wrecking her. We leave the effect of their conduct upon the defendant's liability to be determined, if it should become necessary, upon the new trial; simply saying that the question is worthy of careful consideration, whether the defendant can allege his own incompetency, and at the same time claim that, for any reason, the mate ought not to have taken control of the vessel.

[…] It is an unquestioned rule of law that an insurance company cannot successfully defend an action upon its policy to recover for a loss by showing that the insured destroyed the property while insane, or that its destruction was caused by the carelessness of his agents and servants. The liability of the insured to respond in damages for the loss or destruction of the property of another owner stands upon different principles. […]

Since writing the above, suggestions have been made by some of my brethren which should receive some attention.

The fact that the defendant was a part owner of the vessel can play no part in this discussion. He did not take the vessel as part owner, but under the contract with the other owners; and, as to them, his duties and obligations were such as spring from the relation created by their contract. … Therefore, as I have before said, he must be treated as the charterer, lessee, or bailee of the vessel.

I quite agree, and no one in this case has contended for more, that the defendant was bound, in the navigation and use of the vessel, to bestow only ordinary care, to wit, such care as a reasonably careful and prudent owner would ordinarily give to his own vessel. Such is the standard of care set up for all bailees of personal property for hire. But what is that standard? It is not such care as a lunatic, a blind man, a sick man, or a man otherwise physically or mentally imperfect or impotent, could give. Such a man is not the jural man of ordinary prudence, and he does not furnish the standard. The standard man is no individual man, but an abstract or ideal man, or ordinary mental and physical capacity and ordinary prudence. The particular man whose duty of care is to be measured does not furnish the standard. He may fall below it in capacity and prudence; yet the law takes no account of that, but requires that he should come up to the standard and his duty be measured thereby.

So, when we have defined as above the duty of care resting upon the defendant, we have made no progress in the solution of the question here involved, for it is conceded that he took no care whatever. It is sought, however, to excuse him because he was insane and incapable of care; and the question—and in the end, the sole question—for us to determine is whether that excuse is a good one, and I have heard no argument to sustain it. It is unquestioned that an insane person is civilly liable for his active torts, and is there then any reason for saying that he is not liable for his negligent torts? To uphold this judgment, we must ingraft upon the general rule the exception or qualification that he is not liable for his negligent torts. If the defendant had taken a torch, and fired the vessel, he would have been liable for her destruction, although his act was unconscious, and accompanied by no free will. But if he had negligently fired the vessel, and thus destroyed her, being incapable, from his mental infirmity, from exercising any care, the claim must be that he would not be liable. Such a distinction is not hinted at in any authority, has no foundation whatever in principle or reason, and cannot stand with authorities I have before cited.

My conclusion, therefore, is that the judgment should be reversed, and a new trial granted; costs to abide event.

All concur, except PECKHAM, GRAY, and O'BRIEN, JJ., dissenting.

Judgment reversed.

Hays's legal difficulties concerning his responsibility for the ship were not over. His case was returned to the district court where he was retried under the theory that being insane or being deranged is *not an excuse* under negligence in the tort law. The trial jury found him liable on this rationale. Hays protested because the New York Court of Appeals had suggested a different rationale under which he *might not* be held accountable, even though he had been deranged. Suppose his "mental condition was produced wholly by his efforts to save the vessel during the storm, and it should therefore be held that no fault could be attributed to him on account of what he personally did or omitted to do?"[31] If Hays had done all the law could reasonably expect a law-abiding person to do under the circumstances but had failed, should he be held accountable? As you read the second *Williams v. Hays* case, or what I dub "*Williams v. Hays* (II)," what is the court's decision? Does it seem a reasonable doctrine to endorse for the tort law? What are some pros and cons?

Williams v. Hays (II)

Court of Appeals of New York

5 Am.Negl.Cas. 435 (1899)

Bartlett, J., dissenting.

HAIGHT, J.: This action was brought by the plaintiff, as assignee of the Phoenix Insurance Company, to recover the amount of insurance paid by the company to Parsons and Loud under a policy of insurance issued to them as the owners of one-sixteenth of the brig "Emily T. Sheldon." The brig had been wrecked on Peaked Hill Bar, on Cape Cod, near Provincetown, Mass.; and it is alleged that the loss occurred through the negligence of the defendant, who was the master and part owner of the brig, and who commanded her at the time of the loss. The plaintiff claims the right to recover in this action upon the theory that the insurance company became subrogated to the rights of the owners, whom it had insured. The answer denied the allegations of the complaint that the loss was caused through the negligence, carelessness, misconduct, and improper navigation of the defendant, and alleges that at the time of the wreck he was unconscious of his acts, and irresponsible therefor, and was not in a condition to navigate the brig, on account of sickness, etc. At the conclusion of the evidence, the trial court directed a verdict in favor of the plaintiff, holding that the insanity of the defendant furnished no defense. The defendant's counsel objected to the direction of the verdict, and asked to go to the jury upon the questions: "First, whether or not the defendant became insane solely in consequence of his efforts to save the vessel during the storm; second, whether the defendant became insane solely in consequence

---

31 *Williams v. Hays* (I), 1894, at 452.

of a sickness occasioned by his efforts to save the vessel during the storm, and the quinine which was taken therefor; third, whether the mate was so cognizant of the condition of the master, of the insanity or other incompetency of the master, as to require him to take the command of the vessel away from the master; fourth, whether the mate exercised due judgment in regard to the condition of the master; fifth, whether the defendant, in consequence of his efforts to save the vessel during the storm, became mentally and physically incompetent to give the vessel any further care than he did." These requests were refused by the court, and a verdict was directed, to which rulings the defendant's counsel duly excepted.

On Thursday, the 18th day of March, 1886, the brig "Emily T. Sheldon" left Boothbay, Maine, with a cargo of ice, bound for Annapolis, Md. At the time of sailing, the weather was fair, and remained so for about 16 hours, at which time a storm commenced, with high winds and rain, with a light snow. At the time of the commencement of the storm, the vessel was in George's Channel, and the defendant tacked to work her about, trying to find his way out, until it became practically impossible to tell where he was. He headed her in what was supposed to be the direction of Cape Cod, but, not being able to make the cape, she was hove to, to ride out the gale. This was about 4 o'clock in the afternoon of the 20th, and she remained hove to until about that time in the afternoon of the 21st, and then the defendant stood her off for what was supposed to be Cape Cod. On Monday morning, the 22d, between 4 and 5 o'clock, Thatcher Island lights were sighted by the defendant. The storm had then abated, but there was a heavy roll of the sea. The defendant then turned the vessel over to the mate, telling him to keep her by the wind until he made Cape Cod light. He then went below, and laid down upon a lounge in his cabin, but, before doing so, took 15 grains of quinine. It appears that during the storm he had had but little rest; had not gone to his berth or undressed; had eaten but little, and that for the last 48 hours he had been constantly upon deck; that he was worn out, exhausted, felt sick, and feared he was to have an attack of malaria. At about 11 o'clock, the second mate, to whom the vessel had been turned over, called the mate, saying that the vessel did not act very well. The mate then went upon deck, and about half past 11 the steward called the defendant. He was lying, dressed, upon the lounge. He did not get up at the first call, and subsequently the steward pulled him off from the lounge, in order to arouse him. He then got up, but within a few minutes was again found lying upon the lounge, and the steward went to him again, and finally succeeded in getting him up on the deck of the vessel. There are some little differences in the testimony of the witnesses in reference to the order of events thereafter occurring. According to the recollection of some of the witnesses, the captain came on deck about half past 12, after the crew had been at dinner. After he came on deck, the tug "Storm King" came up on their weather quarter, and said that the rudderpost of the brig was split, and asked the captain if he did not want a tow. He said that he did not; that he guessed "we are all right." The Storm King then went away, and about 1 o'clock another boat came up under the stern of the brig, and offered a tow, but was refused by the captain. McDonald, who kept the log of the vessel, testified: "After the boats went away, the vessel began to go off and come to, and she would not mind her helm at all, and the sea was edging her into the beach all the time. Then I went over, and looked over the stern, but I could see nothing. Then I got into the bowline; that is a rope with a noose in it, being around my waist; and I was let down over the stern, and I looked at the rudderpost, and it was split, but I could not tell how badly. I went back on deck, and said that the rudderpost was split, and the captain said he didn't think it was, and said, 'I can't see it, and you can't, I think.' Then I began to think there was something wrong with the captain; that he did not act as he used to. Still, I could not see anything wrong with his manner, except when he spoke to me about the vessel; and he then told me to square the yards to see if the vessel would go off again, and we did, and she did go off, but she came right back again; and I lowered the main trysail down again, and hove the helm up again, but she did not go off; she went sideways in onto the beach, and struck," at about 2:30 o'clock. Considerable evidence was taken with reference to the condition of the captain, all of which tends to show that he staggered about the vessel, making irresponsive answers to questions, appeared to be in a dazed condition, and to be either drunk or insane. After the brig struck, a life-saving boat came alongside, and offered to take him ashore; but he refused to go, and the crew of the life boat had to remain for several hours before they finally succeeded in coaxing him to go with them. He was taken ashore, but, according to his testimony, remembers nothing that occurred until the next day. The brig became a total wreck.

This action was considered in this court on a former review (143 N. Y. 442, 38 ***N. E.*** 449), at which time the law of the case was settled, except upon two points. It was then held that the defendant, as charterer of the brig, was liable for losses which occurred through his want of care or skill in the navigation of the vessel; that he was required to exercise such care and skill as a reasonably careful and prudent owner would ordinarily give to his own vessel; and that an insane person is responsible for his torts the same as if sane. The opinion contains some comments of the judge, which have been understood as indicating an intention to do away with any distinction between misfeasance and nonfeasance, and to hold that lunatics and infants were just as liable for their failure to act as they were for their affirmative torts. But, when the judge comes to sum up the result of his examination of the authorities, he concludes by stating the rule to be that, if the defendant "caused her destruction by what in sane persons would be called willful or negligent conduct, the law holds him responsible." The final conclusion reached by the judge we accept as the law of this case. Whether a lunatic or a person mentally incapacitated should be held responsible in all instances for his nonfeasance or failure to act, we will not now stop to consider.

The judge then proceeds in his opinion to say: "If the defendant had become insane solely in consequence of his efforts to save the vessel during the storm, we would have had a different case to deal with. He was not responsible for the storm, and, while it was raging, his efforts to save the vessel were tireless and unceasing; and, if he thus became mentally and physically incompetent to give the vessel any further care, it might be claimed that his want of care ought not to be attributed to him as a fault. In reference to such a case we do not now express any opinion. * * * If it should be found upon the new trial of this action that the defendant's mental condition was produced wholly by his efforts to save the vessel during the storm, and it should therefore be held that no fault could be attributed to him on account of what he personally did or omitted to do, then the question would still remain whether the carelessness of his mate and crew, who were his servants, could not be attributed to him, and his liability be thus based upon their carelessness." We thus have two questions presented for consideration: First Did the defendant become mentally and physically incompetent to care for and navigate the vessel, solely in consequence of his efforts to save the vessel during the storm? And, second, if he was thus mentally and physically incapacitated, were his mate and crew guilty of negligence in not taking the command of the vessel, and procuring a tow? Upon directing a verdict in favor of the plaintiff, the trial court said: "Assuming, as we must, for such purpose, that the condition of the defendant was the result of exhaustion, caused by his efforts to save the ship from the perils of the storm, and the heavy dose of quinine which he took as a remedy, I fail to see how that presents any exception to the principle laid down by the court of appeals, that a person of unsound mind is responsible for the consequences of acts which in the case of a sane person would be negligent. In other words, the standard by which he is to be judged is the same as that which must be applied to the actions of a sane person. It certainly seems to be a cruel doctrine; but as it is apparently based upon the principle that, as between two innocent persons, the loss must fall upon him who caused it, rather than upon the other, the best that can be said about it is that it is a rule which serves the convenience of the public, to which individual rights must give way." It will thus be observed that the case was disposed of below upon the ground that the defendant was liable even though assuming that his condition was the result of exhaustion caused by his efforts to save the ship from the perils of the storm, and the question as to whether the mate was guilty of negligence was not considered. The appellate division has affirmed, following in its opinion, the reasoning of the trial judge.

We cannot give our assent to such a view of the law. To our minds it is carrying the law of negligence to a point which is unreasonable, and, prior to this case, unheard of, and is establishing a doctrine abhorent to all principles of equity and justice. In this case, as we have seen, the storm commenced on Friday, continued through Saturday and Sunday, and it was not until 5 o'clock Monday morning that the defendant was relieved from the care of his vessel. For three days and nights he had been upon duty almost continuously, ** and for the last 48 hours had not been below the deck. The man is not yet born in whom there is not a limit to his physical and mental endurance, and, when that limit has been passed, he must yield to laws over which man has no control. When the case was here before, it was said that the defendant was bound to exercise such reasonable care and prudence as a careful and prudent man would ordinarily give to his own vessel. What careful and prudent man could do more than to care for his vessel until overcome by physical and mental exhaustion? To do more was impossible. And yet we are told that he must, or be responsible. Among the familiar legal maxims are the following: The law intends what is agreeable to reason; it does not suffer an absurdity. Impossibility is an excuse in law, and there is no obligation to perform impossible things. … Applying these maxims to the case under consideration, we think the fallacy of the reasoning below is apparent, and that it cannot and ought not to be sustained.

As to whether the mate should be chargeable with negligence is a question which has not as yet been determined. It is said that he did nothing to save the vessel. It appears that he was on deck, obeying the orders of the captain. The circumstances surrounding him were peculiar. Possibly he might have put the captain in irons, and taken the command of the vessel, but mutiny at sea is criminal, and heavily punished. In order to justify such action, he must be satisfied of the derangement of his superior officer, and be able to command the assistance of the crew. Whether the condition of the captain was so apparent at the time as to charge the mate with negligence in not resorting to strong measures, we think, was a question of fact for the determination of the jury, and that it was not within the province of the court to dispose of it as a question of law. The judgment should be reversed, and a new trial granted, with costs to abide the event.

BARTLETT, J. (dissenting).

I am of opinion there was no question for the jury in this case. The learned counsel for the defendant asked to go to the jury on two questions:

First. "Whether or not the defendant became insane solely in consequence of his effort to save the vessel during the storm." It is true that Judge Earl, writing in this case for the court on the former appeal, stated that, if the defendant had become insane solely in consequence of his efforts to save the vessel during the storm, we would have had a different case to deal with. It is, however, undisputed that the record now before us is identical in all essential respects with the one then under examination, and it therefore follows that the determination of this court that the insanity of the defendant was no defense is the law of this case, and was properly followed by the trial judge when he directed a verdict for the plaintiff.

Second. "Whether the defendant became insane solely in consequence of a sickness occasioned by his efforts to save the vessel during the storm, and the quinine which was taken therefor." Judge Earl stated in his opinion upon the former appeal that if it were found upon a new trial that the defendant's mental condition was produced wholly by his efforts to save the vessel during the storm, and it should therefore be held that no fault could be attributed to him on account of what he personally did, or omitted to do, then the question would still remain whether the carelessness of his mates and crew, who were his servants, could not be attributed to him, and his liability be thus based upon their failure to act. There is no conflict of evidence on this latter point, and only a question of law is presented to this court on undisputed facts,—whether the captain was not liable for this loss, not only on account of his insanity, but for the reason that the mates and crew, having full knowledge of the captain's mental incapacity, and that the rudder was useless, failed to intervene and save the vessel, but allowed her to drift with the dead swell upon the beach, with all sails set and no anchors out, in a light wind blowing off shore, in the middle of a pleasant afternoon, with two steam tugs lying by, and offering a tow to a port nine miles distant. There was no request to go to the jury as to the conduct of the crew. The liability of the captain for the acts of his mates and crew is well settled. Story on Agency (section 314) states: "The policy of the maritime law has therefore indissolubly connected his (the master's) personal responsibility with that of all the other persons on board, who are under his command, and are subjected to his authority." With the same record before us as on the former appeal, I am unable to understand why the former decision of this court should not be followed. 143 N. Y. 442, 38 N. E. 449. I vote for affirmance. (Citations omitted)

All concur with HAIGHT, J., for reversal, except BARTLETT, J., who reads for affirmance. Judgment reversed, etc.

The outcome of *Williams v. Hays* (II), while acknowledging there is no defense of insanity, points out (noted in the original case) that it might be impossible for Hays to do more than he did to save the boat in distress. The court notes that even careful and prudent people could only do what they are capable of until they were overcome by physical and mental exhaustion. Legally, to expect more, in short is to expect the defendant to do the impossible, which is not something the law can endorse. It notes, "Among the familiar legal maxims are the following: The law intends what is agreeable to reason; it does not suffer an absurdity. Impossibility is an excuse in law, and there is no obligation to perform impossible things."[32]

32 *Williams v. Hays* (II), 1899, at 548.

Consequently, Captain Hays in the end was not held liable in torts for the loss of the ship. The Court of Appeals considered two different excusing conditions for exonerating him. The trial court found him insane, but the Court of Appeals held that this is not an excusing condition in the tort law, as it is in the criminal. In addition, the Court of Appeals in the second case judged that to require him to do more to exercise the duty of care to save the ship in his circumstances would require him to do the impossible. Thus, this court recognizes that impossibility can be a defense to requiring a person to uphold their tort duty of care and in this case, to co-owners of the ship. The law does not require an absurdity of citizens!

The next case, *Sforza v. Green Bus Lines*, also involves insanity, but with some additional legal doctrine. A bus owned by the Green Bus Lines Corporation and driven by Mr. LaSala hit an ice truck owned by Mr. Mekay, around which Mr. Sforza was working when the bus hit him and the truck. Sometime before the accident, LaSala seems to have experienced some degree of insanity. It does seem odd that "insanity" could appear so quickly, but he also may have become agitated about his wife's impending delivery of their child and also suffered from overwork. LaSala was confined to an insane asylum following the accident. There is no question LaSala was negligent in hitting the truck and Mr. Sforza, making both LaSala and Green Bus Lines negligent as a result of vicarious liability. The company's liability arises under a law of vicarious liability. Under the vicarious liability doctrine even though the company itself did not hit Sforza, it had employed LaSala, and, because the accident occurred while he was working for Green Bus Lines, responsibility is extended to it for his actions. The underlying idea is that if I employ you and in the course of your employment you do something that causes harm to others, as your employer I am responsible for your torts. Employing people to work for me, I have had the opportunity to review their qualifications and whether they are sufficiently responsible persons so I can ensure that they are not likely to commit torts in the course of or arising out of their employment.

However, because LaSala had become insane, the company argued that, because insanity was a defense, he and they could not be held accountable. Of course, this argument was a nonstarter, since insanity in the tort law is not a defense. Insanity does not excuse LaSala's actions, and because the company is vicariously responsible for its employees, it too is responsible for his actions; and since insanity does not excuse LaSala, it does not constitute a defense for the company.

Sforza v. Green Bus Lines, Inc.

Municipal Court of the City of New York, Borough of Queens, Fourth District.

150 Misc. 180 (1934)

Judgment for plaintiffs against both defendants.

PETTE, J.

While operating a bus owned by the corporate defendant, the individual defendant, who had been employed by the corporation eight years, suddenly became insane and apparently lost control of the bus which struck a parked ice truck owned by plaintiff Mekay, upon which plaintiff Sforza was chopping ice. These actions follow to recover for property damage and personal injuries.

The driver was committed for observation and later confined in an insane asylum where he still remained at the time of the trial. Defendants do not deny negligence by the driver, but seek to excuse the negligence, claiming that the driver, having become insane just prior to the accident, was incapable of care, and hence is not responsible for damages, and that therefore the negligence may not be imputed to the company.

Defendants suggest that the insanity may have been produced by a state of mind on the part of LaSala, induced by his wife's expected motherhood that morning. While the evidence as to the unusual and irrational acts of the driver at the time of and immediately following the accident are consistent with a finding that he had become insane just prior to the accident, the facts negative any idea, and defendants do not claim, even if such a distinction exists in the law of torts as a finality, … that the insanity was due in any measure to his occupation or to his exhaustion or other physical or mental condition caused through devotion to duty or by his efforts to save the bus from peril, or to otherwise protect the interests of his employers or himself.

If the driver were sane, his acts in driving the bus into the truck then at a standstill and out of the way would constitute a tort of misfeasance, that is, a willful, negligent conduct which invaded the rights of plaintiffs to be secure in their person and property. Or, the driver may be deemed liable on the theory of nonfeasance for failing to swerve the course of the bus to prevent a collision. For practical purposes, upon the facts at bar, the adoption of one theory or the other will not conflict with the result.

The authorities establish that an insane person is civilly liable for his torts, and whether the tort be one of nonfeasance or misfeasance does not seem to affect the liability which is grounded upon the damage caused by the tort. Williams v. Hays (I), … In a well-written brief, the defense urges that, upon the second appeal of the same case … a distinction is made between torts of misfeasance and torts of nonfeasance when committed by an insane person. I regret that I am unable to agree with that contention. What was said upon the second appeal, at page 546 of 157 N. Y., 52 N. E. 589, 591, does not change, but confirms the refusal in the first opinion to establish any different rule between negligence and affirmative conduct. All that the court said upon the second appeal … has reference to an inquiry which the court did not then deem it necessary to make, as to whether a lunatic is liable "in all instances of nonfeasance or failure to act." That is, the responsibility for the tort of misfeasance was left unquestioned, and it was only adverted that with respect to the tort of misfeasance there might be instances in which the insane person would not be held liable. Whatever rule may be ultimately established, I hold to the opinion that such a distinction would be unreal and unsubstantial, and, if given judicial sanction, would readily induce an influx of simulated or pretended insanity, predicated upon a great variety of anomalous situations, which would work fraud and injustice … It is unfortunate, following the remarks of Cooley on Torts ([4th Ed.], that one should be compelled to respond for that which, for want of the control of reason, he was unable to avoid; that "it is imposing upon a person already visited with the inexpressible calamity of mental obscurity an obligation to observe the same care and precaution respecting the rights of others that the law demands of one in the full possession of his faculties." But, the author continues: "The question of liability in these cases, as well as others, is a question of policy and is to be disposed of as would the question whether the incompetent person is to be supported at the expense of the public, or of his neighbors, or at the expense of his own estate. * * *" The above statement of the rule was adopted in the Hays Case upon the first appeal, and by later cases of which Seals v. Snow (1927), is a noteworthy illustration. The Kansas court there refers to the Hays Case as a leading case among the "well-nigh unanimous, and * * * firmly established" "authorities upholding the doctrine."

The question left open by the second appeal ... as to whether a lunatic is responsible in all cases of negligence, that is, omission or failure to act, is not now before the court for the reason that, not only is there no evidence in the case at bar as to how the insanity was occasioned, but also that upon the second appeal the court accepted the statement of the rule enunciated in the first appeal, after an exhaustive review of the authorities, to the effect that, "if the defendant 'caused the destruction [of the vessel] by what in sane persons would be called willful or negligent conduct, the law holds him responsible.'" Williams v. Hays (II).

I, therefore, conclude that the defendant LaSala is legally responsible for the negligence which is imputable to the corporate defendant. Judgment is rendered against both defendants, in favor of plaintiff Sforza in the amount of $200 for personal injuries sustained by him, and in favor of the plaintiff Mekay in the amount of $225 for property damage. Ten days' stay.

(Citations omitted)

Responsibility of Minors for Harm

Recall our consideration in Chapter 1 of the minimal mental conditions for holding children and adults accountable in the criminal law—general *mens rea*. We have just seen that insanity is no excuse for negligent and some intentional actions in the tort law. However, what is the lower bound for holding youngsters accountable for actions that if done by adults would constitute torts? Jurisdictions differ on this point. We consider two cases: one, *Tyler v. Weed*, which discusses two different models for holding children accountable for contributory negligence in torts and then provides its reasons for following the "common-law" model instead of the "Massachusetts" model. The second case is *Verni v. Johnson*.

The main issue in both cases concerns contributory negligence. In each case, a child ran out into a street and was hit by an oncoming car. In each case the driver was judged to be negligent. However, recall "contributory negligence" from the discussion of Friedman regarding the 19th-century doctrine of contributory negligence in the workplace. According to that older doctrine, if a person contributes to his or her own harm, this exonerates others whose negligence caused the sequence that led to plaintiff's harm. Coming out of employment torts and influenced by 19th-century ideas to protect employers from employees' tort suits, it had a quite worrisome consequence for working people; going forward, it would have an even more worrisome implication for ordinary citizens as in these car accident cases. If injured parties make a negligent contribution to their own injuries, they would be blocked from compensation. Of course, often there are instances in which people make faulty contributions to their own injuries, but the older contributory negligence doctrine completely blocked plaintiffs' compensation in such cases.

In the car accident cases, if a negligent driver hits a child crossing the street, he or she would be required to compensate the child or their parents for the injuries. However, if the child was contributorily negligent in producing the injuries; e.g., he or she failed to watch for cars or only looked one way or just raced into the street, this would prevent the child and/or parents from receiving compensation for the child's injuries. Whether a child may be held for contributory negligence depends upon the jurisdiction and often some details about the child.

In the cases that follow contributory negligence reappears. It continued to survive from its 19th-century origin into the first third of the 20th century. And it continued in its draconian form. You will see in *Tyler v. Weed* and *Verni v. Johnson* that defendants sought to preclude responsibility and compensation for young children injured by negligent drivers.

Given the ages of young children in these cases, should they be judged capable of negligence? If they are, their capability for negligence could preclude compensation for their injuries when they were hit by a negligent driver. In *Tyler v. Weed*, there is a nice discussion of two different approaches to judging the responsibility of a young child less than 7 years of age. What are the differences between the two models for young children? Which do you think is the better model to follow in the tort law?

Tyler v. Weed

Supreme Court of Michigan

285 Mich. 460 (1938)

POTTER, J., dissenting. McALLISTER and BUSHNELL, JJ., dissenting in part.

Opinion: McALLISTER, Justice.

This is an action for damages for negligence, brought by an infant suitor by his next friend. On September 26, 1935, just before noon, plaintiff, a child six years and eight months old, was returning from school to his home in Battle Creek. He was walking in a westerly direction on the north side of Webber Street, which intersects Meachem Avenue, a north and south street. When plaintiff came to the intersection he stepped from the curb and, it is claimed, looked north, took a step or two and then looked south, and started running diagonally across Meachem Avenue in a northwesterly direction.

Defendant, a woman 65 years old, was driving an automobile on Meachem Avenue proceeding in a northerly direction. She testified that when she reached the intersection she glanced to the sidewalk on the right, but saw no one on the corner; but she states that when she arrived in the middle of the intersection she first saw plaintiff two feet from the curb on the right. From the time she first saw plaintiff until she applied her brakes, her car travelled approximately 25 feet. The plaintiff was struck by the left fender of defendant's car after he had run in a northeasterly direction a distance of 51 feet, and after he had passed the center line of the street he was trying to cross. As a result of the accident, plaintiff suffered severe and permanent injuries, including fractures and the loss of an eye.

The case was tried before a jury and resulted in a verdict of no cause of action. On appeal the plaintiff claims error on the part of the trial court in submitting to the jury the question of his contributory negligence, because he was under seven years of age, and also asks reversal on the court's instructions to the jury relative to acts done in emergency and the standard of care required of the defendant. [...]

While such assignment did not explicitly claim that the trial court erred in not holding that plaintiff was presumed to be free from negligence as a matter of law, it nevertheless set forth that the court erred in charging the jury that plaintiff could not recover if he were negligent in any manner, if such negligence contributed to the accident. [...]

We believe that the ground upon which reversal is sought, is fairly indicated and sufficiently complies with the rule, that errors, which are assigned, must be fairly indicated if not precisely stated. ... So presented, it raises the question of whether infant plaintiff in this case, being under the age of seven years, is conclusively presumed to be incapable of negligence; and whether the court erred in submitting such claimed negligence of the infant plaintiff as a question of fact to be determined by the jury.

On this proposition there is a conflict of authorities between those that hold that the question of an infant's negligence is always to be determined as a question of fact regardless of age, and those that follow the so-called common law rule that an infant under the age of seven years is conclusively presumed to be incapable of negligence.

This proposition, in its various phases, has been before our Court on numerous occasions.

In Thornton v. Ionia Free Fair Association, a case involving the alleged contributory negligence of a boy 14 years old, the Court said (page 961): "Plaintiff had passed the years of tender childhood which is protected from contributory negligence by the presumption thrown around its assumed lack of experience, discretion, and capacity to recognize and understand danger. The general rule imputes that lack of capacity up to the age of 7 years, and some courts have applied it as a prima facie presumption until the age of 14 is reached, putting the burden of proof on those claiming contributory negligence."

This would seem to affirm the common law rule in our state. However, the Court further said: "But age alone is not the conclusive test. Experience and capacity are also to be considered. As was said in Trudell v. Railway Co., ... where the injured child was 7 years and 4 months old: 'Age is not the true test in such cases. It is the intelligence of the boy, not his age, that must control.' By the tests of capacity and experience children younger than 7 years have been held guilty of contributory negligence as a matter of law under the undisputed facts." [...]

In Barger v. Bissell, 188 Mich., a child six years, ten months and ten days of age was injured in an automobile accident and received a judgment against the defendant driver, which came before this court for review. The defendant asked reversal on the ground that there was no evidence showing, or having any tendency to show, negligence on the part of the defendant and that the verdict was contrary to the great weight of the evidence. The court reversed the judgment on the ground that there was no showing of negligence on the part of the defendant. But in passing on the case, the court said (page 108): "It is manifest that she [the infant plaintiff] exercised no care at all, and, if an adult, she would clearly be barred from recovery by her own carelessness and negligence; but with a child of her age the question of contributory negligence precluding recovery, in case the defendant is shown guilty of negligence, is usually an issue of fact for the jury. In passing upon the legal questions raised here, the materiality of her conduct in thus suddenly coming upon the street close in front of a passing automobile, in the middle of a block, is its bearing upon the question of defendant's negligence. * * * Drivers upon highways are not held as insurers against accidents arising from negligence of children or their parents, and though in law such negligence in a particular case may not be a defense, as contributory negligence, for a driver also guilty of negligence, the fact of an accident does not establish liability or raise a presumption that the driver is negligent." [...]

Easton v. Medema, marked a turning point in our decisions involving the question of contributory negligence of infant plaintiffs. In that case an evenly divided court disagreed upon whether the contributory negligence of a child five years and eight months old was a question for the jury, and Mr. Justice Fead in his opinion stated the following (page 638): "Regardless of the general principles governing care required of children and the weight and conflict of authority as to the age at which a child may be charged with contributory negligence, it is settled law of this state that a child under six years of age cannot be so charged." [...]

Following Easton v. Medema, supra, it was held that a child four years and three months of age was too young to be guilty of contributory negligence; that an infant three and one-half years of age could not be guilty of contributory negligence; that a child five years and eleven months old could not be guilty of contributory negligence as a matter of laws, ...; and it was held in Benedict v. Rinna, that the question of infant plaintiff's contributory negligence was not involved, he being only five years and eight months old; and later by unanimous opinion it was held in Guscinski v. Kenzie, that a boy five years old was too young to be guilty of contributory negligence. [...]

According to authorities following the common law rule, the age of seven years is arbitrarily fixed as the age under which children are incapable of negligence. "We are of the opinion that there was no error in giving the second instruction, and hold, in analogy to the rule of the common law, which exempts children under seven years of age from criminal responsibility, that up to the age of seven years 'a child is incapable of such conduct as will constitute contributory negligence, and that the court may so declare as a matter of law.'" [...]

In McDonald v. City of Spring Valley, the court said (page 477): "From time immemorial the status of a minor of tender years has been recognized in law to be different from that of one of more mature years. The law recognizes that up to the age of seven years a child is incapable of such conduct as will constitute contributory negligence, and our courts have uniformly so stated the law in their instructions to juries."

In an extensive note on the subject in L.R.A. 1917F, it is said: "There seems to be considerable ground for the position that as matter of law a child under seven years of age is incapable of contributory negligence, not especially because of any analogy to the criminal law that a child under that age cannot commit a crime, although this reason is frequently given, but because, in the case of a child under seven years of age, there is lacking that discretion and judgment, and that appreciation of the probability and extent of the danger, which, as has been shown above, are the essential elements in determining whether a child has exercised due care. And if these elements, are not merely knowledge, receive proper consideration in determining the question of the age at which the rule of conclusive presumption of incapacity ceases to be applicable, it seems that in some cases a higher age limit should have been adopted. It was said on this point in an Alabama case ... in which the court was of the opinion that the doctrine of contributory negligence was not applicable to a child under seven years of age (the child in this instance, however, being only three and one-half years old): "It would seem to follow that a child under the age of seven years should be absolutely exempt from the operation of the principle. Thought, discretion, judgment, or will cannot be legally imputable to him—he cannot be adjudged guilty and punished for crime. * * * Not having an 'independent will,'—incapable of choosing between the right and the wrong, between care and rashness, the creature of instinct and impulse,—there is no ground on which to base negligence. From him duties to others are not exacted, while duties to him are recognized and compulsorily enforced.

Negligence has the same significance, whether applied to a defendant as creating a cause of action, or to a plaintiff in bar of an action for a redress of injuries. * * * A child below the age of seven years, irresponsible, incapable of discretion, could as well be subjected to liability for negligence as to permit one fully sui juris by the imputation of negligence to escape the responsibility of his own wrongful act. The child owes to him no duty, because incapable of performing it."

This rule was transplanted from the civil law to our common law at an early period. In Austin's Jurisprudence the author, in discussing conclusive presumptions of law, mentions the case of infants under the age of seven years and says: "Here, according to the Roman Law, and (semble) according to our own, the infant is presumed juris et de jure incapable of unlawful intention or culpable inadvertence. His incapacity is inferred or presumed from the age wherein he is; and proof to the contrary of that preappointed inference is not admissible by the tribunals." Lectures on Jurisprudence, John Austin, Vol. 1, p. 492 (5th Edition, 1929). [...]

How well founded in the experience of countless centuries, and in the observation of philosophers of antiquity this understanding of incapacity and blamelessness of childhood was, is seen in modern thought and the researches of outstanding scholars of recent years; and it may be pertinent to remark that our state follows, whether consciously or not, the classic idea in the matter of the capacity of childhood for education. According to the statutes providing for the compulsory education of children, the age of seven years is arbitrarily established as the time at which such education must commence. [...]

In cases on review, courts do not usually seek guiding principles from general authorities outside the law. It is the general rule that scientific works and books, cannot be read in evidence on the trial of a case, although it is a practice of some states, and one sustained by very respectable authority to allow attorneys during their argument to the jury, to read from books which have been proved to be standard works upon the subject. ... But the rule is to the contrary in Michigan. [...]

This rule, and its implications, however, should not preclude a reviewing court, from taking cognizance of authorities, generally accepted as outstanding and reputable, as to conclusions reached resulting from scientific observation and research, with the object of testing whether assumptions of fact, relied upon in decisions of cited authorities as self-evident, based presumably on reason and logic, and without supporting evidence, are justifiable.

What is there in actual fact, science, or research to justify a different treatment of children under the age of seven years from those that have passed this age? One cannot fail to be impressed with the fact that these conclusions which crystalized centuries ago regarding the special status of a child of this age, have been confirmed by present day observers and scientists in the specialized field of child care, education and psychology. In recent times, the studies of Alfred Binet, in France, Hans Gross, in Austria, Jean Piaget, in Switzerland, and Maria Montessori, in Italy, have brought a new light upon the mysterious mind of the child, and have elucidated many of the obscure areas in the understanding of mental development and growth in infancy and adolescence.

What is remarkable in the conclusions arrived at by such research, is the fact that the age of seven years marks a transitional line in the mental development of children. In the copious and rich literature devoted to the subject, there repeatedly recurs the emphasis upon this age as marking the inception of thought and reason, the commencement of exchange of ideas, the beginning of concepts of justice. Authorities hold that this age marks the passage from the period of self-centered speech and thought to verbal understanding and social thought and cooperation. In short, the age of seven years can be said to be the threshold over which a human being passes from the realm of imagination and dream to the world of reality and fact. [...]

These considerations bring us to the application of the standard of care required of the infant plaintiff in this case, as set forth in the following instructions of the trial court to the jury: "I charge you that ordinary care has relation to the situation and condition of the parties, and varies according to the exigencies which require vigilance and attention, and when contributory negligence is sought to be attributed to a child, the child can only be held to that degree of care which may be reasonably expected from one under the same conditions and of the same sex, intelligence and judgment. I therefore charge you that the care and discretion to be used by the plaintiff in this case, Edmund Dean Tyler, a child of 6 years and 9 months, must be proportionate to his age and capacity to understand and ability to perform it, therefore in passing upon the question of whether or not the plaintiff was guilty of contributory negligence in this case you will consider all the testimony with relation thereto, his age, ability and intelligence and his experience to recognize and understand danger, and determine whether or not he conducted himself as a child of his age, ability and understanding would reasonably have been expected to, under like circumstances; and if he did, then he would not be guilty of contributory negligence. If, on the other hand, he failed to use that degree of care which a child of his age, ability and understanding would reasonably have been expected to exercise under like circumstances, then he would be guilty of negligence and if his negligence in that regard contributed to the accident, then he would not be entitled to recover."

Much has been written about "the careful and prudent man" as the standard of care in cases involving negligence and such standard has often been criticized as unreliable, logically indefensible and an unjustified fiction originally resorted to evade problems of jurisprudence. Whatever the criticism, or whether it be merited, it has at least the virtue of being an attempt to arrive at an objective standard.

This cannot be said of the same standard when applied to the conduct of infants. In the case before us, the plaintiff was six years and eight months of age. But the standard of care was not laid down as that of the ordinarily careful and prudent child of this age. The jury was instructed that in order to recover, such infant must conduct himself as a child of his age, ability and understanding would reasonably have been expected to act under like circumstances, taking into consideration his age, ability and intelligence.

This is a confusion of the objective standard of care, and the individual standard of care of a particular child. How can any juryman or judge know how a prudent child of such tender years should conduct himself, aside from the reflection of the prudent adult mind of what a child should do. Prudence and tender years are paradoxical and contradictory. How does one take into consideration the intelligence, ability and understanding of this particular child without proof of what such intelligence, ability and understanding actually are? How deceptive logical trappings may be, is well illustrated in the present case, where the record shows that the child was not even a witness; and from any available indications, may not even have been present during the trial. Yet the jury was obliged, in the course of its determination of these most essential issues, to arrive at a finding of what a prudent, careful child at the age of six years, and eight months would do under the circumstances, with which the infant in this case was confronted; and they were then obliged to determine the degree of intelligence, ability and understanding of this particular child in order to ascertain whether, taking into consideration such individual qualities, the infant plaintiff acted as a prudent, careful child would have acted in attempting to cross the street in front of the oncoming automobile. They were further to judge what this particular infant's intelligence, ability and understanding were, without hearing the child as a witness, and it may have been, without even seeing him. Any conclusion arrived at by the jury under such circumstances resulted from piling speculation upon the fiction of a fiction. Therefore, the common law rule is interposed in behalf of this little boy in the tender years of early childhood, suffering blindness and permanent injuries to save him from being the victim of a fruitless and ritualistic determination of his rights.

The fact that the child was not a witness in this case, emphasizes, peculiarly, another reason for the rule so necessary to the protection of infants' rights. The burden of proving freedom from contributory negligence by his own testimony would be almost insuperable for a child barely emerging from babyhood. It is a severe enough test for a mature person of intelligence. For a baby it is unthinkable. It would seem that such a consideration would be of especial importance where the party opposing the infant is the mature wrongdoer who inflicts the injury. While the jury might approach the determination of such a question in a fair minded attitude, it would be more concerned with testimony of complex facts—time, distance, speed, exercise of caution—than with inferences that might be drawn to explain the child's inability to enlighten it on these points. The burden is too heavy for the small child, and in such an unequal contest the law does not permit a wrongdoer to take advantage of the infant's difficulty and inadequacy.

Our court, however, has never yet, on the ground of his own contributory negligence, repudiated the claim of an infant plaintiff under seven years of age for injuries received at the hands of a negligent wrongdoer. On the contrary, it has repeatedly affirmed recovery on the part of such an infant, even though, according to every known standard, the infant would have been guilty of contributory negligence, had the court given consideration in the slightest degree to such defense.

To adopt the Massachusetts rule in this case, we would be obliged to reverse our decisions dating back more than a quarter of a century to Johnson v. Bay City, 1910, supra.

Nor are we impressed with the argument that the common law rule is unjustifiable because it is arbitrary. There is no unfairness from an arbitrary treatment of the matter when it is considered that the cause of the contributory negligence of the infant can come into consideration only after a determination that the defendant himself was negligent. For if the defendant was not negligent, there can be no recovery, as no one is liable for injuries resulting from the sudden and unexpected act of a child. Czarniski v. Security Storage Co.; and if the defendant was negligent he should not be allowed to escape on the ground that an infant who is not fully aware of the consequences of his acts, was also negligent.

The citizen is everywhere hedged about by legal qualifications and disabilities based upon arbitrary rules of age. The law fixes the age of 21 years under which infants are not liable upon their contracts; and in spite of varying degrees of intelligence and capacity, the same age is prescribed as a qualification for the right to vote. Infants can choose their own guardians at 14 years of age. The age at which persons can consummate a legal marriage is arbitrarily fixed by law. The age qualifications for election to Congress is 25 years; to the Senate, 30 years; to the

Presidency, 35 years. If there is any reason for arbitrary age qualifications or disabilities in law, they would certainly be as capable of justification when used in the protection of little children from the infliction of wrongs, as in any other situations above mentioned. [...]

An illuminating article[2] on the subject of the incapacity of children in matters of negligence is found in a law review of recent years, in which the author, in discussing the question, under consideration in the case before us, says:

"The majority of the states set an arbitrary age limit below which no infant can be held guilty of contributory negligence. The minority sends every case to the jury except where the facts are undisputed and can result in but one conclusion. Age is the only fact considered by the majority. The minority treat age as just one of the many facts to be considered by the jury in settling that particular case before the court.

"Which view is preferable? Under which view is the infant accorded the greater amount of protection?

"The writer accepts the majority view for the following reasons: The majority view is administratively expedient. The possible danger of a shifting standard is avoided. The confusion and inconsistency which oftimes mark jury decisions is eliminated. The law is crystallized and defined. The application of the majority view is simple.

"The majority view in setting an arbitrary age attaches full significance to the fact that infants as a class lack that judgment and discretion which comes with age and experience. While the infant may have knowledge of the possibility of injury when he runs in front of a moving trolley, the writer contends that he fails to consider the full consequences, the immediacy of the danger and the severity of the consequences. The infant acts on impulse. Seldom, if ever, does the infant stop to consider the full consequences of any act. The possibility that he may be crippled for life or even killed is not appreciated. All that concerns the infant is his present desire. Deliberation and a sensible choice of alternatives in the light of future consequences are not the attributes of one of tender years.

"The minority view fails to give adequate protection against this youthful deficiency in judgment and discretion. The tendency of the jury in considering the case before it is to attach importance to the fact whether or not the infant had knowledge of the possibility of present danger. The juror is impressed with the immediate facts and the infant's conduct in relation thereto and may not, unless clearly instructed by the court, go beyond those facts which are brought to his attention. The juror fails to consider whether or not the infant plaintiff would have done what he did in this case had he the ability to temper his impulsive action with the judgment and discretion which comes with age and experience. The public charge of tomorrow demands present protection.

"The negligent defendant placed the injurious force in operation. The infant was injured as a result of the defendant's acts. The courts are cognizant of the fact that the infant is not fully able to take care of himself and as a result has set a different standard of care for the infant than it has for the adult. If we agree that infants as a class are to be treated with leniency, why should we strive to relieve a negligent defendant whose only claim to be absolved from liability is based on the alleged fault of that group whom we seek to protect? This argument is practically sound. The complications of modern civilization with its crowding traffic and premium on speed has lessened the odds in favor of safety for infants. Why decrease these odds any further by favoring that negligent adult who initiated the injurious force with knowledge of its capacity to do harm?"

Every consideration further impels a court to determine such questions involving little children from a humane standpoint unless restricted by precedent, vested rights, justice to the opposite party, or because of public policy. None of these considerations arise to prevent the application of the humanitarian common law rule in cases involving children of tender years.

The rule contended for by defendant that the contributory negligence of the infant is always a question of fact regardless of his age, has been adopted by the Supreme Court of Massachusetts, and has come to be known as the "Massachusetts Rule." While we have the utmost respect for the distinguished tribunal of that commonwealth, we are constrained to differ with it in our determination of this question for several reasons. Among these, it may be mentioned that we have uniformly held, directly contrary to the so-called Massachusetts rule, since Easton v. Medema, supra, and in numerous cases involving children under the age of six years, have repeatedly held that such infants were incapable of contributory negligence as a matter of law. We have further found no ground advanced as a basis for the rule that is supported by reason, experience, observation or public policy, or a regard for the protection of the rights of infants. On other matters closely associated with the question of contributory negligence of infants, such as the rule adopted in Massachusetts, imputing the contributory negligence of an adult in charge of the care of the child, to the innocent child itself, preventing in such cases any recovery by the child for injuries caused by a negligent defendant ... "The strong objection to it is its palpable injustice to the infant." [...]

Because of the nature of reasoning, and because of the similar considerations of public policy and protection of infants' rights involved in rules adopted by different authorities as to the imputation of negligence to infants, and their capacity for contributory negligence, it is of interest in a discussion as to whether the common law rule or the Massachusetts rule be followed in Michigan, to note the grounds advanced why we do not follow Massachusetts on the rule of imputing the negligence of a parent to an infant plaintiff. [...]

In Battishill v. Humphreys, Judge Morse said (page 901): "The contrary doctrine would abandon the young and helpless, whom the courts are bound to protect, to the not always tender mercies of parents and guardians, and to wanton ill treatment and injury, without hope of redress. * * * The law aims to guard and shield children of tender years from the abuse of parents as well as of strangers." [...]

This somewhat extensive reference to authorities outside the law, however, is not made for the purpose of establishing a rule but rather to justify and confirm an already established rule that seems to us not only to possess the virtue of approval of times past, but also to be founded upon reason and humane considerations. In a larger sense the burden of establishing the tenet that an infant, under seven years of age, is incapable of contributory negligence is not upon those who assert it. Above the cruelties and carnage of the centuries, History holds aloft the principle of such blameless early childhood. In civil law, in criminal jurisprudence, in the majority rule of our state jurisdictions in matters relating to negligence, the incapacity of children of a certain age is recognized, whether it be a question of intention or inadvertence; and the long experience of humanity has recognized in matters of education, morals, and mental development, a definite age of transition from carefree infancy to that time when a sense of responsibility is born. To surrender that principle one must depart from the sentiments of the past—not from an archaic rule—but from a vital and considered recognition of a transcendent element of human value. It seems, indeed, a paradox to hold the same child incapable of an act of wrongful intention but at the same time to hold him responsible for passive carefree inattention.

In our determination of this case we follow the common law rule announced by the numerous authorities, entitled to eminent respect, which hold that an infant under seven years of age is incapable of contributory negligence. [...]

Such a doctrine recognized at a time when the harshness of the common law was untempered by equity, should not in these days be frittered away be the hazards of metaphysical reflection, or the necessarily dubious speculation of juries in such cases. This ancient bulwark and protection of little children is a vital safeguard of their rights and persons. It warns that no one can negligently cause injury to a child of such tender years with impunity, by casting on his small shoulders the onerous burden of proving his own freedom from negligence.

In this state, our courts, nurturing the rights of infants, will not prescribe and require of them novel standards of care, as a condition precedent to reparation for injuries inflicted by careless wrongdoers, and will not exact from them more severe obligations of conduct than prevailed in the middle ages. In Michigan, the common law rule is reaffirmed, and children under the age of seven years are conclusively presumed to be incapable of contributory negligence.

It follows that the action of the trial court in submitting infant plaintiff's contributory negligence to the jury for determination as a question of fact, was reversible error. [...]

Judgment reversed and new trial granted, with costs to plaintiff.

BUSHNELL, J., concurred with McALLISTER, J.

WIEST, Chief Justice

(concurring in the reversal for exclusion of competent testimony)

I cannot join in the holding that a boy, six years and seven months of age, cannot, under any circumstances, be guilty of contributory negligence as a matter of fact, nor can I subscribe to the statement that: "In Michigan, the common law rule is reaffirmed, and children under the age of seven years are conclusively presumed to be incapable of contributory negligence."

The common law rule with reference to non-responsibility of children under seven years of age, related to criminal acts and ought not, by analogy, because wholly lacking in similarity, be applied to negligence. [...]

"Under a proper instruction the Massachusetts rule is the more sound and the one most likely to insure just result. It does not cast upon the general public any and all risks that may be created by the carelessness of a child. Still it does not go so far as to hold a child to a degree of care not commensurate with its age and experience. Under present day circumstances a child of six is permitted to assume many responsibilities. There is much opportunity for him to observe and thus become cognizant of the necessity for exercising some degree of care. Compulsory school attendance, the radio, the movies, and traffic conditions all tend to have this effect. Under the Illinois rule a child may be guilty of the most flagrant violation of duty and still not be precluded from recovering damages for injuries suffered partly because of such violation. The Massachusetts rule contemplates justice for all parties irrespective of age. Jurors, by virtue of their office, are competent to judge whether or not a child has exercised a degree of care commensurate with its age, capacity, and understanding. The Illinois rule has no basis in sound reason or logic. It is based upon an outworn historical rule of criminal law which refused to acknowledge any capacity on the part of any child under seven years of age to distinguish between right and wrong." [...]

In Milbury v. Turner Centre System, the injured boy was five years of age, and was hit and injured by an automobile as he was crossing the street in a city.

Upon the question of contributory negligence of the boy, the court stated (page 473): "Whether the plaintiff failed to use the care of one of his age and experience was, we think, for the jury. No serious contention was made that he was not of sufficient judgment to be alone upon the street. Certainly his conduct did not measure up to the care to be demanded of an adult. Sullivan v. Chadwick. The law does not require that it should. He was bound to use the care of a prudent boy of his age and experience." [...]

Upon this point the court in the case at bar charged the jury: "I charge you that ordinary care has relation to the situation and condition of the parties, and varies according to the exigencies which require vigilance and attention, and when contributory negligence is sought to be attributed to a child, the child can only be held to that degree of care which may be reasonably expected from one under the same conditions and of the same sex, intelligence and judgment. I therefore charge you that the care and discretion to be used by the plaintiff in this case, Edmund Dean Tyler, a child of 6 years and 9 months, must be proportionate to his age and capacity to understand and ability to perform it, therefore in passing upon the question of whether or not the plaintiff was guilty of contributory negligence in this case you will consider all the testimony with relation thereto, his age, ability and intelligence and his experience to recognize and understand danger, and determine whether or not he conducted himself as a child of his age, ability and understanding would reasonably have been expected to, under like circumstances; and if he did, then he would not be guilty of contributory negligence. If, on the other hand, he failed to use that degree of care which a child of his age, ability and understanding would reasonably have been expected to exercise under like circumstances, then he would be guilty of negligence and if his negligence in that regard contributed to the accident, then he would not be entitled to recover."

We are not called upon to pass upon the age a child may be held guilty of contributory negligence as a matter of law.

I find reversible error in the exclusion of evidence and the judgment should be reversed, with costs to plaintiff.

BUTZEL, SHARPE, and CHANDLER, JJ., concurred with WIEST, C.J.

(Citations omitted)

Verni v. Johnson

Court of Appeals of New York

295 N.Y. 436 (1946)

Opinion: DESMOND, Judge.

The testimony here raised a question of fact as to defendant's negligence. The Trial Justice submitted to the jury that issue and an issue as to contributory negligence of plaintiff's intestate, an infant three years and two months old at the time of the accident. Plaintiff's counsel requested a charge that "a child of the age of three years and two months is non sui juris and incapable of being guilty of negligence." The request was refused. We granted leave to appeal so that we might pass on the correctness of the rule of law contended for in that request to charge.

In every reported case where the question has been squarely raised, this court has held that a three-year-old child is conclusively presumed to be incapable of negligence. ... [T]he second department joined unanimously in an opinion by Justice Hagarty holding that "a child under the age of four years is non sui juris, as a matter of law." We denied leave. The argument for leaving the question of competency to juries is based on certain language in Camardo v. New York State Railways. The Camardo child was just under five years of age and the language of this court's opinion must be read with that in mind. There is no sign in that opinion of any intent to overrule the Mangam, Ihl, Prendegast and McGarry cases, above cited.

Throughout the United States, "as regards a child between three and four years of age, the weight of authority is in favor of a conclusive presumption of incapacity". ...

The rule which refuses to allow such young children to be penalized for supposed faults has been followed in this court at least since 1868. Mangam v. Brooklyn R. Co., supra. It is not an unjust rule or one which changing conditions make obsolete. No reason appears for changing it.

The judgments should be reversed and a new trial granted, with costs to abide the event.

CONWAY, Judge (dissenting): I dissent and vote to affirm upon the ground that the court properly charged the jury that ordinarily a child of less than four years of age is considered to be non sui juris, but that where, as in this instance, the plaintiff introduced evidence as to the memory and intelligence of the child, the question whether or not this particular child was sui juris was a question for the jury ... A child's age does not alone determine its capacity to care for itself and to avoid dangers which may threaten. The law does not disregard variations in capacity among children of the same age, and does not arbitrarily fix an age at which the duty to exercise some care begins or an age at which an infant must exercise the same care as an adult. * * * Determination whether under the particular circumstances in each case reasonable men might differ as to the inferences that can be drawn is decisive of whether upon the evidence a question of fact or of law is presented. It is sometimes said that at least a presumption exists that a particular child is non sui juris, or that another child is not capable of exercising the care which an adult would exercise in the face of the danger which threatened. It would perhaps be more accurate to say that, under some circumstances, in the absence of any evidence bearing upon the capacity of a particular child except its age, an inference may be drawn, in the light of common experience, as to the child's ability to apprehend and avoid the danger which resulted in its injury. (Citing a case.) Here, too, however, it must be noted that from the cases decided in this court **no general rule can be deduced that at a definite and fixed age** the basis for an inference that a child is incapable of caring for itself under particular circumstances fails. * * * **No rule of law fixes an arbitrary age** at which a particular degree of care may be expected, **or** furnishes **a true presumption which takes the place of evidence**, that a child is not chargeable with contributory negligence. Only where the circumstances admit of only one inference may the court decide as a matter of law what inference shall be drawn." (Emphasis supplied.)

LOUGHRAN, C.J., and THACHER and DYE, JJ., concur with DESMOND, J.

CONWAY, J., dissents in memorandum, in which LEWIS, J., concurs.

(Citations omitted)

The following diagram seeks to outline some of the court doctrines concerning whether or not there is a general *mens rea* requirement in the tort law. The general answer is: there is not one that resembles general *mens rea* in the criminal law. However, there are pockets of general *mens rea* as the cases reveal and the diagram displays.

SUMMARY DIAGRAM: **Insanity and Infancy in Tort Liability**

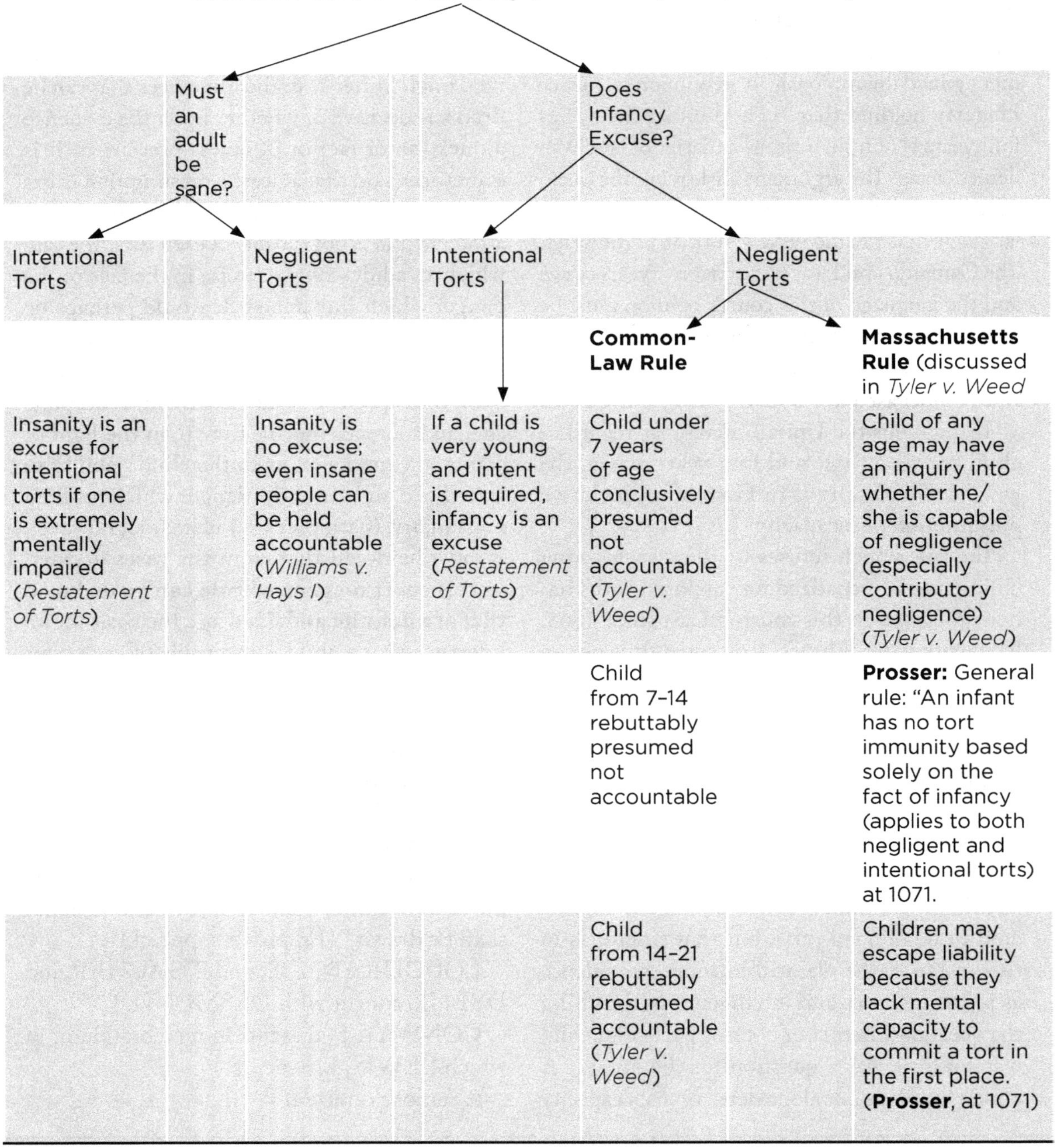

The following chapter considers other legal cases that address additional elements of a tort action.

■ CHAPTER 4

Causation and Proximate Causation in the Tort Law

The Causation Requirement for Tort Law Offenses

An essential element for a cause of action in the tort law is that the plaintiff has to show the defendant in fact caused plaintiff's harm and was the proximate cause of the harm. In this section, we consider a variety of cases that connect plaintiff's harm to a defendant's action. In the next section, we consider cases addressing proximate causation.

To succeed in a tort case, plaintiffs must show that defendants in their case more likely than not caused their harm. Recall, this differs from the criminal law, since not all crimes require a causal element. An assassin may attempt a murder but fail by hitting a bird instead, and the targeted victim may not even know he or she was a target and may not even hear the report from a gun. Thus, the would-be assassin can be convicted of attempted murder without a causal connection between the shooting and any harm to the targeted victim or anyone else. Conspiracy similarly lacks a causal requirement. If you and Al Capone agree to rob a bank and you take some steps toward robbing it, but the police stop you before you even reach the bank, and even if there has been no harm to the bank or anyone else, you have still conspired to rob the bank provided good evidence supports the various elements of the conspiracy.

In the tort law, what must a plaintiff legally show to establish the causal relationship? A classic determination for showing causation is for the finder of fact—the jury, or perhaps a judge hearing all the issues in a case—to consider a hypothetical, "to compare what did occur with what would have occurred if hypothetical contrary-to-fact conditions had existed."[1]

---

1 *Prosser and Keeton on torts* (5th ed.), p. 265. W. Page Keeton et al., Eds. West Publishing.

A common rule utilized by many courts is the "But-For" Rule:

> The defendant's conduct is a cause of the event if the event would not have occurred but for that conduct; conversely, the defendant's conduct is not a cause of the event, if the event would have occurred without it.[2]

Note that this rule excludes causal considerations. Just because defendant's conduct is *a causal factor* in bringing about the harm, there may be other causal contributions, and perhaps some of them might preclude defendant from being liable. On the other hand, if an event would have occurred without defendant's action, this still may not show defendant's action may be excluded from consideration. We will see cases in which this becomes an issue.

In fact, but-for causation is illustrated in *Stubbs v. the City of Rochester.* Mr. Stubbs lived and worked in the city of Rochester, New York, and during the summer of 1910 he only drank Rochester water. However, he contracted typhoid fever and alleged he was sick from this because one waterline for industrial purposes (but not for drinking) was contaminated with the *Typhoid* bacillus, giving him the fever.

The bold terms below name some major events in civil law trials (broader than torts). They begin when someone suffers some adverse event in the world that they think could be remedied in the law. This party—the plaintiff—files a **complaint** against a defendant he or she believes harmed him or her. The defendant files an **answer** to the allegations in the complaint. This is followed by a **discovery** period, in which each side seeks to learn what the other side knows about issues in the case. At the end of discovery, the case might end at that time as it did for Judith Sindell. If it does not end at that time, **plaintiffs present their case-in-chief**—facts and interpretations of the law followed by **defendants' case-in-chief**, a presentation of their facts and legal interpretations. The two sides then sum up their case before a jury, which then retires to deliberate about what it has heard. A **jury verdict** would then be issued, but the trial may not be over because there is the possibility of post-verdict motions. For an abstract timeline of these issues, see the Appendix.

Stubbs v. City of Rochester

Court of Appeals of New York

226 N.Y. 516 (1919)

Opinion: HOGAN, J.

This action was brought by plaintiff to recover damages alleged to have been sustained by him due to drinking contaminated water from the defendant's domestic service.

During the year 1910 and for many years prior thereto the defendant under legislative authority was engaged in the business of selling water to its inhabitants. A duty was imposed on the commissioner of public works to provide an abundant supply of wholesome water for public and private use, to devise plans and sources of water supply, to plan and supervise the distribution of water

2 *Ibid.*, 266.

through the *city*, and to protect it against contamination. The *city* has two systems of water supply: One for potable water brought by it from Hemlock Lake, some distance south of the *city* to reservoirs near the *city*, and thence distributed by gravity to consumers. That system is known as the Hemlock system. The second or Holly system for fire purposes in the business district, the water being pumped from the Genesee river near the center of the *city* into a separate set of distributing pipes. The Holly system carried a pressure of from 60 to 70 pounds to the square inch, which in case of fire was increased to 130 pounds. The pressure in Hemlock system was about 50 pounds to the square inch. The Erie Canal ran through the *city*. A number of lift bridges, including one at Brown street, crossed the same. The bridges were raised by admitting water under pressure to a cylinder forcing a piston out and raising the platform of the bridge. The pipes furnishing water to the cylinders were "Y" shaped; one branch being connected with the Hemlock system and the second branch with the Holley system. Gates were installed in each pipe at a point about 20 feet back from the place of connection with the "Y" pipe to control the flow of waters therein. If the gates in both pipes were open at one time both systems would discharge water into the "Y" pipe. If one gate was closed the discharge would be confined to the other pipe. The employees of the *city* had possession of the wrenches or keys by which these gates could be opened or closed; the water for operating the bridge being furnished by the *city*.

… The water used for the purpose of operating the lift bridges is shut off in the fall of the year at the close of navigation on the Erie Canal, and turned on when navigation is resumed, usually about May. In the year 1910 the gates of the two systems located near the Brown street bridge were opened by direction of the superintendent of waterworks of the *city*. In June, 1910, numerous complaints were received by the superintendent from inhabitants, consumers of the Hemlock water, residing or employed in the vicinity of Brown street bridge, in substance that the water was roily, dirty, and had an offensive odor. No attention was given the matter of complaints until one resident called upon the health commissioner of the *city*, and the latter accompanied the complainant to her home, observed the condition of the water, took a sample of the water from the faucet, and observed that it looked and smelled badly. He thereupon had it analyzed by a chemist, which analysis disclosed a serious condition of contamination. The health officer thereupon notified the public through the newspapers not to drink the water without boiling it, continued his investigation, collected water from a number of houses, and caused an analysis to be made of same, which disclosed contamination, and he thereupon notified the water department that the Hemlock water was contaminated. The latter department started an investigation on October 2d, upwards of three months after many complaints had been made to it, and upon arrival at the Brown street bridge discovered the source of contamination to be at that point, and that water from the Holly system was being discharged through the Hemlock system pipes. The water was thereupon shut off, and a few days later the discovery was made that there was no check valve in the pipe of the Hemlock system, and the water of the two systems commingled and were being furnished to consumers in that locality as potable waters.

The plaintiff, a resident of the City of Rochester and a machinist, was employed by a firm whose place of business was at the corner of Allen and Platt streets, about one block from the Brown street bridge. The factory was supplied with Hemlock Lake water for drinking purposes. Plaintiff drank the water from time to time, using his individual drinking glass. He was taken ill September 6, 1910, with typhoid fever, and was sick in bed for 6 weeks and unable to work for some 12 weeks. Asserting that his illness was caused by reason of drinking contaminated water supplied by the city, he seeks to recover damages by reason thereof. The evidence disclosed upon the trial clearly established that the water furnished by the defendant for potable purposes in the locality of the Brown street bridge was contaminated. The negligence of the defendant charged is that it carelessly and negligently permitted poisonous and polluted water from the Genesee river to flow through the Holly system mains and pipes into the mains and pipes of the Hemlock system, thereby polluting and contaminating the Hemlock water, rendering the same dangerous to life and health of the inhabitants of the city, in violation of its duty to furnish pure and wholesome water; a failure to inspect the pipes from time to time to discover whether or not the check valve was in place and operating, and failure to exercise diligence in a discovery of the nature and source of the contamination, following many complaints as to the condition of the water. The facts adduced upon the trial were ample to permit a consideration of the question of negligence of the *city* by a jury, and if found by a jury to sustain such finding. It is argued by counsel for the *city* that plaintiff's case as to how he contracted typhoid fever rests wholly upon conjecture. Upon the appeal to the Appellate Division after the first trial the latter court reversed the judgment recovered by plaintiff upon that ground … Upon the appeal to the Appellate Division in the case under review two of the justices, who concurred for reversal on the first appeal on the ground stated, dissented from the decision affirming the nonsuit at Trial Term, presumptively indicating that the evidence upon the second trial had been supplemented by additional testimony, and rendered the earlier decision distinguishable from the present record.

The important question in this case is, **Did the plaintiff produce evidence from which inference might reasonably be drawn that the cause of his illness was due to the use of contaminated water furnished by defendant**. Counsel for respondent argues that, even assuming that the *city* may be held liable to plaintiff for damages caused its negligence in furnishing contaminated water for drinking purposes: (a) The evidence adduced by plaintiff fails to disclose that he contracted typhoid fever by drinking contaminated water; (b) that it was incumbent upon the plaintiff to establish that his illness was not due to any other cause to which typhoid fever may be attributed for which defendant is not liable. The evidence does disclose several causes of typhoid fever, which is a germ disease, the germ being known as the typhoid bacillus, which causes may be classified as follows:

First. Drinking of polluted water. Second. Raw fruits and vegetables in certain named localities where human excrement is used to fertilize the soil are sometimes sources of typhoid infection. Third. The consumption of shellfish, though not a frequent cause. Fourth. The consumption of infected milk and vegetables. Fifth. The housefly in certain localities. Sixth. Personal contact with an infected person by one who has predilection for typhoid infection and is not objectively sick with the disease. Seventh. Ice, if affected with typhoid bacilli. Eighth. Fruits, vegetables, etc., washed in infected water. Ninth. The medical authorities recognize that there are still other causes and means unknown. This fact was developed on cross-examination of physicians called by plaintiff.

Treating the suggestions of counsel in their order: (a) That the evidence fails to disclose that plaintiff contracted typhoid fever by drinking contaminated water. The plaintiff, having been nonsuited at the close of his case, **is entitled to the most favorable inference deducible from**

the evidence. That plaintiff, on or about September 6th, 1910, was taken ill, and very soon thereafter typhoid fever developed, is not disputed. That he was employed in a factory located one block distant from the Brown street bridge, in which Hemlock lake water was the only supply of water for potable and other purposes, and that the water drawn from faucets in that neighborhood disclosed that the water was roily and of unusual appearance, is not questioned. And no doubt prevails that the Holly system water was confined to the main business part of the city for use for fire purposes and sprinkling streets, and is not furnished for domestic or drinking purposes.

The evidence of the superintendent of waterworks of the city is to the effect that Hemlock lake water is a pure wholesome water free from contamination of any sort at the lake, and examinations of the same are made weekly; that the Holly water is not fit for drinking purposes, taken as it is from the Genesee river. Further evidence was offered by plaintiff by several witnesses, residents in the locality of Brown street bridge, who discovered the condition of the water at various times during July, August, and September, and made complaint to the water department of the condition of the same. Dr. Goler, a physician and health officer of the city, was called by plaintiff, and testified that in September, when complaint was made to him by a resident of the district, he went to the locality, visited houses in the immediate neighborhood, found that the water drawn from the faucet of the Hemlock supply looked badly and smelled badly. He took a sample of the water to the laboratory, and had it examined by a chemist, who found that it contained an increase in solids, and very many times, that is, 20 to 30 times, as much chlorine or common salt as is found in the domestic water supply—the presence of chlorine in excessive quantities indicates contamination in that quantity, bad contamination and usually sewage contamination. Further examination followed in the district. Water was collected from various houses and a large number of samples, perhaps less than 100, but over 25. ... About the following day, the source of contamination having been discovered, the doctor made an investigation as to the reported cases of typhoid fever in the city in the months of August, September, and October, for the purpose of determining the number of cases, where the cases came from, what gave rise to it, and he stated that in his opinion the outbreak of typhoid was due to polluted water, contaminated as he discovered afterwards by sewage. In answer to a hypothetical question embracing generally the facts asserted by plaintiff the witness testified that he had an opinion as to the cause of the infection of plaintiff, and such opinion was that it was due to contaminated water.

... Dr. Brady, the physician who attended the plaintiff, and Dr. Culkin both testified that in their opinion the plaintiff contracted typhoid fever from drinking polluted water.

... [C]ounsel for defendant stipulated that 57 witnesses which the plaintiff proposed to call ... suffered from typhoid fever, that ... such witnesses need not be called by plaintiff, and the stipulation shall have the same force and effect as though the witnesses had been called and testified to the facts.

The plaintiff resided with his wife some three miles distant from the factory where he was employed. The water consumed by him at his house outside the infected district was Hemlock water. The only water in the factory was Hemlock water, and he had there an individual cup from which he drank. He was not outside of the *city* during the summer of 1910. Therefore, the only water he drank was in the city of Rochester.

A table of statistics as to typhoid fever in the city of Rochester for the years 1901–1910, inclusive, was produced by the health officer and received in evidence. That exhibit was the subject of comment in the opinion of Justice Foote upon the first appeal. The fact is evident from a perusal of his opinion that upon the first trial plaintiff did not undertake to establish the number of cases of typhoid fever in the district where the water was contaminated as compared with the total number of cases in the city in 1910, which evidence was supplied upon this trial. The statistics disclose that the number of typhoid cases in the city in 1910 was 223, an excess of 50 cases of any year of the nine years preceding. Recalling that complaints as to water commenced in the summer of 1910, and as shown by the evidence that typhoid fever does not develop until two or three weeks after the bacilli have been taken into the system, in connection with the fact that the source of contamination was not discovered until October, the statistics disclose that of the 223 cases of typhoid in the city in the year 1910, 180 cases appear during the months of August, September, October, and November as against 43 cases during the remaining eight months, 35 of which were prior to August and 8 in the month of December, two months after the source of contamination of the water was discovered.

The evidence on the trial discloses that at least 58 witnesses, residents of the district, drank the contaminated water and suffered from typhoid fever in addition to plaintiff; thus one-third of the 180 cases during the months stated were shown to exist in that district.

Counsel for respondent asserts that there was a failure of proof on the part of plaintiff, in that he did not establish that he contracted disease by drinking contaminated water, and in support of his argument cites a rule of law that **when there are several possible causes of injury for one or more of which a defendant is not responsible, plaintiff cannot recover without proving that the injury was sustained wholly or in part by a cause for which defendant was responsible. He submits that it was essential for plaintiff to eliminate all other of seven causes from which the disease might have been contracted**. If the argument should prevail and the rule of law stated is not subject to any limitation, the present case illustrates the impossibility of a recovery in any case based upon like facts. One cause of the disease is stated by counsel to be "personal contact with typhoid carriers or other persons suffering with the disease, whereby bacilli are received and accidentally transferred by the hands or some other portion of the person or clothes to the mouth." Concededly a person is affected with typhoid some weeks before the disease develops. The plaintiff here resided three miles distant from his place of employment, and traveled to and from his work upon the street car. To prove the time when he was attacked with typhoid, then find every individual who traveled on the same car with him, and establish by each one of them that he or she was free from the disease even to his or her clothing is impossible. Again, the evidence disclosed that typhoid fever was caused by sources unknown to medical science. If the word of the rule stated is to prevail plaintiff would be required to eliminate sources which had not yet been determined or ascertained. I do not believe the rule stated to be as inflexible as claimed for. **If two or more possible causes exist, for only one of which a defendant may be liable, and a party injured established facts from which it can be said with reasonable certainty that the direct cause of the injury was the one for which the defendant was liable, the party has complied with the spirit of the rule**.

The plaintiff was employed in the immediate locality where the water was contaminated. He drank the water daily. The consumption of contaminated water is a very frequent cause of typhoid fever. In the locality there were a large number of cases of typhoid fever, and near to 60 individuals who drank the water and had suffered from typhoid fever in that neighborhood appeared as witnesses on behalf of plaintiff. The plaintiff gave evidence of his habits, his home surroundings, and his method of living, and the medical testimony indicated that his illness was caused by drinking contaminated water. Without reiteration of the facts disclosed on the trial I do not believe that the case on the part of plaintiff was so lacking in proof as matter of law that his complaint should be dismissed. On the contrary, the most favorable inferences deducible from the plaintiff were such as would justify a submission of the facts to a jury as to the reasonable inferences to be drawn therefrom, and a verdict rendered thereon for either party would rest, not in conjecture, but upon reasonable possibilities.

The judgment should be reversed, and a new trial granted, costs to abide the event. (Citations omitted)

CARDOZO, POUND, and ANDREWS, JJ., concur.

HISCOCK, C. J., and CHASE and McLAUGHLIN, JJ., dissent.

We see that while Stubbs provided evidence of a possible cause of typhoid fever, showing the potable water was a potential factor that could cause his disease, numerous potential contributors to typhoid had to be addressed sufficiently for the case to go to a jury.

This case illustrates several points about causation and more widely about the tort law. First, it illustrates why the "but-for" test for tort law causation is insufficient to establish causation needed for a tort.

Second, it illustrates the need to be cautious about but-for causation; in *Stubbs's* instance, plaintiff might have contracted typhoid fever even if he had not ingested the contaminated water.

Third, we see an appellate court encountering and discussing causal relationships from the world that legal rules may not be sufficient to address and to ensure the aims of the tort law. Events in the world may reveal other causal relationships that sometimes may force judges to modify legal rules to serve the goals of the tort law; namely, to ensure that plaintiffs have a fair opportunity to receive compensation for injuries they suffered from the actions of others.

Fourth, the Court of Appeals found there was sufficient evidence to go to a jury, which required a reversal of the trial court's decision. The Court of Appeals had to create a legal rule to account for the facts of the case and then, in its judgment, provide an opportunity for Stubbs to present his case to a jury to determine whether or not he had been injured by the contaminated water.

Fifth, the case also illustrates a procedural point about civil litigation. That is, once Stubbs had filed his complaint and his lawyer had presented his evidence against Rochester for his disease, Rochester petitioned the judge to end the case because **Stubbs could not prove all the facts needed to establish his case**; his case never went to a jury because the trial judge found his causal evidence wanting, as urged by the defendant. **Stubbs was *nonsuited***. Rochester argued that contaminated water *may* have given Stubbs typhoid fever (thus it was a but-for cause), but Stubbs could not adequately rule out many other sources of the typhoid bacillus that could have caused his disease. As you read the case, you should query whether or not the city's demands for ruling out other causes would be a defensible causal rule for the tort law. The trial judge concurred with the defense, and Stubbs's case was at an end. Stubbs appealed, and the highest court in New York, or the Court of Appeals (not the "Supreme Court" as are the highest courts in most states), granted the appeal. Some procedural stages in civil litigation are summarized in the table in the Appendix, along with some other cases we will read about.

One might say that causation is complex, as indeed it is. Consequently, when there are multiple possible contributing factors in the causal sequence, the "but-for" rule merely ensures that one possible contributor belongs as part of the sequence, but it does not settle the causal issue. The appellate court rejected the defense's proposal about what Stubbs should be required to show in order to rule out other possible causes of his typhoid fever. What did the defense propose? What did the appellate court object to? Was it correct in doing so?

The next case, *Anderson v. Minneapolis, St. P. and S. S. M. Ry. Co.,* poses a somewhat similar issue with fewer other potential contributors to the fire that damaged Anderson's property. The sparks from a railroad engine set Anderson's property on fire, but the railroad company claimed that one or more fires joined the first one and those joint fires, not the railroad's caused fire, harmed Anderson. The rule seemingly endorsed by this court is what one might call a *negligent-innocent* cause rule because one fire was clearly caused by the railroad company and the other might have been innocent of human causation, but due to lightning caused prairie fires or other innocent origins. The court endorses a "material or substantial" cause factor for determining whether or not the defendant railroad company has to compensate Anderson's property damage. This principle concerns what factors a jury can consider when faced with a difficult causation issue in which several causal contributions may have produced it. A generalization from the *Anderson* case is what is often called the "substantial factor rule." Sometimes, causal issues are easy; when a person is killed with a bullet to the head or a car runs over someone, the bullet or the car, respectively, is the cause of death. Other causation events in the world can be more complex as when more than one fire might have contributed to Anderson's house burning. In such cases, when several factors might have caused the damage, courts have articulated a rule for a jury to determine whether a particular causal factor is a "substantial" or "material cause" of the damage, even though other factors might also have contributed.

I have highlighted some civil procedure points about *Anderson* in **bold** in this case that should be considered. The plaintiff filed his **complaint**, which was **answered** by the defendant. The plaintiff then presented his **case in chief,** which provided the law and the evidence that he believed entitled him to compensation for his harms. The defense then presented its **case in chief,** with its view of the facts and law on its side. The case then went to the jury, which decided that plaintiff's law and facts were more likely than not correct compared with the defense's presentation. Defendant then filed a motion with the trial judge for a **judgment notwithstanding the verdict (JNOV), or in the alternative for a new trial (See Table on Civil Procedure in the Appendix)**. The claim of a JNOV is that no reasonable jury could have come to the conclusion the jury did in this case. The claim would have to be that the quality and quantity of evidence so overwhelmingly favored the defense's position that no reasonable jury could decide otherwise. A motion for a new trial urged that there was some major error in how the trial judge conducted the case and a new trial should be ordered. The trial judge rejected both claims, and the defendant appealed the trial court's final judgment to an appellate court and ultimately to the Supreme Court of Minnesota. You will read that opinion.

Anderson v. Minneapolis, St. P. & S. S. M. Ry. Co. et al.

Supreme Court of Minnesota

146 Minn. 430 (1920)

Opinion: LEES, C.: This is a fire case, brought against the defendant railway company and the Director General of Railroads. … Plaintiff had a verdict. The appeal is **from an order denying a motion in the alternative for judgment notwithstanding the verdict or for a new trial**. The *complaint* alleged that early in August, 1918, sparks from one of defendant's locomotive engines set a fire on or near the right of way, and that this fire spread until it finally reached plaintiff's land, where it destroyed some of his property.

The **answer** was a general denial, followed by an allegation that, if plaintiff was damaged by fire, the fire was not due to any act of defendant, was of unknown origin, and, by reason of extraordinary weather conditions, became a huge conflagration.

The reply put these allegations in issue.

Plaintiff's case in chief was directed to proving that in August, 1918, one of defendant's engines started a fire in a bog near the west side of plaintiff's land; that it smoldered there until October 12, 1918, when it flared up and burned his property, shortly before it was reached by one of the great fires which swept through Northeastern Minnesota at the close of that day.

Defendant introduced evidence to show that on and prior to October 12th fires were burning west and northwest of, and were swept by the wind towards, plaintiff's premises. It did not show how such fires originated, neither did it clearly and certainly trace the destruction of plaintiff's property to them.

[…]

> "If you find that bog fire was set by defendant's engine, and that some greater fire swept over it before it reached plaintiff's land, then it will be for you to determine whether the bog fire * * * was a material or substantial factor in causing plaintiff's damage. If it was, defendant was liable. If it was not, defendant was not liable. If the bog fire was set by one of defendant's engines, and if one of defendant's engines also set a fire or fires west of Kettle River, and those fires combined and burned over plaintiff's property, then the defendant is liable."

[…]

[T]he jury returned a sealed verdict in favor of plaintiff. …

Defendant requested the court to instruct that the extraordinary and unusual wind and weather conditions on October 12, 1918, were such an efficient and independent cause of plaintiff's damage as to relieve defendant from liability. …

… Neither [a] drought [in the region] nor [high winds] … would or could have destroyed plaintiff's property without the fire. … Hence, [even] if it can be said that an extraordinary wind coupled with an unusual drought were proximate causes of the injury, still the fire was a material concurring cause, without which there would have been no damage to plaintiff, and defendant is liable under the established rules of law. … That [such an] independent concurring cause was what is termed an act of God does not alter the rule. …

Our attention is invited to a number of cases holding that, if a fire has been spread beyond its natural limits by an unusual or extraordinary wind, carrying it to a place that would have been safe, except for the wind, the person who set the fire is not liable, because he could not reasonably have anticipated a wind of such a nature. … They are … of doubtful application in view of our statute (G. S. 1913, § 4426), which creates liability irrespective of weather conditions, virtually makes railroad companies insurers against damage caused by fires set by their engines … and entirely eliminates the question of negligence. …

The following proposition is stated in defendant's brief and relied on for a reversal:

> "If plaintiff's property was damaged by a number of fires combining, one being the fire pleaded, and the others being of no responsible origin, but of such sufficient or superior force that they would have produced the damage to plaintiff's property, regardless of the fire pleaded, then defendant was not liable."

… The Supreme Court of Michigan has referred to [this assertion form a case] as good law. … The Supreme Court of Idaho says the opinion is logical and well-reasoned, but the discussion is in a large measure theoretical and academic. … Judge Thompson, in his work on Negligence (volume 1, § 739), says that the conclusion reached is so clearly wrong as not to deserve discussion. If the Cook Case merely decides that one who negligently sets a fire is not liable if another's property is damaged, unless it is made to appear that the fire was a material element in the destruction of the property, there can be no question about the soundness of the decision. But if it decides that if such fire combines with another of no responsible origin, and after the union of the two fires they destroy the property and either fire independently of the other would have destroyed it, then, irrespective of whether the first fire was or was not a material factor in the destruction of the property, there is no liability, we are not prepared to adopt the doctrine as the law of this state. If a fire set by the engine of one railroad company unites with a fire set by the engine of another company, there is joint and several liability, even though either fire would have destroyed plaintiff's property. …

We find no error requiring a reversal, and hence the order appealed from is affirmed.

The court in *Anderson* introduces the idea of asking whether the fire caused by the railroad poses a "substantial factor" in burning Anderson's property, even though another fire might have contributed to it. This generic idea is manifested in other cases with different conditions or background issues making possible causal contributions to plaintiff's injuries. Does this principle seem defensible to help juries decide more complex cases such as this one?

Steinhauser v. Hertz presents a somewhat different substantial factor circumstance courts must legally address. There clearly was a car accident, after which Ms. Steinhauser began acting somewhat strangely and erratically. A major question in the case is how to characterize it: Did she have some latent tendency to schizophrenia, which was revealed as a result of the accident? Did the accident *aggravate* the disease; did it *precipitate* her disease; or did the accident *actually cause* the disease by itself? What term might you use for this and other cases in which the *condition of an individual* might contribute to the injury or its seriousness? Do you concur in how the Court of Appeals resolved this case? We will see other cases somewhat resembling this one that are called "eggshell skull cases" because of the particular vulnerability or biological weakness of the plaintiff.

Steinhauser v. The Hertz Corporation

United States Court of Appeals, Second Circuit

421 F.2d 1169 (1970)

Before FRIENDLY, SMITH and ANDERSON, Circuit Judges.

Opinion: FRIENDLY, Circuit Judge: On September 4, 1964, plaintiff Cynthia Steinhauser, a New Jersey citizen then 14 years old, her mother and father were driving south through Essex County, N.Y. A northbound car, owned by defendant Hertz Corporation, a Delaware corporation authorized to do business in New York, and operated by defendant Ponzini, a citizen of New York, crossed over a double yellow line in the highway into the southbound lane and struck the Steinhauser car heavily on the left side. The occupants did not suffer any bodily injuries.

The plaintiffs' evidence was that within a few minutes after the accident Cynthia began to behave in an unusual way. Her parents observed her to be "glassy-eyed," "upset," "highly agitated," "nervous" and "disturbed." When Ponzini came toward the Steinhauser car, she jumped up and down and made menacing gestures until restrained by her father. On the way home she complained of a headache and became uncommunicative. In the following days things went steadily worse. Cynthia thought that she was being attacked and that knives, guns and bullets were coming through the windows. She was hostile toward her parents and assaulted them; becoming depressed, she attempted suicide.

The family physician recommended hospitalization. After observation and treatment in three hospitals, with a final diagnosis of "schizophrenic reaction—acute—undifferentiated," she was released in December 1964 under the care of a psychiatrist, Dr. Royce, which continued until September 1966. His diagnosis, both at the beginning and at the end, was of a chronic schizophrenic reaction; he explained that by "chronic" he meant that Cynthia was not brought to him because of a sudden onset of symptoms. She then entered the Hospital of the University of Pennsylvania and, one month later, transferred to the Institute of Pennsylvania Hospital for long-term therapy. Discharged in January 1968, she has required the care of a psychiatrist. The evidence was that the need for this will continue, that reinstitutionalization is likely, and that her prognosis is bad.

[1] As the recital makes evident, the important issue was the existence of a causal relationship between the rather slight accident and Cynthia's undoubtedly serious ailment.[1] The testimony was uncontradicted that prior to the accident she had never displayed such exaggerated symptoms as thereafter. However, she had fallen from a horse about two years earlier and suffered what was diagnosed as a minor concussion; she was not hospitalized but missed a month of school. The other evidence relied on by the defendants to show prior psychiatric abnormality was derived largely from the history furnished, apparently in large part by Cynthia, at her admission to the first of the three hospitals on September 20, 1964, which we set out in the margin.[2]

Dr. Royce testified that a person may have a predisposition to schizophrenia which, however, requires a "precipitating factor" to produce an outbreak. As a result of long observation he believed this to have been Cynthia's case—that "she was a rather sensitive child and frequently exaggerated things and distorted things that happened within in the family" but that the accident was "the precipitating cause" of her serious mental illness. Under cross-examination he stated that prior to the accident Cynthia had a "prepsychotic" personality but might have been able to lead a normal life. Dr. Stevens, attending psychiatrist at the Institute of Pennsylvania Hospital, who had treated Cynthia, in answer to a hypothetical question which included the incidents relied on by the defendants to show prior abnormality, was of the opinion that the accident "was the precipitating cause of the overt psychotic reaction," "the last straw that breaks the camel's back."[3] In contrast defendants' expert, Dr. Brock, while agreeing that "with a background of fertile soil" schizophrenia can be induced by emotional strain, was of the opinion, based largely on the matters recited in footnote 2, that Cynthia was already schizophrenic at the time of the accident.

At the conclusion of the evidence the judge remarked to counsel, outside the presence of the jury, that, as he saw it, the sole question in the case was whether plaintiff had established that defendants caused Cynthia's condition or aggravated a pre-existing one. Even though plaintiffs' experts had testified in terms of precipitating rather than aggravating, it may be that if matters had been left right there, the jury would have understood. However, defendants' counsel, after correctly noting that "the question is not aggravate but precipitate," went on to say that, while that had been his understanding of plaintiffs' theory as outlined in counsel's opening statement, he now understood plaintiffs to be taking the position that the accident "caused schizophrenia." Taking this up, the judge asked plaintiffs' counsel, "Isn't it your position that this child was perfectly normal before this accident and that this accident caused schizophrenia?" When counsel responded that "this child was a fairly normal child, your Honor, and—" the judge demanded a direct answer whether it was plaintiffs' position that Cynthia "did not have schizophrenia before this accident." After counsel, not unnaturally, had responded in the affirmative, the judge said he would put the case to the jury on the basis of proximate cause. Further efforts by counsel to explain that his theory was one of "precipitating cause of a quiescent disease" proved unavailing; the judge insisted that he choose between saying "that this plaintiff was perfectly normal and that she got this schizophrenia as a result of the accident" or admitting "that she had schizophrenia before this accident, and that this accident only aggravated a pre-existing condition. There is no in between position." Counsel remarked that there were "a host of other positions" between Cynthia's being "the most perfect child" or being schizophrenic before the accident, but the judge was not persuaded. When trial counsel again referred to "precipitating cause," the judge asked for supporting authority. Counsel cited, of all cases, Palsgraf v. Long Island R.R. …

After several hours of deliberation the jury propounded the following question:

If we find the auto accident was the precipitating factor, but not the cause of the illness (schizophrenia) must we find for the plaintiff?

The judge responded by rereading what he had already said on proximate cause. Ten minutes later the jury brought in a defendants' verdict.

It is plain enough that plaintiffs were deprived of a fair opportunity to have the jury consider the case on the basis of the medical evidence they had adduced. The testimony was that before the accident Cynthia was neither a "perfectly normal child" nor a schizophrenic, but a child with some degree of pathology which was activated into schizophrenia by an emotional trauma although it otherwise might not have blossomed. Whatever the medical soundness of this theory may or may not be, and there does not seem in fact to have been any dispute about it, … plaintiffs were entitled to have it fairly weighed by the jury. They could not properly be pinioned on the dilemma of having either to admit that Cynthia was already suffering from active schizophrenia or to assert that she was wholly without psychotic tendencies. The jury's question showed how well they had perceived the true issue. When they were told in effect that plaintiffs could recover only if, contrary to ordinary experience, the accident alone produced the schizophrenia, the result was predestined.

It is unnecessary to engage in exhaustive citation of authority sustaining the legal validity of plaintiffs' theory of the case. Since New York law governs, the oft-cited decision in McCahill v. New York Transportation Co., which plaintiffs' appellate counsel has discovered, would alone suffice. There the defendant's taxicab negligently hit McCahill, broke his thigh and injured his knee. After being hospitalized, he died two days later of delirium tremens. A physician testified that "the injury precipitated his attack of delirium tremens, and understand I mean precipitated not induced"; he explained that by "precipitated," he meant "hurried up,"—just what plaintiffs' experts testified to be the role of the accident here. The Court of Appeals allowed recovery for wrongful death. In Champlin Refining Co. v. Thomas, the court held that "where one who has tubercular germs in his system suffers injuries due to the negligence of another, and the injuries so weaken the resistance of the tissues that as a direct consequence tubercular infection sets up therein, the negligence is the proximate cause of the tubercular infection and renders the negligent person liable in damages therefor." There was no suggestion that plaintiff was required either to admit that he already "had" tuberculosis or to assert that the accident "caused" the development of the germs. ... Our own decision in Evans v. S. J. Groves & Sons Co., (thrombosis of sinus possibly due in part to ear disease but "triggered" by blow to head) is also quite relevant. [...]

We add a further word that may be of importance on a new trial. Although the fact that Cynthia had latent psychotic tendencies would not defeat recovery if the accident was a precipitating cause of schizophrenia, this may have a significant bearing on the amount of damages. The defendants are entitled to explore the probability that the child might have developed schizophrenia in any event. ... In Evans v. S. J. Groves & Sons Company, supra, we noted that if a defendant "succeeds in establishing that the plaintiff's pre-existing condition was bound to worsen * * * an appropriate discount should be made for the damages that would have been suffered even in the absence of the defendant's negligence." ... It is no answer that exact prediction of Cynthia's future apart from the accident is difficult or even impossible. However taxing such a problem may be for men who have devoted their lives to psychiatry, it is one for which a jury is ideally suited. Reversed for a new trial.

Notes

1. The fact that no physical harm was suffered as a result of the accident does not affect plaintiff's right to recover. New York has abandoned the rule disallowing recovery for mental disturbance in the absence of a physical impact, see Battalla v. State, and although some courts deny recovery for mental disturbance unaccompanied by physical injuries, see Prosser, Torts 348–49 (3d ed. 1964); A.L.I. Restatement 2d Torts § 436A, New York allows such recovery if the "mental injury [is] marked by definite physical symptoms, which are capable of clear medical proof," (awarding damages where slight physical impact "aggravated and exacerbated that pre-existing condition" to produce schizophrenia).
2. She was a normal child except one incident when at the age of nine one of the friends of

her uncle molested her three times. Two years before while in camp she fell down from a horse. There she liked one horse called Silverfox, which she wanted to buy and felt much attached to him. Against her wishes, she saw that horse sold to another party. She felt depressed. Food seemed the only answer. She ate and felt better. As a result of it she became fat and felt further depressed. Later on she felt attached to a Riviera automobile but the family bought a Cadillac, which she hated very much. "Horses go away, car goes away but food never does." One year before she got involved with "hoods." They were fast and did everything—also in quotes. Quote, I felt much better among them. I wished to be liked and did everything to please them, unquote

There was evidence that in fact the first incident was exposure by the brother of an uncle rather than molestation.

Evans v. S. J. Groves & Sons Company provides a different example of a substantial causal factor. Ms. Evans at the time of the accident already had some kind of noticeable brain condition, which plaintiffs claimed was exacerbated during the car accident when she hit her head on the windshield. Might existing physical conditions like this, which make an injured party more susceptible to further harm, be taken into account by courts when they consider defendants' liability for harm? What does the court rule? Do you agree?

Evans v. S. J. Groves & Sons Company

United States Court of Appeals Second Circuit

315 F.2d 335 (1963)

Opinion: FRIENDLY, Circuit Judge.

These appeals by an out-of-state defendant from judgments of the District Court for the Northern District of New York in two negligence actions brought by in-state plaintiffs present a number of close questions, mainly of New York law. We have concluded to affirm.

The evidence amply supported the following version of the accident and its immediate sequelae—a version which, indeed, has not been seriously questioned either below or here. On December 10, 1954, one of the plaintiffs, Mrs. Abbie F. Evans, aged 57, was a passenger in the front seat of a farm truck traveling north on a two-lane highway in Oneida County, New York. Her neighbor, Roy Clemons, owned the truck and was driving it; his wife, Jane, sat between Roy and Mrs. Evans. There was slush and snow on the pavement; this was bare in some spots and slippery in others. It was dusk, a little after 5 P.M.; the farm truck had its lights on and was equipped with chains. It was well on the right side of its own lane, indeed with its right wheels on the shoulder, as it traveled uphill at 25 m.p.h. or less. Appellant *Groves'* truck was coming downhill, having rounded the upper portion of an "S" curve. It was in a skid, and as it slipped sideways, it "slew(ed) around" to the left side of the road, with the result that its left rear wheel hit the left front of the Clemons truck. The Groves truck then "bound over" onto its proper side of the road again, and came to a stop some distance beyond the point of impact. The impact cracked the windshield and caused damage to the front end of the Clemons truck, which had to be towed to a garage for repairs; it also lifted Mrs. Evans out of the seat and caused her head to strike the windshield, resulting in a bump on the top of her head one-half to three-quarters of an inch high and two and one-half to three inches long. Neither of the Clemonses was hurt. On December 14 Mrs. Evans consulted Dr. Redmond, her local physician, and, according to the doctor's testimony at the trial, "complained of feeling dizziness, having fainting spells, having blinking spells of vision with her eyes and getting tired after visiting the day before." Mrs. Evans had previously complained to Dr. Redmond of dizziness, grogginess, and other difficulties and, as recently as November 29, 1954, of false and defective hearing. Although Mrs. Evans "also made note that she had been worrying over a head injury she had received in an accident * * * on December 10," Dr. Redmond's records and testimony do not indicate that on the occasion of her December 14 visit either his patient or he attached much significance to this.

[...]

Two weeks later Mrs. Evans again saw Dr. Redmond and complained of head symptoms. From that time on her condition became progressively worse, and there ensued a long history of examinations, consultations, surgery and hospital care, the latter taking place at the Faxton Hospital in Utica, the Albany Medical Center, and, since May 13, 1955, at the Marcy State Hospital, an institution for the mentally ill, where Mrs. Evans was confined at the time of the trial as a legally-adjudged incompetent. As to the nature and cause of her ailment, suffice it here to say that the plaintiffs' theory in these two actions—one by Mrs. Evans through her husband as her Committee, and the other by the husband for loss of services—was that her suffering was due to a thrombosis of the left lateral sinus and that that condition, in turn, was due to the collision with defendant's truck; there was adequate evidence to warrant a jury's finding to this effect—although, as is usual in such cases, there was also adequate evidence to support a contrary decision on either of the two necessary causal factors.

[...]

At the subsequent trial on the merits, Dr. Redmond elaborated on Mrs. Evans' December 14 visit as above described, noting that she complained of fainting and dizziness and was worried about the head injury received in the accident, and Milfred Evans testified that by Christmas time he "could make quite an observation of the change" in his mother—"She used to lay down to sleep, which was very unusual. She said she felt tired all the time and from Christmas on to the last day of December she was gradually getting worse every day, as far as I could see." If this testimony had been before the judge at the preliminary trial, it might well have affected his determination as to the plaintiff's knowledge of the underlying injury on January 5. Whether if he had nevertheless found that both or either of them did not know of it, this ruling would have been "clearly erroneous" under F.R.Civ.Proc. 52, is another question, but one we are not called upon to answer.. [...]

II. SUFFICIENCY OF THE EVIDENCE OF NEGLIGENCE

Defendant's skid appears to have propelled us into one of the most slippery areas of New York tort law—as witness the three opinions written on the subject by distinguished Justices of the Appellate Division for the First Department in a quite similar case, ... which curiously has not been cited to us by either side. [...]

[...] We believe, rather, that under such circumstances the plaintiff would be deemed to have done enough to shift to the defendant the burden of proffering such evidence as is reasonably available to him; if, as here, the defendant fails to do this, the plaintiff then goes to the jury not simply on his own evidence of the skid but with the added help of the inference from the defendant's failure to produce available evidence, ... and we see nothing in New York jurisprudence to indicate that the Court of Appeals will not adopt it when the issue is squarely presented. [...]

III. REFUSAL TO GIVE THE REQUESTED CHARGE AS TO NEGLIGENCE.

The judge charged that plaintiffs must prove "by a fair preponderance of the evidence" that the injury "was caused through the negligence of the defendant Groves Company, or the driver of its automobile, at the time and place we have already mentioned"; that negligence is "carelessness," "a failure to do * * * that which a reasonably prudent person would do under like circumstances"; and that "negligence in the operation of a vehicle under adverse conditions, snow, ice and whatnot" on a country road may be "something else" than negligent operation on a dry highway or a city street. Defendant's counsel made no objection to the charge, but then asked the judge "to charge this jury the sloughing of the rear end of Mr. Mulcay's (the driver's) truck in and of itself is not negligence." The Court refused the request, saying "I will leave that to the jury itself. Consider all the circumstances. They may take into consideration all of the circumstances that existed there in considering that question." All this took place in the presence of the jury, counsel having declined the judge's offer to permit the request to be made outside the jury's presence. [...]

IV. THE JUDGE'S ANSWER TO THE JURY'S REQUEST FOR A FURTHER INSTRUCTION ON CAUSATION.

In contrast to the sparse testimony as to the reason for the accident, the record contained much evidence as to the cause of the heightened intracranial pressure which produced various symptoms of mental deterioration, required long hospitalization and surgery, and eventually led to Mrs. Evans' incompetence. As stated above, plaintiffs' case was that this pressure was due to a thrombosis of the left lateral sinus resulting from the collision, and there was adequate evidence to sustain both elements of this claim. Defendant's prime theory was that Mrs. Evans was suffering from a brain tumor, which had already produced head symptoms prior to the accident and was in no way affected by the impact. Alternatively, defendant submitted some evidence that if thrombosis of the sinus were the correct diagnosis, this condition was due not to the collision but to a disease in the middle ear, which allegedly was evidenced by the hearing difficulties Mrs. Evans had reported to Dr. Redmond before the accident. The judge charged, inter alia, that the plaintiff must show that the accident was the "proximate cause" of Mrs. Evans' condition and, quoting from a text, that this means "the moving or efficient cause without which the accident or the injuries in this case would not have occurred."

The jury, having received the case at about 5:30 p.m. and taken time out for dinner, deliberated further and then sent the judge the following message:

"In your charge to the jury did you state we must decide if the accident and/or injury must be the direct cause of the plaintiff's condition? Or is it our prerogative to consider the injury aggravated a pre-existing condition thereby establishing a causal relationship and on that premise to find damages for the plaintiff."

Considering the jury to have asked two questions, the judge, shortly after midnight, responded to what he termed the first by repeating that the accident "must be a moving or efficient cause without which the injuries would not have occurred." In answer to the "second question," he said, inter alia, that "a defendant is chargeable for all the harm and suffering which his negligent act brought on even though plaintiff's injuries were aggravated by his own predisposition or weakness," and that "a defendant must take a human being as he finds him, and if a human being has a predisposition to an illness and is injured, why of course that does not excuse the defendant for the damages which he himself has caused. It does not of course authorize the awarding of damages for the condition that existed prior to the accident * * *." [...]

Lawyers and judges understand **"aggravation" to refer to cases where a plaintiff already incapacitated in some degree by a disease or injury suffers a worsened condition as a result of the defendant's wrongful act; in such cases the defendant is liable for the additional harm that he caused.** See ... one of the two New York decisions from which the judge stated that he drew his answer to the jury's second question, illustrates a related but slightly different problem—that of a **plaintiff with a special physical condition perhaps in no way permanently disabling, such as pregnancy, which makes the consequences of the negligently inflicted impact much more serious than they would be for the normal victim.5 In such cases the defendant is liable for the entire damage, American Law Institute, Restatement of Torts, 461, unless he succeeds in establishing that the plaintiff's pre-existing condition was bound to worsen, in which event an appropriate discount should be made for the damages that would have been suffered even in the absence of the defendant's negligence.** ... Still different is the case of **concurrent causes, "where defendant's negligence and another cause for which defendant is not responsible would each have caused the whole injury even in the absence of the other cause." 2 Harper & James, supra, at 1122. Although there is division in both judicial and academic authority, the tendency favors imposing liability in such a case if the defendant's act is a substantial causative factor,** ... The proportion of the total damages for which the defendant is liable in such cases seems not to be much discussed, apparently on the theory—generally but perhaps not always true—that apportionment would be either logically or practically impossible.

Although the judge's midnight remarks, as applied to the facts, rather agglomerated these different situations and the legal principles governing them, the question before us is not whether he would have earned an "A" on a law school examination but whether, in the context of the case at hand, his answer was so misleading as to work the material prejudice to the defendant necessary to warrant our directing a new trial. ... We think not.

The jury, quite obviously, was troubled by the evidence that Mrs. Evans had experienced dizziness and other symptoms suggesting a cranial difficulty before the accident. It thus asked whether the accident "must be the direct cause of the plaintiff's condition." The judge's reply to this branch of the inquiry was, if anything, too favorable to defendant, for in requiring that the accident be found to be a cause "without which the injuries would not have occurred," he excluded the possibility of a plaintiffs' verdict based on the theory, sustainable under the law if the evidence warranted, that the accident and the pre-existing ailment were "concurrent causes" of the ultimate injury. If the judge had added only that in fixing damages the jury should take account of the fact that Mrs. Evans was not enjoying perfect health before the accident, and should further reduce its award if it found that her pre-existing ailment would have worsened and independently brought about some of the difficulties that she in fact experienced after the accident, or all of these difficulties but at a later date, defendant could have had no ground for objection. The contention is, however, that in responding to the second branch of the inquiry the judge went beyond this and erroneously gave an affirmative answer to the jury's question whether it could "consider the injury aggravated a pre-existing condition thereby establishing a causal relationship." Insofar as the asserted vice in such an answer is that it authorized the jury to find for the plaintiffs on the basis that the accident "aggravated" a pre-existing tumor—a theory which there was no evidence to support—we think the judge's clear and strict answer to the first part of the question, as applied to the evidence, makes it quite inconceivable that the jury could have rendered its verdict on such a view. There is more likelihood, however, that the jury understood the second answer to authorize a plaintiffs' verdict if, accepting thrombosis of the sinus as the proper diagnosis, it found that while this condition would not have occurred "but for" the accident, the condition would also not have occurred "but for" a preexisting ear disease, so that the defendant's conduct was a contributing cause of the harm but would not alone have sufficed to bring it about.

This is certainly not bad law; it merely assimilates the present case to that of the 'special physical condition' which makes the consequences of the impact more serious for the particular victim than they would be for others, a situation which, as we have seen, warrants the imposition of full liability in the absence of proof that the condition would have developed in any event. Appellant contends, however, that such a result is bad medicine; such a theory of liability must be excluded, it asserts, because, while "there was evidence of a pre-existing condition * * *, (there was) no evidence at all that this accident could aggravate or trigger this condition so as to produce the intracranial pressure." But there was medical evidence that thrombosis, or blockage, of the sinus could be caused by ear disease or by head injury; that both causes were common ones; and that the condition could develop "when circulation is at a low ebb from any cause." We think the jury could infer from this evidence, at least in the absence of proof that such an occurrence was medically impossible, that in a given case the two causes had cooperated to bring about the result— that the pre-existing ear disease had, for example, produced a partial blockage or lowered the circulation before the accident and thus created a weakened condition which contributed, along with the head injury, to causing the thrombosis. It is true that no medical expert testified specifically as to the possibility of such cooperative causation; but the inference is a rational one from evidence in the record, and we see no reason why the expert medical nature of that evidence should restrict the jury's customary power to draw rational inferences. So long as the decision of complex medical issues is left to laymen, it must be expected that juries will occasionally provide news for doctors. We would view this with some equanimity if all juries were as diligent and objective in analyzing the factual issues before them as, judging by the searching nature of its question and the extent of its deliberation, this one was.

Affirmed.

(Citations omitted)

A broader principle from the tort law unites the above cases and others with a concern to protect individuals who have some kind of vulnerability or susceptibility, even one that is hidden and not apparent, that might be precipitated, aggravated, or triggered by the negligent actions of others, or that makes the encounter between defendant and plaintiff worse than might be supposed. As summarized by *Prosser and Keeton on Torts*, when a victim is within the scope of a risk created by a defendant, the defendant is held accountable for all the harm done to the victim even though it was not foreseeable that the victim was extremely vulnerable, including those with "eggshell skulls."

> It is as if a magic circle were drawn about the person, and one who breaks it, even by so much as a cut on the finger, becomes liable for all resulting harm to the person although it may be death. The defendant is held liable when the defendant's negligence operates upon a concealed physical condition, such as pregnancy, or a latent disease, or susceptibility to disease (psychotic or neurotic predispositions, predisposition to amnesia, ruptured disc, delirium tremens), to produce consequences which the defendant could not reasonably anticipate. The defendant is held liable for unusual results of personal injuries which are regarded as unforeseeable, such as tuberculosis, paralysis, pneumonia, heart or kidney disease, blood poisoning, cancer or the loss of hair from fright ... One of the illustrations which runs through the English cases is that of the plaintiff with the "eggshell skull", who suffers death where a normal person would have had only a bump on the head ...[3]

The defendant is, however, liable "only for the extent to which the defendant's conduct has resulted in an aggravation of the pre-existing condition, and not for the condition as it was ..."[4] This limitation was explicitly expressed in *Steinhauser.*

A case I have found quite revelatory of the eggshell skull principle concerns a teenaged woman who quickly went bald as a result of a farm accident.

Ominsky v. Chas. Weinhagen & Co.

Supreme Court of Minnesota.

113 Minn. 422 (1911)

Opinion: 423 SIMPSON, J.

While working for defendant, Tillie Ominsky, then 14 years of age, had her dress caught in a machine near which she was standing, and was drawn towards the machine, and a lever attachment struck her in the face with sufficient force to cause a slight abrasion. She was badly frightened by the accident. She went home, and was nervous and hysterical for several days, and at intervals thereafter for several weeks. About ten days after the accident her hair, which had previously been abundant and in good condition, began to fall out very rapidly, and

3 *Ibid.*, 291–292.

4 *Ibid.*, 265.

within three weeks after the accident her body was devoid of hair, and remained substantially in that condition up to the time of trial, a period of upwards of four years.

This action was brought by the father of Tillie Ominsky to recover from the defendant damages for the injury resulting to her from the accident above described; it being claimed that the accident was caused by defendant's negligence. On the trial plaintiff recovered a substantial verdict, which cannot be supported unless the loss of hair suffered by the girl was shown to be attributable to the described accident. Whether the evidence sufficiently established that fact is the single question raised in this court, on the appeal of the defendant from the order denying its alternative motions for judgment or a new trial.

The medical testimony on the trial was to the effect that alopecia areata universalis, or general baldness, the condition of this girl, is a mysterious trouble, the cause of which is not fully understood, and its origin is obscure and conjectural; that medical authorities generally agree, however, that sometimes the trouble has a neuropathic origin, such as nervous shock, fright, or grief, sometimes, and in the larger percentage of cases it is due to parasitic or germ disease, and sometimes it is attributable to heredity. From this evidence, together with the evidence concerning this particular case, the jury were warranted in finding as a fact that fright and nervous shock are an adequate cause for a condition of general baldness. The relation of cause and effect may be established, though the theory of such relationship is not understood. It is a matter of general information that the causes or morbid processes are still unknown in many diseases, and that from our present viewpoint such processes in many other diseases were, until recently, either shrouded in mystery or in error. Yet it does not follow that medical science is unable, with reasonable certainty, to ascribe the development of such diseases to the existence of certain preceding conditions or injuries.

... [A] general consensus of opinion of medical authorities ... recognized and established that this trouble did have its origin in fright and nervous shock. A court cannot assume, either that this conclusion is not well founded, because the morbid processes involved are not understood, or that this conclusion of medical experts is based on insufficient data, because the experience and observation of laymen do not furnish sufficient data to establish such conclusion.

It also appeared from the testimony that it was impossible to determine in a particular case of general baldness, by a physical examination, what caused the condition, and that therefore the cause in each case could only be determined, if at all, by the history of the case. Upon the question of the cause of the trouble in the case of this girl, each of the experts called by plaintiff gave it as his opinion that in view of the history of the case, as above given, the condition of baldness was caused by the fright and nervous shock incident to her said accident, and the experts called by the defendant stated that it was possible that it was so caused. The evidence did not show the existence of any other circumstance or condition in her case that is recognized as a cause of this disease. By the evidence, then, an adequate cause resulting from defendant's negligence for the condition of baldness was shown to be present in the case of this girl, and there was no evidence of the presence of any other adequate cause for the condition. Clearly this took the question of the cause of the baldness of this girl out of the realm of conjecture, and the jury were warranted in finding that the present adequate cause in fact produced the condition. The plaintiff, to make a prima facie case, is not bound, in addition to establishing that the negligent act is an adequate proximate cause of the injury, to negative the existence of any other adequate cause. On this point the present case is distinguishable from the cases in which it has been held that, two adequate causes being present, one cannot arbitrarily or as a matter of conjecture be found to be the responsible cause. The jury were warranted by the evidence in finding that fright and nervous shock are an adequate cause of the condition of general baldness, and that this condition in Tillie Ominsky was produced by the fright and nervous shock from the accident occasioned through defendant's negligence. Affirmed.

This case also has some similarities to issues that arise in discussion of proximate causation, so we will consider it further at that point in the readings.

The next case, *McAllister v. Workmen's Compensation Appeals Board*, continues the theme of an individual potentially harmed by the actions of another, in this case by his employment as a firefighter, but developing an injury (illness of lung cancer) that might have been caused by his employment, but also might have been caused by something else; namely, his smoking habit.

Consider first what workers' compensation is. Early the 20th century, companies, courts, and injured employees found that when employees were required to sue in the tort law for injuries suffered at the workplace this was inefficient and unjust. Injured workers typically could not afford lawyers, making it difficult for them to bring tort cases. Employers had every incentive to delay engaging in litigation for as long as possible. If they succeeded, injured employees might give up or change jobs, but in both cases, they might go uncompensated for their injuries. We noted that Friedman discussed the various barriers 19th-century judges erected that tend to bar employees from receiving compensation for workplace injuries.

Workers' compensation is in effect an insurance institution to substitute for tort law compensation. Companies contribute to an insurance fund based on the nature of the business and typical risks of employees' possible injuries. If workers are injured, they may seek funds for their injuries in accordance with a schedule of harms and be authorized to seek medical treatment and time off from work to permit their injuries to heal. This arrangement provides more reliable, but possibly lesser, compensation to injured employees than the tort law might, saves employers and workers the costs of litigation, and typically delivers compensation much quicker to injured employees than they could receive through the tort law, if they would ever be compensated at all. If a company's workplace was revealed as riskier than the basis for initial insurance premiums, they could face increased contributions to the insurance pool. This gave them incentives to improve the safety of their work environment.

Nonetheless, there could be litigation regarding whether or not compensation should be permitted under the workers' compensation law; this is the issue in *McAllister*. This case stands out because both McAllister's longtime smoking habit and his employment exposed him to toxic products, both of which could contribute to lung cancer. The California Supreme Court permitted his widow to receive compensation for his death from lung cancer, but some shortcomings of the defendant's case may have made this easier for Mrs. McAllister. Defendant did not do much to challenge her claim, did not present alternative evidence regarding the toxicity of cigarette smoke, and did not compare the lung cancer death rates of smoking firefighters versus nonsmoking firefighters, which would be more likely in today's world.

Importantly, however, the court ruled in favor of Mrs. McAllister, even though her husband's personal habit could have caused precisely the same lung cancer. The *McAllister* court adds something new to the foregoing discussion of substantial-factor causation. To decide causation in this scenario, the court compares the victim's employment risks to risks of ordinary persons, and if victim's risks are more common at McAllister's place of employment than those one would encounter in ordinary life, this would be enough to treat victim's employment as a contributing cause.

McAllister v. Workmen's Compensation Appeals Board

Supreme Court of California

69 Cal.2d 408 (1968)

Opinion: TOBRINER, Justice.

Petitioner seeks review of the appeals board's decision after reconsideration in which the board held that the death of petitioner's husband did not arise out of his employment. We conclude that, since the board's decision lacks the support of substantial evidence and involves errors of law, it cannot stand.

Petitioner's husband, Arthur McAllister, worked for the San Francisco Fire Department for 32 years beginning in 1934. On October 31, 1966, Mr. McAllister died of lung cancer. Subsequently Mrs. McAllister filed this application for death benefits and burial expenses, alleging that smoke inhalation during the course of decedent's employment had caused his death.

At the hearing before a trial referee, petitioner testified that the decedent had worked as a fireman during the period in question, that he had suffered terrible coughing spells, and that he had complained about the smoke that he had inhaled at the fires. Petitioner called as her witness one Jerome Mahoney, a fireman who had worked with decedent; Mahoney testified as to the frequency and nature of the fires which decedent and he had fought together. Mahoney further stated that he had seen decedent affected by smoke many times and that he had observed him being carried out of a burning building in a semiconscious condition. Dr. Mortimer Benioff, also called by petitioner, stated that the referee could reasonably assume that the fire smoke which the decedent had inhaled had caused his death. Respondent offered no evidence.

The referee found in favor of petitioner. Subsequently the respondent City and County of San Francisco filed a petition for reconsideration with the appeals board. The board granted the petition and annulled the referee's award on the ground that the evidence had not shown that decedent's illness arose out of and in the course of his employment. The board concluded that the record did not disclose sufficient evidence as to the toxicity of the smoke inhaled or as to the amount of decedent's exposure to smoke, that a letter written by Dr. Benioff failed to support petitioner's contentions, and that petitioner had not adduced a satisfactory and detailed showing of the manner in which smoke inhalation may cause lung cancer.

We hold that the uncontradicted evidence in this case compelled the board to rule in petitioner's favor as to both toxicity and exposure, that Dr. Benioff's letter did possess evidentiary value, and that the exact mechanism of industrial causation need not be shown. We reject, as inconsistent with our statements on contributory causes, respondents' contention that the application must be denied because decedent smoked cigarettes.

1. Petitioner's uncontradicted evidence established the toxicity of the smoke.

The board based its conclusion in large part on the alleged inadmissibility, or ineffectuality, of Dr. Benioff's belief in a statistical correlation between lung cancer[1] and the specific pollutants which firemen would normally inhale. The board noted Dr. Benioff's expert testimony as to the statistical correlation between air pollution (or cigarette smoke) and lung disease. The board reasoned, however, that petitioner had introduced no "convincing" evidence to show that the smoke that firemen commonly inhale contains the same substances as those in cigarette smoke or in polluted air. It therefore concluded that Dr. Benioff's expert opinion as to the industrial causation depended upon facts not established in the record.

The record did contain evidence that the smoke that firemen inhale contains the same substances as in air pollution or cigarette smoke. Dr. Benioff testified that smoke from burning tar or creosote "may well" contain the same type of carcinogen found in cigarette smoke, and petitioner introduced testimony by Fireman Mahoney that the fires which decedent fought involved creosote. Similarly, petitioner introduced expert opinion by a Dr. Prindle to demonstrate that many of the carcinogens found in "air pollution" are "produced by almost any type of incomplete combustion of almost any product." Respondent City and County of San Francisco, on the other hand, introduced no evidence whatever to suggest that the smoke inhaled by firemen is always or usually benign.

We examine this evidence in the light of our holding that the applicant need only establish the **reasonable probability of industrial causation**. [...]

This case presents the problem of how to apply the well established "substantial evidence rule" to a case in which the prevailing party has introduced no evidence. We recognize that self-consistent testimony introduced by one party alone can raise factual questions: (a) Is the testimony and other evidence introduced to be believed? (b) What did the person whose statements or writings are introduced intend as their meanings? (c) What are the proper inferences of fact to be drawn from the testimony and other evidence? We believe the policy basis of the substantial evidence rule implies that we should resolve these questions in favor of the board wherever there is a substantial reason for doing so. Of course, as indicated in Wilhelm v. Workmen's Comp. App. Bd. (1967), ... the board must accept as true the intended meaning of testimony both uncontradicted and unimpeached.

In this case, however, even the indulgence of the substantial evidence rule will not permit us to uphold the board's decision. We note at the outset that no effort was ever made—either by way of allegation or evidence—to question the honesty or competence of any of petitioner's witnesses. Accordingly we, as the board, in view of the City's failure to introduce any contradictory evidence, must assume the accuracy of the testimony. Likewise, the meaning of the testimony, and the inferences to be drawn from it, cannot be disputed.

Dr. Benioff stated in writing that it was "probable" that the smoke inhaled contained carcinogens, and he testified that the carcinogens in cigarette smoke "may well" be in tar or creosote, which Fireman Mahoney's undisputed testimony established as being in most buildings. We cannot conjure up a plausible reason to believe the degree of likelihood intended by "probable" and "may well" is less than that in the requirement of "reasonable probability," especially in view of Dr Benioff's testimony that an inference of industrial causation would be a reasonable one.

The absence of testimony as to whether the smoke which firemen inhale contains incompletely oxidized materials does not lessen the import of Dr. Prindle's views. Especially in the absence of conflicting testimony, we think that the petitioner's offered evidence that firemen inhale smoke sufficed. [...]

In the case before us we think that both common knowledge and ordinary language support our recognition that smoke is visible, and that, as a matter beyond scientific dispute, smoke is visible precisely because it contains incompletely oxidized materials. [...]

2. Petitioner's uncontradicted evidence established decedent's exposure to smoke.

The board suggested as a further reason for denying the application its view that the evidence of decedent's exposure to smoke was "singularly scanty." We find this argument difficult to understand and impossible to uphold.

The board may be suggesting that the fact that a man spent 32 years fighting fires, often without a gas mask, presents no reason to believe that he ever inhaled any smoke. Thus, of the nine-year period from 1944 to 1953 the board said, "There is no specific evidence of exposure whatsoever." Yet we think that proof of 32 years as a firefighter constitutes very weighty evidence of exposure to smoke. We judicially notice that fires cause smoke, that firefighters must stand near or enter burning buildings, and that one standing near or in a burning building would be extremely likely to inhale smoke being produced there.

Fireman Mahoney, who served with the decedent for 13 years, testified as to details of some of the fires they had fought, although in the interest of brevity he did not attempt to cover all fires during that period. Mahoney stated that he had seen decedent affected by smoke on many occasions. The board stressed, however, that he could not recall whether decedent was ever treated at the scene of a fire for smoke inhalation. ... The board seems to have thought exposure to smoke not requiring medical assistance unlikely to be dangerous. Such an assumption lacks foundation; indeed, all the evidence supports the opposite conclusion.

Although the City contends that evidence of inhalation should have been more detailed, the City was in the best position readily to secure such information. In such a situation the employer should be encouraged to come forward with all relevant data available to it. [...]

4. The causal mechanism need not be proved in detail.

Finally, the board expressed concern because petitioner did not produce a more detailed account of the alleged industrial causation, the exact amount of each type of smoke inhaled, and the precise danger to decedent from such inhalation. Of course, such a detailed account would have been desirable, but it was not a prerequisite to recovery. Such a burden on applicants would often be unbearable. The exact amount and kinds of pollutants inhaled by decedent could only be known if a chemist had gone with him to each fire over his 32 years as a fireman. The precise toxicity of each type of pollutant, alone or in combination with others, is still not known.

In order to cover such unavoidable uncertainties, we require applicants to establish no more than that industrial causation is reasonably probable. Thus the commission allowed recovery in early cancer cases when our understanding of the disease was even less complete than it is now. ... [Citing additional cases for same conclusion.]

5. Decedent's smoking does not bar recovery.

Respondents urge us to deny the application in view of decedent's history as a smoker. They note that decedent smoked about a pack of cigarettes a day for some 42 years, although they admit that during at least part of that period he did not inhale. Respondents further point out the statistical correlation between smoking and lung cancer. The board, however, although well aware of these facts, declined to rely upon them as the basis of its decision.

We cannot doubt that the more smoke decedent inhaled—from whatever source—the greater the danger of his contracting lung cancer. His smoking increased that danger, just as did his employment. Given the present state of medical knowledge, we cannot say whether it was the employment or the cigarettes which "actually" caused the disease; we can only recognize that both contributed substantially to the likelihood of his contracting lung cancer. As we noted, however, in Employers, etc., Ins. Co. of Wis. v. Industrial Acc. Comm. (1953), the decedent's employment **need only be a "contributing cause"** of his injury. And in Bethlehem Steel Co. v. Industrial Acc. Comm., we pointed out a particular instance of this principle when we stated that it was enough that "the employee's risk of contracting the disease by virtue of the employment must be materially greater than that of the general public." Thus in Bethlehem we allowed an award to an employee who contracted a contagious eye disease, since he had shown that the disease was more common at his place of employment than among the public.

Although decedent's smoking may have been inadvisable, respondents offer no reason to believe that the likelihood of contracting lung cancer from the smoking was so great that the danger could not have been materially increased by exposure to the smoke produced by burning buildings.

Conclusion

In deciding this case we obviously do not hold that all firemen contracting lung cancer can obtain compensation benefits from their employers. In the case before us respondent City elected to introduce no evidence of its own; we conclude that no substantial evidence supports a finding that there is not a reasonable probability that decedent's illness arose out of his employment.

Future scientific developments will tell us more about lung cancer. Ultimately it may be possible to pinpoint with certainty the cause of each case of the disease. But the Legislature did not contemplate years of Damnum absque injuria pending such scientific certainty. Accordingly, we and the Workmen's Compensation Appeals Board are bound to uphold a claim in which the proof of industrial causation is reasonably probable, although not certain or "convincing". We must do so even though the exact causal mechanism is unclear or even unknown.

The decision of the Workmen's Compensation Appeals Board is annulled and the cause is remanded to that board for further proceedings consistent with the views herein expressed.

TRAYNOR, C.J., and PETERS, MOSK, BURKE and SULLIVAN, JJ., concur.

(Citations omitted)

To this point, we have considered one plaintiff potentially exposed to more than one circumstance or cause that could contribute to harm: *Stubbs* (other causes of typhoid); *Anderson* (a railway set fire and fires of legally innocent origin); *Steinhauser* (latent schizophrenia and car accident); *Evans* (likely preexisting condition exacerbated by car accident); and *Ominsky* (machine accident and surprising psychological and physical reaction to the scary accident); and the general eggshell skull principle.

The eggshell skull principle argues that a defendant's negligent act operating on a concealed physical condition; e.g., pregnancy, or "a latent disease, or susceptibility to disease (psychotic or neurotic predispositions, predisposition to amnesia, ruptured disc, delirium tremens), to produce consequences which the defendant could not reasonably anticipate," could be held accountable for the full costs of the harm unless the hidden condition was bound to worsen and defendant was not responsible for it.[5] *McAllister* requires workers' compensation insurance to compensate harms arising out of the workplace that produced the same outcome as the plaintiff's smoking habits, provided the probability of lung cancer among firefighters was higher than in the general public; plaintiff's smoking did not undermine compensation for lung disease arising out of his work as a fireman.

Now we will consider a different set of causation issues in tort law. Who should the tort law hold accountable when *two* hunters who shoot in the direction of plaintiff and inflict *one* serious injury on plaintiff? Normally, plaintiffs have the burden of proof to show that defendants' actions caused their harm in order to hold them accountable. However, what if plaintiffs cannot identify which if any negligently acting defendants caused their harm? What if several defendants market a pharmaceutical known to cause harm, but plaintiff who is in fact harmed cannot identify which company's drug caused her particular harm? Does she have a remedy in the tort law? In effect, some of these cases pose questions about the **"but-for" rule for causation**. If a particular defendant cannot be identified as causing harm because of the possible contribution of another or others, should this exonerate one or more of the possible defendants?

We first have two hunting cases in which one plaintiff was harmed (*Summers v. Tice* and *Leuer v. Johnson*) and then take up the rightly famous pharmaceutical case, *Sindell v. Abbott Labs,* in which a number of young women suffered from vaginal/cervical cancer about twenty years later as a result of their mothers taking a synthetic estrogen when they were pregnant with their daughters. However, although their cancers were clearly caused by *in utero* exposure to the pharmaceutical, they could not identify which manufacturer caused the damage to each of them. What should a court do in a circumstance like this?

Also, when reading *Summers v. Tice,* recall the discussion of *State v. Newberg* from the discussion of criminal homicide. What similarities and differences are there between that case and *Summers*?

Summers v. Tice

Supreme Court of California

33 Cal.2d 80 (1948)

Opinion: CARTER, Justice.

Each of the two defendants appeals from a judgment against them in an action for personal injuries. Pursuant to stipulation the appeals have been consolidated.

Plaintiff's action was against both defendants for an injury to his right eye and face as the result of being struck by bird shot discharged from a shotgun. The case was tried by the court without

5 *Ibid.*, 291–292.

a jury and the court found that on November 20, 1945, plaintiff and the two defendants were hunting quail on the open range. Each of the defendants was armed with a 12 gauge shotgun loaded with shells containing 7 1/2 size shot. Prior to going hunting plaintiff discussed the hunting procedure with defendants, indicating that they were to exercise care when shooting and to "keep in line." In the course of hunting plaintiff proceeded up a hill, thus placing the hunters at the points of a triangle. The view of defendants with reference to plaintiff was unobstructed and they knew his location. Defendant Tice flushed a quail which rose in flight to a ten foot elevation and flew between plaintiff and defendants. Both defendants shot at the quail, shooting in plaintiff's direction. At that time defendants were 75 yards from plaintiff. One shot struck plaintiff in his eye and another in his upper lip. Finally it was found by the court that as the direct result of the shooting by defendants the shots struck plaintiff as above mentioned and that defendants were negligent in so shooting and plaintiff was not contributorily negligent.

First, on the subject of negligence, defendant Simonson contends that the evidence is insufficient to sustain the finding on that score, but he does not point out wherein it is lacking. There is evidence that both defendants, at about the same time or one immediately after the other, shot at a quail and in so doing shot toward plaintiff who was uphill from them, and that they knew his location. That is sufficient from which the trial court could conclude that they acted with respect to plaintiff other than as persons of ordinary prudence. The issue was one of fact for the trial court. See, Rudd v. Byrnes.

Defendant Simonson urges that plaintiff was guilty of contributory negligence and assumed the risk as a matter of law. He cites no authority for the proposition that by going on a hunting party the various hunters assume the risk of negligence on the part of their companions. Such a tenet is not reasonable. It is true that plaintiff suggested that they all "stay in line," presumably abreast, while hunting, and he went uphill at somewhat of a right angle to the hunting line, but he also cautioned that they use care, and defendants knew plaintiff's position. We hold, therefore, that the trial court was justified in finding that he did not assume the risk or act other than as a person of ordinary prudence under the circumstances. [...]

The problem presented in this case is whether the judgment against both defendants may stand. It is argued by defendants that they are not joint tort feasors, and thus jointly and severally liable, as they were not acting in concert, and that there is not sufficient evidence to show which defendant was guilty of the negligence which caused the injuries—the shooting by Tice or that by Simonson. Tice argues that there is evidence to show that the shot which struck plaintiff came from Simonson's gun because of admissions allegedly made by him to third persons and no evidence that they came from his gun. Further in connection with the latter contention, the court failed to find on plaintiff's allegation in his complaint that he did not know which one was at fault—did not find which defendant was guilty of the negligence which caused the injuries to plaintiff.

Considering the last argument first, we believe it is clear that the court sufficiently found on the issue that defendants were jointly liable and that thus the negligence of both was the cause of the injury or to that legal effect. It found that both defendants were negligent and "That as a direct and proximate result of the shots fired by defendants, and each of them, a birdshot pellet was caused to and did lodge in plaintiff's right eye and that another birdshot pellet was caused to and did lodge in plaintiff's upper lip." In so doing the court evidently did not give credence to the admissions of Simonson to third persons that he fired the shots, which it was justified in doing. It thus determined that the negligence of both defendants was the legal cause of the injury or that both were responsible. Implicit in such finding is the assumption that the court was unable to ascertain whether the shots were from the gun of **one** defendant or the other or **one** shot from each of them. The one shot that entered plaintiff's eye was the major factor in assessing damages and that shot could not have come from the gun of both defendants. It was from one or the other only.

It has been held that where a group of persons are on a hunting party, or otherwise engaged in the use of firearms, and two of them are negligent in firing in the direction of a third person who is injured thereby, both of those so firing are liable for the injury suffered by the third person, although the negligence of only one of them could have caused the injury. ... The same rule has been applied in criminal cases (State v. Newberg), and both drivers have been held liable for the negligence of one where they engaged in a racing contest causing an injury to a third person ... These cases speak of the action of defendants as being in concert as the ground of decision, yet it would seem they are straining that concept and the more reasonable basis appears in Oliver v. Miles, supra. There two persons were hunting together. Both shot at some partridges and in so doing shot across the highway injuring plaintiff who was travelling on it. The court stated they were acting in concert and thus both were liable. The court then stated: "We think that * * * each is liable for the resulting injury to the boy, although no one can say definitely who actually shot him. To hold otherwise would be to exonerate both from liability, although each was negligent, and the injury resulted from such negligence. (It is said in the Restatement: "For harm resulting to a third person from the tortious conduct of another, a person is liable if he * * * (b) knows that the other's conduct constitutes a breach of duty and gives substantial assistance or encouragement to the other so to conduct himself, or (c) gives substantial assistance to the other in accomplishing a tortious result and his own conduct, separately considered, constitutes a breach of duty to the third person." Under subsection (b) the example is given: "A and B are members of a hunting party. Each of them in the presence of the other shoots across a public road at an animal, this being negligent as to persons on the road. A hits the animal. B's bullet strikes C, a traveler on the road. A is liable to C." [...]

The real reason for the rule that each joint tortfeasor is responsible for the whole damage is the practical unfairness of denying the injured person redress simply because he cannot prove how much damage each did, when it is certain that between them they did all; let them be the ones to apportion it among themselves. Since, then, the difficulty of proof is the reason, the rule should apply whenever the harm has plural causes, and not merely when they acted in conscious concert. * * * (Wigmore, Select Cases on the Law of Torts) [...]

When we consider the relative position of the parties and the results that would flow if plaintiff was required to pin the injury on one of the defendants only, a requirement that the burden of proof on that subject be shifted to defendants becomes manifest. They are both wrongdoers—both negligent toward plaintiff. They brought about a situation where the negligence of one of them injured the plaintiff, hence it should rest with them each to absolve himself if he can. The injured party has been placed by defendants in the unfair position of pointing to which defendant caused the harm. If one can escape the other may also and plaintiff is remediless. Ordinarily defendants are in a far better position to offer evidence to determine which one caused the injury.

This reasoning has recently found favor in this Court. In a quite analogous situation this Court held that a patient injured while unconscious on an operating table in a hospital could hold all or any of the persons who had any connection with the operation even though he could not select the particular acts by the particular person which led to his disability. Ybarra v. Spangard. There the Court was considering whether the patient could avail himself of res ipsa loquitur, rather than where the burden of proof lay, yet the effect of the decision is that plaintiff has made out a case when he has produced evidence which gives rise to an inference of negligence which was the proximate cause of the injury. It is up to defendants to explain the cause of the injury. It was there said: "If the doctrine is to continue to serve a useful purpose, we should not forget that 'the particular force and justice of the rule, regarded as a presumption throwing upon the party charged the duty of producing evidence, consists in the circumstance that the chief evidence of the true cause, whether culpable or innocent, is practically accessible to him but inaccessible to the injured person.'" Similarly in the instant case plaintiff is not able to establish which of defendants caused his injury …

Cases are cited for the proposition that where two or more tort feasors acting independently of each other cause an injury to plaintiff, they are not joint tort feasors and plaintiff must establish the portion of the damage caused by each, even though it is impossible to prove the portion of the injury caused by each. … In view of the foregoing discussion it is apparent that defendants in cases like the present one may be treated as liable on the same basis as joint tort feasors, and hence the last cited cases are distinguishable inasmuch as they involve independent tort feasors.

In addition to that, however, it should be pointed out that the same reasons of policy and justice shift the burden to each of defendants to absolve himself if he can relieving the wronged person of the duty of apportioning the injury to a particular defendant, apply here where we are concerned with whether plaintiff is required to supply evidence for the apportionment of damages. If defendants are independent tort feasors and thus each liable for the damage caused by him alone, and, at least, where the matter of apportionment is incapable of proof, the innocent wronged party should not be deprived of his right to redress. The wrongdoers should be left to work out between themselves any apportionment. […]

The judgment is affirmed.

GIBSON, C. J., and SHENK, EDMONDS, TRAYNOR, SCHAUER, and SPENCE, JJ., concur.

(Citations omitted)

Summers v. Tice further highlights a legal doctrine at the time to address causal relationships that developed in the world. The doctrine of but-for causation would seem to preclude both Tice and Simonson from accountability unless a court decides to modify how these facts in the world should be addressed by the legal system. The answer: this court shifts the burden of proof to negligent defendants in cases involving multiple sufficient causes of injury to exonerate themselves (as contributors of the harm), *if they can.*

This is another instance in which courts must confront causal issues presented by the world but then decide what the best legal approach to them should be. The following Minnesota case distinguishes *Leuer v. Johnson* from *Summers v. Tice*. What are the distinguishing features? Do these seem correct?

Leuer v. Johnson

Court of Appeals of Minnesota

450 N.W.2d 363 (1990)

Syllabus by the Court

1. Summary judgment is appropriate on a claim of res ipsa loquitur where neither the identity of the instrumentality causing the accident nor the identity of the controller of that instrumentality can be established.
2. Summary judgment is appropriate on a claim of joint enterprise when there is no common control of the means used to achieve the common purpose.
3. Summary judgment is appropriate on a claim of duty to warn where the facts indicate that a warning would have been superfluous.
4. Summary judgment is appropriate on a claim of joint and several liability where there is only one tortfeasor.

OPINION: HUSPENI, Judge.

Appellant was injured by a bullet fired by one of the two respondents; the tortfeasor could not be identified. Respondent moved for summary judgment in response to appellant's claims of res ipsa loquitur, joint enterprise, duty to warn and joint and several liability. This motion was granted. We affirm.

Appellant Randall Leuer, his brother respondent Kelin Leuer and respondent Todd Johnson went deer hunting in November, 1981. The men separated, having agreed to return to the car at the end of the day. After respondents returned to the car, they went to tell appellant they were ready to leave. Appellant, who had remained near the car, was pursuing a deer he believed he had wounded. As respondents approached him, they both thought they saw a deer and fired almost simultaneously. One of their bullets hit appellant. The bullet was never found; none of the three men knows who fired it. Appellant sued on the theories of res ipsa loquitur, joint enterprise, duty to warn, and joint and several liability. The trial court granted respondent Johnson's motions for summary judgment on each of the four theories.

ISSUES

1. Is appellant entitled to argue the theory of res ipsa loquitur?
2. Is appellant entitled to argue the theory of joint enterprise?
3. Is appellant entitled to argue the theory of duty to warn?
4. Is there a basis for declaring respondents jointly and severally liable for appellant's injury?

ANALYSIS

The standard of review for an appeal from summary judgment appears at Betlach v. Wayzata Condominium: this court can reverse only if there are genuine issues of material fact or if the trial court erred in its application of law. There are no issues of fact, so the application of the law to each of the four theories is the only question before this court.

1. Res Ipsa Loquitur

The three elements of res ipsa loquitur are that the event must not generally occur unless someone is negligent, must be caused by an instrumentality within the exclusive control of the defendant, and must not have been due to any voluntary action or contribution of the plaintiff. Spannaus v. Otolaryngology Clinic, 308 Minn. The danger inherent in hunting with high-powered rifles does not preclude the application of res ipsa loquitur to hunting injuries: they are held not to occur absent negligence. [...]

[...] This case involves two hunters, one of them innocent and the other a tortfeasor. A California case with similar facts, Summers v. Tice, involved a plaintiff hit with birdshot from the guns of one or both defendants. The Summers court found that

> a requirement that the burden of proof on [appellant] be shifted to [respondents] becomes manifest. * * * They brought about a situation where the negligence of one of them injured [appellant], hence it should rest with them each to absolve himself if he can.

This reasoning was derived from an earlier California case, Ybarra v. Spangard, (1944), which extended res ipsa loquitur to a plaintiff who had been injured while unconscious on the operating table by an unidentifiable instrumentality in the control of an unidentifiable tortfeasor.

> If the doctrine is to continue to serve a useful purpose, we should not forget that "the particular force and justice of the rule, regarded as a presumption throwing upon the party charged the duty of producing evidence, consists in the circumstance that the chief evidence of the true cause, whether culpable or innocent, is practically accessible to him but inaccessible to the injured person."

This passage is quoted in Summers as the basis for its application of res ipsa loquitur when exclusive control of the instrumentality by a specific defendant could not be established.

Ybarra has been the subject of frequent comment for the appellate courts of this state, particularly in malpractice cases. It was distinguished in Wallstedt v. Swedish Hospital, on the grounds that the Ybarra plaintiff's injury had no possible cause other than someone's negligence, while the injury to the Wallstedt plaintiff "could have been the result of one of several causes." [...]

> In the present case, * * * we must decide whether to follow the majority of jurisdictions which have adopted the Ybarra rule. Because we agree with the rationale of those cases, we hold that the trial court erred.

(Hoven.) However, the supreme court explicitly rejected the Ybarra rule when it overturned this decision in Hoven v. Rice Memorial Hospital (1986), stating the court of appeals had based its decision

> on the almost absolute liability of the modified res ipsa loquitur doctrine applied by the California Supreme Court. * * * Adoption of that analysis would put the burden on defendants to show how plaintiff's injury occurred and that the injury was caused by no negligence on the part of any team member—in most cases creating what would amount to absolute liability.

The facts here are similar to those in Summers. However, because the Summers decision had as its basis Ybarra, and because Ybarra has been consistently rejected by the Minnesota Supreme Court, we must reject Summers as well.

We note, however, that Summers was cited in Mahowald v. Minnesota Gas Company, as an example of

> shift[ing] the burden of proof where the plaintiff was blameless but the instrumentality causing the harm could not be readily identified or was not exclusively in control of a charged

> defendant, although the person charged was responsible to see the instrumentality was not negligently used so as to cause harm to others.

The Mahowald decision addressed gas company liability specifically, and its sole application has been in another gas company case, Spinett, Inc. v. Peoples Natural Gas Company, 385 N.W.2d 834 (Minn.Ct.App. 1986). Furthermore, although Mahowald cited Summers, Mahowald did not follow the holding of Summers. In any event, Minnesota's rejection of Ybarra, on which Summers is based, must be interpreted to weaken further any reliance formerly placed upon Summers. We conclude that the burden of proving each respondent's liability remains with appellant. Appellant cannot meet that burden here, because the instrumentality which caused the harm cannot be identified, and therefore it is impossible to determine who was in control of that instrumentality.

Because the doctrine of res ipsa loquitur cannot be invoked unless all three of its elements are present, appellant's inability to establish the second element of "exclusive control" renders moot the question of whether his conduct contributed to the accident. [...]

2. Joint Enterprise

The two elements of vicarious liability under joint enterprise are set out in another hunting case, Delgado v. Lohmar (1970).

> (1) a mutual understanding for a common purpose, and (2) a right to a voice in the direction and control of the means used to carry out the common purpose.

The Delgado holding renders it virtually impossible for joint enterprise to be found in a hunting expedition, since

> the shotgun of each defendant [is] at all times under the independent care, custody and control of its owner. Each hunter [is] confronted with his own split-second decisions as to whether or not to shoot.

The trial court correctly found no joint enterprise here.

3. Duty to Warn

Appellant argues that duty to warn is a question of fact, and therefore not appropriate for summary judgment. Gabrielson v. Warnemunde (1989) examines the roles of the jury and the court:

It is not, however, the jury's function to determine whether the facts give rise to a duty. Rather the jury's role is to resolve disputed facts, upon which the court then determines whether a duty of care exists.

It is undisputed that each man saw the other two shortly before the accident. Given this fact, the trial court appropriately determined that there was no duty to warn.

4. Joint and Several Liability

Had any of the other three theories advanced by appellant been viable, joint and several liability would have resulted. However, here there is a single tortfeasor: only one bullet struck appellant. The trial court correctly declined to impose joint and several liability.

DECISION

Appellant's claim of res ipsa loquitur fails because Minnesota's rejection of the Ybarra rule requires that appellant bear the burden of proving respondent's exclusive control of the instrumentality and appellant cannot meet that burden under the facts of this case. Appellant's claim of joint enterprise fails because there was no common control of an instrumentality to achieve a common purpose; his claim of duty to warn fails because warnings would have been superfluous; and his claim of joint and several liability fails because there was only one tortfeasor. The trial court's grant of respondent's motion for summary judgment is therefore affirmed.

(Citations omitted)

Proximate Causation in the Tort Law

As we considered in the elements of a tort action, plaintiffs must show both that defendant caused and was the proximate cause of harm plaintiff suffered. We turn from the extent to which a defendant may be held accountable for negligent acts but for which plaintiff might not have been harmed (but where there were possible other causes that might have contributed to the same harms) to an additional topic related to causation.

Discussion of proximate causation raises different issues: since a causal event modifies the world, if a person negligently causes the event, how far does liability for negligently causing the consequences of the initial act extend in holding a defendant accountable? In some instances, proximate causation is a legal doctrine that limits the scope of actual causes a defendant has set in motion so that defendants are not responsible for "too long or a too extensive" a causal chain connected to his or her initial negligent act. Whereas issues of causation seem to pose reasonably straightforward questions about what events a defendant caused, proximate causation typically raises more normative issues about the limits of defendants' legal responsibility, as we will see in *Palsgraf*.

We introduce the topic by recalling the short presentation from Friedman's *History of American Tort Law*. There we saw that early doctrines of proximate causation, hewing closely to the idea of limiting defendants' accountability for causal consequences they set in motion. Nineteenth-century judges greatly restricted the scope of responsibility for negligent causes that started fires and burned houses or whole towns. Thus, the tort law began with substantially constrained ideas about proximate causation to protect budding industries during the Industrial Revolution. Since the time of those 19th-century proximate cause cases, there has been a liberalizing of the idea of proximate causation.

The first case disabuses us of the idea that "proximate" causation must be limited in space if not time. In *Ramsey v. Carolina-Tennessee Power Co.*, the Louisville and Nashville Railroad Company permitted the power company to place a power line in the railroad company's right of way at the end of a siding or spur track. One day the railroad pushed cars onto the spur, which lacked a barrier to stop cars from rolling off the end of the rails. The cars kept rolling, hit a guy wire that held an electric pole, which in turn sent an electrical shock down the electric line, and miles away, Mr. Ramsey, who worked for a laundry with electric washing machines, was electrocuted and killed.

Mr. Ramsey was not proximate in geographic space to the location of the accident, but was clearly harmed by the conjoint actions of the electric company and railroad that caused the initial electrical short, which killed him. Should the two companies be held to have caused and been the proximate cause of Ramsey's death, even though the initial accident and his death were miles apart? Put another way, were the two events sufficiently "proximate" to hold the companies accountable for Ramsey's death?

Ramsey v. Carolina-Tennessee Power Company

Supreme Court of North Carolina

195 N.C. 788 (1928)

Action for personal injury resulting in death. ... [P]rior to April 19, 1927, the power company, with the knowledge and consent of the railroad company, had erected, and was then maintaining, one of its poles (to which were affixed transformers and wires of high voltage) within a few feet of the end of a spur track over which the railroad company switched and moved its cars; that there was no bumper, embankment, or other device to prevent cars from running off the track; that the pole was on the right of way of the railroad company, as was also the anchor to which the guy or cable was fastened; that the guy extended from the anchor to the pole and was directly over the right of way; that both defendants were negligent, in that one erected the post and put up the guy on the right of way and the other permitted its right of way to be used for this purpose ... [O]n April 18, 1927, the railroad company negligently shunted cars on the spur track so as to cause one of them to run off the rails at the end of the track and to strike the guy with great force, thereby injuring the transformers on the pole, and other electrical appliances, and causing the electric current transmitted on the high voltage wires to flow along the wire leading to the plant of the steam laundry; that, ... [where] the laundry company used washers which were operated by electricity and which was connected with .. the power line ...; that on April 19, 1927, the plaintiff's intestate in doing the work assigned him as an employee of the laundry company suffered an electric shock of such intensity as to cause his instant death; and that the negligence of both defendants was the proximate cause thereof. [The trial court found for plaintiff] but ... the defendants appealed, assigning error, which is set out in the opinion.

OPINION: ADAMS, J.

Since both the power company and the railroad company moved in compliance with the statute for judgment of **nonsuit**, it becomes necessary to examine the evidence in its relation to the alleged negligence of each defendant. One of the contentions of the plaintiff is this: That the power company was negligent in putting up its post and its guy on or near the roadbed of the railroad company and that the latter company was negligent in permitting them to be put there. While there is some evidence in support of this contention, there are other circumstances which in our opinion justify a denial of the motion. There was evidence that the intestate's death occurred in this way: Two washers were outside the laundry; one was connected by means of a cord or cable to a three-way socket midway between the washer and the laundry building where there was a switch or little button; connected with this was a cord or "green twisted wire" which extended through the window of the laundry and "was pushed into a plug." The deceased was in charge of the washing machine; he had gone into the house and had returned when a colored woman told him the motor was smoking. He took hold of the switch with his right hand, said, "Lord, have mercy," quivered, shook, caught the wire with his left hand, "crumpled up against the washing machine," and instantly died. These circumstances, if accepted by the jury, were sufficient to make a case of prima facie negligence against the power company, subject of course to any explanation it should make, or, in the absence of explanation, to the hazard of an adverse verdict. …

The power company says that the maxim, "res ipsa loquitur," never applies where the cause of the accident is known and that the verdict establishes the negligence of the railroad company as the proximate cause of the injury and death. An answer is given in Electric Co. v. Letson, 68 C.C.A., 453, quoted in Houston v. Traction Co., supra: "The contention of the company amounts to this: That if the wires were properly installed it cannot be held responsible for their being out of repair, unless it is proved they got out of repair through its fault. But this loses sight of the duty of the company not only to make the wires safe at the start, but to keep them so. They must not only be put in order, but kept in order. The obligation is a continuing one. The safety of patrons and public permits no intermission. Constant oversight and repair are required and must be furnished." The company was required on its own responsibility to make reasonable inspection and what is reasonable inspection is generally a question for the jury.

That there is evidence of negligence on the part of the railroad company in "shunting" or "kicking" its cars needs no citation of authority; the contested question is whether such negligence proximately caused or concurred in causing the intestate's death. On this point there was evidence tending to show that, when the derailed car struck the guy or cable, the post was jarred and "looked like it might fall"; that a little blaze ran up a few minutes about the second cross-arm on the pole, on which two loose wires were hanging; that a noise like "spitting" or "a racket something like frying" was heard; that the blaze was evidence of an arc, that is, electricity passing from one wire to another; that, if wires of high and low voltage crossed and there was an arc between them, an electric current could pass from the wire of high voltage to the one of low voltage; that the flame was probably caused by a short circuit; that, if there is no atmospheric disturbance, there will be no flame "if everything is functioning properly"; and that, if a "frying sound was heard, there was something wrong." There was evidence that the cable was struck about 2 or 3 o'clock on the afternoon of April 18, and that soon thereafter electrical disturbance was noticed in a garage, a hardware store, and on a clothesline, each separate wire communicating with the transformer on the pole. Proof of these circumstances was competent in corroboration of the plaintiff's contention.

The evidence precluded dismissal of the action. **In a motion to nonsuit, the plaintiff must be given the advantage of every inference that may reasonably be drawn from the testimony of the witnesses**; and the testimony thus considered is susceptible of the construction that the intestate's death was proximately caused by the concurring negligence of the defendants. The motion for nonsuit was therefore properly denied.

The exception to the court's apportionment of challenges is addressed to the exercise of discretion, which has not been abused, if it be admitted that the interests of the defendants are antagonistic. Moreover, the decision of the judge as to the nature of the interests and the number of challenges is final. […]

Exception was taken to the instruction that there may be more than one proximate cause; but in the law of negligence no rule is better settled than this: There may be more than one efficient proximate cause of an injury. […]

We have given to each of the other exceptions our careful attention and are of opinion that the record presents no error entitling the defendants or either of them to a new trial.

We are aware of the uncertainty with which the defendants say their evidence has clothed the circumstances of the intestate's death, including the time that elapsed between the alleged damage to the transformer and the injury to the deceased; but, unless reversible error in law was committed, it is not our province to interfere with the verdict or judgment and to award the defendants another hearing. We find the record, presenting the exceptions of both defendants, to be free from error.

(Citations omitted)

In the next case, one of the best known in tort law, its majority and dissenting opinions raise substantial questions about what constitutes negligence and also what constitutes proximate causation. This case also creates conceptual complexity for the idea of proximate causation. For negligence torts, must a defendant have some degree of awareness of the *risks* his actions might create to others to have a duty to protect others from harm? Does the majority opinion think that the railroad company was negligent toward Mrs. Palsgraf and should be held accountable for her injuries, surprising though they were? Or might a defendant be held accountable for harms befalling others even though at the time of acting defendant did not have any idea that his or her actions posed risks of harm to someone in the vicinity even though defendant might well have been aware of the possibility of some risks to some others, just not the person actually harmed?

Without question, in this case, Mrs. Helen Palsgraf was injured because the railway officials assisted a late-arriving passenger boarding a departing train; he dropped a package of fireworks, which exploded, sending percussive forces though the train station that caused some scales to fall on Mrs. Palsgraf and injure her. The actions of railway officials set in motion a causal sequence that unquestionably injured her, but did they act negligently and legally could they be the proximate cause of her injuries?

The majority in *Palsgraf* argues that there was no negligence by defendants because they were unaware and could not be aware of a risk toward Mrs. Palsgraf from the late-boarding passenger, and, thus proximate causation would not need to be addressed. The dissenters argue there was both negligence and proximate causation. According to the majority what factors should go into a judgment of proximate causation? Which do you think is the more defensible view for the tort law? Does this case differ sufficiently from *Ramsey* to reach a different conclusion? In *Ramsey,* did either the railway or electricity company have in mind the slightest possibility that Mr. Ramsey or someone else might have been killed from damage to the electric line miles away?

Palsgraf v. Long Island R.R. Co.

Court of Appeals of New York

248 N.Y. 339 (1928)

Opinion: CARDOZO, C. J.

Plaintiff was standing on a platform of defendant's railroad after buying a ticket to go to Rockaway Beach. A train stopped at the station, bound for another place. Two men ran forward to catch it. One of the men reached the platform of the car without mishap, though the train was already moving. The other man, carrying a package, jumped aboard the car, but seemed unsteady as if about to fall. A guard on the car, who had held the door open, reached forward to help him in, and another guard on the platform pushed him from behind. In this act, the package was dislodged, and fell upon the rails. It was a package of small size, about fifteen inches long, and was covered by a newspaper. In fact it contained fireworks, but there was nothing in its appearance to give notice of its contents. The fireworks when they fell exploded. The shock of the explosion threw down some scales at the other end of the platform many feet away. The scales struck the plaintiff, causing injuries for which she sues.

The conduct of the defendant's guard, if a wrong in its relation to the holder of the package, was not a wrong in its relation to the plaintiff, standing far away. Relatively to her it was not negligence at all. Nothing in the situation gave notice that the falling package had in it the potency of peril to persons thus removed. Negligence is not actionable unless it involves the invasion of a legally protected interest, the violation of a right. "Proof of negligence in the air, so to speak, will not do." … The plaintiff, as she stood upon the platform of the station, might claim to be protected against intentional invasion of her bodily security. Such invasion is not charged. She might claim to be protected against unintentional invasion by conduct involving in the thought of reasonable men an unreasonable hazard that such invasion would ensue. These, from the point of view of the law, were the bounds of her immunity, with perhaps some rare exceptions, survivals for the most part of ancient forms of liability, where conduct is held to be at the peril of the actor. Sullivan v. Dunham. … If no hazard was apparent to the eye of ordinary vigilance, an act innocent and harmless, at least to outward seeming, with reference to her, did not take to itself the quality of a tort because it happened to be a wrong, though apparently not one involving the risk of bodily insecurity, with reference to some one else. "In every instance, before negligence can be predicated of a given act, back of the act must be sought and found a duty to the individual complaining, the observance of which would have averted or avoided the injury." … The plaintiff sues in her own right for a wrong personal to her, and not as the vicarious beneficiary of a breach of duty to another. […]

The argument for the plaintiff is built upon the shifting meanings of such words as "wrong" and "wrongful," and shares their instability. What the plaintiff must show is "a wrong" to herself; i. e., a violation of her own right, and not merely a wrong to some one else, nor conduct "wrongful" because unsocial, but not "a wrong" to any one. We are told that one who drives at reckless speed through a crowded city street is guilty of a negligent act and therefore of a wrongful one, irrespective of the consequences. Negligent the act is, and wrongful in the sense that it is unsocial, but wrongful and unsocial in relation to other travelers, only because the eye of vigilance perceives the risk of damage. If the same act were to be committed on a speedway or a race course, it would lose its wrongful quality. The risk reasonably to be perceived defines the duty to be obeyed, and risk imports relation; it is risk to another or to others within the range of apprehension. … This does not mean, of course, that one who launches a destructive force is always relieved of liability, if the force, though known to be destructive, pursues an unexpected path. "It was not necessary that the defendant should have had notice of the particular method in which an accident would occur, if the possibility of an accident was clear to the ordinarily prudent eye." … Some acts, such as shooting are so imminently dangerous to any one who may come within reach of the missile however unexpectedly, as to impose a duty of prevision not far from that of an insurer. Even to-day, and much oftener in earlier stages of the law, one acts sometimes at one's peril. … Under this head, it may be, fall certain cases of what is known as transferred intent, an act willfully dangerous to A resulting by misadventure in injury to B. … These cases aside, wrong is defined in terms of the natural or probable, at least when unintentional. … The range of reasonable apprehension is at times a question for the court, and at times, if varying inferences are possible, a question for the jury. Here, by concession, there was nothing in the situation to suggest to the most cautious mind that the parcel wrapped in newspaper would spread wreckage through the station. If the guard had thrown it down knowingly and willfully, he would not have threatened the plaintiff's safety, so far as appearances could warn him. His conduct would not have involved, even then, an unreasonable probability of invasion of her bodily security. Liability can be no greater where the act is inadvertent.

Negligence, like risk, is thus a term of relation. Negligence in the abstract, apart from things related, is surely not a tort, if indeed it is understandable at all. Negligence is not a tort unless it results in the commission of a wrong, and the commission of a wrong imports the violation of a right, in this case, we are told, the right to be protected against interference with one's bodily security. But bodily security is protected, not against all forms of interference or aggression, but only against some. One who seeks redress at law does not make out a cause of action by showing without more that there has been damage to his person. If the harm was not willful, he must show that the act as to him had possibilities of danger so many and apparent as to entitle him to be protected against the doing of it though the harm was unintended. Affront to personality is still the keynote of the wrong. […]

The law of causation, remote or proximate, is thus foreign to the case before us. The question of liability is always anterior to the question of the measure of the consequences that go with liability. If there is no tort to be redressed, there is no occasion to consider what damage might be recovered if there were a finding of a tort. We may assume, without deciding, that negligence, not at large or in the abstract, but in relation to the plaintiff, would entail liability for any and all consequences, however novel or extraordinary. … There is room for argument that a distinction is to be drawn according to the diversity of interests invaded by the act, as where conduct negligent in that it threatens an insignificant invasion of an interest in property results in an unforeseeable invasion of an interest of another order, as, e. g., one of bodily security. Perhaps other distinctions may be necessary. We do not go into the question now. The consequences to be followed must first be rooted in a wrong.

The judgment of the Appellate Division and that of the Trial Term should be reversed, and the complaint dismissed, with costs in all courts.

ANDREWS, J. (dissenting).

Assisting a passenger to board a train, the defendant's servant negligently knocked a package from his arms. It fell between the platform and the cars. Of its contents the servant knew and could know nothing. A violent explosion followed. The concussion broke some scales standing a considerable distance away. In falling, they injured the plaintiff, an intending passenger.

Upon these facts, may she recover the damages she has suffered in an action brought against the master? The result we shall reach depends upon our theory as to the nature of negligence. Is it a relative concept—the breach of some duty owing to a particular person or to particular persons? Or, where there is an act which unreasonably threatens the safety of others, is the doer liable for all its proximate consequences, even where they result in injury to one who would generally be thought to be outside the radius of danger? This is not a mere dispute as to words. We might not believe that to the average mind the dropping of the bundle would seem to involve the probability of harm to the plaintiff standing many feet away whatever might be the case as to the owner or to one so near as to be likely to be struck by its fall. If, however, we adopt the second hypothesis, we have to inquire only as to the relation between cause and effect. We deal in terms of proximate cause, not of negligence.

Negligence may be defined roughly as an act or omission which unreasonably does or may affect the rights of others, or which unreasonably fails to protect one's self from the dangers resulting from such acts. Here I confine myself to the first branch of the definition. …

There must be **both the act or the omission, and the right**. It is the act itself, not the intent of the actor, that is important. … In criminal law both the intent and the result are to be considered. Intent again is material in tort actions, where punitive damages are sought, dependent on actual malice—not one merely reckless conduct. But here neither insanity nor infancy lessens responsibility. Williams v. Hays, 143 N. Y. 442, 38 N. E. 449, 26 L. R. A. 153, 42 Am. St. Rep. 743.

As has been said, except in cases of contributory negligence, **there must be rights which are or may be affected**. Often though injury has occurred, no rights of him who suffers have been touched. A licensee or trespasser upon my land has no claim to affirmative care on my part that the land be made safe. … Where a railroad is required to fence its tracks against cattle, no man's rights are injured should he wander upon the road because such fence is absent … An unborn child may not demand immunity from personal harm.

But we are told that "there is no negligence unless there is in the particular case a legal duty to take care, and this duty must be one which is owed to the plaintiff himself and not merely to others." … This I think too narrow a conception. Where there is the unreasonable act, and some right that may be affected there is negligence whether damage does or does not result. That is immaterial. Should we drive down Broadway at a reckless speed, we are negligent whether we strike an approaching car or miss it by an inch. The act itself is wrongful. It is a wrong not only to those who happen to be within the radius of danger, but to all who might have been there—a wrong to the public at large. Such is the language of the street. Such the language of the courts when speaking of contributory negligence. Such again and again their language in speaking of the duty of some defendant and discussing proximate cause in cases where such a discussion is wholly irrelevant on any other theory … As was said by Mr. Justice Holmes many years ago:

"The measure of the defendant's duty in determining whether a wrong has been committed is one thing, the measure of liability when a wrong has been committed is another." […]

Due care is a duty imposed on each one of us to protect society from unnecessary danger, not to protect A, B, or C alone.

It may well be that there is no such thing as negligence in the abstract. "Proof of negligence in the air, so to speak, will not do." In an empty world negligence would not exist. It does involve a relationship between man and his fellows, but not merely a relationship between man and those whom he might reasonably expect his act would injure; rather, a relationship between him and those whom he does in fact injure. If his act has a tendency to harm some one, it harms him a mile away as surely as it does those on the scene. We now permit children to recover for the negligent killing of the father. It was never prevented on the theory that no duty was owing to them. A husband may be compensated for the loss of his wife's services. To say that the wrongdoer was negligent as to the husband as well as to the wife is merely an attempt to fit facts to theory. [...]

In the well-known [English] Polhemis Case, [1921] Scrutton, L. J., said that the dropping of a plank was negligent, for it might injure "workman or cargo or ship." Because of either possibility, the owner of the vessel was to be made good for his loss. The act being wrongful, the doer was liable for its proximate results. Criticized and explained as this statement may have been, I think it states the law as it should be and as it is. [...]

The proposition is this: Every one owes to the world at large the duty of refraining from those acts that may unreasonably threaten the safety of others. Such an act occurs. Not only is he wronged to whom harm, might reasonably be expected to result, but he also who is in fact injured, even if he be outside what would generally be thought the danger zone. There needs be duty due the one complaining, but this is not a duty to a particular individual because as to him harm might be expected. Harm to some one being the natural result of the act, not only that one alone, but all those in fact injured may complain. We have never, I think, held otherwise. Indeed in the Di Caprio Case we said that a breach of a general ordinance defining the degree of care to be exercised in one's calling is evidence of negligence as to every one. We did not limit this statement to those who might be expected to be exposed to danger. Unreasonable risk being taken, its consequences are not confined to those who might probably be hurt.

[...]

The right to recover damages rests on additional considerations. The plaintiff's rights must be injured, and this injury must be caused by the negligence. We build a dam, but are negligent as to its foundations. Breaking, it injures property down stream. We are not liable if all this happened because of some reason other than the insecure foundation. But, when injuries do result from our unlawful act, we are liable for the consequences. It does not matter that they are unusual, unexpected, unforeseen, and unforeseeable. But there is one limitation. The damages must be so connected with the negligence that the latter may be said to be the proximate cause of the former.

These two words have never been given an inclusive definition. What is a cause in a legal sense, still more what is a proximate cause, depend in each case upon many considerations, as does the existence of negligence itself. Any philosophical doctrine of causation does not help us. A boy throws a stone into a pond. The ripples spread. The water level rises. The history of that pond is altered to all eternity. It will be altered by other causes also. Yet it will be forever the resultant of all causes combined. Each one will have an influence. How great only omniscience can say. You may speak of a chain, or, if you please, a net. An analogy is of little aid. Each cause brings about future events. Without each the future would not be the same. Each is proximate in the sense it is essential. But that is not what we mean by the word. Nor on the other hand do we mean sole cause. There is no such thing.

Should analogy be thought helpful, however, I prefer that of a stream. The spring, starting on its journey, is joined by tributary after tributary. The river, reaching the ocean, comes from a hundred sources. No man may say whence any drop of water is derived. Yet for a time distinction may be possible. Into the clear creek, brown swamp water flows from the left. Later, from the right comes water stained by its clay bed. The three may remain for a space, sharply divided. But at last inevitably no trace of separation remains. They are so commingled that all distinction is lost.

[...]

A cause, but not the proximate cause. What we do mean by the word "proximate" is that, because of convenience, of public policy, of a rough sense of justice, the law arbitrarily declines to trace a series of events beyond a certain point. This is not logic. It is practical politics. Take our rule as to fires. Sparks from my burning haystack set on fire my house and my neighbor's. I may recover from a negligent railroad. He may not. Yet the wrongful act as directly harmed the one as the other. We may regret that the line was drawn just where it was, but drawn somewhere it had to be. We said the act of the railroad was not the proximate cause of our neighbor's fire. Cause it surely was. The words we used were simply indicative of our notions of public policy. Other courts think differently. But somewhere they reach the point where they cannot say the stream comes from any one source.

[...]

There are some hints that may help us. The proximate cause, involved as it may be with many other causes, must be, at the least, something without which the event would not happen. The court must ask itself whether there was a natural and continuous sequence between cause and effect. Was the one a substantial factor in producing the other? Was there a direct connection between them, without too many intervening causes? Is the effect of cause on result not too attenuated? Is the cause likely, in the usual judgment of mankind, to produce the result? Or, by the exercise of prudent foresight, could the result be foreseen? Is the result too remote from the cause, and here we consider remoteness in time and space. ... where we passed upon the construction of a contract—but something was also said on this subject. Clearly we must so consider, for the greater the distance either in time or space, the more surely do other causes intervene to affect the result. When a lantern is overturned, the firing of a shed is a fairly direct consequence. Many things contribute to the spread of the conflagration—the force of the wind, the direction and width of streets, the character of intervening structures, other factors. We draw an uncertain and wavering line, but draw it we must as best we can.

Once again, it is all a question of fair judgment, always keeping in mind the fact that we endeavor to make a rule in each case that will be practical and in keeping with the general understanding of mankind.

Here another question must be answered. In the case supposed, it is said, and said correctly, that the chauffeur is liable for the direct effect of the explosion, although he had no reason to suppose it would follow a collision. "The fact that the injury occurred in a different manner than that which might have been expected does not prevent the chauffeur's negligence from being in law the cause of the injury." But the natural results of a negligent act—the results which a prudent man would or should foresee—do have a bearing upon the decision as to proximate cause. We have said so repeatedly. What should be foreseen? No human foresight would suggest that a collision itself might injure one a block away. On the contrary, given an explosion, such a possibility might be reasonably expected. I think the direct connection, the foresight of which the courts speak, assumes prevision of the explosion, for the immediate results of which, at least, the chauffeur is responsible.

If may be said this is unjust. Why? In fairness he should make good every injury flowing from his negligence. Not because of tenderness toward him we say he need not answer for all that follows his wrong. We look back to the catastrophe, the fire kindled by the spark, or the explosion. We trace the consequences, not indefinitely, but to a certain point. And to aid us in fixing that point we ask what might ordinarily be expected to follow the fire or the explosion.

This last suggestion is the factor which must determine the case before us. The act upon which defendant's liability rests is knocking an apparently harmless package onto the platform. The act was negligent. For its proximate consequences the defendant is liable. If its contents were broken, to the owner; if it fell upon and crushed a passenger's foot, then to him; if it exploded and injured one in the immediate vicinity, to him also as to A in the illustration. Mrs. Palsgraf was standing some distance away. How far cannot be told from the record—apparently 25 or 30 feet, perhaps less. Except for the explosion, she would not have been injured. We are told by the appellant in his brief, "It cannot be denied that the explosion was the direct cause of the plaintiff's injuries." So it was a substantial factor in producing the result—there was here a natural and continuous sequence—direct connection. The only intervening cause was that, instead of blowing her to the ground, the concussion smashed the weighing machine which in turn fell upon her. There was no remoteness in time, little in space. And surely, given such an explosion as here, it needed no great foresight to predict that the natural result would be to injure one on the platform at no greater distance from its scene than was the plaintiff. Just how no one might be able to predict. Whether by flying fragments, by broken glass, by wreckage of machines or structures no one could say. But injury in some form was most probable.

Under these circumstances I cannot say as a matter of law that the plaintiff's injuries were not the proximate result of the negligence. That is all we have before us. The court refused to so charge. No request was made to submit the matter to the jury as a question of fact, even would that have been proper upon the record before us.

The judgment appealed from should be affirmed, with costs.

POUND, LEHMAN and KELLOGG, JJ., concur with CARDOZO, Ch. J.; ANDREWS, J., dissents in opinion in which CRANE and O'BRIEN, JJ., concur.

Judgment reversed, etc.

(Citations omitted)

An issue of justice underlies the disagreement between the majority and minority views in *Palsgraf*. The majority view likely rests on two concerns. First, that because the railway employees had no idea, not the slightest clue, that the late-arriving passenger had a package that, should it fall when he was trying to get on the train, might pose a risk of harm. The majority based its view on the idea of negligence: if the objective duty of reasonable due care that every citizen must exercise toward others did not include even a hint of risk from the passenger's package, the railway employees (and thus the railway) could not be charged with negligence for the harm to Mrs. Palsgraf that resulted from the exploding package. In short, if ordinary reasonable care in the circumstances would not reveal unforeseeable risks to the actor toward some parties, it would be unjust for the actor to compensate those parties for ensuing harm. The scope of risks revealed by ordinary and prudent due care toward others thus places limits on negligence for surprising causal consequences to others.

Second, the railroad did not *create* the risk to Mrs. Palsgraf. Of course, railroads have a general duty to protect their passengers from harms, but it would be *unjust* to defendants to hold them accountable for surprising and unforeseeable risks that materialize into harm that ordinary due care would not have revealed.

However, implicit in the dissenting view is the idea that it would surely be *unjust* to a plaintiff, such as Mrs. Palsgraf, to be prevented from being compensated for injuries suffered from a causal sequence that so obviously and directly resulted from railway agents. And, on balance, they might argue, as between an innocent and unsuspecting injured plaintiff and innocent railway agents whose reasonable care would not have revealed the slightest hint of risk to others by assisting the late arriving passenger, practical issues plus reasonable care as something owed to the world at large suggests that the balance of justice would favor awarding Mrs. Palsgraf compensation for injuries so directly caused by the agents. Either innocent defendants would be treated unjustly by having to compensate for unforeseeable risks of harm or innocent plaintiffs who suffered harms when unforeseeable risks materialized would be treated unjustly.

Both sides have legitimate concerns. The majority seeks a principle to limit negligence for which defendants who weren't aware of risks and did not create them would be required to compensate others; the minority seeks to ensure that plaintiffs harmed even in a manner that resulted from unforeseeable risks should receive compensation for their injuries.

Moreover, there are legal cases on both sides of the issues, although Prosser suggests that much legal opinion is on the side for limiting compensation to plaintiffs for whom consequences are foreseeable with reasonable due care.

Interestingly, this disagreement regarding proximate causation in tort law debates echoes two earlier issues we have met. Recall in *Williams v. Hays* that insane defendants may be held accountable in torts on the principle that between innocent defendants (who negligently caused harm while insane) and innocent plaintiffs who suffered harm caused by insane actors, the tort law favors compensation for innocent plaintiffs. The balance of justice between two parties, both innocent but for different reasons, favors plaintiffs. This is a widespread, perhaps universally held, view for negligent torts.

Analogously, we considered eggshell skull cases in which negligent actors are required to compensate plaintiffs who have hidden or *unforeseeable* vulnerabilities (of which defendants cannot be aware) for those injuries. As Prosser summarizes it

> The defendant is held liable for unusual results of personal injuries which are regarded as unforeseeable, such as tuberculosis, paralysis, pneumonia, heart or kidney disease, blood poisoning, cancer or the loss of hair from fright ... One of the illustrations which runs through the English cases is that of the plaintiff with the "eggshell skull", who suffers death where a normal person would have had only a bump on the head ...[6]

In the eggshell skull and related cases, the defendants are more culpable than in insanity cases. They negligently caused plaintiff some harm; it just turned out to be worse than an initial event would have suggested. However, the tort law has strongly endorsed the view that harmed and innocent plaintiffs should be compensated for greater injuries because of unforeseeable and hidden vulnerabilities. Thus, for eggshell skull cases, the tort law is committed to ensuring compensation for injured parties even when they have unforeseeable or hidden vulnerabilities about which defendants could not know.

The juxtaposition of these three different kinds of cases suggests that at some deep level there may be inconsistencies in the tort law between different topic areas. By and large innocent plaintiffs who have eggshell skulls and those who are harmed by the insane are "protected" in the sense that compensation is authorized for their harm (except for a plaintiff's existing eggshell skull condition, which was bound to worsen, for which defendant would not be held accountable). In contrast, under *Palsgraf,* innocent

6 *Ibid.*, 291–292.

plaintiffs, such as Mrs. Palsgraf, are not protected from the harmful effects of a causal sequence set in motion by a person who had no awareness of any risks to third parties. In effect, in Cardozo's view, defendants' implausible awareness of possible risks to third parties exonerates defendants. For Cardozo, the injustice of imposing liability on defendant in *Palsgraf* kinds of cases outweighs (it's not even considered) unjust harm to a seeming injustice to plaintiff.

Would Cardozo's approach to duty in *Palsgraf* preclude defendants' having a duty to repair all (or most) of the damage to a plaintiff with an eggshell skull? Since a vulnerability is hidden, would Cardozo's view preclude compensation for injuries resulting from a "hidden" and unforeseeable vulnerability in a plaintiff? One might argue that if a defendant causes injuries to an eggshell plaintiff, the defendant need only compensate for typical or average injuries that might occur to such individuals. If an ordinary car crash killed a person with special vulnerability because of a skull with a hole in it, should the victim only be permitted to recover for damages typical of a person with an "average" or "typical" skull, not a particularly fragile one? I would not favor this, so I tend to find some tension in the tort law between underlying approaches in these three different areas of the law.

The next case is a wild and unexpected proximate cause case that adds to some of the tensions created by *Palsgraf*. If I just described the next case to you, you would not believe me and think I was making up a science-fiction-type case. However, read it and consider whether or not you think the driver of the negligently parked truck should be held accountable for the second negligent driver shooting a Good Samaritan who came to assist the victims of the accident.

Lynch v. Fisher, et al.

Court of Appeal of Louisiana, Second Circuit

34 So.2d 513 (1947)

Opinion: HARDY, Judge.

This matter comes before us on appeal from judgment of the Eleventh Judicial District Court of Louisiana sustaining exceptions of no cause or right of action filed on behalf of all defendants and **dismissing plaintiff's action as of nonsuit.**

[The issues follow.] That about 9:00 p.m. on July 3, 1945, an employee of the defendants, Wheless and Fisher, (whose insurer is the defendant, Lumbermen's Mutual Casualty Company of Chicago, Ill.) at the time engaged within the general scope and course of his employment, parked a pulpwood truck which he was driving on the right-hand side of highway No. 171, some twelve miles north of Mansfield, De Soto Parish, Louisiana;

That, while said truck was thus parked, a passenger car owned and driven by the defendant, Robert Joe Gunter, collided violently with the rear end thereof;

That the driver of the parked truck was guilty of negligence, imputable to his employers, on numerous grounds, specifically in parking the truck entirely on the highway without leaving a clearance of fifteen feet on the pavement; in failing to have warning lights on the parked truck; in leaving the truck parked on the highway, thereby constituting a menace to traffic, and in failing to set out flares, or to have same available and ready for service.

That the negligence of the defendant, Robert Joe Gunter consisted of driving and operating his automobile at an excessive, unreasonable and unlawful rate of speed; in failing to keep and maintain a proper lookout; operating his vehicle without adequate brakes; and failing to take any action to avoid the collision;

That the concurrent acts of negligence of the driver of the truck and the driver of the passenger car were the proximate causes of the accident;

That plaintiff seeing the collision ran to the scene thereof, succeeded in opening the doors of the badly damaged Gunter car, and, with the aid of another party, extricated both Mrs. Gunter and the defendant, Robert Joe Gunter, from the automobile, which had meanwhile caught fire;

That, in the effort to further assist the fatally injured Mrs. Gunter, plaintiff attempted to pull a floor mat out of the car to be used as a cushion for her head as she lay upon the roadside; that in the performance of this act plaintiff found a pistol on the floor of the car and handed the same to the defendant Gunter, who, being delirious and temporarily mentally deranged by reason of the shock of the accident, fired the pistol at plaintiff, the bullet passing through plaintiff's left ankle and inflicting serious injuries, for which damages are claimed in this action. [...]

Plaintiff herein has properly alleged the concurrent negligence of the several defendants and there is ample authority in this State for the proposition that a third person may recover from either or all parties alleged to be guilty of concurrent negligence.

The rule is plainly stated in Comment (a) on page 472 of Volume 2 of the Restatement of the Law of Torts as follows: "A plaintiff who intervenes to rescue a third person is not affected by the fact that the third person has been a legally contributing cause in putting plaintiff in peril."

Determination of the issue of proximate cause must of necessity be considered with relation to the allied doctrine of intervening cause which is clearly material under the alleged facts of this case.

It is quite true, as contended by learned counsel for defendants, as a general proposition of law that only that negligence which directly causes the injury is deemed to be proximate. But a resolution of this point must perforce depend upon the particular facts of each case.

In the matter before us there are three elements that must be determined:

(a). Did the original negligence of the driver of the parked truck set in motion a chain of circumstances following consecutively one upon the other which led to plaintiff's injury?
(b). Was the act of original negligence superseded by an intervening act breaking the chain of causation leading to plaintiff's injury?
(c). Is the fact that plaintiff's injuries resulted from an improbable and unforeseeable incident sufficient to eliminate the original act of negligence from consideration as a proximate cause?

The answer to these queries will dispose of all the claims based upon the doctrines of proximate and intervening causes and foreseeability.

Upon the basis of the allegations there is no room for any reasonable contravention of the proposition that the circumstances following the negligent parking of the truck down to the removal of the pistol from the car by plaintiff were natural, probable and reasonably to be expected. But at this point an imponderable enters into consideration. The rescuer hands a pistol to the rescued and is shot by the latter. Certainly under the general rule, this action could not be within the reasonable contemplation of any normal individual and the specific incident therefore could not be imputed to the negligent truck driver as a probable result flowing from his negligence. But, unfortunately, the proposition does not admit of being disposed of so easily, for it is well established in the jurisprudence of the State of Louisiana and a majority of other jurisdictions that the general rule must yield to specific instances.

Of course, no Court could reasonably hold that the driver of a vehicle, no matter how gross his negligence, could have contemplated the shooting of a third party as a normal and natural result of such negligence. Nor, indeed, could the rescuer himself be held to have assumed the risk of such a strange, unnatural and unusual result flowing from his gallant efforts.

But, if the results of accidents were normal, usual and predictable, the burden of both Bar and Bench would be made immeasurably lighter.

To determine whether or not the shooting incident is susceptible of being distinguished and set apart from the general law of proximate cause, we must base our conclusions not upon those elements which would be applicable as between parties to the collision itself but as affecting the injury inflicted upon an innocent third party, himself without fault.

[...]

[T]he laws of probability were overwhelmingly against the occurrence of the character and nature of the incident and resulting injury to plaintiff under the actual facts of this case. But, certainly, plaintiff is without fault, and, certainly, the negligence of some party or the concurrent negligence of several parties combined to set up the unfortunate situation which resulted in his injury.

In our opinion the general doctrine of proximate cause cannot be applied under the alleged facts and chain of circumstances herein presented. Under the tenor of the allegations, it is quite clear that plaintiff would not have been shot if originally the truck driver had not negligently parked his truck in such manner as to constitute a menace and hazard to vehicles rightfully traveling the highway.

The proximate cause of the injury to one who voluntarily interposes to save the lives of persons imperiled by the negligence of others is the negligence which causes the peril. 19 A.L.R., page 13.

[6] In determining the question as to the efficiency of the intervening act, that is, in this case, the shooting of plaintiff by one of the defendants, we must consider the well established principle that an intervening cause is not necessarily a superseding cause. The intervening cause, in order to supersede original negligence, must have alone produced injury.

Under paragraph (B) of the Comment on Section 440 of the Restatement of the Law of Torts this proposition is set forth: "Therefore, if in looking back from the harm and tracing the sequence of events by which it was produced, it is found that a superseding cause has operated, there is no need of determining whether the actor's antecedent conduct was or was not a substantial factor in bringing about the harm."

In the instant case there is no question but that in tracing back from the point of the actual injury to plaintiff we would ordinarily be compelled to conclude that the shooting by one of the defendants was unquestionably a superseding cause were it not for the allegation that the defendant inflicting the injury at the time was temporarily insane by reason of shock resulting from the collision caused by the initial negligence of the truck driver.

Section 455 of the Restatement of the Law of Torts submits the principle:

"If the actor's negligent conduct so brings about the delirium or insanity of another as to make the actor liable for it, the actor is also liable for harm done by the other to himself while delirious or insane, if his delirium or insanity.

(a). Prevents him from realizing the nature of his act * * *."

We think it must logically and inevitably follow that under such circumstances the actor is not only liable for harm done in a fit of delirium or insanity by such deranged person to himself, but also for any harm caused by him to another. [...]

In every consideration of the point which has come to our attention in the study of this case, the qualities of the relieving or superseding act are repeatedly and unfailingly designated as being intervening and voluntary, by a person responsible for his acts.

Since we must accept the well pleaded allegations of the petition as being true for the purpose of determining the exception, we are constrained to hold that plaintiff has met the requirements established by these several factors and has negatived the possibility that the act which immediately resulted in the harm was the voluntary action of a person responsible for his acts.

Under the allegations of the petition it is inescapable that plaintiff has properly alleged that the defendant Gunter was mentally deranged and rendered temporarily insane as the result of the collision of his car with the parked truck. Plaintiff by his allegations has further definitely asserted that such a condition was brought about by the concurrent negligence of the several defendants. In order to affirm the holding of the lower court it would be necessary for us to find that the temporary insanity of the defendant Gunter, which led to the shooting, was not caused by the collision. Clearly, this is a question of fact to be determined by trial on the merits, and, meanwhile, any conclusion must be governed by the plain allegations of the petition.

Any attempt to determine at what point, with relation to the actual injury to plaintiff, the negligence of the original actor, namely, the driver of the truck, ceased and a new and independent tortious act intervened and superseded the original negligence, conclusively impresses us with the impossibility of such a severance of causes. The chain is complete and whole, link by link, and though tested with the utmost care no break is revealed in the succession of circumstances.

The consecutive order of the related circumstances and events may be briefly outlined:

1. Negligence of the truck driver in parking his truck on the highway, resulting in
2. Collision, superinduced by the concurrent negligence of the defendant Gunter, resulting in
3. a. attempted rescue by the plaintiff.
   b. Temporary mental derangement of the defendant Gunter as a result of the shock of the collision, resulting in
4. The shooting of plaintiff and the injury sustained thereby.

If there is any break in the continuity of the incidents flowing from the original act of negligence, we are unable to point out such a circumstance.

We think it is well established that the general doctrine of foreseeability is not applicable to the extent of relieving one who sets in motion, through the agency of a negligent act, a chain of circumstances leading to the final resultant injury. [...]

We do not believe that the theory of foreseeability is applicable to the facts of this case. Referring again to the Restatement of the Law of Torts, we find in Section 435 a plain and unambiguous statement of the principle which refutes the requirement of foreseeability: "If the actor's conduct is a substantial factor in bringing about harm to another, the fact that the actor neither foresaw nor should have foreseen the extent of the harm or the manner in which it occurred does not prevent him from being liable."

In our opinion the original act of negligence alleged upon is so inextricably interwoven with the subsequent occurrences involved that it cannot be disassociated from any of them. Nor can we consider, in the light of the authorities cited, the act of a temporarily insane or deranged person as being such a character of an independent, voluntary and responsible action as would stand alone as the proximate cause of plaintiff's injury.

While the burden of this opinion has been concerned with the question of negligence of the defendants, employers of the truck driver, and their insurer, the reasons advanced apply even more strongly and with greater force in maintaining plaintiff's right and cause of action against the defendant, Gunter.

For the reasons assigned, the judgment appealed from is reversed and set aside, and there is now judgment overruling the exceptions of no cause or right of action filed on behalf of all defendants and remanding this cause to the District Court for further proceedings. The costs of this appeal are to be borne by defendants and all other costs are to await final determination of the suit.

[...]

In conclusion we can only reiterate the observation which we made in our original opinion herein: "While the burden of this opinion has been concerned with the question of negligence of the defendants, employers of the truck driver, and their insurer, the reasons advanced apply even more strongly and with greater force in maintaining plaintiff's right and cause of action against the defendant, Gunter."

For the reasons assigned our original opinion herein is reinstated and made the judgment of this Court.

(Citations omitted)

In contrast to *Palsgraf,* in *Lynch* the court acknowledges that Harry Fisher, driver of the negligently parked truck, could not have had in mind the possibility that risks from his action would lead to Good Samaritan Lynch being shot as a result. Might Cardozo disagree with this case? Fisher negligently created risks by how he parked his truck. However, did he have a duty in negligence to Lynch because it is extremely unlikely he would have thought of the possibility of a Good Samaritan being shot as a consequence? It seems just as implausible as the possibility of harm to Mrs. Palsgraf in that case.

Make sure you understand the quite persuasive argument of this court for holding Fisher accountable for injuries to Lynch.

Proximate Causation in the Criminal Law Versus Tort Law

In the following case regarding proximate causation in the criminal law, keep in mind both the proximate causation cases we have read plus cases from the tort law the court references in *Commonwealth v. Root*. It is important that this is a case from the criminal law; we are taking it up in this section since you will already have some background concerning proximate causation in the tort law. As the Pennsylvania Supreme Court lays out in *Root*, the contrast between the two areas of the law is important. Although the court does not indicate what is important about the differences in proximate causation in torts compared with the criminal law, other than providing examples it thinks are quite persuasive, what principle or rationale can you think of that might make the difference between the two kinds of cases?

Commonwealth v. Root

Supreme Court of Pennsylvania

22 Ill.403 Pa. 571(1961)

Opinion: CHARLES ALVIN JONES, Chief Justice.

The appellant was found guilty of involuntary manslaughter for the death of his competitor in the course of an automobile race between them on a highway. The trial court overruled the defendant's demurrer to the Commonwealth's evidence and, after verdict, denied his motion in arrest of judgment. On appeal from the judgment of sentence entered on the jury's verdict, the Superior Court affirmed. We granted allocatur because of the important question present as to whether the defendant's unlawful and reckless conduct was a sufficiently direct cause of the death to warrant his being charged with criminal homicide.

The testimony, which is uncontradicted in material part, discloses that, on the night of the fatal accident, the defendant accepted the deceased's challenge to engage in an automobile race; that the racing took place on a rural 3-lane highway; that the night was clear and dry, and traffic light; that the speed limit on the highway was 50 miles per hour; that, immediately prior to the accident, the two automobiles were being operated at varying speeds of from 70 to 90 miles per hour; that the accident occurred in a no-passing zone on the approach to a bridge where the highway narrowed to two directionally-opposite lanes; that, at the time of the accident, the defendant was in the lead and was proceeding in his right hand lane of travel; that the deceased, in an attempt to pass the defendant's automobile, when a truck was closely approaching from the opposite direction, swerved his car to the left, crossed the highway's white dividing line and drove his automobile on the wrong side of the highway head-on into the oncoming truck with resultant fatal effect to himself.

This evidence would of course amply support a conviction of the defendant for speeding, reckless driving and, perhaps, other violations of The Vehicle Code of May 1, 1929, as amended. In fact, it may be noted, in passing, that the Act of January 8, 1960, P.L (1959) … makes automobile racing on a highway an independent crime punishable by fine or imprisonment or both up to $500 and three years in jail. As the highway racing in the instant case occurred prior to the enactment of the Act of 1960, cit. supra, that statute is, of course, not presently applicable. In any event, unlawful or reckless conduct is only one ingredient of the crime of involuntary manslaughter. Another essential and distinctly separate element of the crime is that the unlawful or reckless conduct charged to the defendant was the direct cause of the death in issue. The first ingredient is obviously present in this case but, just as plainly, the second is not.

While precedent is to be found for application of the tort law concept of "proximate cause" in fixing responsibility for criminal homicide, the want of any rational basis for its use in determining criminal liability can no longer be properly disregarded. When proximate cause was first borrowed from the field of tort law and applied to homicide prosecutions in Pennsylvania, the concept connoted a much more direct causal relation in producing the alleged culpable result than it does today. Proximate cause, as an essential element of a tort founded in negligence, has undergone in recent times, and is still undergoing, a marked extension. More specifically, this area of civil law has been progressively liberalized in favor of claims for damages for personal injuries to which careless conduct of others can in some way be associated. To persist in applying the tort liability concept of proximate cause to prosecutions for criminal homicide after the marked expansion of civil liability of defendants in tort actions for negligence would be to extend possible criminal liability to persons chargeable with unlawful or reckless conduct in circumstances not generally considered to present the likelihood of a resultant death. [...]

The instant case is one of first impression in this State; and our research has not disclosed a single instance where a district attorney has ever before attempted to prosecute for involuntary manslaughter on facts similar to those established by the record now before us. The closest case, factually, would seem to be Commonwealth v. Levin, 1957, which affirmed the defendant's conviction of involuntary manslaughter. In the Levin case two cars were racing on the streets of Philadelphia at speeds estimated at from 85 to 95 miles per hour. The defendant's car, in the left hand lane, was racing alongside of the car in which the deceased was a passenger when the defendant turned his automobile sharply to the right in front of the other car thereby causing the driver of the latter car to lose control and smash into a tree, the passenger being thrown to the road and killed as a result of the impact. It is readily apparent that the elements of causation in the Levin case were fundamentally different from those in the present case. Levin's act of cutting his automobile sharply in front of the car in which the deceased was riding directly forced that car off of the road and into the tree. The defendant's reckless and unlawful maneuver was the direct cause of the crucial fatality. In the instant case, the defendant's conduct was not even remotely comparable. Here, the action of the deceased driver in recklessly and suicidally swerving his car to the left lane of a 2-lane highway into the path of an oncoming truck was not forced upon him by any act of the defendant; it was done by the deceased and by him alone, who thus directly brought about his own demise. The Levin case was properly decided but it cannot, by any ratiocination, be utilized to justify a conviction in the present case.

Legal theory which makes guilt or innocence of criminal homicide depend upon such accidental and fortuitous circumstances as are now embraced by modern tort law's encompassing concept of proximate cause is too harsh to be just. A few illustrations should suffice to so demonstrate.

In Mautino v. Piercedale Supply Co.,—a civil action for damages—we held that where a man sold a cartridge to a person under 16 years of age in violation of a State statute and the recipient subsequently procured a gun from which he fired the cartridge injuring someone, the injury was proximately caused by the act of the man who sold the cartridge to the underage person. If proximate cause were the test for criminal liability and the injury to the plaintiff in the Mautino case had been fatal, the man who sold the bullet to the underage person (even though the boy had the appearance of an adult) would have been guilty of involuntary manslaughter, for his unlawful act would, according to the tort law standard, have been the proximate cause of the death.

In Schelin v. Goldberg, 1958, it was held that the plaintiff, who was injured in a fight, could recover in tort against the defendants, the owners of a taproom who prior to the fight had unlawfully served the plaintiff drinks while he was in a visibly intoxicated condition, the unlawful action of the defendants being held to be the proximate cause of the plaintiff's injuries. Here, again, if proximate cause were the test for criminal liability and the plaintiff had been fatally injured in the fight, the taproom owners would have been guilty of involuntary manslaughter, for their unlawful act would have been no less the proximate cause of death.

In Marchl v. Dowling Company, 1945, it was held that where a truck driver had double parked his truck and the minor plaintiff was struck by a passing car when she walked around the double parked truck, the truck driver's employer was held liable in tort for the plaintiff's injuries on the ground that the truck driver's act of double parking, which violated both a State statute and a city ordinance, was the proximate cause of the plaintiff's injuries. Here, also, if proximate cause were the test for criminal liability and the plaintiff's injuries had been fatal, the truck driver would have been guilty of involuntary manslaughter since his unlawful act would have been the proximate cause of the death for which his employer was held liable in damages under respondeat superior. To be guilty of involuntary manslaughter for double parking would, of course, be unthinkable, yet if proximate cause were to determine criminal liability, such a result would indeed be a possibility.

Even if the tort liability concept of proximate cause were to be deemed applicable, the defendant's conviction of involuntary manslaughter in the instant case could not be sustained under the evidence. The operative effect of a supervening cause would have to be taken into consideration. Commonwealth v. Redline, supra, 391. But, the trial judge refused the defendant's point for charge to such effect and erroneously instructed the jury that "negligence or want of care on the part of [the deceased] is no defense to the criminal responsibility of the defendant * * *."

[…]

If the tort liability concept of proximate cause were to be applied in a criminal homicide prosecution, then the conduct of the person whose death is the basis of the indictment would have to be considered, not to prove that it was merely an additional proximate cause of the death, but to determine, under fundamental and long recognized law applicable to proximate cause, whether the subsequent wrongful act superseded the original conduct chargeable to the defendant. If it did in fact supervene then the original act is so insulated from the ensuing death as not to be its proximate cause.

Under the uncontradicted evidence in this case, the conduct of the defendant was not the proximate cause of the decedent's death as a matter of law. In Kline v. Moyer and Albert, 1937, the rule is stated as follows: "Where a second actor has become aware of the existence of a potential danger created by the negligence of an original tort-feasor, and thereafter, by an independent act of negligence, brings about an accident, the first tort-feasor is relieved of liability, because the condition created by him was merely a circumstance of the accident and not its proximate cause." …

In the case last above cited, while Angretti was driving his truck eastward along a highway, a bus, traveling in the same direction in front of him, stopped to take on a passenger. Angretti swerved his truck to the left into the lane of oncoming traffic in an attempt to pass the bus but collided with a tractor-trailer driven by the plaintiff's decedent, who was killed as a result of the collision. In affirming the entry of judgment n.o.v. in favor of the defendant bus company, we held that any negligence on the part of the bus driver, in suddenly bringing his bus to a halt in order to pick up a passenger, was not a proximate cause of the death of the plaintiff's decedent since the accident "was due entirely to the intervening and superseding negligence of Angretti in allowing his truck to pass over into the pathway of the westbound tractor-trailer * * *."

In the case now before us, the deceased was aware of the dangerous condition created by the defendant's reckless conduct in driving his automobile at an excessive rate of speed along the highway but, despite such knowledge, he recklessly chose to swerve his car to the left and into the path of an oncoming truck, thereby bringing about the head-on collision which caused his own death.

To summarize, the tort liability concept of proximate cause has no proper place in prosecutions for criminal homicide and more direct causal connection is required for conviction. (Commonwealth v. Redline). In the instant case, the defendant's reckless conduct was not a sufficiently direct cause of the competing driver's death to make him criminally liable therefor.

The judgment of sentence is reversed and the defendant's motion in arrest of judgment granted.

BELL, J., files a concurring opinion.

EAGEN, J., files a dissenting opinion.

[...]

EAGEN, Justice (dissenting): The opinion of the learned Chief Justice admits, under the uncontradicted facts, that the defendant, at the time of the fatal accident involved, was engaged in an unlawful and reckless course of conduct. Racing an automobile at 90 miles per hour, trying to prevent another automobile going in the same direction from passing him, in a no-passing zone on a two-lane public highway, is certainly all of that. Admittedly also, there can be more than one direct cause of an unlawful death. To me, this is self-evident. But, says the majority opinion, the defendant's recklessness was not a direct cause of the death. With this, I cannot agree.

If the defendant did not engage in the unlawful race and so operate his automobile in such a reckless manner, this accident would never have occurred. He helped create the dangerous event. He was a vital part of it. The victim's acts were a natural reaction to the stimulus of the situation. The race, the attempt to pass the other car and forge ahead, the reckless speed, all of these factors the defendant himself helped create. He was part and parcel of them. That the victim's response was normal under the circumstances, that his reaction should have been expected and was clearly foreseeable, is to me beyond argument. That the defendant's recklessness was a substantial factor is obvious. All of this, in my opinion, makes his unlawful conduct a direct cause of the resulting collision.

(Citations omitted)

[...]

Given the discussion in *Root* contrasting criminal and tort liability, what accounts for different treatment by this court? The opinion does not provide reasons, but it strongly suggests that for proximate cause in the criminal law, the defendant must have some knowledge, or perhaps probable knowledge, of what the teenager who buys a bullet will do with it. Given the general doctrines of the criminal law, this seems one explanation. Another possibility might be that there must be a more proximate connection (in the ordinary sense) between an agent's action and harm to an unknown victim. This might better support reasons for inflicting the burdens of punishment on the agent.

After *Root* was decided, Pennsylvania legislators concluded that the laws concerning drag racing should be amended. You see the result of this in the following case.

Commonwealth v. Jackson

Superior Court of Pennsylvania

744 A.2d 271 (1999)

Opinion: DEL SOLE, J.:

1 This appeal is taken from a judgment of sentence imposed after Appellant was convicted in a bench trial of Homicide by Vehicle, Involuntary Manslaughter, Recklessly Endangering Another Person, Criminal Conspiracy and summary traffic violations.

2 Appellant contends that he was not responsible for the fatal automobile accident which gave rise to the charges against him, and therefore his conviction cannot be supported by law or by the weight of the evidence presented. Appellant's convictions result from a collision which occurred in April of 1996. The trial court recounted the evidence presented at trial detailing the events which culminated in the fatal accident.

> [T]he evidence presented by the Commonwealth established that the Defendant and his brother, Stephen Jackson, engaged in a drag race in the Brookline Boulevard area of the City of Pittsburgh. Numerous witnesses testified to conduct from which it could be readily inferred that the Defendant and his brother were racing their vehicles on roadways of this Commonwealth. Eyewitness testimony placed the Defendant's vehicle and his brother's vehicle in close proximity shortly before the time of the accident in question.

Testimony presented by Commonwealth witnesses revealed that shortly before the two brothers' vehicles disappeared from the sight of onlookers, these vehicles were neck and neck at a high rate of speed. Once these vehicles disappeared from eyesight, witnesses heard the unmistakable sound of an automobile collision. Within a matter of seconds, observers noted that the vehicle of Stephen Jackson had collided with a vehicle driven by the decedent, Mr. Richard Smith. Smith was apparently in the process of making a u-turn (sic) at the time of the collision.

The Defendant's vehicle was seen a short distance beyond the site of the accident, and did not physically impact with either his brother's vehicle or that driven by the decedent.

Expert testimony presented by the Commonwealth established that the speed of Stephen Jackson's vehicle was seventy-six (76) miles per hour prior to impact with Mr. Smith's vehicle. The Defendant's expert opined that Stephen's vehicle was traveling at a speed of seventy (70) miles per hour, rather than the seventy-six (76) miles per hour as reported by the Commonwealth expert. In either event, this disparity is insignificant, as the posted speed limit in this area is twenty-five (25) miles per hour.

Mr. Smith ultimately died from the injuries sustained in this accident, resulting in charges being filed against both Stephen Jackson as a juvenile and his brother, the Defendant herein, as an adult. Trial Court Opinion 11/6/98 at 2-3.

3 Appellant initially alleges that the trial court failed to consider the decedent's actions as possibly diminishing Appellant's responsibility as the direct and substantial cause of death. Appellant alleges the decedent was performing an illegal U-turn close to the crest of a hill and near a bend in the road at the time his vehicle was struck. Appellant claims that the trial court failed to consider the concept that the victim's

actions can serve to diminish a defendant's criminal responsibility.

4 Our Supreme Court … determined that a defendant charged with Homicide by Vehicle must be permitted to introduce evidence of the decedent's intoxication and the resulting inference that it was the decedent's own disregard of his circumstances which caused the accident. Likewise in another case …: "In a criminal trial where the jury has the responsibility of determining the 'direct cause' of death in order to decide whether or not to covict [sic] the defendant of homicide by vehicle, evidence of other factors which may have been the direct cause of death is clearly appropriate.

5 Thus, it was proper for the trial court in this case to admit and consider evidence of the decedent's driving, including the illegal U-turn and evidence of his consumption of alcoholic beverages. However, upon review of the record and the trial court's statements in its opinion, it is evident that the court allowed the admission of this evidence and considered it, but ultimately rejected it as the legal cause of the accident. …

6 Appellant further contends that he cannot be held responsible for the crimes for which he was convicted under an accomplice liability theory. Appellant claims his conviction … cannot rest on the fact that he was an accomplice to the drag race, where his vehicle did not strike the victim or the victim's vehicle. In support of his position Appellant cites to Commonwealth v. Root, 403 Pa. 571, 170 A.2d 310 (1961). There the defendant and decedent were engaged in a high-speed race on a rural highway. The decedent attempted to pass the defendant, crossed the centerline and drove head-on into an oncoming truck. The court ruled that the defendant's conduct was not the proximate cause of the decedent's death. It remarked that "the deceased was aware of the dangerous condition created by the defendant's reckless conduct in driving his automobile at an excessive rate of speed along the highway, but despite such knowledge, he recklessly chose to swerve his car to the left and into the path of an oncoming truck, thereby bringing about the head-on collision which caused his own death." Id. at 314.

7 The trial court distinguished the Root decision from the present case. First, … the decedent in Root was one of the racing drivers and that he chose to attempt to pass the defendant, resulting in his driving into the path of an oncoming truck. Thus, the driver in Root was responsible for his own death. Secondly, the trial court noted that the Root decision was made prior to the existence of the Pennsylvania Crimes Code which now provides:

> *(a) General rule.*—a person is guilty of an offense if it is committed by his own conduct or by the conduct of another person for which he is legally accountable, or both.
>
> *(b) Conduct of another.*—A person is legally accountable for the conduct of another person when:
>
> [...]
>
> (3) he is an accomplice of such other person in the commission of the offense.
>
> *(c) Accomplice defined.*—a person is an accomplice of another person in the commission of an offense if:
>
> (1) with the intent of promoting or facilitating the commission of the offense, he: (ii) aids or agrees or attempts to aid such other person in planning or committing it. [...]

8 The trial court noted that … Appellant and his brother agreed to engage in a high-speed race and that they should have been aware that their

conduct could result in an accident involving death or serious bodily injury. We find support for this conclusion in the record and agree with the trial court that this ruling does not conflict with our Supreme Court's decision in Root.

[...]

10 The trial court concluded that Appellant's conduct, as well as his brother's, was a direct and substantial factor in Mr. Smith's death. ... Appellant's actions in engaging in this high-speed race, in violation of the laws designed to protect vehicular and pedestrian travelers, made it entirely foreseeable that he or another could be seriously killed or injured as a result of his conduct. Thus, it is appropriate that Appellant be held responsible for Mr. Smith's death. Accordingly, we affirm Appellant's convictions and judgment of sentence.

11 Judgment of sentence affirmed.

(Citations omitted)

Strict Liability in Torts

Eventually, after the 19th century courts have generally endorsed holding defendants **strictly accountable** in the tort law for three classes of offenses: for injuries resulting from widely distributed products, for ultrahazardous activities, and for trespass. (Recall from Chapter 3 that strict liability in torts is "liability that is imposed apart from any recovery on a theory that defendant knowingly or purposely interfered with a legally protected interest or was negligent."[7]) We consider cases from each of these topic areas. The cases are not considered in historical order. Instead, the first case shows an imaginative justice of the California Supreme Court developing a solution to holding producers of products accountable for injuries their products cause. Justice Traynor in a concurring opinion provides some important insights into justifications for holding producers accountable for injuries and simultaneously recognizing the difficulties plaintiffs would have in identifying a producer's negligence, which better serves the overall goal of torts to repair tortiously injured plaintiffs. Although Traynor's opinion on these issues was only a concurrence with the majority view, it came to dominate the law of product liability for decades.

Product Liability

Escola v. Coca Cola Bottling Co. of Fresno

Supreme Court of California

24 Cal.2d 453(1944)

Opinion: GIBSON, Chief Justice.

Plaintiff, a waitress in a restaurant, was injured when a bottle of Coca Cola broke in her hand. She alleged that defendant company, which had bottled and delivered the alleged defective bottle to her employer, was negligent in selling "bottles containing said beverage which

7 *Ibid.*, 554.

on account of excessive pressure of gas or by reason of some defect in the bottle was dangerous * * * and likely to explode." This appeal is from a judgment upon a jury verdict in favor of plaintiff.

Defendant's driver delivered several cases of Coca Cola to the restaurant, placing them on the floor, one on top of the other, under and behind the counter, where they remained at least thirty-six hours. Immediately before the accident, plaintiff picked up the top case and set it upon a near-by ice cream cabinet in front of and about three feet from the refrigerator. She then proceeded to take the bottles from the case with her right hand, one at a time, and put them into the refrigerator. Plaintiff testified that after she had placed three bottles in the refrigerator and had moved the fourth bottle about 18 inches from the case "it exploded in my hand." The bottle broke into two jagged pieces and inflicted a deep five-inch cut, severing blood vessels, nerves and muscles of the thumb and palm of the hand. [...]

One of defendant's drivers, called as a witness by plaintiff, testified that he had seen other bottles of Coca Cola in the past explode and had found broken bottles in the warehouse when he took the cases out, but that he did not know what made them blow up.

Plaintiff then rested her case, having announced to the court that being unable to show any specific acts of negligence she relied completely on the doctrine of res ipsa loquitur.

Defendant contends that the doctrine of res ipsa loquitur does not apply in this case, and that the evidence is insufficient to support the judgment.

Many jurisdictions have applied the doctrine in cases involving exploding bottles of carbonated beverages. [...]

Res ipsa loquitur does not apply unless (1) defendant had exclusive control of the thing causing the injury and (2) the accident is of such a nature that it ordinarily would not occur in the absence of negligence by the defendant. [...]

Many authorities state that the happening of the accident does not speak for itself where it took place some time after defendant had relinquished control of the instrumentality causing the injury. Under the more logical view, however, the doctrine may be applied upon the theory that defendant had control at the time of the alleged negligent act, although not at the time of the accident, provided plaintiff first proves that the condition of the instrumentality had not been changed after it left the defendant's possession. [...]

Upon an examination of the record, the evidence appears sufficient to support a reasonable inference that the bottle here involved was not damaged by any extraneous force after delivery to the restaurant by defendant. It follows, therefore, that the bottle was in some manner defective at the time defendant relinquished control, because sound and properly prepared bottles of carbonated liquids do not ordinarily explode when carefully handled.

[...] The question is whether under the evidence there was a probability that defendant was negligent in any of these respects. If so, the doctrine of res ipsa loquitur applies.

[...]

Although it is not clear in this case whether the explosion was caused by an excessive charge or a defect in the glass there is a sufficient showing that neither cause would ordinarily have been present if due care had been used. Further, defendant had exclusive control over both the charging and inspection of the bottles. Accordingly, all the requirements necessary to entitle plaintiff to rely on the doctrine of res ipsa loquitur to supply an inference of negligence are present.

[...] It is well settled, however, that when a defendant produces evidence to rebut the inference of negligence which arises upon application of the doctrine of res ipsa loquitur, it is ordinarily a question of fact for the jury to determine whether the inference has been dispelled. [...]

The judgment is affirmed.

SHENK, CURTIS, CARTER, and SCHAUER, JJ., concurred.

TRAYNOR, Justice.

I concur in the judgment, but I believe the manufacturer's negligence should no longer be singled out as the basis of a plaintiff's right to recover in cases like the present one. In my opinion it should now be recognized that a manufacturer incurs an absolute liability when an article that he has placed on the market, knowing that it is to be used without inspection, proves to have a defect that causes injury to human beings. MacPherson v. Buick Motor Co., (1916) established the principle, recognized by this court, that irrespective of privity of contract, the manufacturer is responsible for an injury caused by such an article to any person who comes in lawful contact with it ... In these cases the source of the manufacturer's liability was his negligence in the manufacturing process or in the inspection of component parts supplied by others. Even if there is no negligence, however, public policy demands that responsibility be fixed wherever it will most effectively reduce the hazards to life and health inherent in defective products that reach the market. It is evident that the manufacturer can anticipate some hazards and guard against the recurrence of others, as the public cannot. Those who suffer injury from defective products are unprepared to meet its consequences. The cost of an injury and the loss of time or health may be an overwhelming misfortune to the person injured, and a needless one, for the risk of injury can be insured by the manufacturer and distributed among the public as a cost of doing business. It is to the public interest to discourage the marketing of products having defects that are a menace to the public. If such products nevertheless find their way into the market it is to the public interest to place the responsibility for whatever injury they may cause upon the manufacturer, who, even if he is not negligent in the manufacture of the product, is responsible for its reaching the market. However intermittently such injuries may occur and however haphazardly they may strike, the risk of their occurrence is a constant risk and a general one. Against such a risk there should be general and constant protection and the manufacturer is best situated to afford such protection. [...]

[An] inference of negligence may be dispelled by an affirmative showing of proper care. If the evidence against the fact inferred is "clear, positive, uncontradicted, and of such a nature that it can not rationally be disbelieved, the court must instruct the jury that the nonexistence of the fact has been established as a matter of law." ... An injured person, however, is not ordinarily in a position to refute such evidence or identify the cause of the defect, for he can hardly be familiar with the manufacturing process as the manufacturer himself is. In leaving it to the jury to decide whether the inference has been dispelled, regardless of the evidence against it, the negligence rule approaches the rule of strict liability. It is needlessly circuitous to make negligence the basis of recovery and impose what is in reality liability without negligence. If public policy demands that a manufacturer of goods be responsible for their quality regardless of negligence there is no reason not to fix that responsibility openly. [...]

In the words of Judge Cardozo in the MacPherson case ...: "The dealer was indeed the one person of whom it might be said with some approach to certainty that by him the car would not be used. Yet the defendant would have us say that he was the one person whom it was under a legal duty to protect. The law does not lead us to so inconsequent a conclusion." While the defendant's negligence in the MacPherson case made it unnecessary for the court to base liability on warranty, Judge Cardozo's reasoning recognized the injured person as the real party in interest and effectively disposed of the theory that the liability of the manufacturer incurred by his warranty should apply only to the immediate purchaser. It thus paves the way for a standard of liability that would make the manufacturer guarantee the safety of his product even when there is no negligence.

This court and many others have extended protection according to such a standard to consumers of food products, taking the view that the right of a consumer injured by unwholesome food does not depend "upon the intricacies of the law of sales" and that the warranty of the manufacturer to the consumer in absence of privity of contract rests on public policy. [...]

As handicrafts have been replaced by mass production with its great markets and transportation facilities, the close relationship between the producer and consumer of a product has been altered. Manufacturing processes, frequently valuable secrets, are ordinarily either inaccessible to or beyond the ken of the general public. The consumer no longer has means or skill enough to investigate for himself the soundness of a product, even when it is not contained in a sealed package, and his erstwhile vigilance has been lulled by the steady efforts of manufacturers to build up confidence by advertising and marketing devices such as trade-marks. ... Consumers no longer approach products warily but accept them on faith, relying on the reputation of the manufacturer or the trade mark. ... Manufacturers have sought to justify that faith by increasingly high standards of inspection and a readiness to make good on defective products by way of replacements and refunds. ... The manufacturer's obligation to the consumer must keep pace with the changing relationship between them; it cannot be escaped because the marketing of a product has become so complicated as to require one or more intermediaries. Certainly there is greater reason to impose liability on the manufacturer than on the retailer who is but a conduit of a product that he is not himself able to test. [...]

The manufacturer's liability should, of course, be defined in terms of the safety of the product in normal and proper use, and should not extend to injuries that cannot be traced to the product as it reached the market.

(Citations omitted)

The Evolution of Liability for Injuries from Products:
From Warranties to *MacPherson v. Buick Motors* to *Escola v. Coca Cola*

Before *MacPherson*				
Manufacturer	**Wholesaler**	**Retailer**	**Consumer**	**C. injured**
Manufacturer ←	Wholesaler sues Mfr ←	Retailer sues wholesaler ←	Consumer must sue Retailer in contract warranty	
MacPherson v. Buick Motors				
Manufacturer ←——————			Consumer can directly sue Mfr in *negligence*	
Escola v. Coca Cola				
Manufacturer ←——————			Consumer can directly sue Mfr in *strict liability*	

This diagram represents how liability for injuries from products evolved from arising from a contractual duty to warrant the safety of products to being a doctrine that much better recognized who should be held accountable—the manufacturer of a product as Justice Traynor argues. The reasons for this were articulated in *Escola v. Coca Cola*.

I have inserted a case in which plaintiffs asserted that defendant driving a car and who suddenly suffers an unexpected convulsion should be strictly liable for injuries inflicted on plaintiffs because plaintiffs argued for an analogy with strict products liability. Defendant argued that the law did not hold a person accountable when unconscious from a sudden seizure; in short, he should not be held strictly liable for injuries he caused while unconscious. This California case shows that in the tort law, a person must have voluntarily committed a tort in negligence before being held accountable while driving a car. *Hammontree* is one case showing that the tort law has a voluntary act requirement. It does not have quite the same overall function in torts as it does in the criminal law (discussed in Chapter 3).

Hammontree v. Jenner

Court of Appeal, Second District, Division 1, California

20 Cal.App.3d 528 (1971)

Action for personal injuries and property damage sustained when automobile driven by defendant who claimed he had become unconscious during epileptic seizure crashed through the wall of the bicycle shop owned and operated by plaintiffs and struck one plaintiff. The Superior Court, Los Angeles County, Kenneth A. White, J., rendered judgment on jury verdict in favor of defendant, and plaintiffs appealed. The Court of Appeal, Lillie, J., held that defendant was not absolutely liable for injuries and property damage sustained. Affirmed.

LILLIE, Associate Justice.

Plaintiff Maxine Hammontree and her husband sued defendant for personal injuries and property damage arising out of an automobile accident. The cause was tried to a jury. Plaintiffs appeal from judgment entered on a jury verdict returned against them and in favor of the defendant.

The evidence shows that on the afternoon of April 25, 1967, defendant was driving his 1959 Chevrolet home from work; at the same time plaintiff Maxine Hammontree was working in a bicycle shop owned and operated by her and her husband; without warning defendant's car crashed through the wall of the shop, struck Maxine and caused personal injuries and damages to the shop.

Defendant claimed he became unconscious during an epileptic seizure losing control of his car. He did not recall the accident but his last recollection before it, was leaving a stop light after his last stop, and his first recollection after the accident was being taken out of his car in plaintiffs' shop. Defendant testified he has a medical history of epilepsy and knows of no other reason for his loss of consciousness except an epileptic seizure; prior to 1952 he had been examined by several neurologists whose conclusion was that the condition could be controlled and who placed him on medication; in 1952 he suffered a seizure while fishing; several days later he went to Dr. Benson Hyatt who diagnosed his condition as petit mal seizure and kept him on the same medication; thereafter he saw Dr. Hyatt every six months and then on a yearly basis several years prior to 1967; in 1953 he had another seizure, was told he was an epileptic and continued his medication; in 1954 Dr. Kershner prescribed dilantin and in 1955 Dr. Hyatt prescribed phelantin; from 1955 until the accident occurred (1967) defendant had used phelantin on a regular basis which controlled his condition; defendant has continued to take medication as prescribed by his physician and has done everything his doctors told him to do to avoid a seizure; he had no inkling or warning that he was about to have a seizure prior to the occurrence of the accident.

In 1955 or 1956 the Department of Motor Vehicles was advised that defendant was an epileptic and placed him on probation under which every six months he had to report to the doctor who was required to advise it in writing of defendant's condition. In 1960 his probation was changed to a once-a-year report.

Dr. Hyatt testified that during the times he saw defendant, and according to his history, defendant "was doing normally" and that he continued to take phelantin; that "(t)he purpose of the (phelantin) would be to react on the nervous system in such a way that where, without the medication, I would say to raise the threshold so that he would not be as subject to these episodes without the medication, so as not to have the seizures. He would not be having the seizures with the medication as he would without the medication compared to taking medication"; in a seizure it would be impossible for a person to drive and control an automobile; he believed it was safe for defendant to drive.

Appellants' contentions that the trial court erred in refusing to grant their motion for summary judgment on the issue of liability and their motion for directed verdict on the pleadings and counsel's opening argument are answered by the disposition of their third claim that the trial court committed prejudicial error in refusing to give their jury instruction on absolute liability.[1]

Under the present state of the law found in appellate authorities beginning with Waters v. Pacific Coast Dairy, Inc., … (driver rendered unconscious from sharp pain in left arm and shoulder) through Ford v. Carew & English, … (fainting spells from strained heart muscles), Zabunoff v. Walker, … 463 (sudden sneeze), and Tannyhill v. Pacific Motor Trans. Co. … (heart attack), the trial judge properly refused the instruction. The foregoing cases generally hold that liability of a driver, suddenly stricken by an illness rendering him unconscious, for injury resulting from an accident occurring during that time rests on principles of negligence. However, herein during the trial plaintiffs withdrew their claim of negligence and, after both parties rested and before jury argument, objected to the giving of any instructions on negligence electing to stand solely on the theory of absolute liability. The objection was overruled and the court refused plaintiffs' requested instruction after which plaintiffs waived both opening and closing jury arguments. […]

Appellants seek to have this court override the established law of this state which is dispositive of the issue before us as outmoded in today's social and economic structure, particularly in the light of the now recognized principles imposing liability upon the manufacturer, retailer and all distributive and vending elements and activities which bring a product to the consumer to his injury, on the basis of strict liability in tort expressed first in Justice Traynor's concurring opinion in Escola v. Coca Cola Bottling Co., and then in Greenman v. Yuba Power Products, Inc., Vandermark v. Ford Motor Co., and Elmore v. American Motors Corp. These authorities hold that "A manufacturer (or retailer) is strictly liable in tort when an article he places on the market, knowing that it is to be used without inspection for defects, proves to have a defect that causes injury to a human being." … Drawing a parallel with these products liability cases, appellants argue, with some degree of logic, that only the driver affected by a physical condition which could suddenly render him unconscious and who is aware of that condition can anticipate the hazards and foresee the dangers involved in his operation of a motor vehicle, and that the liability of those who by reason of seizure or heart failure or some other physical condition lose the ability to safely operate and control a motor vehicle resulting in injury to an innocent person should be predicated on strict liability.

We decline to superimpose the absolute liability of products liability cases upon drivers under the circumstances here. The theory on which those cases are predicated is that manufacturers, retailers and distributors of products are engaged in the business of distributing goods to the public and are an integral part of the over-all producing and marketing enterprise that should bear the cost of injuries from defective parts. … This policy hardly applies here and it is not enough to simply say, as do appellants, that the insurance carriers should be the ones to bear the cost of injuries to innocent victims on a strict liability basis. In Maloney v. Rath, … appellant urged that defendant's violation of a safety provision (defective brakes) of the Vehicle Code makes the violator strictly liable for damages caused by the violation. While reversing the judgment for defendant upon another ground, the California Supreme Court refused to apply the doctrine of strict liability to automobile drivers. The situation involved two users of the highway but the problems of fixing responsibility under a system of strict liability are as complicated in the instant case as those in Maloney v. Rath, and could only create uncertainty in the area of its concern. As stated in Maloney .. "To invoke a rule of strict liability on users of the streets and highways, however, without also establishing in substantial detail how the new rule should operate would only contribute confusion to the automobile accident problem. Settlement and claims adjustment procedures would become chaotic until the new rules were worked out on a case-by-case basis, and the hardships of delayed compensation would be seriously intensified. Only the Legislature, if it deems it wise to do so, can avoid such difficulties by enacting a comprehensive plan for the compensation of automobile accident victims in place of or in addition to the law of negligence."

The instruction tendered by appellants was properly refused for still another reason. Even assuming the merit of appellants' position under the facts of this case in which defendant knew he had a history of epilepsy, previously had suffered seizures and at the time of the accident was attempting to control the condition by medication, the instruction does not except from its ambit the driver who suddenly is stricken by an illness or physical condition which he had no reason whatever to anticipate and of which he had no prior knowledge.

The judgment is affirmed.

(Citations omitted)

Note

1 "When the evidence shows that a driver of a motor vehicle on a public street or highway loses his ability to safely operate and control such vehicle because of some seizure or health failure, that driver is nevertheless legally liable for all injuries and property damage which an innocent person may suffer as a proximate result of the defendant's inability to so control or operate his motor vehicle. "This is true even if you find the defendant driver had no warning of any such impending seizure or health failure."

Summary: Product Liability in Torts

1. A product is defective as marketed in the kind of way that makes it unreasonably dangerous for any of the following reasons:
    a. a flaw in the product that was present in the product at the time the defendant sold it;
    b. a failure by the producer or assembler of a product adequately to warn of a risk or hazard related to the way the product was designed; or
    c. a defective design.
2. A flaw in a product is defined as an abnormality or a condition that was unintended, and makes the product more dangerous than it would have been as intended (defendant is liable without proof that there was any negligence).
3. A product can be defective in the kind of way that makes it unreasonably dangerous by failing to warn or failing adequately to warn about a risk or hazard related to the way a product is designed (here plaintiff must show that defendant was negligent in failing to warn, because defendant knew or should have known about the risk in question).
4. Design defect (this is more complicated and not discussed).

The next case, *Sindell v. Abbott Labs*, is quite important for its treatment of causation and for it being a product liability case. However, to understand it, we need to introduce an additional distinction regarding causation; namely the difference between *general causation* and *specific causation*. This issue is especially pertinent when invisible entities like molecules, typically of pharmaceutical products, or other invisible entities, like toxic substances such as pesticides, cause harm.

The tort law has been modified to recognize this important difference. Recall that a plaintiff must show that defendant's action or product was the cause, and the proximate cause of plaintiff's harm. This idea works fine for many interactions between macro objects, such as car accidents or accidents between cars and trains. For invisible particles, this will not work. For large objects, we humans have some understanding of what one car can do to another car when they collide, or what a car can do to a person if it hits her or what a train can do to a person or car if it hits it.

However, with invisible particles, we lose the advantage of visually understanding what occurs when they are the source of harm. Consequently, the tort law doctrine for causation in such cases is that showing causation typically requires two steps:

> **General Causation** to establish that exposure to substance S *can cause* the kind of harm that plaintiff has experienced; and
>
> **Specific Causation** to show that exposures to substance S *did cause* the actual harm that plaintiff suffers from.

Thus, if someone has been exposed to benzene, an industrial chemical that causes various kinds of bone and other cancers, to receive compensation for exposure to benzene, a plaintiff would have to show she had contracted a disease typically caused by benzene, such as acute myelogenous leukemia and also show that her leukemia more likely than not had been caused by *defendant's* benzene. The *Sindell* plaintiffs faced having to show both general and specific causation from exposure to the pharmaceutical diethylstilbestrol (or DES, for short) *in utero*.

A physician at a Massachusetts obstetrical and gynecological clinic treated a number of young women in his clinic between the ages of 18 and perhaps 30 that had an unusual disease—vaginal or cervical cancer. Most women the age of his patients are highly unlikely to exhibit this disease until they are much older, perhaps typically after menopause. However, this evidence was quite solid; no scientific questions about it. As he investigated, he found that all or perhaps all but one of the women with the disease had been born to mothers who had taken the pharmaceutical DES, a synthetic estrogenic hormone, during their pregnancy with their daughters. This substance could and did cause cervical cancer in a subset of daughters about 20 years after their *in utero* exposure. In the case, it's noted that the manufacturers of DES knew, or should have known, that it was a carcinogenic substance.

General causation could be easily established for a tort suit to compensate the women for their diseases. However, under the tort law causation requirement, plaintiff must show that defendant's action or product caused *her* harm. Thus, even though general causation had been established, each plaintiff had to show specific causation in her own case and in particular whose pharmaceutical caused it. This was problematic, however, because DES was a generic drug and could be manufactured and sold by any firm that used the proper Food and Drug Administration (FDA) approved formula for it. With many firms selling DES nationwide and in California, plaintiffs could have considerable difficulty showing which defendant had made and sold the DES taken by each person's mother and exposed the women *in utero* to it.

When Judith Sindell and others brought their suit against several defendant pharmaceutical manufacturers, the firms immediately petitioned the court to remove the suit as a matter of law. The reason, an important element of causation could not be proven, even if the court accepted all that plaintiffs were alleging in their complaint; they could not show *which* firm manufactured the DES that each of their mothers took. Defendants requested that the case be ended because even accepting all the plaintiffs' claims, they could not establish a critical element. The trial court agreed; plaintiffs' cases were at an end. They had to appeal their lawsuit to higher-level appellate courts, ending in the California Supreme Court. For a graphic illustrating these issues, see the table in the appendix.

Read the following case carefully because it is an important high-water mark in addressing a new causal question that facts in the world put before courts for legal resolution. As you read it, what is the California Supreme Court's resolution to the causal issues it faces? What similarities and differences are there between *Sindell* and the *Summers* case you read earlier in this chapter?

Sindell v. Abbott Laboratories

Supreme Court of California

26 Cal.3d 588 (1980)

Opinion: MOSK, Justice.

This case involves a complex problem both timely and significant: may a plaintiff, injured as the result of a drug administered to her mother during pregnancy, who knows the type of drug involved but cannot identify the manufacturer of the precise product, hold liable for her injuries a maker of a drug produced from an identical formula?

Plaintiff Judith Sindell brought an action against eleven drug companies and Does 1 through 100, on behalf of herself and other women similarly situated. The complaint alleges as follows:

Between 1941 and 1971, defendants were engaged in the business of manufacturing, promoting, and marketing diethylstilbesterol (DES), a drug which is a synthetic compound of the female hormone estrogen. The drug was administered to plaintiff's mother and the mothers of the class she represents,[1] for the purpose of preventing miscarriage. […]

DES may cause cancerous vaginal and cervical growths in the daughters exposed to it before birth, because their mothers took the drug during pregnancy. The form of cancer from which these daughters suffer is known as adenocarcinoma, and it manifests itself after a minimum latent period of 10 or 12 years. It is a fast-spreading and deadly disease, and radical surgery is required to prevent it from spreading. DES also causes adenosis, precancerous vaginal and cervical growths which may spread to other areas of the body. The treatment for adenosis is cauterization, surgery, or cryosurgery. Women who suffer from this condition must be monitored by biopsy or colposcopic examination twice a year, a painful and expensive procedure. […]

During the period defendants marketed DES, they knew or should have known that it was a carcinogenic substance, that there was a grave danger after varying periods of latency it would cause cancerous and precancerous growths in the daughters of the mothers who took it, and that it was ineffective to prevent miscarriage. Nevertheless, defendants continued to advertise and market the drug as a miscarriage preventative. They failed to test DES for efficacy and safety; the tests performed by others, upon which they relied, indicated that it was not safe or effective. In violation of the authorization of the Food and Drug Administration, defendants marketed DES on an unlimited basis rather than as an experimental drug, and they failed to warn of its potential danger.[2]

Because of defendants' advertised assurances that DES was safe and effective to prevent miscarriage, plaintiff was exposed to the drug prior to her birth. She became aware of the danger from such exposure within one year of the time she filed her complaint. As a result of the DES ingested by her mother, plaintiff developed a malignant bladder tumor which was removed by surgery. She suffers from adenosis and must constantly be monitored by biopsy or colposcopy to insure early warning of further malignancy.

The first cause of action alleges that defendants were jointly and individually negligent in that they manufactured, marketed and promoted DES as a safe and efficacious drug to prevent miscarriage, without adequate testing or warning, and without monitoring or reporting its effects.

[…]

Plaintiff seeks compensatory damages of $1 million and punitive damages of $10 million for herself. For the members of her class, she prays for equitable relief in the form of an order that defendants warn physicians and others of the danger of DES and the necessity of performing certain tests to determine the presence of disease caused by the drug, and that they establish free clinics in California to perform such tests.

Defendants demurred to the complaint. [Defendants' demurrer was granted because of plaintiffs' inability to identify who manufactured the drug responsible for her injures.]… This appeal involves only five of ten defendants named in the complaint. […]

[1] We begin with the proposition that, as a general rule, the imposition of liability depends upon a showing by the plaintiff that his or her injuries were caused by the act of the defendant or by an instrumentality under the defendant's control. The rule applies whether the injury resulted from an accidental event … or from the use of a defective product. […]

There are, however, exceptions to this rule. Plaintiff's complaint suggests several bases upon which defendants may be held liable for her injuries even though she cannot demonstrate the name of the manufacturer which produced the DES actually taken by her mother. The first of these theories, classically illustrated by Summers v. Tice (1948) ..., places the burden of proof of causation upon tortious defendants in certain circumstances. The second basis of liability emerging from the complaint is that defendants acted in concert to cause injury to plaintiff. There is a third and novel approach to the problem, sometimes called the theory of "enterprise liability," but which we prefer to designate by the more accurate term of "industry-wide" liability,[9] which might obviate the necessity for identifying the manufacturer of the injury-causing drug. We shall conclude that these doctrines, as previously interpreted, may not be applied to hold defendants liable under the allegations of this complaint. However, we shall propose and adopt a fourth basis for permitting the action to be tried, grounded upon an extension of the Summers doctrine.

I

Plaintiff places primary reliance upon cases which hold that if a party cannot identify which of two or more defendants caused an injury, the burden of proof may shift to the defendants to show that they were not responsible for the harm. This principle is sometimes referred to as the "alternative liability" theory.

The celebrated case of Summers v. Tice, supra, … a unanimous opinion of this court, best exemplifies the rule. In Summers, the plaintiff was injured when two hunters negligently shot in his direction. It could not be determined which of them had fired the shot which actually caused the injury to the plaintiff's eye, but both defendants were nevertheless held jointly and severally liable for the whole of the damages. We reasoned that both were wrongdoers, both were negligent toward the plaintiff, and that it would be unfair to require plaintiff to isolate the defendant responsible, because if the one pointed out were to escape liability, the other might also, and the plaintiff-victim would be shorn of any remedy. In these circumstances, we held, the burden of proof shifted to the defendants, "each to absolve himself if he can" [...]

In Summers, we relied upon Ybarra v. Spangard (1944). ... There, the plaintiff was injured while he was unconscious during the course of surgery. He sought damages against several doctors and a nurse who attended him while he was unconscious. We held that it would be unreasonable to require him to identify the particular defendant who had performed the alleged negligent act because he was unconscious at the time of the injury and the defendants exercised control over the instrumentalities which caused the harm. Therefore, under the doctrine of res ipsa loquitur, an inference of negligence arose that defendants were required to meet by explaining their conduct.

The rule developed in Summers has been embodied in the Restatement of Torts. [...]

In Summers, the circumstances of the accident themselves precluded an explanation of its cause. To be sure, Summers states that defendants are "(o)rdinarily ... in a far better position to offer evidence to determine which one caused the injury" than a plaintiff ..., but the decision does not determine that this "ordinary" situation was present. Neither the facts nor the language of the opinion indicate that the two defendants, simultaneously shooting in the same direction, were in a better position than the plaintiff to ascertain whose shot caused the injury. As the opinion acknowledges, it was impossible for the trial court to determine whether the shot which entered the plaintiff's eye came from the gun of one defendant or the other. Nevertheless, burden of proof was shifted to the defendants.

[...]

It is important to observe, however, that while defendants do not have means superior to plaintiff to identify the maker of the precise drug taken by her mother, they may in some instances be able to prove that they did not manufacture the injury-causing substance. In the present case, for example, one of the original defendants was dismissed from the action upon proof that it did not manufacture DES until after plaintiff was born.

Thus we conclude that the fact defendants do not have greater access to information which might establish the identity of the manufacturer of the DES which injured plaintiff does not per se prevent application of the Summers rule.

Nevertheless, plaintiff may not prevail in her claim that the Summers rationale should be employed to fix the whole liability for her injuries upon defendants, at least as those principles have previously been applied.[15] There is an important difference between the situation involved in Summers and the present case. There, all the parties who were or could have been responsible for the harm to the plaintiff were joined as defendants. Here, by contrast, there are approximately 200 drug companies which made DES, any of which might have manufactured the injury-producing drug.[16]

Defendants maintain that, while in Summers there was a 50 percent chance that one of the two defendants was responsible for the plaintiff's injuries, here since any one of 200 companies which manufactured DES might have made the product which harmed plaintiff, there is no rational basis upon which to infer that any defendant in this action caused plaintiff's injuries, nor even a reasonable possibility that they were responsible.[17]

These arguments are persuasive if we measure the chance that any one of the defendants supplied the injury-causing drug by the number of possible tortfeasors. In such a context, the possibility that any of the five defendants supplied the DES to plaintiff's mother is so remote that it would be unfair to require each defendant to exonerate itself. There may be a substantial likelihood that none of the five defendants joined in the action made the DES which caused the injury, and that the offending producer not named would escape liability altogether. While we propose, infra, an adaptation of the rule in Summers which will substantially overcome these difficulties, defendants appear to be correct that the rule, as previously applied, cannot relieve plaintiff of the burden of proving the identity of the manufacturer which made the drug causing her injuries.

II

The second principle upon which plaintiff relies is the so-called "concert of action" theory.

[...] The elements of this doctrine are prescribed in section 876 of the Restatement of Torts. The section provides, "For harm resulting to a third person from the tortious conduct of another, one is subject to liability if he (a) does a tortious act in concert with the other or pursuant to a common design with him, or (b) knows that the other's conduct constitutes a breach of duty and gives substantial assistance or encouragement to the other so to conduct himself, or (c) gives substantial assistance to the other in accomplishing a tortious result and his own conduct, separately considered, constitutes a breach of duty to the third person." With respect to this doctrine, Prosser states that "those who, in pursuance of a common plan or design to commit a tortious act, actively take part in it, or further it by cooperation or request, or who lend aid or encouragement to the wrongdoer, or ratify and adopt his acts done for their benefit, are equally liable with him. (P) Express agreement is not necessary, and all that is required is that there be a tacit understanding. ..." (Prosser, Law of torts (4th ed. 1971).)

[...]

It is difficult to understand how these allegations can form the basis of a cause of action for wrongful conduct by defendants, acting in concert. The formula for DES is a scientific constant. [...]

What the complaint appears to charge is defendants' parallel or imitative conduct in that they relied upon each others' testing and promotion methods. But such conduct describes a common practice in industry: a producer avails himself of the experience and methods of others making the same or similar products. Application of the concept of concert of action to this situation would expand the doctrine far beyond its intended scope and would render virtually any manufacturer liable for the defective products of an entire industry, even if it could be demonstrated that the product which caused the injury was not made by the defendant .[...]

Thus, there was no concert of action among defendants within the meaning of that doctrine.

III

A third theory upon which plaintiff relies is the concept of industry-wide liability, or according to the terminology of the parties, "enterprise liability." This theory was suggested in Hall v. E. I. Du Pont de Nemours & Co., Inc. (E.D.N.Y.1972). ... In that case, plaintiffs were 13 children injured by the explosion of blasting caps in 12 separate incidents which occurred in 10 different states between 1955 and 1959. The defendants were six blasting cap manufacturers, comprising virtually the entire blasting cap industry in the United States, and their trade association. [...]

The court reasoned ... that defendants, acting independently, had adhered to an industry-wide standard with regard to the safety features of blasting caps, that they had in effect delegated some functions of safety investigation and design, such as labelling, to their trade association, and that there was industry-wide cooperation in the manufacture and design of blasting caps. In these circumstances, the evidence supported a conclusion that all the defendants jointly controlled the risk. Thus, if plaintiffs could establish by a preponderance of the evidence that the caps were manufactured by one of the defendants, the burden of proof as to causation would shift to all the defendants. ... [This] theory of liability applied to industries composed of a small number of units, and that what would be fair and reasonable with regard to an industry of five or ten producers might be manifestly unreasonable if applied to a decentralized industry composed of countless small producers.[23][...]

We decline to apply this theory in the present case. At least 200 manufacturers produced DES; Hall, which involved 6 manufacturers representing the entire blasting cap industry in the United States, cautioned against application of the doctrine espoused therein to a large number of producers. Moreover, in Hall, the conclusion that the defendants jointly controlled the risk was based upon allegations that they had delegated some functions relating to safety to a trade association. There are no such allegations here, and we have concluded above that plaintiff has failed to allege liability on a concert of action theory.

Equally important, the drug industry is closely regulated by the Food and Drug Administration, which actively controls the testing and manufacture of drugs and the method by which they are marketed, including the contents of warning labels. To a considerable degree, therefore, the standards followed by drug manufacturers are suggested or compelled by the government. Adherence to those standards cannot, of course, absolve a manufacturer of liability to which it would otherwise be subject. (Stevens v. Parke, Davis & Co. (1973).) But since the government plays such a pervasive role in formulating the criteria for the testing and marketing of drugs, it would be unfair to impose upon a manufacturer liability for injuries resulting from the use of a drug which it did not supply simply because it followed the standards of the industry.

IV

If we were confined to the theories of Summers and Hall, we would be constrained to hold that the judgment must be sustained. Should we require that plaintiff identify the manufacturer which supplied the DES used by her mother or that all DES manufacturers be joined in the action, she would effectively be precluded from any recovery. ... There are, however, forceful arguments in favor of holding that plaintiff has a cause of action.

In our contemporary complex industrialized society, advances in science and technology create fungible goods which may harm consumers and which cannot be traced to any specific producer. The response of the courts can be either to adhere rigidly to prior doctrine, denying recovery to those injured by such products, or to fashion remedies to meet these changing needs. Just as Justice Traynor in his landmark concurring opinion in Escola v. Coca Cola Bottling Company (1944) ..., recognized that in an era of mass production and complex marketing methods the traditional standard of negligence was insufficient to govern the obligations of manufacturer to consumer, so should we acknowledge that some adaptation of the rules of causation and liability may be appropriate in these recurring circumstances. The Restatement comments that modification of the Summers rule may be necessary in a situation like that before us.

The most persuasive reason for finding plaintiff states a cause of action is that advanced in Summers: as between an innocent plaintiff and negligent defendants, the latter should bear the cost of the injury. Here, as in Summers, plaintiff is not at fault in failing to provide evidence of causation, and although the absence of such evidence is not attributable to the defendants either, their conduct in marketing a drug the effects of which are delayed for many years played a significant role in creating the unavailability of proof.

From a broader policy standpoint, defendants are better able to bear the cost of injury resulting from the manufacture of a defective product. As was said by Justice Traynor in Escola, "(t)he cost of an injury and the loss of time or health may be an overwhelming misfortune to the person injured, and a needless one, for the risk of injury can be insured by the manufacturer and distributed among the public as a cost of doing business." … The manufacturer is in the best position to discover and guard against defects in its products and to warn of harmful effects; thus, holding it liable for defects and failure to warn of harmful effects will provide an incentive to product safety. … These considerations are particularly significant where medication is involved, for the consumer is virtually helpless to protect himself from serious, sometimes permanent, sometimes fatal, injuries caused by deleterious drugs.

Where, as here, all defendants produced a drug from an identical formula and the manufacturer of the DES which caused plaintiff's injuries cannot be identified through no fault of plaintiff, a modification of the rule of Summers is warranted. … [but], an undiluted Summers rationale is inappropriate to shift the burden of proof of causation to defendants.

[…] [W]e hold it to be reasonable in the present context to measure the likelihood that any of the defendants supplied the product which allegedly injured plaintiff by the percentage which the DES sold by each of them for the purpose of preventing miscarriage bears to the entire production of the drug sold by all for that purpose. Plaintiff asserts in her briefs that Eli Lilly and Company and 5 or 6 other companies produced 90 percent of the DES marketed. If at trial this is established to be the fact, then there is a corresponding likelihood that this comparative handful of producers manufactured the DES which caused plaintiff's injuries, and only a 10 percent likelihood that the offending producer would escape liability.[28]

If plaintiff joins in the action the manufacturers of a substantial share of the DES which her mother might have taken, the injustice of shifting the burden of proof to defendants to demonstrate that they could not have made the substance which injured plaintiff is significantly diminished. While 75 to 80 percent of the market is suggested as the requirement by the Fordham Comment, we hold only that a substantial percentage is required.

The presence in the action of a substantial share of the appropriate market also provides a ready means to apportion damages among the defendants. Each defendant will be held liable for the proportion of the judgment represented by its share of that market unless it demonstrates that it could not have made the product which caused plaintiff's injuries. In the present case, as we have seen, one DES manufacturer was dismissed from the action upon filing a declaration that it had not manufactured DES until after plaintiff was born. Once plaintiff has met her burden of joining the required defendants, they in turn may cross-complaint against other DES manufacturers, not joined in the action, which they can allege might have supplied the injury-causing product.

Under this approach, each manufacturer's liability would approximate its responsibility for the injuries caused by its own products. Some minor discrepancy in the correlation between market share and liability is inevitable; therefore, a defendant may be held liable for a somewhat different percentage of the damage than its share of the appropriate market would justify. It is probably impossible, with the passage of time, to determine market share with mathematical exactitude. But just as a jury cannot be expected to determine the precise relationship between fault and liability in applying the doctrine of comparative fault ... or partial indemnity, ... the difficulty of apportioning damages among the defendant producers in exact relation to their market share does not seriously militate against the rule we adopt. As we said in Summers with regard to the liability of independent tortfeasors, where a correct division of liability cannot be made "the trier of fact may make it the best it can."

We are not unmindful of the practical problems involved in defining the market and determining market share, ... but these are largely matters of proof which properly cannot be determined at the pleading stage of these proceedings. Defendants urge that it would be both unfair and contrary to public policy to hold them liable for plaintiff's injuries in the absence of proof that one of them supplied the drug responsible for the damage. Most of their arguments, however, are based upon the assumption that one manufacturer would be held responsible for the products of another or for those of all other manufacturers if plaintiff ultimately prevails. But under the rule we adopt, each manufacturer's liability for an injury would be approximately equivalent to the damages caused by the DES it manufactured.[30] The judgments are reversed.

BIRD, C. J., and NEWMAN and WHITE,* JJ., concur.

RICHARDSON, Justice, dissenting.

I respectfully dissent. In these consolidated cases the majority adopts a wholly new theory which contains these ingredients: The plaintiffs were not alive at the time of the commission of the tortious acts. They sue a generation later. They are permitted to receive substantial damages from multiple defendants without any proof that any defendant caused or even probably caused plaintiffs' injuries.

Although the majority purports to change only the required burden of proof by shifting it from plaintiffs to defendants, the effect of its holding is to guarantee that plaintiffs will prevail on the causation issue because defendants are no more capable of disproving factual causation than plaintiffs are of proving it. "Market share" liability thus represents a new high water mark in tort law. ... In my view, the majority's departure from traditional tort doctrine is unwise.

The applicable principles of causation are very well established. A leading torts scholar, Dean Prosser, has authoritatively put it this way: "An essential element of the plaintiff's cause of action for negligence, or for that matter for any other tort, is that there be some reasonable connection between the act or omission of the defendant and the damage which the plaintiff has suffered." [...]

The [majority view] is directly contrary to long established tort principles. Once again, in the words of Dean Prosser, the applicable rule is: "(Plaintiff) must introduce evidence which affords a reasonable basis for the conclusion that it is more likely than not that the conduct of the defendant was a substantial factor in bringing about the result. A mere possibility of such causation is not enough; and when the matter remains *one* of pure speculation or conjecture, or the probabilities are at best evenly balanced, it becomes the duty of the court to direct a verdict for the defendant." [...]

[The majority's position is], "each manufacturer's liability for an injury would be approximately equivalent to the damages caused by the DES it manufactured." In other words, because each defendant's liability is proportionate to its market share, supposedly "each manufacturer's liability would approximate its responsibility for the injuries caused by his own products." ... However, ... are not so easily ducked, for they relate not to evidentiary matters but to the fundamental question of liability itself.

Additionally, it is readily apparent that "market share" liability will fall unevenly and disproportionately upon those manufacturers who are amenable to suit in California. [...]

Furthermore, several other important policy considerations persuade me that the majority holding is both inequitable and improper. ... Plaintiff in the ordinary tort case must take a chance that defendant can be reached and can respond financially. On what principle should those plaintiffs who wholly fail to prove any causation, an essential element of the traditional tort cause of action, be rewarded by being offered both a wider selection of potential defendants and a greater opportunity for recovery?

The majority attempts to justify its new liability on the ground that defendants herein are "better able to bear the cost of injury resulting from the manufacture of a defective product." ... This "deep pocket" theory of liability, fastening liability on defendants presumably because they are rich, has understandable popular appeal and might be tolerable in a case disclosing substantially stronger evidence of causation than herein appears. But as a general proposition, a defendant's wealth is an unreliable indicator of fault, and should play no part, at least consciously, in the legal analysis of the problem. In the absence of proof that a particular defendant caused or at least probably caused plaintiff's injuries, a defendant's ability to bear the cost thereof is no more pertinent to the underlying issue of liability than its "substantial" share of the relevant market. [...]

An important and substantial countervailing public policy in defendants' favor was very recently expressed in a similar DES case, ... "Application of the comments to the Restatement Second of Torts, section 402A, to this situation compels a rejection of the imposition of liability. As the comment states, '... It is also true in particular of many new or experimental drugs as to which, because of lack of time and opportunity for sufficient medical experience, there can be no assurance of safety, or perhaps even of purity of ingredients, but such experience as there is justifies the marketing and use of the drug notwithstanding a medically recognizable risk. The seller of such products, again, with the qualification that they are properly prepared and marketed, and proper warning is given, where the situation calls for it, is not to be held to strict liability for unfortunate consequences attending their use, merely because he has undertaken to supply the public with an apparently useful and desirable product, attended with a known but apparently reasonable risk.' [...]"

In the present case the majority imposes liability more than 20 years after ingestion of drugs which at the time they were used, after careful testing, had the full approval of the United States Food and Drug Administration. It seems to me that liability in the manner created by the majority must inevitably inhibit, if not the research or development, at least the dissemination of new pharmaceutical drugs. Such a result, as explained by the Restatement, is wholly inconsistent with traditional tort theory. [...]

I am not unmindful of the serious medical consequences of plaintiffs' injuries, and the equally serious implications to the class which she purports to represent. In balancing the various policy considerations, however, I also observe that the incidence of vaginal cancer among "DES daughters" has been variously estimated at one-tenth of 1 percent to four-tenths of 1 percent. (13 Suffolk L.Rev., supra.) These facts raise some penetrating questions. Ninety-nine plus percent of "DES daughters" have never developed cancer. Must a drug manufacturer to escape this blanket liability wait for a generation of testing before it may disseminate drugs? If a drug has beneficial purposes for the majority of users but harmful side effects are later revealed for a small fraction of consumers, will the manufacturer be absolutely liable? If adverse medical consequences, wholly unknown to the most careful and meticulous of present scientists, surface in two or three generations, will similar liability be imposed? In my opinion, common sense and reality combine to warn that a "market share" theory goes too far. Legally, it expects too much.

I believe that the scales of justice tip against imposition of this new liability because of the foregoing elements of unfairness to some defendants who may have had nothing whatever to do with causing any injury, the unwarranted preference created for this particular class of plaintiffs, the violence done to traditional tort principles by the drastic expansion of liability proposed, the injury threatened to the public interest in continued unrestricted basic medical research as stressed by the Restatement, and the other reasons heretofore expressed.

The majority's decision effectively makes the entire drug industry (or at least its California members) an insurer of all injuries attributable to defective drugs of uncertain or unprovable origin, including those injuries manifesting themselves a generation later, ... I would affirm the judgments of dismissal.

(Citations omitted)

CLARK and MANUEL, JJ., concur.

Notes

1 The plaintiff class alleged consists of "girls and women who are residents of California and who have been exposed to DES before birth and who may or may not know that fact or the dangers" to which they were exposed. Defendants are also sued as representatives of a class of drug manufacturers which sold DES after 1941.

2 It is alleged also that defendants failed to determine if there was any means to avoid or treat the effects of DES upon the daughters of women exposed to it during pregnancy, and failed to monitor the carcinogenic effects of the drug.

9 The term "enterprise liability" is sometimes used broadly to mean that losses caused by an enterprise should be borne by it. (Klemme, Enterprise Liability Theory of Torts (1976) 47 Colo. L.Rev. 153, 158.)

15 Plaintiff relies upon three older cases for the proposition that the burden of proof may be shifted to defendants to explain the cause of an accident even if less than all of them are before the court. (Benson v. Ross (1906); Moore v. Foster (1938); Oliver v. Miles (1927).) These cases do not relate to the shifting of the burden of proof; rather, they imposed liability upon one of two or more joint tortfeasors on the ground that they acted in concert in committing a negligent act. This theory of concerted action as a basis for defendants' liability will be discussed infra. In Summers, we stated that these cases were "straining" the concept of concerted action and that the "more reasonable" basis for holding defendants jointly liable when more than one of them had committed a tort and plaintiff could not establish the identity of the party who had caused the damage was the danger that otherwise two negligent parties might be exonerated.

16 According to the Restatement, the burden of proof shifts to the defendants only if the plaintiff can demonstrate that all defendants acted tortiously and that the harm resulted from the conduct of

one of them. (Rest.2d Torts, § 433B.) It goes on to state that the rule thus far has been applied only where all the actors involved are joined as defendants and where the conduct of all is simultaneous in time, but cases might arise in which some modification of the rule would be necessary if one of the actors is or cannot be joined, or because of the effects of lapse of time, or other circumstances.

17 Defendants claim further that the effect of shifting the burden of proof to them to demonstrate that they did not manufacture the DES which caused the injury would create a rebuttable presumption that one of them made the drug taken by plaintiff's mother, and that this presumption would deny them due process because there is no rational basis for the inference.

23 In discussing strict liability, the Hall court mentioned the drug industry, stating, "In cases where manufacturers have more experience, more information, and more control over the risky properties of their products than do drug manufacturers, courts have applied a broader concept of foreseeability which approaches the enterprise liability rationale."

28 The Fordham Comment explains the connection between percentage of market share and liability as follows: "[I]f X Manufacturer sold one-fifth of all the DES prescribed for pregnancy and identification could be made in all cases, X would be the sole defendant in approximately one-fifth of all cases and liable for all the damages in those cases. Under alternative liability, X would be joined in all cases in which identification could not be made, but liable for only one-fifth of the total damages in these cases. X would pay the same amount either way. Although the correlation is not, in practice, perfect [footnote omitted], it is close enough so that defendants' objections on the ground of fairness lose their value." (Fordham Comment, supra, at p. 994.)

30 The dissent concludes by implying the problem will disappear if the Legislature appropriates funds "for the education, identification, and screening of persons exposed to DES." While such a measure may arguably be helpful in the abstract, it does not address the issue involved here: damages for injuries which have been or will be suffered. Nor, as a principle, do we see any justification for shifting the financial burden for such damages from drug manufacturers to the taxpayers of California.

The court's solution was "market share liability." Plaintiffs must join, or bring into the case, all the manufacturers who were making DES during the time their mothers had been taking DES while pregnant. Liability for injuries plaintiffs had suffered would then be allocated to those firms on the basis of their market share of the DES sales they had at the time. Of course, there would be arguments between defendants about who had what market share during the critical period. Some companies may have had small market shares, some may have large market shares, and others intermediate shares. Compensation to individual plaintiffs would be divided up based on a company's market share at the time. If company A had 5%, there might be a calculation for the total costs of injuries for all affected plaintiffs, and then each company would make a contribution into a total pool of needed funding that would then be divided among the plaintiffs.

The attractive feature of the court's solution is that it mimics how causation would have been understood if there had been a god's-eye view of the causal path of the pills. For instance, if Abbott Labs had manufactured 10% of the DES sold in California, another lab 40%, a third 35%, and a fourth one 15%, and the pills could be traced to causing each woman's cervical/vaginal cancer, this would have approximated the causal contribution of each company, *if it could have been traced*. One can imagine scenarios in which this might not have been ideally realized, but it is a close approximation since actual specific causation for each individual could not be established by a preponderance of the evidence.

Of course, if a particular manufacturer could, for example, show legitimately that it was out of the DES business when the mothers were purchasing DES, they would have no liability. Indeed, the court reports that at least one firm was able to establish this point. In that instance, other companies would have to pick up the bill.

We find in this case an instance in which the court was quite innovative in solving a potential legal problem presented by the facts of the world along with an unusual and delayed disease that did not show up until about 20 years after exposures to this potent carcinogen. If existing tort law rules had been rigidly adhered to, plaintiffs likely would have received no compensation or only a small percentage of what they were legitimately entitled to and wrongfully acting companies would have largely escaped liability for the harm they had clearly caused this group of women. The court might have reasoned that as between innocent plaintiffs and liable manufacturers, the justice of the case was straightforward (recall the discussion of insanity and eggshell skull plaintiffs on this justice issue). The court clearly solved a legal problem presented by causal difficulties that the world had posed. However, if the court had merely rested its legal efforts on preexisting legal rules, plaintiffs likely would have received little or nothing for wrongfully inflicted harms.

Ultrahazardous Activities

There are roughly two other categories of activities for which defendants are held accountable in strict liability if they cause harm to others: ultrahazardous or abnormally dangerous activities, and trespass. The background for holding defendants strictly liable for abnormally dangerous activities was provided by an 1868 English case, *Rylands v. Fletcher*. During the early stages of the Industrial Revolution often small landowners would build water mills on their property to provide services to others in the area. The defendants in *Rylands v. Fletcher* built a dam on their property to create a reservoir as a water supply for a mill. They hired engineers of the time to construct the reservoir. As they began to fill it, the weight of the water created pressure and weight on the bottom of the lake that in turn caused the ground over a disused and abandoned mine shaft to collapse, flooding a neighbor's property. The trial court found for defendant. However, on appeal and on analogy with trespassing cattle and dangerous animals, that the defendants had trespassed on the neighbor's property with a dangerous object, which was upheld by an intermediate court. In 1868 the House of Lords, at the time the highest legal court in England, addressed and endorsed the issue as decided for plaintiff by the Exechequer Chamber as an abnormally dangerous activity.

> We think that the true rule of law is, that the person who for his own purposes brings on his lands, and collects and keeps there anything likely to do mischief if it escapes, must keep it at his peril and, if he does not do so, is prima facie answerable for all the damage which is the natural consequence of its escape. He can excuse himself by showing that the escape

> was owing to the plaintiff's default: or perhaps that the escape was the consequence of vis major, or the act of God. ...[8]

Thus, the court imposed strict liability on the defendants for bringing a hazardous object (reservoir) on their lands from which water escaped and harmed plaintiffs. *Rylands v. Fletcher* follows what has come to be called the "caged tiger" rule: if one keeps a dangerous animal (or thing) on one's property and it escapes and harms a person through no fault of the victim, the owner is held strictly liable.

The Rylands v. Fletcher case had considerable influence even in the United States, at least until a New York court considered the issues in *Losee v. Buchanan*. The latter court, considering a boiler brought onto defendant's land that exploded and harmed the plaintiff, held that defendant should not to be subject to strict liability, but held accountability in negligence. The discussion reveals a difference, probably cultural, between the United States and the United Kingdom, with this US court seemingly more committed to fostering budding industries. As you read this case, what considerations move the court to impose a reduced level of liability for exploding boilers than the English court imposed on escaping water from a reservoir?

A more recent list of ultrahazardous activities would include water collected in a dangerous place, explosives, inflammable liquids stored in the midst of a city, blasting, pile driving, crop dusting, drilling wells, excavations letting in the sea, factories emitting smoke, or dust or noxious gases in the midst of a town. According to the *Restatement of Torts,* an ultrahazardous activity is one that "necessarily involves a risk of serious harm to the person, land or chattels of others which cannot be eliminated by the exercise of the utmost care" and "is not a matter of common usage."

The policy for ultrahazardous activities tends to be applied

> where the defendant's activity is unusual and abnormal in the community, and the danger which it threatens to others is unduly great—and particularly where the danger will be great even though the enterprise is conducted with every possible precaution. The basis of the liability is the defendant's intentional behavior in exposing those in his vicinity to such a risk (emphasis added)". [Such conduct is sufficiently] ... socially unreasonable that the defendant is not allowed to carry it on without making good any actual harm which it does to his neighbors. ... [Moreover], Defendant is in a better position to administer the unusual risks by passing them on to the public than is the innocent victim.[9]

Despite the *Rylands v. Fletcher* example from the United Kingdom, a New York court about the same time declined to hold defendants strictly accountable for an exploding boiler that harmed a person. As you read through the next case, according to the court, what accounts for the differences?

---

8 The House of Lords, at the time, the highest court of appeals in the United Kingdom endorsed the decision by the Court of Exchequer Chamber, (1866. E.R. 1. Ex. 265),(as expressed in the quotation) reported as *Rylands v. Fletcher, House of Lords, 1868, L.R, 3 H.L. 330,*

9 *Ibid.*, 537.

Losee v. Buchanan

Court of Appeals of New York

6 Sickels 476 (1873)

Opinion: EARL, C.: Upon the first trial of this action, the presiding judge … held that the … defendants were liable irrespective of negligence, and excluded all evidence to show that they were not guilty of negligence. For this error, upon appeal to the General Term, the judgment was reversed and new trial granted, the court holding that the defendants could be made liable only by proof against them of negligence. … The plaintiff claimed, as he did upon the first trial, that the defendants were liable without the proof of any negligence, and requested the justice so to rule, and the refusal of the justice to comply with this request raises the principal question for our consideration upon this appeal. […]

The claim on the part of the plaintiff is, that the casting of the boiler upon his premises by the explosion was a direct trespass upon his right to the undisturbed possession and occupation of his premises, and that the defendants are liable just as they would have been for any other wrongful entry and trespass upon his premises.

I do not believe this claim to be well founded, and I will briefly examine the authorities upon which mainly an attempt is made to sustain it.

In Farrand v. Marshall (21 Barb., 409) it was held that a man may dig on his own land, but not so near that of his neighbor as to cause the land of the latter to fall into his pit, thus transferring a portion of another man's land to his own. This is upon the principle that every man has the natural right to the use of his land in the situation in which it was placed by nature, surrounded and protected by the soil of the adjacent lots. […]

In the case of McKeon v. Lee (4 Rob. Superior Court R., 449) it was held, that the defendant had no right to operate a steam engine and other machinery upon his premises so as to cause the vibration and shaking of plaintiff's adjoining buildings to such an extent as to endanger and injure them. This case was decided upon the law of nuisances. It was held that the engine and machinery, in the mode in which they were operated, were a nuisance, and the decision has been affirmed at this term of this court. The decision in this case, and in scores of similar cases to be found in the books, is far from an authority that one should be held liable for the accidental explosion of a steam boiler which was in no sense a nuisance.

We are also cited to a class of cases holding the owners of animals responsible for injuries done by them. There is supposed to be a difference as to responsibility between animals mansuetae naturae and ferae naturae. As to the former, in which there can be an absolute right of property, the owner is bound at common law to take care that they do not stray upon the lands of another, and he is liable for any trespass they may commit, and it is altogether immaterial whether their escape is purely accidental or due to negligence. As to the latter, which are of a fierce nature [**like caged tigers**], the owner is bound to take care of them and keep them under control, so that they can do no injury. But the liability in each case is upon the same principle. The former have a known, natural disposition to stray, and hence the owner knowing this disposition is supposed to be in fault if he do not restrain them and keep them under control. … [For both domestic and wild] animals, the owner can usually restrain and keep them under control, and if he will keep them he must do so. If he does not, he is responsible for any damage which their well-known disposition leads them to commit. […]

By becoming a member of civilized society, I am compelled to give up many of my natural rights, but I receive more than a compensation from the surrender by every other man of the same rights, and the security, advantage and protection which the laws give me. So, too, the general rules that I may have the exclusive and undisturbed use and possession of my real estate, and that I must so use my real estate as not to injure my neighbor, are much modified by the exigencies of the social state. We must have factories, machinery, dams, canals and railroads. They are demanded by the manifold wants of mankind, and lay at the basis of all our civilization. If I have any of these upon my lands, and they are not a nuisance and are not so managed as to become such, I am not responsible for any damage they accidentally and unavoidably do my neighbor. He receives his compensation for such damage by the general good, in which he shares, and the right which he has to place the same things upon his lands. I may not place or keep a nuisance upon my land to the damage of my neighbor, and I have my compensation for the surrender of this right to use my own as I will by the similar restriction imposed upon my neighbor for my benefit. I hold my property subject to the risk that it may be unavoidably or accidentally injured by those who live near me; and as I move about upon the public highways and in all places where other persons may lawfully be, I take the risk of being accidentally injured in my person by them without fault on their part. Most of the rights of property, as well as of person, in the social state, are not absolute but relative, and they must be so arranged and modified, not unnecessarily infringing upon natural rights, as upon the whole to promote the general welfare. [...]

But our attention is called to a recent English case, decided in the Exchequer Chamber, which seems to uphold the claim made. In the case of Fletcher v. Rylands (1 Exchequer, 265, Law Reports) the defendants constructed a reservoir on land separated from the plaintiff's colliery by intervening land Mines, under the site of the reservoir and under part of the intervening land, had been formerly worked; and the plaintiff had, by workings lawfully made in his own colliery and in the intervening land, opened an underground communication between his colliery and the old workings under the reservoir. It was not known to the defendants, nor to any person employed by them in the construction of the reservoir, that such communication existed, or that there were any old workings under the site of the reservoir, and the defendants were not personally guilty of any negligence; but, in fact, the reservoir was constructed over five old shafts, leading down to the workings. On the reservoir being filled, the water burst down these shafts and flowed, by the underground communication, into the plaintiff's mines. It was held, reversing the judgment of the Court of Exchequer, that the defendants were liable for the damage so caused, upon the broad doctrine that one who, for his own purposes, brings upon his land, and collects and keeps there, anything likely to do mischief if it escapes, must keep it at his peril, and, if he does not do so, is prima facie answerable for all the damage which is the natural consequence of its escape.

Mr. Justice BLACKBURN, ... says: "The question of law therefore arises, what is the obligation which the law casts on a person who, like the defendants, lawfully brings on his land something which, though harmless whilst it remains there, will naturally do mischief if it escape out of his land? It is agreed on all hands that he must take care to keep in that which he has brought on the land and keeps there, in order that it may not escape and damage his neighbors; but the question arises whether the duty which the law casts upon him, under such circumstances, is an absolute duty to keep it in at his peril, or is, as the majority of the Court of Exchequer have thought, merely a duty to take all reasonable and prudent precautions in order to keep it in, but no more;" and he reaches the conclusion that it is an absolute duty, and that the liability for damage from the escape attaches without any proof of negligence. This conclusion is reached by the learned judge mainly by applying to the case the same rule of liability to which owners are subjected by the escape of their live animals. As I have shown above, the rules of law applicable to live animals should not be applied to inanimate property. [...]

It is sufficient, however, to say that the law, as laid down in those cases, is in direct conflict with the law as settled in this country. Here, if one builds a dam upon his own premises and thus holds back and accumulates the water for his benefit, or if he brings water upon his premises into a reservoir, in case the dam or the banks of the reservoir give away and the lands of a neighbor are thus flooded, he is not liable for the damage without proof of some fault or negligence on his part. [...]

The same rule applies to injuries to the person. No one in such case is made liable without some fault or negligence on his part, however serious the injury may be which he may accidentally cause; and there can be no reason for holding one liable for accidental injuries to property when he is exempt from liability for such injuries to the person. [...]

In support of the plaintiff's claim in this action the rule has been invoked that, where one of two innocent parties must suffer, he who puts in motion the cause of the injury must bear the loss. But, as will be seen by the numerous cases above cited, it has no application whatever to a case like this.

This examination has gone far enough to show that the rule is, at least in this country, a universal one, which, so far as I can discern, has no exceptions or limitations, that no one can be made liable for injuries to the person or property of another without some fault or negligence on his part.

In this case the defendants had the right to place the steam boiler upon their premises. It was in no sense a nuisance, and the jury have found that they were not guilty of any negligence. [...]

(Citations omitted)

Note the argument used by the court in this case. Since we live in a civilized society and need "factories, machinery, dams, canals and railroads ..." [to satisfy our wants and serve our civilization, as long as] "they are not a nuisance and are not so managed as to become such, I am not responsible for any damage they accidentally and unavoidably do my neighbor. He receives his compensation for such damage by the general good, in which he shares, and the right which he has to place the same things upon his lands." In effect, neighbors and others benefiting from a person's factory or dams may only hold defendants accountable if they create a nuisance or exhibit some degree of fault (i.e., negligence) in how they are managed. The judges seem to echo the strong US commitment to holding defendants in negligence for harms they cause to others.

Interestingly, about 25 years later, the same New York court expressed concerns about *Losee v. Buchanan* in deciding a case concerning blasting and trespass. The *Sullivan v. Dunham* court (next reading) seemed to distinguish and isolate the holding of *Losee v. Buchanan* in its opinion; what reasons did the *Sullivan court give* for the distinctions it noted?

Trespass and Ultrahazardous Activities

The following case is labeled both an instance of trespass, which it is as described by the court, but also one in which defendants were engaged in the ultrahazardous activity of dynamiting trees from private land. It's probably better to emphasize trespass (and it does receive the court's attention) because this is a third category of typical strict liability torts.

Sullivan v. Dunham

Court of Appeals of New York

7 Am.Negl.Cas. 126 (1900)

Opinion: VANN, J. (after stating the facts).

The main question presented by this appeal is whether one who, for a lawful purpose, and without negligence or want of skill, explodes a blast upon his own land, and thereby causes a piece of wood to fall upon a person lawfully traveling in a public highway, is liable for the injury thus inflicted.

The statute authorizes the personal representative of a decedent to "maintain an action to recover damages for a wrongful act, neglect, or default, by which the decedent's death was caused, against a natural person who, or a corporation which, would have been liable to an action in favor of the decedent, by reason thereof, if death had not ensued." Code Civ. Proc. § 1902. It covers any action of trespass upon the person which the deceased could have maintained if she had survived the accident. Stated in another form, [are] the defendants ... liable as trespassers.

This is not a new question, for it has been considered, directly or indirectly, so many times by this court that a reference to the earlier authorities is unnecessary. In the leading case upon the subject the defendant, in order to dig a canal authorized by its charter, necessarily blasted out rocks from its own land with gunpowder, and thus threw fragments against the plaintiff's house, which stood upon the adjoining premises. Although there was no proof of negligence or want of skill, the defendant was held liable for the injury sustained. All the judges concurred in the opinion of Gardiner, J., who said: "The defendants had the right to dig the canal; the plaintiff, the right to the undisturbed possession of his property. If these rights conflict, the former must yield to the latter, as the more important of the two, since, upon grounds of public policy, it is better that one man should surrender a particular use of his land than that another should be deprived of the beneficial use of his property altogether, which might be the consequence if the privilege of the former should be wholly unrestricted. The case before us illustrates this principle; for if the defendants, in excavating their canal, in itself a lawful use of their land, could, in the manner mentioned by the witnesses, demolish the stoop of the plaintiff with impunity, they might, for the same purpose, on the exercise of reasonable care, demolish his house, and thus deprive him of all use of his property. The use of land by the proprietor is not, therefore, an absolute right, but qualified and limited by the higher right of others to the lawful possession of their property. To this possession the law prohibits all direct injury, without regard to its extent or the motives of the aggressor. * *

* He may excavate a canal, but he cannot cast the dirt or stones upon the land of his neighbor, either by human agency or the force of gunpowder. If he cannot construct the work without the adoption of such means, he must abandon that mode of using his property, or be held responsible for all damages resulting therefrom. [...]"

These were cases of trespass upon lands, while the case before us involves trespass upon the person of a human being, when she was where she had the same right to protection from injury as if she had been walking upon her own land. As the safety of the person is more sacred than the safety of property, the cases cited should govern our decision, unless they are no longer the law.

The Hay Case was reviewed by the Commission of Appeals in Losee v. Buchanan, 51 N. Y. 476, 479, where it was held that one who, without negligence, and with due care and skill, operates a steam boiler upon his own premises, is not liable to his neighbor for the damages caused by the explosion thereof. That was not a case of intentional, but of accidental, explosion. A tremendous force escaped, so to speak, from the owner, but was not voluntarily set free. The court, commenting upon the Hay Case, said: "It was held that the defendant was liable for the injury, although no negligence or want of skill in executing the work was alleged or proved. This decision was well supported by the clearest principles. The acts of the defendant in casting the rocks upon plaintiff's premises were direct and immediate. The damages was the necessary consequence of just what the defendant was doing, and it was just as much liable as if it had caused the rocks to be taken by hand, or any other means, and thrown directly upon plaintiff's land."

"[...] The case of Hay v. Cohoes Co. (supra) shows that, unless there is a right to the use of the adjacent lands for the purposes of the work, it matters not that the mode adopted of carrying on the work was necessary. * * * It follows, then, that the defendant having no right to invade the premises, which, for the purposes of this case, were the possession of the plaintiff, it matters not whether or no he made his invasion without negligence." [...]

This case is analogous to the one before us, because the person injured did not own the land upon which he stood when struck, but he had a right to stand there, the same as the plaintiff's intestate had a right to walk in the highway. We see no distinction in principle between the two cases. [...]

We think that the Hay Case has always been recognized by this court as a sound and valuable authority. After standing for 50 years as the law of the state upon the subject, it should not be disturbed, and we have no inclination to disturb it. It rests upon the principle, founded in public policy, that the safety of property generally is superior in right to a particular use of a single piece of property by its owner. It renders the enjoyment of all property more secure, by preventing such a use of one piece by one man as may injure all his neighbors. It makes human life safer, by tending to prevent a landowner from casting, either with or without negligence, a part of his land upon the person of one who is where he has a right to be. It so applies the maxim of sic utere tuo as to protect person and property from direct physical violence, which, although accidental, has the same effect as if it were intentional. It lessens the hardship by placing absolute liability upon the one who causes the injury. The accident in question was a misfortune to the defendants, but it was a greater misfortune to the young woman who was killed. The safety of travelers upon the public highway is more important to the state than the improvement of one piece of property, by a special method, is to its owner. [...]

We think the courts below were right in holding the defendants liable as trespassers, regardless of the care they may have used in doing the work. Their action was a direct invasion of the rights of the person injured, who was lawfully in a public highway, which was a safe place until they made it otherwise by throwing into it the section of a tree.

We find no reversible error in the record before us. While the complaint suggests negligence as the gravamen of the action, it was tried upon the theory of trespass, and no ruling was made or exception taken which raised any question as to the scope of the pleadings, or suggested the propriety of a motion for leave to amend. We can consider no objection unless it was taken upon the trial and saved by an exception. … Moreover, if every allegation relating to negligence were struck from the complaint, it would still set forth a cause of action in trespass. […]

(Citations omitted)

As one can determine from reading this case, it emphasizes trespassing on another person on a public highway analogous to trespassing on a person on private land, but of course the defendants were also engaged in the ultrahazardous activity of blasting trees out of the ground, which ultimately caused the harm. However, despite two major issues in the case, the court tends to treat what occurred as one of trespass for which a person can be held strictly liable.

Administrative Law–Tort Law Interactions (Tort Law Backup Function)

At the end of the discussion of the tort law, we consider a tort case that is interesting on multiple fronts. First, it falls within the class of torts concerning ultrahazardous activities and thus is a strict liability case. Moreover, it is an instance of a very old cause of action in strict liability based on an analogue to the "caged tiger" rule that we met in the previous section, but in new garb. Karen Silkwood was not harmed by a real uncaged tiger, but a modern variant to which the plaintiff's lawyer appealed; namely, a very poisonous type of radiation, plutonium. Plutonium is a radioactive element used in nuclear power plants to generate electricity.[10] At the Kerr-McGee nuclear power plant, plutonium was only used as a material for generating heat in the nuclear reactor.

A second interesting feature of this case is that plutonium escaped and contaminated Karen Silkwood and her apartment. However, before she could bring a tort action against Kerr-McGee, she was killed in a car accident while driving to meet with a *New York Times* reporter to reveal poor control of plutonium in the Kerr-McGee plant. Her parents sued in Oklahoma tort law to receive compensation for the injuries she suffered from the exposures. By bringing a tort action under the caged-tiger rule, Kerr-McGee would face a tort action in strict liability. If the plutonium escaped and contaminated Karen, she (or her loved ones, since she had died) would be entitled to compensation for any injuries she incurred, as long as she did not release the plutonium that harmed her—as long as she did not let the "tiger" of plutonium out of its cage. A trial court found that she had not been responsible for the release of the plutonium.

---

10 Plutonium is so poisonous that at US nuclear weapons laboratories, the Department of Energy has to create working conditions so that people do not come into contact with the substance. Workers creating the core of nuclear weapons deal with plutonium by using glove boxes through which they manipulate robotic arms that touch, shape, and modify plutonium to create the radioactive material that ultimately would explode as a bomb. (From the author's experience on a safety oversight committee of some National Energy Laboratories.)

Third, we see the interaction of two different parts of the legal system at play: the Nuclear Regulatory Commission (NRC)—a federal administrative agency that issues regulatory laws to ensure private nuclear power plants are properly constructed and run safely—and the tort law. One of the NRC's major concerns is to protect employees from radiation exposure. Because Karen Silkwood was exposed, Kerr-McGee could face some legal actions by the NRC, especially if it was found to have violated safety rules that permitted the plutonium escape. However, NRC laws do not provide any compensation for employees harmed by escaping nuclear material. Typically, this would be provided by the Workers' Compensation Program we met in *McAllister*. And, as we see in the text of the case, Kerr-McGee argued, successfully, before the US Court of Appeals, Tenth Circuit, that compensation for Silkwood's family from radiation contamination should be covered by Workers' Compensation (note that on appeal the US Supreme Court disagreed with this).

In addition, and quite importantly, there is the question of which area of law—torts or workers' compensation or NRC administrative law—should guide what compensation, if any, and how much compensation the Silkwood family should receive for Karen's death. The major issue in the case is whether Oklahoma tort law should even be permitted to address Silkwood's injuries from radiation exposure. The reason for this is that in the United States, with different legal systems—state laws and federal laws—laws sometimes can conflict with one another; as a general matter, which law should apply and prevail to address a problem needing legal resolution when there are conflicts? And when they are in conflict and the conflict between them is sufficiently significant, which should prevail? Consequently, a major question for the US Supreme Court is, "Does federal regulatory or administrative law, governed by congressional legislation incorporated into the laws administered by the NRC, preempt or preclude the use of the Oklahoma tort law to provide compensation for Karen Silkwood's family; or should NRC laws plus workers' compensation be the appropriate area for compensating her family?

Finally, because of the interaction between administrative (or regulatory law) and the tort law, we see two different parts of the legal system that could address injuries to Karen Silkwood. Moreover, a much larger issue is more general: what strengths and limitations are there in different areas of the law for providing some degree of protections for citizens like Karen Silkwood? The course will close by raising some of these questions for different areas of the law we will have considered in this book. *Silkwood v. Kerr-McGee* is one datum we will consider in introducing these issues.

Silkwood v. Kerr-McGee Corporation

Supreme Court of the United States

104 S.Ct. 615 (1984)

Opinion:

Justice WHITE delivered the opinion of the Court.

Last term, this Court examined the relationship between federal and state authority in the nuclear energy field and concluded that states are precluded from regulating the safety aspects of nuclear energy. … This case requires us to determine whether a state-authorized award of punitive damages arising out of the escape of plutonium from a federally-licensed nuclear facility is preempted either because it falls within that forbidden field or because it conflicts with some other aspect of the Atomic Energy Act.

I

Karen Silkwood was a laboratory analyst for Kerr-McGee[1] at its Cimmaron plant near Crescent, Okla. The plant fabricated plutonium fuel pins for use as reactor fuel in nuclear power plants. Accordingly, the plant was subject to licensing and regulation by the Nuclear Regulatory Commission (NRC) pursuant to the Atomic Energy Act, [...][2]

During a three-day period of November 1974, Silkwood was contaminated by plutonium from the Cimmaron plant. On November 5, Silkwood was grinding and polishing plutonium samples, utilizing glove boxes designed for that purpose.[3] In accordance with established procedures, she checked her hands for contamination when she withdrew them from the glove box. When some contamination was detected, a more extensive check was performed. A monitoring device revealed contamination on Silkwood's left hand, right wrist, upper arm, neck, hair, and nostrils. She was immediately decontaminated, and at the end of her shift, the monitors detected no contamination. However, she was given urine and fecal kits and was instructed to collect samples in order to check for plutonium discharge.

The next day, Silkwood arrived at the plant and began doing paperwork in the laboratory. Upon leaving the laboratory, Silkwood monitored herself and again discovered surface contamination. Once again, she was decontaminated.

On the third day, November 7, Silkwood was monitored upon her arrival at the plant. High levels of contamination were detected. Four urine samples and one fecal sample submitted that morning were also highly contaminated.[4] Suspecting that the contamination had spread to areas outside the plant, the company directed a decontamination squad to accompany Silkwood to her apartment. Silkwood's roommate, who was also an employee at the plant, was awakened and monitored. She was also contaminated, although to a lesser degree than Silkwood. The squad then monitored the apartment, finding contamination in several rooms, with especially high levels in the bathroom, the kitchen, and Silkwood's bedroom.

The contamination level in Silkwood's apartment was such that many of her personal belongings had to be destroyed. Silkwood herself was sent to the Los Alamos Scientific Laboratory to determine the extent of contamination in her vital body organs. She returned to work on November 13. That night, she was killed in an unrelated automobile accident. [...]

Bill Silkwood, Karen's father, brought the present diversity action in his capacity as administrator of her estate. The action was based on common law tort principles under Oklahoma law and was designed to recover for the contamination injuries to Karen's person and property. Kerr-McGee stipulated that the plutonium which caused the contamination came from its plant, and the jury expressly rejected Kerr-McGee's allegation that Silkwood had intentionally removed the plutonium from the plant in an effort to embarrass the company. However, there were no other specific findings of fact with respect to the cause of the contamination.

During the course of the trial, evidence was presented which tended to show that Kerr-McGee did not always comply with NRC regulations. One Kerr-McGee witness conceded that the amount of plutonium which was unaccounted for during the period in question exceeded permissible limits. ... An NRC official testified that he did not feel that Kerr-McGee was conforming its conduct to the "as low as reasonably achievable" standard. Ibid. There was also some evidence that the level of plutonium in

Silkwood's apartment may have exceeded that permitted in an unrestricted area such as a residence. Ibid.

However, there was also evidence that Kerr-McGee complied with most federal regulations. The NRC official testified that there were no serious personnel exposures at the plant and that Kerr-McGee did not exceed the regulatory requirements with respect to exposure levels that would result in significant health hazards. In addition, Kerr-McGee introduced the Commission's report on the investigation of the Silkwood incident in which the Commission determined that Kerr-McGee's only violation of regulations throughout the incident was its failure to maintain a record of the dates of two urine samples submitted by Silkwood.

The trial court determined that Kerr-McGee had not shown that the contamination occurred during the course of Silkwood's employment. Accordingly, the court precluded the jury from deciding whether the personal injury claim was covered by Oklahoma's Workers' Compensation Act, which provides the sole remedy for accidental personal injuries arising in the course of employment. ... Instead, the court submitted the claims to the jury on alternative theories of strict liability and negligence.[7]

The court also instructed the jury with respect to punitive damages, explaining the standard by which Kerr-McGee's conduct was to be evaluated in determining whether such damages should be awarded:

"[T]he jury may give damages for the sake of example and by way of punishment, if the jury finds the defendant or defendants have been guilty of oppression, fraud, or malice, actual or presumed. [...]

"Exemplary damages are not limited to cases where there is direct evidence of fraud, malice or gross negligence. They may be allowed when there is evidence of such recklessness and wanton disregard of another's rights that malice and evil intent will be inferred. If a defendant is grossly and wantonly reckless in exposing others to dangers, the law holds him to have intended the natural consequences of his acts, and treats him as guilty of a willful wrong." [...]

The jury returned a verdict in favor of Mr. Silkwood, finding actual damages of $505,000 ($500,000 for personal injuries and $5,000 for property damage) and punitive damages of $10 million. The trial court entered judgment against Kerr-McGee in that amount.

Kerr-McGee then moved for judgment n.o.v. or a new trial. In denying that motion, 485 F.Supp. 566 (W.D.Okl.1979), the court rejected Kerr-McGee's contention that compliance with federal regulations precluded an award of punitive damages. The court noted that Kerr-McGee "had a duty under part 20 of Title 10 of the Code of Federal Regulations to maintain the release of radiation 'as low as reasonably achievable.' Compliance with this standard cannot be demonstrated merely through control of escaped plutonium within any absolute amount." Id., at 585. Therefore, the court concluded, it is not "inconsistent [with any congressional design] to impose punitive damages for the escape of plutonium caused by grossly negligent, reckless and willful conduct." Ibid.

Kerr-McGee renewed its contentions with greater success before the Court of Appeals for the Tenth Circuit. That court, by decision of a split panel, affirmed in part and reversed in part. ... The court first held that recovery for Silkwood's personal injuries was controlled exclusively by Oklahoma's workers' compensation law. It thus reversed the $500,000 judgment for those injuries. The court then affirmed the property damage portion of the award, holding that the workers' compensation law applied only to personal injuries and that Oklahoma law permitted an award under a theory of strict liability in the circumstances of this case. Finally, the court held that because of the federal statutes regulating the Kerr-McGee plant, "punitive damages may not be awarded in this case," id., at 923.

In reaching its conclusion with respect to the punitive damages award, the Court of Appeals adopted a broad preemption analysis. It concluded that "any state action that competes substantially with the AEC (NRC) in its regulation of radiation hazards associated with plants handling nuclear material" was impermissible. Ibid. Because "[a] judicial award of exemplary damages under state law as punishment for bad practices or to deter future practices involving exposure to radiation is not less intrusive than direct legislative acts of the state," the court determined that such awards were preempted by federal law. Ibid.

Mr. Silkwood appealed, seeking review of the Court of Appeals' ruling with respect to the punitive damages award. We noted probable jurisdiction and postponed consideration of the jurisdictional issue until argument on the merits. [...]

III

As we recently observed in Pacific Gas Electric Co. v. State Energy Resources Conservation & Development Comm'n, (1983), state law can be preempted in either of two general ways. If Congress evidences an intent to occupy a given field, any state law falling within that field is preempted. ... If Congress has not entirely displaced state regulation over the matter in question, state law is still preempted to the extent it actually conflicts with federal law, that is, when it is impossible to comply with both state and federal law ..., or where the state law stands as an obstacle to the accomplishment of the full purposes and objectives of Congress ... Kerr-McGee contends that the award in this case is invalid under either analysis. We consider each of these contentions in turn.

In Pacific Gas Electric, an examination of the statutory scheme and legislative history of the Atomic Energy Act convinced us that "Congress ... intended that the federal government regulate the radiological safety aspects involved ... in the construction and operation of a nuclear plant." ... Thus, we concluded that "the federal government has occupied the entire field of nuclear safety concerns, except the limited powers expressly ceded to the states." [...]

Kerr-McGee argues that our ruling in Pacific Gas Electric is dispositive of the issue in this case. Noting that "regulation can be as effectively asserted through an award of damages as through some form of preventive relief," ..., Kerr-McGee submits that because the state-authorized award of punitive damages in this case punishes and deters conduct related to radiation hazards, it falls within the prohibited field. However, a review of the same legislative history ... convinces us that the preempted field does not extend as far as Kerr-McGee would have it. [...]

More importantly, the only congressional discussion concerning the relationship between the Atomic Energy Act and state tort remedies indicates that Congress assumed that such remedies would be available. After the 1954 law was enacted, private companies contemplating entry into the nuclear **industry expressed concern over potentially bankrupting state-law suits arising out of a nuclear incident**. As a result, in 1957 Congress passed the **Price-Anderson Act**, an amendment to the Atomic Energy Act. ... That Act established an indemnification scheme under which operators of licensed nuclear facilities could be required to obtain up to $60 million in private financial protection against such suits. The government would then provide indemnification for the next $500 million of liability, and the resulting $560 million would be the limit of liability for any one nuclear incident.

Although the Price-Anderson Act does not apply to the present situation, the discussion preceding its enactment and subsequent amendment indicates that Congress assumed that persons injured by nuclear accidents were free to utilize existing state tort law remedies. [...]

"Since the rights of third parties who are injured are established by State law, there is no interference with the State law until there is a likelihood that the damages exceed the amount of financial responsibility required together with the amount of the indemnity. At that point the Federal interference is limited to the prohibition of making payments through the state courts and to prorating the proceeds available." [...]

Congress clearly began working on the Price-Anderson legislation with the assumption that in the absence of some subsequent legislative action, state tort law would apply.[14] This was true even though Congress was fully aware of the Commission's exclusive regulatory authority over safety matters. As the Joint Committee explained in 1965:

The belief that the NRC's exclusive authority to set safety standards did not foreclose the use of state tort remedies was reaffirmed when the Price-Anderson Act was amended in 1966. The 1966 amendment was designed to respond to concerns about the adequacy of state law remedies. [...]

Describing the effect of the 1966 amendment, the Joint Committee stated:

"By requiring potential defendants to agree to waive defenses the defendants' rights are restricted; concomitantly, to this extent, the rights of plaintiffs are enlarged. Just as the rights of persons who are injured are established by State law, the rights of defendants against whom liability is asserted are fixed by State law. What this subsection does is to authorize the [NRC] to require that defendants covered by financial protection and indemnity give up some of the rights they might otherwise assert." [...]

Similarly, when the Committee outlined the rights of those injured in nuclear incidents which were not extraordinary nuclear occurrences, its reference point was again state law. "Absent ... a determination [that the incident is an 'extraordinary nuclear occurrence'], a claimant would have exactly the same rights that he has today under existing law—including, perhaps, benefit of a rule of strict liability if applicable State law so provides." ... Indeed, the entire discussion surrounding the 1966 amendment was premised on the assumption that state remedies were available notwithstanding the NRC's exclusive regulatory authority. [...]

Kerr-McGee focuses on the differences between compensatory and punitive damages awards and asserts that, at most, Congress intended to allow the former. This argument, however, is misdirected because ... [p]unitive damages have long been a part of traditional state tort law. As we noted above, Congress assumed that traditional principles of state tort law would apply with full force unless they were expressly supplanted. [...]

In sum, it is clear that in enacting and amending the Price-Anderson Act, Congress assumed that state-law remedies, in whatever form they might take, were available to those injured by nuclear incidents. [...]

We do not suggest that there could never be an instance in which the federal law would preempt the recovery of damages based on state law. But insofar as damages for radiation injuries are concerned, preemption should not be judged on the basis that the federal government has so completely occupied the field of safety that state remedies are foreclosed but on whether there is an irreconcilable conflict between the federal and state standards or whether the imposition of a state standard in a damages action would frustrate the objectives of the federal law. We perceive no such conflict or frustration in the circumstances of this case. [...]

We also reject Kerr-McGee's submission that the punitive damages award in this case conflicts with Congress' express intent to preclude dual regulation of radiation hazards. ... As we explained in part A, Congress did not believe that it was inconsistent to vest the NRC with exclusive regulatory authority over the safety aspects of nuclear development while at the same time allowing plaintiffs like Silkwood to recover for injuries caused by nuclear hazards. We are not authorized to second-guess that conclusion.

IV

We conclude that the award of punitive damages in this case is not preempted by federal law. On remand Kerr-McGee is free to reassert any claims it made before the Court of Appeals which were not addressed by that court or by this opinion, including its contention that the jury's findings with respect to punitive damages were not supported by sufficient evidence and its argument that the amount of the punitive damages award was excessive. The judgment of the Court of Appeals with respect to punitive damages is therefore reversed, and the case is remanded to the Court of Appeals for proceedings consistent with this opinion. It is so ordered.

[Omitted citations and several dissenting opinions]

Notes

2 Under 42 U.S.C. § 2073, the Commission is authorized to issue licenses to those who handle special nuclear materials like the plutonium processed in Kerr-McGee's plant. Section 2201(b) empowers the Commission to set standards and issue instructions to govern the possession and use of such materials. On April 2, 1970, Kerr-McGee obtained a license to receive and possess special nuclear materials at its Cimmaron plant. It closed the plant in 1975.

3 A glove box is a supposedly impervious box surrounding the plutonium processing equipment which has glove holes permitting the operator to work on the equipment or the plutonium from outside the box.

4 At trial, the parties stipulated that the urine samples had been spiked with insoluble plutonium, i.e., plutonium which cannot be excreted from the body. However there was no evidence as to who placed the plutonium in the vials.

6 Federal regulations require that "persons engaged in activities under licenses issued by the Nuclear Regulatory Commission ... make every reasonable effort to maintain radiation exposures, and releases of radioactive materials in effluents to unrestricted areas, as low as is reasonably achievable." 10 CFR 20.1(c) (1983). In 1974, the regulation required reasonable efforts to maintain exposures and releases "as far below the limits specified [in other portions of the regulations] as practicable." The difference in the terminology is not significant. 40 Fed.Reg. 33029 (1975).

7 In an effort to avoid a new trial in the event that the Court of Appeals disagreed with its ruling on the applicability of strict liability principles, the court instructed the jury to answer a special interrogatory as to whether Kerr-McGee negligently allowed the plutonium to escape from its plant. The jury answered in the affirmative.

Some Criminal Law–Tort Law Comparisons

We close this chapter by reviewing some of the similarities and differences between the criminal law and tort law. We have discussed these points in the chapters to this point, but it may be useful to draw out some more general similarities and differences in one place.

In the criminal law, a voluntary act is a necessary condition for all criminal liability, with the possible exception of strict liability. This requirement ensures an agent's acts are properly attributable to *choices* of the agent as opposed to bodily movements not resulting from choices, which in turn helps to ensure that the agent exhibits proper guilt and is properly condemned via punishment. Although the tort law presupposes that an agent acts voluntarily, this is less explicit than in the criminal law, probably because tort liability is less fine-grained than criminal liability and because the sanctions are quite different, reducing the need for sanctioning explicit states of mind as in the criminal law because of punishment.

The two areas of the law differ substantially on a general *mens rea* requirement. Having the minimal capacity to understand the law and conform to it are necessary conditions of a criminal offense; insanity is a complete defense to a crime. Having the mental capacity of a child is also a complete defense to a crime, although different jurisdictions differ on the minimal age for criminal accountability. Diminished mental capacity reduces the severity of some homicides even though a person is not judged insane. The rationale is that proper guilt and condemnation are only attributable to persons who choose with sound minds to violate the law and are mature enough to make sound choices. The tort law is quite different, as we have seen.

There is no general *mens rea* requirement for all torts, as we saw in *Williams v. Hays* I (insanity is no defense). In some instances, sufficient insanity might excuse some intentional torts. Thus, there are "pockets" of the tort law with a general *mens rea*. For the responsibility of children, two broadly different rules seem to be the "common-law rule," under which children below the age of 7 are conclusively presumed incapable of tort responsibility, but under the Massachusetts rule we met in *Tyler v. Weed*, there seems to be no age below which a child is presumed to be incapable of tortious acts; this has to be judged based on the age and maturity of the child and the circumstances in question. Prosser argues that the liability of infants resembles the Massachusetts rule: "an infant has no immunity based on the fact of infancy" with a qualification for intentional torts and a point we have not considered concerning contracts.[11]

Central to the criminal law is that for "core" crimes there must be a "specific *mens rea*." This both defines the crime in question and enters into judgments about proper punishment. As we noted, *generally* at the time of acting, this requires that an agent act knowingly or intentionally quite broadly construed as explained in *Morissette*. That is, agents must have been "aware" at the time of acting they were about to cause harm or violate the law or had a risk of doing so (the Model Penal Code's definitions of a person's acting intentionally in a narrow sense, knowingly or recklessly, captures these ideas). Some lesser crimes may be committed with negligence or gross negligence, but negligence is controversial because of its similarity to strict liability; at the time of acting, an agent need not be aware of the possibility of harm to others; he or she *should* have been aware of risks from his or her activities. The rationale for specific *mens rea* is related to finding persons properly guilty of making culpable choices that deserve the harsh sanction of some degree of punishment. There is no analogous specific *mens rea* in torts except for

11 *Prosser and Keeton on torts* (5th ed.), p. 1071. W. Page Keeton et al., Eds. West Publishing.

intentional torts, such as libel, slander, battery, assault, or malicious prosecution, about which we have said little. For most torts, a defendant is held liable for simple negligence or is held strictly accountable for certain torts, such as the actions of defendant's domestic or wild animals, trespass, product liability, and ultrahazardous activities. The different sanction for the tort law has some explanatory role for the absence of specific *mens rea* in torts.

Causation is an essential element of torts because it connects defendant's actions to plaintiff's injuries. Because of the complexity of the world, courts have developed various legal doctrines to address the causal complexity presented by events in the world, as some legal cases have illustrated. Court-developed rules also have permitted plaintiffs to establish causation in order to provide tort compensation that in the view of judges is warranted and that better serves the aims of torts. Causation is not an essential element of every crime (recall attempted crimes, conspiracies, and planning a crime), but of course, causation will be required for many crimes; e.g., various homicides, rape, burglary, robbery, and theft.

Proximate causation doctrines are different between the two areas of the law. There is a less expansive doctrine of proximate causation in the criminal law than in torts, as the decision and discussion in *Commonwealth v. Root* shows. For instance, the court in *Root* found it would be unjust to hold a storeowner for involuntary manslaughter simply because he sold cartridges to a teenager they hypothesize killed another. They quit with citing this and other examples, but it seems likely that a more extensive idea of proximate cause would be inconsistent with finding persons, e.g., the store owner, properly guilty of involuntary manslaughter where he had no idea what the teen would do with the bullet. It also seems that the harshness of the criminal sanction probably influences their judgments concerning the criminal law. In contrast, the tort law has a more expansive or liberal conception of proximate causation doctrine, probably to better serve the aim of torts and because the tort sanction is less harsh and intrusive. This point is nicely illustrated by *Lynch v. Fisher* (which if this were a criminal case, the first negligent driver would not have been responsible at all for the second negligent driver shooting the Good Samaritan), some tort law examples in *Commonwealth v. Root*, and language from *Williams v. Hays I* discussing insanity illustrate these issues: the tort "law looks to the person damaged by another, and seeks to make him whole, without reference to the purpose or the condition, mental or physical, of the person causing the damage." Thus, one might think of the importance in torts of extending liability through proximate causation to better achieve compensation for damage caused by another

What accounts for these differences? I have suggested that the condemnation and hard treatment of the criminal sanction likely accounts for many of the differences; the law must be much more careful in holding people accountable for crimes because of the intrusiveness and harshness of criminal punishment. Of course, we should also recall that strict liability is quite controversial in the criminal law because it could be applied to quite innocent persons, but this seems not to be true in torts or much less so. The aim of torts is different and it has a much less severe sanction for the defendant than the criminal law. Together, these result in more relaxed conceptions of accountability, and the tort law has developed doctrines to make it easier for victims to "put matters right" (within the general burden of proof) after they have been injured.

Underlying the two areas of the law may be different conceptions of responsibility. The criminal law seems much closer to our considered moral judgments of blame, praise and condemnation than the tort law. In some wide views of responsibility revealed in some tort cases, defendants who "without justification harm others by their conduct should put the matter right, even if they were not at fault."

That is, there is a less robust degree of fault in torts than in the criminal law. As one author puts it, "[W]e are responsible for the outcome of our conduct ... and ... a just distribution of risks requires us to make good the harm that our conduct causes to others in return for the benefit and credit that accrues to us when our plans come off."[12] These views are more in the nature of a proposal, but they seem to point to a broader underlying conception of responsibility for harms done to others compared with blaming with which we might be more familiar and that seems closer to criminal law ideas.

In the next chapter, we consider some shortcomings of torts and criminal law, leading to a consideration of a third area of law, administrative, or regulatory, law.

12 Tony Honore, The morality of tort law—Questions and answers. In *Philosophical foundations of tort law* (1995), pp. 73–95, 94. David G. Owen, Ed. Clarendon Press.

■ CHAPTER 5

Administrative Law and Some Broader Issues

If we think of the law as both guiding behavior and protecting people or institutions in the community from various kinds violations or "border crossings," typically, but not always, resulting in harms, different areas of the law can provide the protections in different ways. We have considered some ways in which both the criminal law and the tort law seek to protect us against violations of our person and property, but do it with different doctrinal presuppositions and different penalties for the violations. Other areas of law can also act to secure our bodies, possessions, and legal interests from others. In a short while, we will consider how administrative law achieves some of these goals, and we should be aware of some of the limitations of the criminal law and tort law in providing protections.

Shortcomings of Criminal Law and Torts

To begin, both criminal and tort actions are importantly and essentially retrospective. There are a few components of these laws. First, there are legislatively created or judicially decided laws whose importance is that they inform the public and put all of us on notice that certain kinds of behavior would be in violation of the criminal law and of torts (although different for the two areas). This is part of what is called *general deterrence*; that is, instilling caution or even greater or lesser degrees of fear of violating torts or the criminal law, so that individual citizens who might be tempted to commit a crime or have careless habits would modify their behavior because of the threat of being discovered and held accountable.

Note, however, that legal actions in both areas are retrospective—if individuals are injured, they must seek either criminal or tort redress *after the fact of legal violation (and often harm)*. General deterrence has failed; someone typically harmed the victim. The only prospective protections come from laws on the books and any accompanying threats of sanctions should violations occur. If one is harmed, one could seek compensation in the tort law, provided that the kind of harm suffered is legally authorized and provided one can establish the elements of a tort. Similarly, one could seek the satisfaction of seeing a criminal violator arrested, tried, found guilty beyond a reasonable doubt, and punished. But in each case, one has already suffered harm.

Of course, if either a criminal prosecution or a tort action is successful, it could send a *deterrence-by-example* message to others who might be similarly tempted to violate either kind of law. It's difficult to determine how well deterrence by example functions because there are always people who will commit other crimes or other torts, and in either case, both general deterrence and deterrence by example will have failed.

Consider some difficulties with the tort law and then think about what analogies there might be for the criminal law. Some studies of torts leave one with concerns. For example, receiving compensation requires a decision to claim that one has been harmed, seeking out legal assistance in the effort, taking a case to court, and then settling out of court or going to trial. While the steps are easy to state, people rarely utilize the tort law. With regard to medical malpractice, in some studies, only about 10% of negligently injured patients sought compensation, and for those with the most serious injuries, only about 1 in 6, or 16%, filed claims. A Harvard Medical Practice study found that only about 1 in 16 injured patients received compensation through the tort system.[1] In another study over a wider range of tort cases, only 10% of 1000 grievances in which an injury was noticed was the harm brought to the attention of a lawyer and only 5% filed cases. A RAND Corporation study found that of every 100 people suffering disabling injuries, 81% were not heard from by insurers or injurers, with others taking (or not taking) different actions, but only 2% filing a lawsuit.[2] If cases are not filed or brought to successful conclusion, likely little or no deterrence by example occurs. Thus, Michael Saks concludes, "A tiny fraction of accidental deaths and injuries become claims for compensation; even known actionable injuries rarely become lawsuits."[3] Moreover, "[a]t nearly every stage, the tort litigation system operates to diminish the likelihood that injurers will have to compensate their victims. Only a small fraction of the costs created by actionable injuries will ever be paid by the injurers." However, he adds that deterrence may be somewhat more efficient than these numbers suggest.[4]

In addition, proof of causal connections in some cases concerning toxic exposures is difficult and becoming more so, despite some of the doctrinal modifications discussed above. When plaintiffs are dispersed but have exposure to similar products, proof is more difficult. Thus, not all individuals harmed may receive any kind of compensation because of dispersed plaintiffs and exposures. When there are latency periods for the harms involved, this increases the hurdles in showing harm. Recall Judith *Sindell,* who had about a 20-year latency period between exposure to diethylstilbestrol (DES) *in utero*

---

1 Michael J. Saks, Do we really know anything about the behavior of the tort litigation system—and why not? *140 University of Pennsylvania Law Review 1147* (1992), at 1183–1184, citing Harvard Medical Practice Study, Patients, Doctors, And Lawyers: Medical Injury, Malpractice Litigation, And Patient Compensation In New York, The Report Of The Harvard Medical Practice Study To The State Of New York 3 (1990).

2 Saks, *ibid.*, 1184, citing Deborah R. Hensler et al., *Compensation for accidental injuries in the United States 31* (1991), p. 122.

3 Saks, *ibid.*, 1287.

4 Saks, *ibid.*, 1287–1288.

and contraction of vaginal/uterine cancer, or consider the latency period of 45 years between asbestos exposure and appearance of lung cancer or mesothelioma. It's simply difficult to identify the major cause of disease when long time periods have elapsed. Furthermore, when there is a low level of harm but many may be exposed, this increases legal burdens in bringing a case. When there is statistical proof of causation (because of tort law proof requirements), somewhat analogous to the issues in *Stubbs*, this too presents challenges. Recall Stubbs had to show that proof of causation for his typhoid fever was more likely than not the result of drinking contaminated tap water, but as a statistical matter, he would have had difficulty ruling out all alternative exposures to the *Typhoid* bacillus.

Furthermore, the US Supreme Court increased the barriers for using scientific evidence in legal cases, but especially in torts in three decisions from 1993 to 1999.[5] These decisions have increased barriers for introducing scientific evidence in support of a case and motivated lawyers to seek out favorable jurisdictions for their cases.[6]

Enforcement (administrative) costs are typically on the plaintiffs' attorneys (and sometimes on plaintiffs); thus, suits may not be brought if the probable returns to the attorney or the victims are too low. The costs would then lie where they fell on the plaintiff/victim.

Moreover, even if one successfully brings a tort suit, defendants may be judgment proof—unable to pay court-awarded compensation.

Quite importantly, the tort law is *atomistic*; it addresses harms occurring to individuals who believe they can show they were harmed. Others may have been similarly harmed, but if they do not bring their legal actions or they are not part of an existing action, their injuries are not addressed and would receive no compensation, unless they took their own legal action. While the tort law has a limited means of addressing many people who have been subjected to harm with *class action litigation*, even this legal tool has been restricted. If some go uncompensated, the defendants who injured them escape responsibility for their actions. There is a slight possibility that a tort action favoring one plaintiff, *by example*, will motivate other injured parties to bring legal action against the same or similar defendants. This has occurred with litigation concerning asbestos, a quite toxic substance. Importantly, however, outside of class actions each person would need to bring separate legal cases to receive any compensation.

The limitations for the tort law to comprehensively and systemically address more complicated problems suggest even greater issues for the criminal law. Defendants who actually have violated the law must be charged, tried, and if guilty, found guilty, and then punished. Thus, *individuals* or *small groups* who break the law can be addressed (as groups through conspiracy or other group charges), but apart from any general deterrence or deterrence by example, this area of law is difficult to use for more comprehensive protections. Moreover, the standard of proof—proving violation of a law beyond a reasonable doubt—for criminal convictions is more difficult to meet than the tort law's preponderance of the evidence standard. The main hope for using the criminal law would rest with legislation prohibiting behaviors that would help reduce social effects.

---

5 Carl F. Cranor, *Toxic torts: Science, law and the possibility of justice* (2016). (2nd ed.) Cambridge University Press, along with *Daubert v. Merrell Dow Pharmaceuticals, Inc.*, 509 U.S. 579 *(1993), *General Elec. Co. v. Joiner*, 522 U.S. 136 (1997), and *Kumho Tire Co. v. Carmichael*, 526 U.S. 137, 152 (1999).

6 Andrew Jurs & Scott DeVito, The stricter standard: An empirical assessment of Daubert's effect on civil defendants (2013). *62 Cath. U. L. Rev.* 675–731.

Perhaps even more important, the tort law does not address problems in a *comprehensive manner* and does not typically provide *systemic solutions or protections*. Consider two kinds of problems. Tiny particles, so called $PM_{2.5}$ of air pollution, are surprisingly toxic. When we breathe them in, they can penetrate deeply into our lungs and damage them, ultimately contributing to emphysema, chronic bronchitis, or more generally to chronic obstructive lung disease and some other chronic illnesses. For instance, the US Environmental Protection Agency estimates that current standards for exposures to $PM_{2.5}$ are "responsible for tens of thousands of premature deaths in the United States each year."[7] Air pollution also contributes to heart disease because the particles can penetrate the arteries in the lungs to narrow and restrict blood flow. They can also travel through blood vessels and contribute to similar contractions in coronary and cerebral arteries, potentially having similar effects on blood flow and likely setting the stage for coronary or cerebral events.[8]

It would probably be impossible for some tort action to reduce air pollution in the United States because it is so widespread and pervasive that this atomistic area of the law is poorly suited to address problems for all affected in a comprehensive manner to protect the public's health. Use of the criminal law would also be out of the question unless there were really unusual circumstances of a major polluter deliberately contaminating a geographic area.

Consider a second example. Having legal tools to protect employees from asbestos in workplaces or to protect the citizenry from air pollution–caused diseases can be addressed within national borders, but not well with the criminal or tort laws, although there has been more success with tort suits in recent years.

In addition, there are much broader and more complicated problems calling for legal solutions that simply cannot be addressed by means of the criminal law or torts. For example, polychlorinated biphenyls that cause a variety of diseases can travel long distances from their point of origin, typically making their way to the northern latitudes of the world, contaminating the environment, and sickening the Inuit peoples who live there.[9] To control these substances requires a legal tool adequate to the problem plus cooperation between the nations of the world. Some kind of coordinated international action would have to address such issues.

Administrative Law

We thus need different kinds of laws to address some of these problems. In this last part of the book, we consider administrative, or regulatory, laws. Begin with the account of administrative law from *Black's Law Dictionary*: Administrative law governs

> [T]he organization and operation of administrative agencies ... and the relations of administrative agencies with the legislature, the executive, and judiciary and the public. ...

---

7 Independent Particulate Matter Review Panel, The need for a tighter particulate-matter air-quality standard. *The New England Journal of Medicine*, June 10, 2020. https://doi.org/10.1056/NEJMsb2011009, 2; (policy assessment for the review of the National Ambient Air Quality Standards for particulate matter: EPA-452/R-20-002. Research Triangle Park, NC: Environmental Protection Agency, January 2020).

8 Physicians for Social Responsibility, *Coal's assault on human health*, 22–23.

9 Carl F. Cranor, *Legally poisoned: How the law puts us at risk from toxicants* (2011, 2013). Harvard University Press.

> [Administrative law is typically divided into three parts]: 1) the statutes endowing agencies and powers and establishing rules of substantive law relating to those powers; 2) the body of agency-made law, consisting of administrative rules, regulations, reports, opinions, containing findings of fact and orders; and 3) the legal principles governing the acts of public agents when those acts conflict with private rights (emphasis added).[10]

Administrative laws are created by legislatures with statutes, either state or federal, but our focus is on federal law. Congress passes such laws to address and solve problems that existing institutions do not address well, such as the tort law. Administrative agencies issue regulations that have the force of law that are too particular and probably require too much detailed expertise for legislators adequately to address.

To illustrate administrative laws, consider a "down-home" example. All of us live, work, and study in buildings of one kind or another. Those buildings stand up because there is a set of regulatory or administrative laws that specify how buildings must be designed and constructed. Legally, at any rate, a person may not build just any old house or community center, university building, or church however they want to. They are legally required to build their edifice in accordance with some fairly strict and specific building codes. The structure they erect is not just for one moment and one inhabitant in time, but it must be sufficiently well built that it will protect others who enter it, subsequent purchasers of houses, or university buildings for many years. Moreover, it must withstand particular threats where it is built: floods near rivers, high tides near oceans, earthquakes in California, and hurricanes near the Gulf of Mexico.

The various features of single-family homes, condominiums, apartment buildings, classrooms, and so on have to be built to particular specifications, guided by good engineering techniques for the area, and contractors have to follow very specific rules about how to erect buildings that they construct. This all has to be specified by law and by regulations issued following the guidance of appropriate laws that created them. If any of you have been in construction or been around construction on a house in which you were living, you know that on a time schedule, building inspectors visit and review the construction at various steps in the process to ensure it is being constructed properly.

The point about building codes and laws is to remind us that regulatory laws pervade our lives in many ways where we live, work, and play. Administrative or regulatory laws guide our lives and provide protections probably more than most other areas of the law. Federal administrative laws are everywhere, governing labor relations, social security, disability and disability accommodations, equal employment, electronic communications, energy production and use, the banking system with various agencies, agriculture, natural resources, the military and defense, education, immigration, transportation, veterans' affairs, trade, the safety of foods, drugs, and cosmetics, consumer products, the air we breathe, and the water we drink—to name a few. There are also analogous state agencies in each of the 50 state jurisdictions.

We will not discuss even a small percentage of these. Instead, the following discussion focuses on aspects of two environmental health laws: protections for employees in the workplace from the toxic substance asbestos, and protection of the public from toxic air pollutants. Before beginning that discussion, consider a broader background.

---

10 *Black's Law Dictionary* (2004). (8th ed.), p. 47. Bryan A. Garner, Ed. West Publishing.

Environmental Health Laws

In the 1970s, Congress created a variety of laws to protect the public from toxic substances, ranging from carcinogens to pollutants in the air to developmental toxicants to toxic substances in the workplace, ambient air, drinking water, consumer products, and other areas of our lives. These included the Occupational Safety and Health Act [OSHA] (1970), the Clean Air Act [CAA] (1970), the Clean Water Act (1972), the Consumer Product Safety Act (1972), the Safe Drinking Water Act (1976), and the Toxic Substances Control Act (1976), as well as significant amendments to the Federal Insecticide, Fungicide and Rodenticide Act (1972) and the Food, Drug, and Cosmetic Act (1968). We will briefly consider two of these laws—the Clean Air Act (CAA), administered by the US Environmental Protection Agency, and the Occupational Safety and Health Act, administered by the Occupational Safety and Health Administration.

Congress passes laws authorizing administrative agencies to carry out the general law and policies of a legislature under the guidance of the executive branch of government or under the guidance of an agency independent of the executive (so-called "'independent" agencies). There is something of an explicit preventive goal of administrative laws. They typically are authorized to identify problems or harms in a certain area of public life and address them. They seek to protect us from intrusions on protected areas (or rights) by trying to prevent problems from arising, solving problems that exist, and preventing harms from materializing (that typically affect large numbers or people). They aim to place a greater emphasis on providing prospective guidance and protections compared with retrospective liability or punishments. However, under many administrative laws, issues do arise to which an administrative agency must respond or react to problems, so there can be an aspect of retrospective lawmaking. Congress has choices concerning the extent to which administrative laws are more or less preventive in nature.[11]

In outline, we might say that Congress passes enabling legislation, authorizing the creation of an administrative agency, such as the Occupational Safety and Health Administration (OSHA), or the Environmental Protection Agency (EPA), or extending the authority of an existing agency to address some new problems of social concern. Those agencies in turn are authorized to address a group of problems and conduct appropriate scientific inquiries to identify and remedy them. A few more specific features of these complex laws follow next.

In creating administrative agencies, Congress recognized two major issues. First, legislators did not have the expertise or skill set needed to address the problems at issue with all their particularity and detail. For instance, does Congress have the understanding and expertise to determine the components

11 How well administrative laws prevent harms depends upon their provisions; consider exposures to toxic substances. Most environmental health laws are so-called "postmarket laws." Agencies such as the US Environmental Protection Agency administering many of these laws typically responds to evidence of a problem or harm that should be addressed. Once the agency identifies and then reduces, say, a toxic exposure, citizens in the future will have the protection of the legal action. Before such an action is taken, however, people were exposed to a toxicant and might have suffered illnesses. In contrast, the Food and Drug Administration, in reviewing pharmaceuticals for commercialization, requires that such products must be assessed for their "safety" and "effectiveness" *before* entering the market and the public is exposed. These are called "premarket testing and licensing laws." People typically are not exposed to medicines with significant adverse effects because they have been reviewed for their safety and effectiveness before they enter the market. This approach much better protects the public from harms than postmarket laws can achieve.

of air pollution, their size, and how they should be regulated? Just posing the question makes the answer obvious—experts in various fields are needed to make such assessments. Second, however, Congress in creating separate institutions with experts and lawyers for implementing legislative authority poses some risk of a "fourth branch of government" (in addition to the legislative, the executive, and the judicial components).

To address the first issue, Congress authorized the appropriate agencies with legal resources and the authority to address issues within their purview.

To address the second, Congress also created the Administrative Procedure Act (1946) to guide how agencies should carry out their legal tasks by staying within the boundaries of the substantive law. The APA "applies to all executive branch and independent agencies, prescribes procedures for agency rulemakings and adjudications, as well as standards for judicial review of final agency actions."[12] Two common types of agencies are those in the executive branch and so-called 'independent agencies." The first group answers directly to the president of the United States, while independent agencies do not.

Administrative agencies can issue protective rules by several procedures. The most common one is "informal rule-making." Agencies are "required to provide the public with adequate *notice* of a proposed rule [typically published in the *Federal Record*] followed by a meaningful opportunity to *comment* on the rule's content [by written or oral comments] [emphases added]."[13] Once comments have been received, an agency must provide a general statement of the rule as well as its justification. It need not respond to every submitted comment, but those that are characterized as "significant."[14] It would then issue a *final* rule.

Final administrative regulations are subject to review by a Federal Circuit Court of Appeals. "Informal rule-making" is upheld by courts as long as it is not "arbitrary and capricious." This is a narrow standard of review "in which a court may not substitute its judgment for that of the agency."[15] Rather, a court should only invalidate agency determinations that fail to "examine the relevant data and articulate a satisfactory explanation for [the] action including a 'rational connection' between the facts found and the choice made."[16] There are other kinds of rule-making, but we need not pursue these here. Sometimes Congress specifies an unusual kind of rule-making as it did for the Occupational Safety and Health Act (considered below).

There are various reasons a reviewing court might find a regulation unlawful and set aside the rule, including, *inter alia,* that it is, "(A) arbitrary, capricious, an abuse of discretion, or otherwise not in accordance with law; (B) contrary to constitutional right, power, privilege, or immunity; (C) in excess of statutory jurisdiction, authority, or limitations, or short of statutory right; (D) without observance of procedure required by law ..."[17] We do not need to pause these issues to provide some understanding of the role of administrative agencies in the legal system.

---

12 Todd Garvey (2017-03-27). A Brief Overview of Rulemaking and Judicial Review (PDF) (Report). Washington, DC: US Congressional Research Service. R41546.

13 *Ibid.*, at 2.

14 *Ibid.*, at 3.

15 *Motor Vehicle Manufacturers Association v. State Farm Auto Mutual Insurance Co.*, 463 U.S. 29, 43 (1983).

16 *Ibid.*, at 43.

17 Garvey, A Brief Overview of Rulemaking and Judicial Review, 13.

Administrative agencies and the regulations they issue differ from the criminal law and torts we have considered. For one thing, administrative agencies have substantial capacities and "the talent, knowledge, and energy of many persons to achieve a common goal," such as reducing or eliminating particulate air particles or lead in the air in a comprehensive manner so they do not damage the health of the public.[18] In addition, their goal is not to adjudicate or resolve individualized disputes between private parties as occurs in the tort law or between a public prosecutor and an individual defendant as in the criminal law.

One other topic should be briefly mentioned in this context. In addition to administrative regulations, the President of the United States may and often does issue "executive orders," often hundreds in a four- or eight-year period of an adminisation. This is a written instrument the President can use, within limits, to shape federal policy, especially concerning the functioning of the executive branch and largely affecting domestic policy, that does not encroach on congressional authority, and that has the "force and effect of law."[19] Such orders may be issued independently of Congressional actions (unlike regulatory actions following Congressional legislation). Tyically, an executive order would be reviewed by the Office of Management and Budget, the Attorney General, and the Director of the Office of the Federal Register, but this need not be the case.

There is no specific authority for Presidential executive orders, but on occasion Congress may authorize them, and Presidential authority is generally supported by Article II of the Constituton.[20] Generic Constitutional authority rests with the President to "take Care that the Laws be faithfully executed," required by oath to "faithfully execute the Office of President of the United States," and, to the best of his "Ability, preserve, protect and defend the Constitution of the United States."[21] Presidents have utilized executive orders over many years to address a variety of issues. Notable executive orders include President Lincoln's *Emancipation Proclamation,* President Rosevelt's creation of internment camps for Japanese citizens during World War II, President Kennedy's order banning discrimination in federally funded housing, and President Johnson's Order banning discrimination in government hiring of contractors.[22]

Regulatory actions properly created under the requirements of the Administrative Procedure Act and the relevant law have an important staying power. Particular regulations can remain in effect for a long time. They can be modified or overturned by a future Presidential administration, but any changes must be made in accordance with and addressing the same issues as the initial administrative action on the topic. The syllabus of a major administrative law case, *Motor Vechicle Manufacturers Association v. State Farm*, provided below outlines major requirements for changing a duly created regulation. The Reagan administration, under the influence of automobile manufacturers, sought by changing a regulation issued by a previous administration to eliminate so-called "passive restraints" in automobiles (such as automatic seatbelts or airbags) to protect vehicle occupants. The U.S. Supreme Court did not permit this, arguing that to change a regulation the new administration had to address the same issues considered by the

---

18 Jerry L. Mashaw & Richard A. Merrill, *Administrative law: The American public law system, cases and materials* (1983). (2nd ed.), p. 224. West Publishing.

19 Jonathan M. Gaffney, *Congressional Research Service*, "Executive Orders: An Introduction," at p. 1, located at https://crsreports.congress.gov/product/pdf/R/R46738.

20 Ibid., at 1.

21 Ibid. at 5.

22 Contact Team, *Legal Dictionary, "Executive Orders"*, July 29, 2016

previous administration and persuasively show why they should be changed, before this action could be taken. Thus, administrative regulations issued by one Presidential administration can have a kind of staying power as a result of this legal case.

The same cannot be said of Presidential executive orders. A previous President's executive order can be changed by the stroke of a pen cancelling it or creating a contrary order. Thus, executive orders are much less permanent than administrative regulations enacted under the authority of Congress or the Administrative Procedure Act.

Turn now to some more detailed examples of administrative actions that aim to protect the public's health in the workplace and in the environment after considering some general features of these laws in outline.

Some of the regulatory tasks under the Occupational Safety and Health Act, or the OSH Act for short, are to identify potential physical harms as well as hazardous substances in the workplace and issue rules to protect employees. Two hazardous substances addressed early in the history of this law were vinyl chloride and asbestos. The agency had to consider whether or not exposures should be reduced to better protect workers from diseases. Or under laws administered by the US EPA, such as the Clean Air Act, the EPA would consider whether exposures to air pollutants, including the tiny $PM_{2.5}$ particulates to which citizens are exposed and penetrate deeply into the lungs, or lead in the ambient air, should be reduced to better protect the public's health.

While an administrative agency like the EPA has broad powers, it cannot exceed the authority Congress delegated to it (noted above). In *Whitman v. American Trucking*, which we consider, the Supreme Court indicates that the US Constitution vests "[a]ll *legislative* powers herein granted ... in a Congress of the United States [emphasis added]."[23] Because regulations issued by administrative agencies must be authorized by the Congress in the case of federal legislation, the regulations issued by an agency must not exceed what Congress has authorized, and the agency in issuing legal constraints on activities must not engage in "legislation," but only act within the *discretion* conferred by Congress.[24]

That is, the statute authorizing an agency to address a range of problems must implement its guidance and intentions and not violate it by going outside the statutory limitations as just discussed.

How Do Protective Regulations from an Agency Come into Existence?

Once a problem is identified as being appropriate for an agency to take up, such as excessive levels of asbestos in workplaces or small particulates in the air we breathe, the agency has the authority to issue a **notice of a proposed regulation** addressing it; e.g., reducing concentrations of asbestos in the workplace (OSHA) or particulates in the ambient air (EPA). Because typical administrative actions require both factual (usually scientific data) and policy judgments, the law typically authorizes appropriate fact-finding (e.g., the scientific task) and the creation of regulations in accordance with the legal policies specified or implicit in the law following a **procedural and substantive *blueprint***. The procedural steps indicate how the agency must make a regulation and the substantive blueprint specifies the congressionally mandated legal standards the regulations must meet to protect the public according to the law.

---

23 US Constitution, Article I, § 1, cited in *Whitman v. American Trucking*, 121 S.Ct. 903, at 907.

24 *Motor Vehicles v. State Farm*, 103 S.Ct. 2856 (Supreme Court of the United States, 2001), at 2866.

For instance, Congress authorized OSHA to ensure that employees exposed to toxic substances in the workplace "must adequately ensure, to the extent feasible, that no employee suffer material impairment of health or functional capacity" even if the employee is exposed for a working lifetime, assumed to be 45 years. Thus, OSHA must issue health protections for the working environment to protect against toxic substances, such as asbestos, that are in accordance with the "material impairment standard" of the OSH Act.

The Clean Air Act (CAA) initially passed by Congress in 1970 required the US Environmental Protection Agency to issue exposure standards for some air pollutants that protect the public health "with an ample margin of safety," including sensitive subpopulations.[25] The EPA must "identify the maximum airborne concentration of a pollutant that the public health can tolerate, decrease the concentration to provide an 'adequate' margin of safety, and set the standard at that level."[26] The EPA followed this section of the CAA in setting standards for air pollutants such as *small particulate matter* and, in a different case, *airborne lead* so that the public health would be protected "with an ample margin of safety."

Once a **notice** of a proposed regulation is issued and publicized in the *Federal Register*, the legislation normally provides for a **comment period** (typically at least 30 days, sometimes up to 60 to 90 days), during which an agency is obliged to hear and take written comments from the public at large, including interested parties, such as industries that might be affected by the regulation, as well as public health or union interest groups that might be on the other side of the issue.[27]

Following this, the agency, taking into account and evaluating submitted comments, would then issue **a final regulation** that has the force of law and can be enforced by the agency, unless there is a legal challenge.[28] An agency's **issuing a regulation** is an act of creating a law quite specific to the problem it was addressing and under the auspices of enabling legislation.

The substantive legal provisions specifying the extent of risk permitted under the law implicitly establish a congressionally enacted philosophy about the distribution of benefits and burdens from toxic substances and sometimes the costs of controlling them under the statute.

The Occupational Safety and Health Act

For instance, the Occupational Safety and Health Act requires OSHA to protect workers from toxic materials or harmful physical agents in the workplace, including asbestos. To carry out the legislative mandate, OSHA

> shall set the [health] standard which most adequately assures, to the extent feasible, on the basis of the best available evidence, that no employee will suffer material impairment

25 Clean Air Act, § 109(b)(1).

26 *Whitman v. American Trucking*, 121 S.Ct. 903 (Supreme Court of the United States, 2001).

27 This is called "notice and comment" rule-making.

28 Only legislative rules (which go through notice and comment) have the force of law. Interpretive rules do not go through notice and comment and simply interpret what Congress has already said. They do not create new rights or obligations and do not have the force of law.

> of health or functional capacity even if such employee has regular exposure to the hazard dealt with by such standard for the period of his working life [assumed to be 45 years].[29]

Focusing first on the OSH Act reveals notable ideas about how the Occupational Safety and Health Administration works: 1) To protect employees from health hazards, the agency must issue health standards that "most adequately assure that no employee will suffer material impairment of health or functional capacity" even with 45 years of exposure to it. In principle, this sets a decent goal for health protection. It does not require that employees must have the same life expectancy as the wider public, but it seeks to ensure no impairment of health while the person is working. Will such a person have good health in retirement? That's outside the scope of the law. A more protective standard might have been to ensure that employees' life expectancy not be lower than that of analogous people in the general public, thus setting an employment standard that seeks to ensure that a person's health not suffer diminution because of where they work. Recall in *McAllister v. Workmen's Compensation Appeals Board* that the firefighter, Mr. McAllister, died comparatively young from smoke inhalation from his job (and his own smoking). Although the OSHA standard was not applicable to him, he likely did not have as long a life as the average man in the general population.

2) However, to have safe workplaces, OSHA must address numerous toxic substances required by the law to which working people would be exposed, and there are many. That is, the scope of the OSH Act covers *all toxic substances* encountered in the workplace. Yet, OSHA has addressed few toxic or hazardous substances during its existence because it is typically subjected to intense lobbying by the affected companies. For instance, in 27 years, it issued only eight rules to protect employees from toxic substances. Moreover, "*workplace exposures remain significantly above even the relatively lax limits OSHA has set* [emphasis in original]," and "OSHA has regulated only a vanishingly small fraction of all the chemicals workers are exposed to."[30] The lobbying pressures on OSHA represent one of its major weaknesses as a law for protecting workers exposed to toxicants. We return to this in the last chapter.

3) Once a final regulation has been issued, it becomes a law that must be obeyed by affected individuals or businesses, unless one of the parties affected by the regulation appeals it to a US Circuit Court of Appeals. If it is appealed, typically a court would review it to determine whether it was made **in accordance with the procedures** specified in the enabling legislation and whether it satisfied the **substantive requirements of the law**. On appeal, it may be upheld by the court in toto, upheld in part and overturned in part, or overturned by the court in toto on procedural or substantive grounds.

If the regulation is not appealed, it becomes the law that companies must follow. If it is appealed and upheld, legally it goes into effect. If it is overturned, the agency would have to revise it as specified by the court of appeals.

In order to have a better idea about how the Occupational Safety and Health law would function, consider an early regulation of exposures to asbestos in the workplace. I have substantially edited the

---

29 Occupation Safety and Health Act, Code of Federal Regulations, Chapter 16, OCCUPATIONAL SAFETY AND HEALTH, section 655 (b)(5), p. 999.

30 Adam M. Finkel, Testimony of Adam M. Finkel Before the U.S. House of Representatives, Committee on Energy and Commerce, Environment and Climate Change Subcommittee, Hearing on "Mismanaging Chemical Risks: EPA's Failure to Protect Workers," March 13, 2019.

legal opinion that follows to assist the reading and to highlight only a few issues. (I have left in headings so you can see some of the complexity faced by administrative agencies in trying to provide (in this case) protections to employees from the toxic substance, asbestos.) It must address a number of issues that can quickly become complex.

In the first part of the legal opinion, the court of appeals outlines some of the main features of the OSH Act and how it should function. The main issue of importance in this litigation is whether OSHA can take economic costs into account in how long it permits companies to implement the new exposure rules, and the extent to which economic feasibility of a health standard may be considered. The court holds that economic costs of delaying a safer exposure to asbestos are practical concessions allowed under the law. However, very important in this discussion is the court's account of the permissibility of taking economic considerations into account—it is legally permissible to do so under this law, but read the **bolded** section carefully because the costs of implementing the protections do not trump all other legal considerations. Moreover, the court notes that protecting employees will cost money and profits, arguing that Congress rightly saw this point. In particular, note the boundaries the court sketches for imposing costs on companies (when they are permitted) along with some of the limitations (when imposed costs might become too great).

Industrial Union Department, Afl-Cio, et al. v. Hodgson, Secretary, Department of Labor

United States Court of Appeals, District of Columbia Circuit

499 F.2d 467 (1974)

Opinion: McGOWAN, Circuit Judge:

This direct review proceeding presents a classic case of what Judge Friendly has aptly termed "a new form of uneasy partnership" between agency and court that results whenever Congress delegates decision making of a legislative character to the one, subject to review by the other. … **The angularity of this relationship is only sharpened when, as here, Congress—with no apparent awareness of anomaly—has explicitly combined an informal agency procedure with a standard of review traditionally conceived of as suited to formal adjudication or rulemaking. The federal courts, hard pressed as they are by the flood of new tasks imposed upon them by Congress, surely have some claim to be spared additional burdens deriving from the illogic of legislative compromise. At the least, it would have been helpful if there had been some recognition by Congress that the quick answer it gave to a legislative stalemate posed serious problems for a reviewing court, and that there would inevitably have to be some latitude accorded it to surmount those problems consistently with the legislative purposes.** The duty remains, in any event, to decide the case before us in accordance with our statutory mandate, however dimly the rationale, if any, underlying it can be perceived.

The petition before us seeks review of standards promulgated by the Secretary of Labor under the Occupational Safety and Health Act of 1970, (hereinafter OSHA). The standards in question regulate the atmospheric concentrations of asbestos dust in industrial workplaces.

Petitioners are unions whose members are affected by the health hazards of asbestos dust. They challenge the timetable established by the standards for the achievement of permissible levels of concentration, and object to portions of the standards concerning methods of compliance, monitoring intervals and techniques, cautionary labels and notices, and medical examinations and records. We remand two of such issues to the Secretary for further consideration. In all other respects, the petition is denied.

I.

A. The Occupational Safety and Health Act

Technological progress in industry appears not to have been accompanied uniformly by corresponding reductions in the health hazards of industrial working conditions. More than 2.2 million persons are disabled on the job each year, and in 1967 the Surgeon General estimated that approximately 400,000 new cases of occupational disease would occur in each succeeding year. The Chairman of the Committee on Labor and Public Welfare summarized the problem as follows:

Not only are occupational diseases which first came to light at the beginning of the Industrial Revolution still undermining the health of workers, but new substances, new processes, and new sources of energy are presenting health problems of ever-increasing complexity. […]

OSHA, the first comprehensive attempt by Congress to deal with these problems, covers every employer whose business affects interstate commerce. Eschewing any attempt to establish substantive provisions to control all these various employers, the **Act erects a general framework to govern the development of regulations**, and delegates the task of formulating particular health and safety standards to the Secretary of Labor. Civil and criminal sanctions are provided to enforce compliance.

OSHA specifies the procedure to be followed in the promulgation of standards, and provides for the establishment of a research institute and the appointment of advisory committees to assist the Secretary.[4] The **substantive provisions of the Act impose a general obligation upon employers to provide safe working conditions**. … The Secretary is required to promulgate standards to control particular health hazards that come to his attention. Certain types of controls, including monitoring, medical examinations, warnings, record keeping, and specific protective measures are specified by the statute itself, but the decision as to when and how they should be required with regard to particular health hazards is left to the Secretary.

B. Asbestos

Asbestos is a generic term applicable to a number of fibrous, inorganic, silicate minerals that are incombustible in air. Its commercial value is high, and its uses are many and varied. Asbestos can be woven into cloth, used in powder form, or incorporated into materials of various shapes and consistencies. Almost one million tons of asbestos are used in this country annually; and, for many purposes, it cannot easily be replaced with other substances.

Unfortunately, asbestos is as hazardous to health as it is useful to industry. During its production and use, tiny asbestos fibers are released as a dust in the air, and, over the course of this century, thousands of workers have been killed or disabled by the effects of inhaling these fibers. There are no precise figures concerning the number of workers involved, but it is estimated that three to five million workers are exposed to some extent to asbestos fibers in the building construction and shipyard industries alone. While OSHA was under consideration in Congress, the health hazards of the asbestos industry were among the examples used to stress the need for legislation.

C. Proceedings before the Secretary

Within a few months of the effective date of OSHA, petitioners [unions] requested the Secretary to establish an emergency standard to control concentrations of asbestos dust.[8] The Secretary promptly issued a temporary standard and set in motion the procedure for establishment of a permanent standard. Notice of the proposed rulemaking was published, and interested persons were invited to submit their views. NIOSH [National Institute for Occupational Safety & Health] submitted its recommendations, as did the Advisory Committee. These were made public, and the Secretary conducted a hearing at which various representatives and experts appeared on behalf of interested parties. On the basis of these recommendations and a formidable record of documents and oral testimony, including highly technical statements by expert witnesses, the Secretary established the standards in question. His statement of reasons covers some four and one-half pages of the Federal Register.

Petitioners allege no procedural errors in the promulgation of these standards, but they characterize them as inadequate to protect the health of employees **as required by the Act**. They attack the Secretary's interpretation of OSHA in certain particulars, as well as the enforcement measures he has selected.

II

OSHA is a self-contained statute in the sense that it does not depend upon reference to the Administrative Procedure Act [APA] for specification of the procedures to be followed. It prescribes that the process of promulgating a standard is to be initiated by the publication of a proposed rule. Interested persons are given a period of 30 days thereafter within which to submit written data or comments. Within this period any interested person may submit written objections, and may request a public hearing thereon. In such event, the Secretary shall publish a notice specifying the particular standard involved and stating the time and place of the hearing. Within 60 days after the completion of such hearing, the Secretary shall make his decision. Judicial review by the courts of appeals is provided.

This procedure is characteristic of the **informal rulemaking** contemplated by Section 4 of the APA, and it was so understood by the Congress. [I]nferences of policy drawn from those although describing it as "legislative in type," has provided that the oral hearing called for in the statute shall contain some elements normally associated with the adjudicatory or **formal rulemaking** model. [...]

The substantial evidence test has customarily been directed to adjudicatory proceedings or **formal** rulemaking. The hybrid nature of OSHA in this respect can be explained historically, if not logically, as a legislative compromise. The Conference Report reflects that the Senate bill called for informal rulemaking, but the House version specified formal rulemaking and substantial evidence review. The House receded on the procedure for promulgating standards, but the substantial evidence standard of review was adopted.[14] [...]

Faced with the fact that his determinations were commanded by Congress to be reviewed under a substantial evidence standard, the Secretary did voluntarily move his procedures significantly towards the formal model. He directed that (1) a qualified hearing examiner should preside over the oral hearing, (2) cross-examination should be permitted, and (3) a verbatim transcript made. The total record in this case was in part created under the conditions that obtain in a formal proceeding. [The record also contains] a melange of written statements, letters, reports, and similar materials received outside the bounds of the oral hearing and untested by anything approaching the adversary process.

Thus, in some degree the record approaches the form of one customarily conceived of as appropriate for substantial evidence review. In other respects, it does not. [...]

[The] OSH Act sets forth general policy objectives and establishes the basic procedural framework for the promulgation of standards, but the formulation of specific substantive provisions is left largely to the Secretary. The Secretary's task thus contains "elements of both a legislative policy determination and an adjudicative resolution of disputed facts." [...]

Decision making must in that circumstance depend to a greater extent upon policy judgments and less upon purely factual analysis.[18] Thus, in addition to currently unresolved factual issues, the formulation of standards involves **choices that by their nature require basic policy determinations** rather than resolution of factual controversies. Judicial review of inherently legislative decisions of this sort is obviously an undertaking of different dimensions.

For example, in this case the evidence indicated that reliable data is not currently available with respect to the precisely predictable health effects of various levels of exposure to asbestos dust; nevertheless, the Secretary was obligated to establish some specific level as the maximum permissible exposure. After considering all the conflicting evidence, the Secretary [adopted]... a relatively low limit in terms of the severe health consequences which could result from over-exposure. Inasmuch as the protection of the health of employees is the overriding concern of OSHA, this choice is doubtless sound, but it rests in the final analysis on an **essentially legislative policy judgment**, rather than a factual determination, concerning the relative risks of underprotection as compared to overprotection.

Regardless of the manner in which the task of judicial review is articulated, policy choices of this sort are not susceptible to the same type of verification or refutation by reference to the record as are some factual questions. Consequently, the court's approach must necessarily be different no matter how the standards of review are labeled. ... "The paramount [court] objective is to see whether the agency, given an essentially legislative task to perform, has carried it out in a manner calculated to negate the dangers of arbitrariness and irrationality in the formulation of rules for general application in the future.

[W]e do not understand that we should] treat the Secretary's decision making under OSHA as something different from what it is, namely, the exercise of delegated power to make within certain limits decisions that Congress normally makes itself, and by processes, as the courts have long recognized and accepted, peculiar to itself. A due respect for the boundaries between the legislative and the judicial function dictates that we approach our reviewing task with a flexibility informed and shaped by sensitivity to the diverse origins of the determinations that enter into a legislative judgment.

What we are entitled to at all events is a careful identification by the Secretary, when his proposed standards are challenged, of the reasons why he chooses to follow one course rather than another. Where that choice purports to be based on the existence of certain determinable facts, the Secretary must, in form as well as substance, find those facts from evidence in the record. By the same token, when the Secretary is obliged to make policy judgments where no factual certainties exist or where facts alone do not provide the answer, he should so state and go on to identify the considerations he found persuasive. [...]

III

Before addressing the specific challenges made to the Secretary's action, we examine two further problems raised by petitioners involving statutory construction. One has to do with the weight to be accorded by the Secretary to the NIOSH recommendations [not included]. The other relates to whether the Secretary may take economic considerations into account. [...]

In connection with the second issue, we note that the statutory authority for the promulgation of standards reads in relevant part:

The Secretary ... shall set the standard which most adequately assures, **to the extent feasible**, on the basis of the best available evidence, that no employee will suffer material impairment of health or functional capacity ...

[...] The Secretary explained his decision to delay, two years longer than the period suggested by NIOSH, implementation of the tougher standard as "necessary to allow employers to make the needed changes for coming into compliance," and petitioners argue that the Secretary improperly considered economic factors in reaching this conclusion. **We conclude that the factors entering into the Secretary's conclusion could properly include problems of economic feasibility.**

There can be no question that OSHA represents a decision to require safeguards for the health of employees even if such measures substantially increase production costs. This is not, however, the same thing as saying that Congress intended to require immediate implementation of all protective measures technologically achievable without regard for their economic impact. To the contrary, it would comport with common usage to say that a standard that is prohibitively expensive is not "feasible." [...]

[P]ractical considerations can temper protective requirements. Congress does not appear to have intended to protect employees by putting their employers out of business—either by requiring protective devices unavailable under existing technology or by making financial viability generally impossible.

This qualification is not intended to provide a route by which recalcitrant employers or industries may avoid the reforms contemplated by the Act. Standards may be economically feasible even though, from the standpoint of employers, they are financially burdensome and affect profit margins adversely. Nor does the concept of economic feasibility necessarily guarantee the continued existence of individual employers. It would appear to be consistent with the purposes of the Act to envisage the economic demise of an employer who has lagged behind the rest of the industry in protecting the health and safety of employees and is consequently financially unable to comply with new standards as quickly as other employers. As the effect becomes more widespread within an industry, the problem of economic feasibility becomes more pressing. For example, if the standard requires changes that only a few leading firms could quickly achieve, delay might be necessary to avoid increasing the concentration of that industry. Similarly, if the competitive structure or posture of the industry would be otherwise adversely affected—perhaps rendered unable to compete with imports or with substitute products[24]— the Secretary could properly consider that factor. These tentative examples are offered not to illustrate concrete instances of economic unfeasibility but rather to suggest the complex elements that may be relevant to such a determination.[25]

With the aid of the foregoing analytic background of the procedural and substantive provisions of the Act, we turn to the specific objections raised by petitioners to the standards.

1. Effective Date for the Two Fiber Standard

The most important aspect of setting the standards was the determination of an acceptable dust concentration level. Under the **emergency standards**, the eight hour time-weighted average airborne concentration of asbestos dust had been limited to five fibers greater than five microns in length per milliliter of air (hereinafter "the five fiber standard"). A principal issue at the hearings on the **permanent standards was whether the standard should remain at five fibers or be lowered to two**. Proponents of standards ranging from zero to twelve fibers appeared, and it is fair to say that the evidence did not establish any one position as clearly correct. The Secretary decided to resolve this doubt in favor of greater protection of the health of employees, and established the two fiber standard recommended by NIOSH and his Advisory Committee as the level ultimately to be achieved.

Industry representatives testified that they simply could not reduce concentrations to the two fiber level in the foreseeable future. ... The Secretary decided to retain the five fiber standard for approximately four years (July 1, 1976) before requiring the reduction to two fibers, in order to give employers time to prepare for the lower limit. Petitioners assert that the four year delay permitted by the Secretary is too long because (1) the health of employees is endangered thereby, and (2) employers do not need that much time.

a. Health Hazards Occasioned by the Delay

The Secretary solicited the views of several experts on the question of the predictable health effects of maintaining a five fiber standard until 1976. The experts differed sharply in some of their opinions, but their responses are generally cautious and reflect deficiencies in available data concerning the relationship between exposure to asbestos dust and the likelihood of disease. The record indicates that no precise prediction of increased harm can be made at this time.

The Secretary must establish those standards that most adequately ensure that no employee will suffer material impairment of health. **We cannot say**, on the basis of the conflicting testimony in the record, **that the Secretary erred in his prediction of the health effect** of the four year delay, but neither can we say that employees are not exposed to some additional risk of disease because of greater exposure. In view of the Act's express allowance for problems of feasibility, the Secretary's decision to allow a four year delay is **not irrational** with regard to those industries that require that long to meet the standard. It is appropriate to allow sufficient time to permit an orderly industry-wide transition since, in those cases, the indeterminate degree of risk involved is counterbalanced by considerations of feasibility; it is not, however, a risk to which employees should be needlessly exposed.

b. Industrial Compliance Capability

The evidence indicates that significant inter-industry, as well as intra-industry, differences exist concerning the time needed by employers to meet a two fiber standard. Within particular industries the concentration levels at some plants, usually newer ones, are much lower than at others. More importantly, some industries could implement a two fiber standard more quickly than others. [...]

[T]he Secretary issued a single uniform effective date for all employers in all industries. He explained this decision as follows:

"It is concluded there should be one minimum standard of exposure to asbestos applicable to all workplaces exposed to any kind of mixture of kinds of asbestos. Reasons of practical administration preclude a variety of standards for different kinds of asbestos and of workplaces."

We cannot say on this record that an attempt to assign differing effective dates to employers within an industry based on the time needed by each employer to alter his plant would be practicable. However, insofar as inter-industry differences are concerned, those reasons of practical administration are neither explained nor readily apparent. [...]

Separate standards for different industries would not appear to create opportunities for employers in one industry to challenge their standards on the grounds that standards for another industry were less demanding. The only relevant question would be whether the time schedule established for each industry was feasible for that industry; therefore, comparisons with the standards established for a different industry with different technological problems would be pointless unless the two industries were in competition with one another. If one industry could gain a competitive advantage over another by virtue of differing standards, employers in the disadvantaged industry might challenge the standards on a comparative basis, but the threat of problems of that type does not appear on the basis of the record before us to justify a uniform standard for all industries.

It may be that the task of devising categories and classifying employers by industry would be unmanageable in view of the many diverse uses of asbestos. However, there is no evidence to that effect in the record, and it is not for the court to guess at the Secretary's reasoning or to supply justifications for his action. We have noted his cryptic reference to "reasons of practical administration," but, insofar as inter-industry distinctions are concerned, those reasons are not self-evident. Therefore, we remand this aspect of the standards to the Secretary for clarification or reconsideration.

2. Monitoring Requirements

Within six months of publication of the standards, all employers are required to monitor workplaces to determine whether the concentrations of asbestos dust are within the allowable limits; [...]

The monitoring provisions are especially important because the results of that process often determine when and what protective measures are required. [...]

Periodic monitoring is important to ensure that concentration levels have not been allowed to increase since the initial monitoring. Further, monitoring techniques may not be entirely uniform, and, in any event, concentrations of asbestos in the air may not remain stable throughout a working day or from one day to the next. [...]

Petitioners seem to fear that, because of the imprecise language of this requirement, the six months maximum interval between monitoring samples will in practice become the minimum as well, and they consider that inappropriate. The imprecision is perhaps unavoidable, however, in view of the multitude of diverse industrial situations involved. The most effective manner in which to deal with problems of this sort would appear to be to invoke the procedures for detecting and correcting violations in particular workplaces. In the context of a claim concerning a specific situation, it would be possible to develop a record on the question of the adequacy of the monitoring interval for that particular workplace—a record necessarily absent in the context of these proceedings to establish a general guideline.

3. Methods of Compliance—Scope of Applicability [...]

4. Use of Moisturization as a Control Method […]

Further, this aspect of the Secretary's standards is consistent with the general Congressional scheme. OSHA applies to an estimated 4 million employers and 57 million employees, but the Secretary **has only about 600 inspectors and 100 industrial hygienists**. In this situation some reliance on self-policing by employers is clearly necessary. Although this self-regulatory aspect of the statute would make specific, objective standards desirable, devising standards of this sort that will be generally applicable to thousands of different situations involves enormous practical difficulties. Setting forth inflexible requirements of particular methods would be effective only if the Secretary could anticipate all possible problems and devise a uniform approach appropriate to each. … [The] Secretary has in some instances employed a somewhat open-ended scheme to allow development of different methods for different workplaces. […]

5. Labels and Warnings

In order to ensure that employees handle materials likely to produce asbestos dust carefully and to prevent persons from entering areas where they will be exposed to such dust needlessly, cautionary labels and warning signs are required by the Secretary's standards. Petitioners assert that the language selected by the Secretary is not strong enough for these purposes, … [however], we cannot say it is required by OSHA. … they are within the range of the Secretary's discretion.

6. Medical Examinations

The standards require that all employers provide a medical examination (1) when an employee is first assigned to a job involving exposure to asbestos, (2) when he leaves that job, and (3) annually during his employment in the position. […]

5. The Recordkeeping Requirements

…

a. Medical Records …
b. Records of Exposure Levels Detected by Monitoring …

Except for the remand we order for reexamination of (1) the uniform application of the 1976 effective date for the two fiber standard and (2) the three year retention period for monitoring records, the petition for review is denied. **All of the challenged features of the standards appear to partake of an essentially legislative type of decision making by the Secretary in the performance of the broad delegation made to him by Congress. Had any one of these decisions been made in the first instance by Congress itself and embodied in the statute, its vulnerability to judicial scrutiny would have been dubious indeed**. In this context, therefore, judicial review inevitably runs the risk of becoming arbitrary supervision and revision of the Secretary's efforts to effectuate the legislative purposes in an area where variant responses might each be legitimate in the sight of Congress.

What, in our view, differentiates the two provisions we have remanded from those we have left untouched is that the record, examined closely in relation to the relevant concerns of the Act, leaves nagging questions—even for the inexpert observer—as to the reason and rationale for the Secretary's particular choices. However the statutory standard for our review may be characterized, we consider that our dispositions fall within it.

(Citations omitted)

Notes

4 The Act establishes within the Department of Health, Education, and Welfare a National Institute for Occupational Safety and Health (NIOSH) which is authorized to "develop and

establish recommended occupational safety and health standards" for transmission to the Secretary of Labor. 29 U.S.C. 671. The Secretary of Labor may also appoint an advisory committee to assist him in his standard-setting functions.

8 Under 29 U.S.C. § 655(c), the Secretary can issue an immediately effective emergency standard without observing the procedural requirements for a permanent standard if (1) employees are exposed to grave danger, and (2) the emergency standard is necessary to protect them. The Secretary must then publish a permanent standard within six months.

14 This combination is made even more confusing by a statement in the report that seems to indicate that the Conference Committee thought the substantial evidence standard was less exacting then the standard of rationality ordinarily applicable to the results of informal rulemaking. ... For a more detailed discussion of these legislative events, see Associated Industries, 470 supra, where the Second Circuit said that the Congressional intention was clear "to adopt the substantial evidence test for review as a tradeoff for the House's abandoning its insistence on rule-making on the record ..." 487 F.2d at 349.

18 Where existing methodology or research in a new area of regulation is deficient, the agency *necessarily enjoys broad discretion to attempt to formulate a solution to the best of its ability on the basis of available information*. Permian Basin Area Rate Cases, 390 U.S. 747, 811, 88 S. Ct. 1344, 20 L.Ed.2d 312 (1968).

25 Since technological progress is here linked to objectives other than the traditional competitive, profit-oriented concerns of industry, accommodation of both sets of values will sometimes involve novel economic problems. International Harvester Co. v. Ruckelshaus (1973), illustrates some of these problems in the context of the automobile emissions standards of the Clean Air Act. In the highly concentrated automobile industry the court deemed it likely that, by virtue of their size and importance to the economy, any one of the three major companies could obtain a relaxation of the automobile emissions standards if it could not meet them. If this occurred after other manufacturers had prepared to comply with the standard, the technological laggard would enjoy a competitive advantage because installation of the control devices renders the vehicles less efficient to operate. This circumstance justified insuring that the standards could be met by all major producers before they became effective.

37 Employees may report to the Secretary conditions that they believe to be in violation of the standards, and request an inspection. 29 U.S.C. § 657(f)(1). Coupled with the sanctions available for violations, these provisions are designed to deter employers from ignoring their responsibilities.

What can we learn from *Hodgson*? First, we see the need to address exposures to asbestos in a wide range of workplaces in a more comprehensive manner than could be done in tort law cases (and this would be even less plausible in a criminal case) (you should consider why).

Second, the DC Circuit complains that Congress has given it a particularly difficult task because of inconsistencies in how the law was written (a small point). However, a larger issue related to this is that courts are required to review what an administrative agency has done and whether or not this is consistent with the procedures specified in the law and protections properly specified in the legislation.

Third, we begin to understand some of the scientific and legal complexities administrative agencies must address as they grapple with determining how to make workplaces sufficiently safe where employees will be exposed to a toxicant such as asbestos. Administrative agencies must address some quite complex issues, and courts reviewing them must have sufficient understanding to review administrative actions properly.

Fourth, unlike the next case we consider, *Whitman v. American Trucking*, the court permits OSHA to take costs of compliance with its regulations and their timing into account under the OSH Act's "feasibility" clause, but it clearly indicates that, of course, protecting employees from harm is going to cost money and reduce profits and some firms that cannot do this efficiently may go out of business. The discussion of economic feasibility is interesting because it outlines, but does not set hard boundaries on, what costs are legally permitted as part of issuing a regulation.

The Clean Air Act

For another example of how administrative law functions, we consider a case concerning the regulation of ozone and particulate matter in the air we breathe, regulated under the Clean Air Act administered by the US Environmental Protection Agency.

Air pollution is a quite significant and likely a much underappreciated health problem brought to us via particulate matter that the EPA was seeking to reduce with the air standards discussed under *Whitman v. American Trucking*.

As background for this case, consider some of the adverse health effects of fine (small) particulates in the air on our bodies, one of the components the EPA addressed that became litigated in *Whitman*. Obviously, air pollution can both affect a person's lungs on its own and exacerbate existing breathing difficulties and some other disease endpoints, such as smoking. Chronic obstructive pulmonary disease (COPD) is an umbrella term for several lung diseases. Consider only one, emphysema. This disease of the lungs is typically caused by smoking cigarettes, environmental tobacco smoke, indoor and outdoor air pollution, or other lung irritants such as workplace dusts, fumes, or chemicals. Smoking is the most frequent cause of emphysema. However, emphysema can be aggravated or exacerbated by air pollution.

Emphysema diminishes lung capacities, reducing our ability to process oxygen and carbon dioxide. When one breathes, oxygenated air passes down the bronchial tubes leading to small air sacs called alveoli (about the thinness of a single cell), where oxygen in the air enters the bloodstream through small blood vessels called capillaries. The oxygen then travels to myriad bodily organs. Various lung pollutants can damage the alveoli, making them less elastic and reducing their effectiveness. As alveoli become less elastic and less able to expel carbon dioxide from the lungs,[31] they restrict oxygen exchange. Eventually, the invisible physiological changes in the alveoli may intrude on our lives as emphysema and impose other limitations. In advanced stages, emphysema impairs one's breathing. This can lead to shortness of breath during minor physical activities, more labored breathing while climbing stairs, or a persistent cough. More labored breathing may force one to avoid some activities. Eventually, this could induce wheezing, chest tightness, lightheadedness, and/or fatigue. "Flare-ups" of emphysema may lead to hospital visits to treat infections because of fluid accumulation in the lungs.[32] Eventually, a person may even have difficulty walking across the room.

---

31 Healthline, What is the pathophysiology of COPD?

32 Personal communication with Crystal A. Cranor, cardiac critical care nurse, April 8, 2021.

The adverse effects of $PM_{2.5}$ are not restricted to the lungs. They influence heart disease, the leading cause of death in the United States, by increasing inflammation in heart or pulmonary arteries, accelerating atherosclerosis, and altering autonomic controls of the heart, such as rhythms.[33] Exposures could create risks of myocardial or cerebral infarctions or they may increase the thickness of the blood that can lead to similar results.[34] Peak air pollution levels are associated with "potentially fatal" cardiac events for those with heart disease.[35] The probability of myocardial infarctions rises with increasing concentrations of $PM_{2.5}$.

Surprisingly, particulate air pollution adversely affects diabetes. A large international study across 10 countries "found that substantial risks exist [between $PM_{2.5}$ and diabetes] at concentrations well below those outlined in the air quality standards of WHO and national and international regulatory agencies."[36]

Clearly, $PM_{2.5}$ needs attention and reduction in the air we breathe. In 1997, the US EPA set exposure standards for $PM_{2.5}$ at 15 µg/m^3 based on a 3-year average of exposure information that was reviewed by the US Supreme Court in *Whitman v. American Trucking*.[37] The EPA's standards were opposed by a variety of companies. They argued that the agency should take into account the costs of implementing these standards. Companies often make this argument because they can point to total costs across an industry that can be very high, but assessing the benefits to people from reduced adverse health effects is much more difficult to determine. Making a policy decision solely based on costs would not likely carry out the mission of the law. They also argued that contrary to the constitution that invests federal legislative authority in Congress, EPA had exercised legislative power in coming to these air pollution standards. There were other, more technical issues we will not consider.

The appeal of EPA's rule-making on particulate and ozone standards at the first level was heard by the US Federal Court of Appeals for the District of Columbia. That court agreed with the companies who appealed that the EPA had taken on **legislative authority in rule-making that violated constitutional provisions**. However, it held that under the Clean Air Act, the EPA *may not take* the costs of implementing its ozone and particulate standards into account. The statutory language and a line of appellate courts cases agreed that this was not permissible.

Because the EPA lost some important issues at the DC Circuit, it appealed that decision to the Supreme Court of the United States.[38] The Supreme Court agreed that **cost factors are** "both so indirectly related to public health and **[importantly]** ***so full of potential for canceling the conclusions drawn from direct health effects*** **that it would have been expressly mentioned [emphasis and bold added]"** in the relevant sections of the act had **Congress meant it** to be considered.

---

33 C. Arden Pope III, Richard T. Burnett, George D. Thurston, Michael J. Thun, Eugenia E. Calle, Daniel Krewski, & John J. Godleski (2004). Cardiovascular mortality and long-term exposure to particulate air pollution: Epidemiological evidence of general pathophysiological pathways of disease. *Circulation*, *109*:71–77. https://doi.org/10.1161/01.CIR.0000108927.80044.7

34 Physicians for Social Responsibility, *Coal's assault on human health*, 22–23; see also, C. Arden Pope III, Richard T. Burnett, George D. Thurston, Michael J. Thun, Eugenia E. Calle, Daniel Krewski, & John J. Godleski (2004). Cardiovascular mortality and long-term exposure to particulate air pollution: Epidemiological evidence of general pathophysiological pathways of disease. *Circulation*, *109*:71–77. https://doi.org/10.1161/01.CIR.0000108927.80044.7F

35 Physicians for Social Responsibility, *Coal's assault on human health*, 24–25.

36 Yan Yan, Hong Xian, & Ziyad Al-Aly (2018). The 2016 global and national burden of diabetes mellitus attributable to PM2·5 air pollution. *Lancet Planet Health*, 2:e301–12. Located at www.thelancet.com/planetary-health.

37 Supreme Court of the United States, 121 S.Ct. 903 (2001).

38 Supreme Court of the United States, 121 S.Ct. 903, at 905.

The Court also **found that the EPA did *not* engage in legislative behavior (actually legislating) contrary to the Constitution**. In contrast, since the agency was merely exercising properly delegated discretion in applying the Clean Air Act, the Court overturned the DC Circuit decision on this point, finding that "the scope of discretion that § 109(b)(1) allows is well within the outer limits of the Court's nondelegation precedents, ... Statutes need not provide a determinate criterion for saying how much of a regulated harm is too much to avoid delegating legislative power."[39]

The Court did find the EPA's final implementation of the law in issuing its particulate and ozone policy was unlawful and must be revised. Against powerful commercial interests the EPA largely prevailed.

Whitman v. American Trucking Associations, Inc., et al.

Supreme Court of the United States

121 S.Ct. 903 (2001)

Syllabus

Section 109(a) of the Clean Air Act (CAA) requires the Environmental Protection Agency (EPA) Administrator to promulgate national ambient air quality standards (NAAQS) for each air pollutant for which "air quality criteria" have been issued under § 108. Pursuant to § 109(d)(1), the Administrator in 1997 revised the ozone and particulate matter NAAQS. Respondents ... private parties and several States (hereinafter respondents), challenged the revised NAAQS on several grounds. The District of Columbia Circuit found that, under the Administrator's interpretation, § 109(b)(1)—which instructs the EPA to set standards "the attainment and maintenance of which ... are requisite to protect the public health" with "an adequate margin of safety"—delegated legislative power to the Administrator in contravention of the Federal Constitution, and it remanded the NAAQS to the EPA. The Court of Appeals also declined to depart from its rule that the EPA may not consider implementation costs in setting the NAAQS. And it held that, although certain implementation provisions for the ozone NAAQS contained in Part D, Subpart 2, of Title I of the CAA did not prevent the EPA from revising the ozone standard and designating certain areas as "nonattainment areas," those provisions, rather than more general provisions contained in Subpart 1, constrained the implementation of the new ozone NAAQS. The court rejected the EPA's argument that it lacked jurisdiction to reach the implementation question because there had been no "final" implementation action.

Held:

1. Section 109(b) does not permit the Administrator to consider implementation costs in setting NAAQS. Because the CAA often expressly grants the EPA the authority to consider implementation costs, a provision for costs will not be inferred from its ambiguous provisions. ... And since § 109(b)(1) is the engine that drives nearly all of Title I of the CAA, the textual commitment of costs must be clear; Congress does not alter a regulatory scheme's fundamental details in vague terms or ancillary provisions, ... Respondents' arguments founder

39 Supreme Court of the United States, 121 S.Ct. 903, at 905.

upon this principle. It is implausible that § 109(b)(1)'s modest words "adequate margin" and "requisite" give the EPA the power to determine whether implementation costs should moderate national air quality standards. Cf. ibid. And the **cost factor is both so indirectly related to public health and so full of potential for canceling the conclusions drawn from direct health effects that it would have been expressly mentioned in §§ 108 and 109 had Congress meant it** to be considered [emphases added]. [...]

2. **Section 109(b)(1) does not delegate** legislative power to the EPA. When conferring decisionmaking authority upon agencies, Congress must lay down an intelligible principle to which the person or body authorized to act is directed to conform. ... An agency cannot cure an unlawful delegation of legislative power by adopting in its discretion a limiting construction of the statute ... [T]he scope of discretion that § 109(b)(1) allows is well within the outer limits of the Court's nondelegation precedents, ... Statutes need not provide a determinate criterion for saying how much of a regulated harm is too much to avoid delegating legislative power. Pp. 11–15.

3. The Court of Appeals had jurisdiction to consider the implementation issue under § 307 of the CAA. The implementation policy constitutes final agency action under § 307 because it marked the consummation of the EPA's decisionmaking process, [...]

4. The implementation policy is unlawful. Under Chevron U.S.A. Inc. v. Natural Resources Defense Council, Inc., if the statute resolves the question whether Subpart 1 or Subpart 2 applies to revised ozone NAAQS, that ends the matter; but if the statute is ambiguous, the Court must defer to a reasonable agency interpretation. Here, the statute is ambiguous concerning the interaction between Subpart 1 and Subpart 2, but the Court cannot defer to the EPA's interpretation, which would render Subpart 2's carefully designed restrictions on EPA discretion nugatory once a new ozone NAAQS has been promulgated. The principal distinction between the subparts is that Subpart 2 eliminates regulatory discretion allowed by Subpart 1. The EPA may not construe the statute in a way that completely nullifies textually applicable provisions meant to limit its discretion. [...]

[...]

Opinion: Justice SCALIA delivered the opinion of the Court.

These cases present the following questions: (1) Whether § 109(b)(1) of the Clean Air Act (CAA) delegates **legislative power** to the Administrator of the Environmental Protection Agency (EPA). (2) Whether the Administrator may consider the costs of implementation in setting national ambient air quality standards (NAAQS) under § 109(b)(1). (3) Whether the Court of Appeals had jurisdiction to review the EPA's interpretation of Part D of Title I of the CAA, 42 U.S.C. §§ 7501–7515, with respect to implementing the revised ozone NAAQS. (4) If so, whether the EPA's interpretation of that part was permissible.

Section 109(a) of the CAA, ... requires the Administrator of the EPA to promulgate NAAQS for each air pollutant for which "air quality criteria" have been issued under § 108,. ... Once a NAAQS has been promulgated, the Administrator must review the standard (and the criteria on which it is based) "at five-year intervals" and make "such revisions ... as may be appropriate." These cases arose when, on July 18, 1997, the Administrator revised the NAAQS for particulate matter and ozone. ... American Trucking Associations, Inc., and its co-respondents ...—challenged the new standards in the

Court of Appeals for the District of Columbia Circuit. [...]

The District of Columbia Circuit accepted some of the challenges and rejected others. It agreed with the No. 99–1257 respondents (hereinafter respondents) that § 109(b)(1) delegated legislative power to the Administrator in contravention of the United States Constitution, Art. I, § 1, because it found that the EPA had interpreted the statute to provide no "intelligible principle" to guide the agency's exercise of authority. American Trucking Assns., Inc. v. EPA. [...]

The Administrator and the EPA petitioned this Court for review of the first, third, and fourth questions described in the first paragraph of this opinion. Respondents conditionally cross-petitioned for review of the second question. We granted certiorari on both petitions, ... , and scheduled the cases for argument in tandem. We have now consolidated the cases for purposes of decision.

II

In Lead Industries Assn., Inc. v. EPA, supra, at 1148, the District of Columbia Circuit held that **"economic considerations [may] play no part in the promulgation of ambient air quality standards under Section 109" of the CAA**. In the present cases, the court adhered to that holding. ... Respondents argue that these decisions are incorrect. We disagree [...]

Section 109(b)(1) instructs the EPA to set primary ambient air quality standards "the attainment and maintenance of which ... are requisite to protect the public health" with "an adequate margin of safety." Were it not for the hundreds of pages of briefing respondents have submitted on the issue, one would have thought it fairly clear that this text does not permit the EPA to consider costs in setting the standards. The language, as one scholar has noted, "is absolute." ... The EPA, "based on" the information about health effects contained in the technical "criteria" documents compiled under § 108(a)(2), 42 U.S.C. § 7408(a)(2), is to identify the maximum airborne concentration of a pollutant that the public health can tolerate, decrease the concentration to provide an "adequate" margin of safety, and set the standard at that level. **Nowhere are the costs of achieving such a standard** made part of that initial calculation.

Against this most natural of readings, respondents make a lengthy, spirited, but ultimately unsuccessful attack.

[...] Respondents' textual arguments ultimately founder upon this principle. [...]

III

Section 109(b)(1) of the CAA instructs the EPA to set "ambient air quality standards the attainment and maintenance of which in the judgment of the Administrator, based on [the] criteria [documents of § 108] and allowing an adequate margin of safety, are requisite to protect the public health." The Court of Appeals held that this section as interpreted by the Administrator did not provide an "intelligible principle" to guide the EPA's exercise of authority in setting NAAQS. "[The] EPA," it said, "lack[ed] any determinate criteria for drawing lines. It has failed to state intelligibly how much is too much." ... The court hence found that the EPA's interpretation (but not the statute itself) violated the nondelegation doctrine. Id., at 1038. *We disagree.*

In a delegation challenge, ***t*he constitutional question is whether the statute has delegated legislative power to the agency**. Article I, § 1, of the *Constitution vests* **"[a]ll legislative Powers herein granted ... in a Congress of the United States."** This text permits no delegation of those powers ..., and so we repeatedly have said that **when Congress confers decisionmaking authority upon agencies Congress must "lay down by legislative act an intelligible principle to which the person or body authorized to [act] is directed**

to conform." ... We have never suggested that an agency can cure an unlawful delegation of legislative power by adopting in its discretion a limiting construction of the statute. [...]

We agree with the Solicitor General that the text of § 109(b)(1) of the CAA at a minimum requires that "[f]or a discrete set of pollutants and based on published air quality criteria that reflect the latest scientific knowledge, [the] EPA must establish uniform national standards at a level that is requisite to protect public health from the adverse effects of the pollutant in the ambient air." ... These limits on the EPA's discretion are strikingly similar to the ones we approved, ... [and] also resemble the Occupational Safety and Health Act of 1970 provision requiring the agency to "'set the standard which most adequately assures, to the extent feasible, on the basis of the best available evidence, that no employee will suffer any impairment of health'"—which the Court upheld in Industrial Union Dept., AFL–CIO v. American Petroleum Institute, 448 U.S. 607, 646, 100 S.Ct. 2844, 65 L.Ed.2d 1010 (1980), [...]

The scope of discretion § 109(b)(1) allows is in fact well within the outer limits of our nondelegation precedents. In the history of the Court we have found the requisite "intelligible principle" lacking in only two statutes, one of which provided literally no guidance for the exercise of discretion, and the other of which conferred authority to regulate the entire economy on the basis of no more precise a standard than stimulating the economy by assuring "fair competition." ... ... And we have found an "intelligible principle" in various statutes authorizing regulation in the "public interest." [...]

We therefore reverse the judgment of the Court of Appeals remanding for reinterpretation that would avoid a supposed delegation of legislative power. It will remain for the Court of Appeals—on the remand that we direct for other reasons—to dispose of any other preserved challenge to the NAAQS under the judicial-review provisions contained in 42 U.S.C. § 7607(d)(9).

IV ... * ***

To summarize our holdings in these unusually complex cases: (1) The EPA *may not consider implementation costs in setting primary and secondary* NAAQS under § 109(b) of the CAA. (2) Section 109(b)(1) *does not delegate legislative power to the EPA in contravention of Art. I, § 1, of the Constitution.* (3) The Court of Appeals had jurisdiction to review the EPA's interpretation of Part D of Title I of the CAA, relating to the implementation of the revised ozone NAAQS. (4) The EPA's interpretation of that Part is unreasonable.

The judgment of the Court of Appeals is affirmed in part and reversed in part, and the cases are remanded for proceedings consistent with this opinion.

It is so ordered.

We have seen how the US Supreme Court concluded that the EPA had issued its ozone and particulate standard in a manner that was not *arbitrary and capricious*. However, what if an administrative agency sought to modify an existing standard that a current presidential administration did not approve of? When, and in what manner, may a later administrative action overturn a previous administrative decision? This occurred in an earlier case, *Motor Vehicle Manufacturers Association v. State Farm.* The Reagan administration sought to modify seatbelt requirement for new cars that would enter the market by not requiring "passive restraints" (such as automatic seatbelts or airbags) to protect vehicle occupants. It argued that automatic restraints would have no safety benefits beyond manual seatbelts and proposed to eliminate the requirement. The Supreme Court found that this proposal was arbitrary and capricious because the secretary of transportation failed to consider safer alternatives, such as nondetachable seatbelts or even airbags.

The recent significance of this decision is that the Trump administration sought to overturn a number of previously established regulations concerning environmental health hazards and other environmental hazards. Courts overturned these attempts because they were not supported in the record by all the factors that the congressional enactments required. To change an existing regulation, an agency may not merely issue a regulation that says it will no longer follow the earlier regulation. Instead, it must give good reasons why it should be changed or dropped, and similarly good reasons for an alternative approach. In effect, the Trump administration ran afoul of the requirements of the Supreme Court's much earlier decision in *Motor Vehicle Manufacturers Association v. State Farm*.

Here is an excerpt from the syllabus of that case:

Motor Vehicle Manufacturers Association v. State Farm

Supreme Court of the United States

103 S.Ct. 2856 (1983)

Syllabus: The National Traffic and **Motor Vehicle** Safety Act of 1966 (Act) directs the Secretary of Transportation to issue *motor vehicle* safety standards that "shall be practicable, shall meet the need for **motor vehicle** safety, and shall be stated in objective terms." In issuing these standards, the Secretary is directed to consider "relevant available **motor vehicle** safety data," whether the proposed standard is "reasonable, practicable and appropriate" for the particular type of **motor vehicle** for which it is prescribed, and "the extent to which such standards will contribute to carrying out the purposes" of the Act. The Act authorizes judicial review, under the Administrative Procedure Act, of "all orders establishing, amending, or revoking" a **motor vehicle** safety standard. The National Highway Traffic Safety Administration (NHTSA), to which the Secretary has delegated his authority to promulgate safety standards, rescinded the requirement of Modified Standard 208 that new **motor vehicles** produced after September 1982 be equipped with passive restraints (automatic seatbelts or airbags) to protect the safety of the occupants of the vehicle in the event of a collision. In explaining the rescission, NHTSA maintained that it was no longer able to find, as it had in 1977 when Modified Standard 208 was issued, that the automatic restraint requirement would produce significant safety benefits. In 1977, NHTSA had assumed that airbags would be installed in 60% of all new cars and automatic seatbelts in 40%. But by 1981 it became apparent that automobile manufacturers planned to install automatic seatbelts in approximately 99% of the new cars and that the overwhelming majority of such seatbelts could be easily detached and left that way permanently, thus precluding the realization of the life-saving potential of airbags and requiring the same type of affirmative action that was the stumbling block to achieving high usage of manual belts. For this reason, NHTSA concluded that there was no longer a basis for reliably predicting that Modified Standard 208 would lead to any significant increased usage of restraints. Hence, in NHTSA's view, the automatic restraint requirement was no longer reasonable or practicable. Moreover, given the high expense of implementing such a requirement and the limited benefits arising therefrom, NHTSA feared that many consumers would regard Modified Standard 208 as an instance of ineffective regulation. [...]

Held: NHTSA's rescission of the passive restraint requirement in Modified Standard 208 was arbitrary and capricious; **the agency failed to present an adequate basis and explanation for rescinding the requirement and must either consider the matter further or adhere to or amend the Standard along lines which its analysis supports.**

(a) The **rescission of an occupant crash protection standard is subject to the same standard of judicial review—the "arbitrary and capricious" standard—as is the promulgation of such a standard**, and should not be judged by, as petitioner **Motor Vehicle** Manufacturers Association contends, the standard used to judge an agency's refusal to promulgate a rule in the first place. The Act expressly equates orders "revoking" and "establishing" safety standards. The Association's view would render meaningless Congress' authorization for judicial review of orders revoking safety standards. An agency changing its course by rescinding a rule is obligated to supply a reasoned analysis for the change beyond that which may be required when an agency does not act in the first instance. While the scope of review under the "arbitrary and capricious" standard is narrow and a court is not to substitute its judgment for that of the agency, the agency nevertheless must examine the relevant data and articulate a satisfactory explanation for its action. In reviewing that explanation, a court must consider whether the decision was based on a consideration of the relevant factors and whether there was a clear error of judgment.

(b) [...]

(c) The first reason for finding NHTSA's rescission of Modified Standard 208 was arbitrary and capricious is that ***it* apparently gave no consideration to modifying the Standard to require that airbag technology be utilized**. Even if NHTSA's conclusion that detachable automatic seatbelts will not attain anticipated safety benefits because so many individuals will detach the mechanism were acceptable in its entirety, standing alone it would not justify any more than an amendment of the Standard to disallow compliance by means of one technology which will not provide effective passenger protection. It does not cast doubt on the need for a passive restraint requirement or upon the efficacy of airbag technology. The airbag is more than a policy alternative to the passive restraint requirement; it is a technology alternative within the ambit of the existing standard.

(d) NHTSA was **too quick to dismiss the safety benefits of automatic seatbelts**. Its explanation for rescission of the passive restraint requirement is not sufficient to enable this Court to conclude that the rescission was the product of reasoned decisionmaking. The agency **took no account of the critical difference between detachable automatic seatbelts and current manual seatbelts, failed to articulate a basis for not requiring nondetachable belts, and thus failed to offer the rational connection between facts and judgment required to pass muster under the "arbitrary and capricious standard.** [...]

Vacated and remanded."

[Full judicial opinion and citations are omitted]

Rights Protection Under Administrative Laws

We have seen how our rights might be protected under the criminal law and torts, but how can we assess the justice of administrative laws, how protective of the public they might be?

First, we should look at the protective standards in the legislation; if those were implemented, how well would we be protected from air pollutants under the CAA or from toxic exposures in workplaces under the OSH Act? Recall the OSH Act seeks to ensure that no person in a workplace should suffer *material impairment of health or functional capacity* even if they work in such exposures for a working lifetime. As already noted, this is a reasonably protective legal standard. The CAA protects us from particulate air pollutants "with an ample margin of safety." This degree of protection is less clear but the US Supreme Court provided some guidance: the EPA must "identify the maximum airborne concentration of a pollutant that the public health can *tolerate*, decrease the concentration to provide an 'adequate' margin of safety, and set the standard at that level [emphasis added]." A concern with this interpretation is that the concentration should be set at a level humans can "tolerate"—not a level that protects everyone's health or 95% of the population. Does this standard sufficiently protect the public?

Second, once we understand the legislative goals, does the agency issue protective rules at all in carrying out its mandate? And do those rules provide the requisite protections?

Third, does the agency issue rules sufficient to protect the public or workforce well? Recall that OSHA has issued few protections from toxic substances; this suggests that despite the OSH Act language, employees will not likely be well protected because so few health protections have been implemented in the last 27 years. Particularly in seemingly major industrial plants like oil refineries, there will probably be numerous toxicants in the workplace for which employees would need protection. Are they well enough protected?

Fourth, are the regulations in accordance with the science needed under the law? In protecting the public from fine particulate matter, as we saw above in the prelude to these issues, the EPA has not kept its legal standards commensurate with the science of the adverse effects from these particles.

Fifth, have there been administrative failures as judged by individuals or companies losing tort cases, or even worse, having been charged with crimes for failures to protect employees? In *Silkwood,* we saw that Nuclear Regulatory Commission standards might have been insufficient to protect Karen Silkwood. In *Sindell,* we saw that the Food and Drug Administration missed the toxicity of DES. Were these failures to issue protective regulations insufficiently protective regulations, or local failures to abide by perfectly good rules?

Some Shortcomings of Administrative Laws

When we discussed the criminal law and torts, we considered some of their limitations and shortcomings. We can see somewhat different shortcomings or difficulties with administrative laws. They are perhaps most visible concerning the EPA. Implementing the Clean Air Act to set *ambient* air pollution exposure levels that will prevent health harms can be complicated. The agency has to determine about five steps in assessing those risks. 1) A planning and scoping process along with research indicates what must be done. 2) It must identify what hazards it seeks to control and how harmful they might be. 3) Next comes dose-response assessment, which determines a numerical relationship between a hazard and its effects, or how potent a toxicant is. 4) Then the agency must assess what is known about human or environmental exposures to the hazard, how frequently they occur, and what levels of contact occur. Finally, 5) there must be an overall characterization of how well data support the nature and extent of the risks from the exposure. These five points are easy to state, but just reading our highly edited *Whitman v. American Trucking* case hints at the extensive effort that goes into setting comprehensive nationwide standards for ozone and particulate pollutants.

However, there is one advantage the EPA has compared with the tort law: in regulating the tiny $PM_{2.5}$ particles, it need only show that exposure to them adversely affects human health. This contrasts with the tort law, under which, if a plaintiff brought a case for adverse effects from $PM_{2.5}$ (if this were even possible), she would have to show the general causal connection between exposure and disease, which science has established, but also show that *her particular disease* was caused by the defendant's $PM_{2.5}$ emissions. Thus, in terms we considered in *Sindell v. Abbott Labs,* for particulate air pollutants, the EPA need only show *general causation*, not the *specific causation* that was needed in *Sindell.*

Moreover, issuing a health standard that affects hundreds, perhaps thousands, of companies that produce air pollutants ensures that there will be substantial pressures against the EPA's efforts, which will result in constant pressures against the total exercise and probably even endeavors to modify particular portions of proposals. Pushback from affected companies is guaranteed and likely to be massive.

In addition, some of the pushback is likely to be successful. For example, in 1997, the agency sought to set standards for $PM_{2.5}$ particulate particles at 15 $\mu g/m^3$.[40] I do not expect the reader to understand much of this, but for comparative purposes, I indicate this measure of protection from the toxicity of fine particulate matter.

In 2013, 20 years later, the agency finally lowered the permitted concentration to "12.0 micrograms per cubic meter (mg/m^3) so as to provide better protection against the adverse health effects of $PM_{2.5}$ associated with long- and short-term exposures."[37] This was a 20% decrease in exposures to $PM_{2.5}$ in 20 years, but since then, agency activities have stalled out. How well was the public protected during that 20-year period?

In 2020, the EPA reported, "[A]fter carefully reviewing the most recent available scientific evidence and technical information, and consulting with the Agency's independent scientific advisors, EPA announced its decision to retain, without revision, the existing primary (health-based) and secondary (welfare-based) National Ambient Air Quality Standards (NAAQS) for particulate matter [at 12.0 $\mu g/m^3$]."[41] Seven years of data and study did not move the agency to increase protections for the public.

Unfortunately, these most recent "protections" for the US public seem quite inadequate according to independent scientists who analyzed particulate air standards. These exposures to $PM_{2.5}$ are "responsible for tens of thousands of premature deaths in the United States each year."[42] And even the EPA's own analysis shows the $PM_{2.5}$ standards are simply inadequate to protect the public. With $PM_{2.5}$ standards at 12.0 $\mu g/m^3$ all-cause mortality in the United States from air pollution, "ranges from 13,500 to 52,100 deaths annually."[43] The high-end estimate is somewhat higher than lives lost to car accidents in the United States per year and about equivalent to annual deaths from influenza in a typical year.

---

40 U.S. Environmental Protection Agency (1997). National Ambient Air Quality Standards for Particulate Matter, 40 CFR Part 50 [AD–FRL–5725–2] RIN 2060–AE66, located at 38652 Federal Register, Vol. 62, No. 138, July 18, 1997. Rules and Regulations.

41 U.S. Environmental Protection Agency (2020. National Ambient Air Quality Standards for Particulate Matter, December 7, 2020. Located at https://www.epa.gov/pm-pollution/national-ambient-air-quality-standards-naaqs-pm.

42 Independent Particulate Matter Review Panel (2020. The need for a tighter particulate-matter air-quality standard. *The New England Journal of Medicine*, June 10, 2020. Located at https://doi.org/10.1056/NEJMsb2011009, 2; (policy assessment for the review of the National Ambient Air Quality Standards for particulate matter: EPA-452/R-20-002. Research Triangle Park, NC: Environmental Protection Agency, January 2020).

43 Independent Particulate Matter Review Panel, p. 2. The need for a tighter particulate-matter air-quality standard.

■ CHAPTER 6

Assessing Components of the Legal System

A major goal of the legal system, but not the only one, is to secure legally protected "border crossings" from violations. We now have some understanding of how the criminal law, the tort law, and administrative health laws might protect us from various invasions and typically harm. In this closing chapter, consider some dimensions on which the different areas of the law can be assessed, some strengths and weaknesses of each as it were. I try to comment on each area of the law along similar dimensions to provide comparable bases of judgment about how well they each carry out this task.

The aims of different components of the legal system, while perhaps similar in the broadest strokes, carry them out in different ways with different institutional and procedural commitments. The criminal law seeks to secure the rightful borders of our possessions and ourselves by *penalizing individuals* who *culpably* cross the borders defined by our rights. The tort law has a similar goal, but aims to assure our rightful borders by *setting matters right* with the injured party should he or she suffer damages from others crossing their legal borders. Perhaps in greater contrast, administrative health laws seek to protect our rights by more explicitly having a preventive stance by aiming to identify harms that do or could affect large numbers of people and by specifying how to modify potentially harmful activities to reduce or eliminate them. Regulatory agencies must follow *blueprints* specified by *legislation* to provide ideas about protection from legislatures. Administrative law aims to provide more prospective guidance to citizens as compared with retrospective compensation in the tort law or criminal punishments, although these two areas of the law have some deterrence effects. This point is developed further below.

Sanctions

Criminal laws are enforced by punishing those who violate them or threatening to do so, which as Murphy argues can have substantial adverse effects. Punishment typically imposes deprivation of liberty, hard treatment, and some degree of social condemnation, along with creating social isolation of defendants. These features of punishment can be quite harsh and intrusive. Both actual criminal punishment and its threats constitute "gravely serious assaults on the fundamental rights of persons, stigmatize and humiliate [them], and typically cause [them] great personal unhappiness. Even ... the possibility that they might be inflicted may be sufficient to generate enough fear in that individual to cause him to refrain from acting in ways he otherwise would have found desirable."[1] However, just because defendants are punished does not mean they have necessarily waived all their rights as citizens under the law and, indeed, on a standard account of guilt, those who are punished have paid their debt to the community and may be readmitted as a full citizen (although this theory is not always honored in practice).[2]

Because of its likely fear-inspiring nature and any resulting deterrence, criminal sanctions are the most severe of the sanctions we have considered from the different areas of the law. They can be quite devastating and perhaps even scary for those held accountable; because of their seriousness, the law makes invoking them more difficult to prove, requiring proof beyond a reasonable doubt.

The tort law sanctions are less severe, inflicting no loss of liberty, no harsh treatment, no or little condemnatory aspect (except perhaps where punitive damages are awarded). Instead, the tort law typically requires defendants found liable to provide monetary compensation to those harmed, or less commonly, to face injunctions for what has been done and to prevent future tortious behavior. The differences between criminal and tort sanctions lead Jeffrie Murphy and Jules Coleman to argue that in seeking to prohibit border crossings, if there is a way to discourage them short of using criminal sanctions, a community should do so. Criminal sanctions should only be reserved for "injuries that are incompensable" or for potential transgressions that are quite "fear-inspiring" for citizens or in a few instances, for backing up the laws of other institutions; e.g., such as car theft, that mere tort law compensation would be insufficient to discourage.[3] For instance, they ask would it be good legal policy to permit an individual to tear off another's arm and then pay compensation after the fact; they think not. Instead, such behavior should be forbidden outright, backed up by the more severe criminal sanctions instead of the liability rules of the tort law.

Administrative law guidance first comes in the form of regulations that require safer behavior from those whose actions harm others in the workplace or from broader health threats, such as air pollution. Once administrative regulations have been issued, they must be followed and are backed by what are called "civil" or "criminal" penalties specified within the enabling statute. Both classes of penalties fall well short of the typical sanctions of the criminal and tort laws.

Criminal laws require voluntary actions in violation of the laws, hold persons accountable for intentionally (in a broad sense) harming others or at least recklessly taking risks toward others, although there

1 Jeffrie Murphy & Jules Coleman (1984). *The philosophy of law: An introduction to jurisprudence*, p. 113. Roman and Allenheld.

2 Herbert Morris (1988). The decline of guilt. *Ethics 99* (October 1988): 62–76.

3 Jeffrie Murphy & Jules Coleman (1984). *The philosophy of law: An introduction to jurisprudence*, pp. 112–113. Roman and Allenheld.

are sanctions for grossly negligent, or more rarely, merely negligent, actions. Strict liability is permitted for a small class of crimes, but its use tends to be controversial.

In contrast, although the tort law recognizes some intentional torts, most offenses hold people for acting negligently. Strict liability has a broader application and is much less controversial because of the more central aim of providing recompense for injured parties.

Standards of culpability are less frequently part of administrative law. Mere violations of issued regulations are effectively strict liability offenses with comparatively minor fines. For intentional flaunting of the laws issued by administrative agencies, there are so-called criminal penalties, which, though called "criminal," tend to be comparatively minor by contrast with traditional criminal law, as the court in *Chicago Magnet Wire* argued.

Because of the intrusiveness and often severity of criminal sanctions, to be held accountable in the criminal law an official acting in the name of the community at large must establish a person's guilt *beyond a reasonable doubt* because of the transcendent values at stake for defendants to be found guilty—life, liberty, and good name. In the tort law, plaintiffs who decide to pursue a private action against defendants who have harmed them need only show defendants were liable by a preponderance of the evidence. According to the US Supreme Court, "In a civil suit between two private parties for money damages, for example, we view it as no more serious in general for there to be an erroneous verdict in the defendant's favor than for there to be an erroneous verdict in the plaintiff's favor ..."[4]

Administrative agencies we have considered do not make laws subjected to standards of proof in the same sense as those terms are used for the criminal and tort litigation. Instead, they must issue regulations implementing statutory authority. Regulations must not be "arbitrary and capricious" under many legislative statutes, such as the Clean Air Act, or must withstand court scrutiny (under more demanding standards) based on "substantial evidence in the record" that OSHA may face. These legal standards seek to ensure that a non-legislative entity such as OSHA or EPA follows the law under which they are issuing regulations and not acting contrary to what Congress specified in the legislation. For example, to act without being arbitrary and capricious, an agency must not

> [rely] on factors which Congress has not intended it to consider, entirely [fail] to consider an important aspect of the problem, offer an explanation for its decision that runs counter to the evidence before the agency, or is so implausible that it could not be ascribed to a difference in view or the product of agency expertise.[5]

Since only Congress may issue federal legislation, an administrative agency answering to the president of the United States, as head of the executive branch of government, must follow guidelines that are reviewable by appellate courts, so that legislative authority is not usurped by this part of the executive branch.

4 *In re Winship*, 397 U.S. 358, at 371–372 (1970).

5 *Motor Vehicles v. State Farm*, 103 S.Ct. 2856 (Supreme Court of the United States (2001) at 2866.

Establishing Causation

Causation is treated somewhat differently in criminal, tort, and regulatory law. Not all criminal offenses require that there must be a causal connection between a crime the person committed and some harm to individuals because not every crime causes harm to others—e.g., attempts, conspiracies, some aiding and abetting, and planning a crime, to note a few. The tort law requires for every tort that a plaintiff seeking compensation for harm suffered must show a causal connection between defendant's actions or products and the harm. For molecular products such as DES (*Sindell*) or the *Typhoid bacillus* (*Stubbs*), a plaintiff must show both that exposure to the molecular product *can cause the kind of injury* from which the plaintiff suffered and that defendant's activities or product in fact *did cause plaintiff's* injury. In contrast, to reduce exposures to harmful tiny substances, non-macro objects (as we discussed in the tort section), an administrative agency carrying out congressional legislation to reduce or prevent molecules from harming the public or workforce need only show the equivalent of general causation—a somewhat easier task than in the tort law because there need be no showing that a particular person's or company's product caused a traceable harm to a particular person.

On causation, one might say that administrative agencies have a modestly easier time establishing causal harm from an activity because agencies need only show a general causal connection between an activity and harm, and for molecularly caused harms, they need not show specific causation as the tort law would require. Moreover, although it is not discussed in quite these terms, a similar showing of specific causation would likely be needed in the criminal law if one were accused of poisoning another person, but that showing that would have to be established by a higher standard of proof than in torts.

Consider a real-world murder case for some context on these points, a case I have discussed elsewhere for different purposes.[6]

Several members of the family of a woman who had rejected the romantic advances of a man suddenly became ill after ingesting lemonade following a family outing. Following ingestion of the lemonade, Chad Shelton, an 11-month-old child, quickly suffered from "gastroenteritis, ...and Reye's syndrome (a disease characterized 'by vomiting, central nervous system damage and liver damage') [inter alia], and died shortly [after]. ... A pathologist who performed the autopsy, noting the poor condition of the liver, suggested a, 'pattern is more consistent with a toxic ingestion of an unknown agent rather than Reye's syndrome or other infectious etiologies.'"[7]

Duane Johnson, uncle of Chad Shelton, was treated at a different hospital. After exhibiting symptoms of chills, diarrhea, vomiting, and severe nosebleeds, he became comatose and went "into ... a neurological situation" and died. His 3-year-old daughter was sick with stomach pains and vomiting, as was his sister-in-law.

Among those who died, the liver was the only organ affected. Most toxic substances that affect the liver also affect other organs, but that was not the case here. The substance seemed soluble in water,

---

6 Carl F. Cranor (2016). *Toxic torts: Science, law and the possibility of justice, 2d Edition*, pp. 121–123. Cambridge University Press. Sometimes citing Berton Roueché (1982). The lemonade mystery, p. 59. *The Saturday Evening Post* (May/June 1982). The next paragraphs are taken from these pages with heavy editing.

7 Berton Roueché (1982). The lemonade mystery, p. 59. *The Saturday Evening Post* (May/June 1982).

since it likely had been in the lemonade that only some family members ingested. The substance was more or less tasteless, and it left no traces in their bodies; only certain kinds of organ damage were noted.

Toxicologists narrowed the potential murderous substance to "readily modifiable hydrocarbons called alkylating agents."[8] The list of eight potential alkylating agents was further narrowed. Several were judged too weak, and one was rejected because it caused damage to red blood cells, which were not seen. Another was inconsistent with the kind of liver damage seen. This left dimethylnitrosamine that fit all the facts of the case. Moreover, the liver lesions microscopically identified from the autopsy were identical to textbook examples from animal studies. Finally, a blind test of several tissue samples identified the substance as dimethylnitrosamine.

This was a murder caused by dimethylnitrosamine placed in the family's lemonade by the jilted boyfriend. Since he worked at a cancer institute and understood something about carcinogens, he intended to give the family cancer over a much longer period of time; he miscalculated and killed two immediately.

In order to convict the defendant of murder, a prosecutor would have had to show *beyond a reasonable doubt* that dimethylnitrosamine could cause the kinds of symptoms and harms experienced by the victims (general causation), which the scientific data showed, and further that the victims died specifically from the murderer's administration of the substance (specific causation).

If this family had brought a tort suit for the deaths and serious diseases caused in the family, they would have had to show both general and specific causation by a preponderance of the evidence. The murder conviction succeeded because he ultimately confessed, but the family might not have brought a tort suit because the defendant was likely judgment proof; that is, without sufficient resources to make a suit plausible.

In contrast, if an administrative agency had sought to show dimethylnitrosamine could cause serious diseases and death, including cancer in the workplace, it would only need to show the toxicological data without having to show specific causation. In general, once an agency has the toxicological data and is properly authorized to protect workers (under the OSH Act), it can take legal action. The agency would not have to show people were sickened or killed by exposures (but often there is this kind of record) and could regulate dimethylnitrosamine exposure, even if no one had been harmed by it in plants.

A challenge facing litigation in tort cases or analogously in criminal cases is that if a person suffers a *common* malady, such as lung cancer in a workplace, one would have to rule out major alternative explanations of the disease before one could successfully win a tort suit, which would pose problems resembling those faced by Stubbs, who contracted typhoid fever that had numerous causes).

For a different example, consider a hypothetical scenario for a pharmaceutical, X, that causes birth defects. Suppose X is a morning-sickness drug for pregnant women that causes shortened limb defects at a rate of about 1.2 times higher than the background rate of these dysfunctions. Suppose also that the "natural" rate of shortened limb defects when X is *not* taken is 2% of natural births, or 2/100. Assume further that there are 2,000,000 live births in the United States each year. A 2% shortened limb effect would result in about 40,000 children with this condition in absence of mothers taking X.

If substance X caused shortened limbs in 20% of children born with them, this would be 8,000 children and their families per year, who should be compensated for their injuries or the injuries should be prevented by a regulatory action.

8 Roueché, The lemonade mystery, 120.

However, in order for plaintiffs to recover compensation in the tort law for exposures to toxic substances in many jurisdictions, they must show by a preponderance of the evidence that exposure to the substance *could cause* harm (general causation) and that exposure to a defendant's product *did cause* plaintiffs' *harm* (specific causation) (recall *Sindell*). In *some* jurisdictions, for plaintiffs to recover compensation, they must show, based on human epidemiological statistical studies, that exposure to the substance *doubles the rate of adverse effects* (in this case, shortened limb defects) for both general causation and specific causation (this is a mistaken scientific view). However, on the above scenario, it would not be possible for families whose children suffered from shortened limb birth defects to show this, simply because an elevated risk of 1.2 is not sufficient (is less than a legally required relative risk of 2 in some jurisdictions).

Consequently, while in some or many jurisdictions plaintiffs would be precluded from compensation for injuries to children, demonstration of a relative risk of 1.2 that X caused this kind of birth defect would be quite sufficient for a regulatory agency such as the Food and Drug Administration to take the drug off the market once evidence of harm had occurred because so many people would be affected. Consequently, when there is statistical evidence of harm from toxic products, but it is short of standards of evidence that some tort law jurisdictions require for showing causation, action by an appropriate regulatory agency might well provide protections (although for some, it would be after the fact of injury).

Environmental tobacco smoke caused lung cancer (relative risk =1.2) in flight attendants exposed to smoke when it was still permitted on airplanes, but experts involved with this case faced a different issue. General causation can be clearly established because environmental tobacco smoke is a well-known cause of lung cancer. Specific causation would need to be shown by ruling out other possible causes of lung cancers, such as exposure to radon or environmental tobacco smoke at home, or perhaps a history of lung cancer in a family, or environmental tobacco smoke when one was growing up. If alternative causes of disease can be sufficiently ruled out, something that would be more difficult in the hypothetical case of pharmaceutical X above, this relative risk would be sufficient to establish city, state, and federal regulatory actions to eliminate exposures to environmental tobacco smoke.

With the above as background, consider some assessments of the three areas of the law. We can use the tort law as a foil, not because it is superior to other institutions for protecting people against border crossings, but because a number of other writers compare one area of the law or another with torts.

Intrusiveness

An area of the law could be intrusive to people in a few different ways. First, the criminal law is particularly intrusive because of its sanction. Criminal sanctions are the most severe because they inflict deprivation of liberty, social isolation, harsh treatment (to some extent), and social condemnation of those convicted. One might say these sanctions "force" citizens to obey the law or suffer severe, or at least quite unpleasant, consequences. Second, it has a fairly elaborate state apparatus to investigate, prosecute, and punish violators. Some aspects of this, especially its investigative institutions, provide considerable room for intervention in people's lives; e.g., by electronic surveillance, police overreach, police conducting illegal searches, and even police brutality.

Administrative law can be intrusive because it tends to specify in some detail how certain activities should be done; e.g., to protect employees or the general public from toxic substances in the workplace or in the general environment, respectively, or how a product, such as cars or houses, should be created (e.g., with car safety laws or building codes). All areas of the law tend to constrain persons' totally free choices, but perhaps both the criminal and administrative laws do so somewhat more obviously. If a person or company seeks to engage in certain activities, like chemical or petroleum manufacturing, or emitting air pollutants, they must be done in such a manner that employees and the broader public are not harmed by its activities. Second, environmental health administrative agencies are institutions with state authority, personnel to investigate problems, conduct scientific investigations, issue rules to carry out congressional laws, and to inspect companies to ensure laws are followed and enforced. Substantial institutions are needed to implement congressional laws requiring administrative agencies, but we cannot live without them. Some parties subjected to administrative rules may well find them intrusive, much like any law might be, but often such rules apply *inter alia* to a company's operations, specifying that employees should be protected from toxicants and in some instances how this should occur; companies may have less choice in how they comply with the laws.

The penalties for administrative law violations are quite different from criminal sanctions. They are hardly severe, which poses a problem. Too often, Congress passes laws seeking to ensure the public or workforce is protected, but the sanctions imposed under the law, either what are called, "civil" or "criminal" penalties specified by legislation, have the reputation of being so minimal that they are often seen as light "slaps on the wrist" or perhaps tiny "costs of doing business." To ensure that administrative rules ensure better protections they promise, penalties for violation should be more severe than they typically are.

In contrast with both the criminal law and administrative laws, the tort law requires little in the nature of state institutions to carry out its tasks, largely needing only court fora for adjudicating disputes between plaintiffs and defendants, and any appeals that follow from initial adjudication. Of course, since tort actions must be implemented by a party who believes she has been injured, whether or not a person is even brought into court is a low probability event. Michael Saks provides data showing that among people clearly injured by tortious actions of others, few ever approach an attorney seeking redress of their injuries (between 4% and 8%), and fewer still pursue a legal case (about 2%).[9] And even if a party ends up in court and has to pay for injuries to a plaintiff, tort sanctions do not have the severity of criminal penal sanctions, requiring only loss of money if a defendant is found liable, or in rare cases, injunctions if conduct is too threatening to others. Monetary losses to companies via the tort law such as we saw *in Silkwood v. Kerr-McGee* could be greater in the tort law than civil or criminal penalties under a typical administrative law. However, neither tort nor administrative penalties approach the severity of criminal sanctions.

Backup Functions

Each of the three areas of law can provide a certain kind of backup for one or more other areas of the law, but these relationships are complicated. Some of these backups occur simply because of overlaps in the areas of the law—the criminal law punishes various homicides, while the tort law holds people accountable for "wrongful death" and both areas make assault and battery illegal. Other backups occur

9 Michael J. Saks (1992). Do we really know anything about the behavior of the tort litigation system—and why not?" 1183–1190, 1284–1286. *Pennsylvania Law Review, 140.*

because there are some general provisions in the Constitution for those, while others may be forbidden because of different constitutional clauses.

Begin with the criminal law. Jeffrie Murphy argues that the criminal law is needed to prevent certain kinds of harm to others simply because some harms are simply incompensable, such as homicide or particularly violent assaults. We need the criminal law to simply *prohibit* such kinds of activities from occurring, to make the threat of legal action sufficiently great with its intrusive punishment that, one hopes, people will simply not think about committing such acts. Or there might be behavior that is so sufficiently terror-inducing that it too should simply be prohibited, instead of addressed by tort law compensation—e.g., such laws might prohibit quite serious and scary assaults like ripping off a person's arm or raping them. Consequently, while many kinds of harms may be subject to the tort law, in some instances the threat of tort sanctions may be too minimal to sufficiently discourage such behavior. In short, the criminal law with its severe sanctions "backs up" other areas of the law that inadequately sanction some particularly harmful or scary behavior.

At the same time, because of the stringent *mens rea* requirements and the severe punishments of the criminal law, both of which must be established beyond a reasonable doubt, there may be circumstances in which the criminal law cannot successfully punish wrongful behavior. For instance, O.J. Simpson was charged with murdering his ex-wife, Nicole Brown Simpson, and a friend, Ron Goldman, but a jury found Simpson not guilty, in part because of concerns about the sufficiency of the evidence. Within a short period of time, Simpson's former in-laws brought a tort lawsuit against Simpson for the wrongful death of Nicole Simpson and their children's loss of love from their mother. A tort jury found O.J. Simpson liable for those actions. While the Brown family probably did not believe that justice had been done under the criminal law, perhaps some measure of justice for the family resulted from the successful tort suit, but what they thought of it is not clear. The upshot is that the criminal law can back up harmful actions that also constitute torts by having more threatening penalties, yet the tort law may provide some backup when analogous convictions in the criminal law simply cannot be successful.

At the beginning of this chapter, we considered that the tort law and criminal law in some instances simply cannot address some problems that need comprehensive and systemic solutions that would need federal or state administrative law to address. Thus, for example, protecting *everyone* occupationally exposed to asbestos in workplaces needs a more comprehensive approach than atomistic tort or criminal laws can provide. And, of course, since both laws function retrospectively, their preventive effects are limited. Consequently, because of the limitations of these two areas, this becomes a social problem that administrative law could address via the Occupational Safety and Health Administration (and, by the way, exposure to asbestos was one of the serious health threats that motivated its enactment). *Hodgson* (considered in Chapter 5) represents one of the early efforts to reduce the scourge of asbestos. The OSHA effort was an attempt to take a more proactive and preventive approach to protecting employees' health from asbestos exposures by reducing the concentrations of asbestos fibers in the air of plants. However, for individuals who had already contracted asbestos-based diseases, OSHA legally could not help them, but the tort law could provide compensation for their diseases and the burdens on their families. The first such case occurred in *Borel v. Fibreboard Paper Products Corporation* in 1957.[10] This

10 *Borel v. Fibreboard Paper Products Corporation et al.*, 493 F.2d 1076 (5th Cir. 1973).

turned out to be an important case because it showed tort lawyers that their tort actions could bring some degree of redress to those harmed by asbestos.

However, because the tort law retrospectively remedies harms already done and depends upon who files tort actions, it is limited in preventing harm. However, if companies see similar firms losing asbestos cases because of injuries to their employees, they may not wish to face tort suits, which may motivate them to better protect their employees. The "early" case of *Borel v. Fibreboard Paper Products Corporation* served this purpose, 30 or 40 years after asbestos-caused diseases were well known. This would be some element of general deterrence from threatened tort actions or deterrence by example of successful litigation against other companies.

We considered *Silkwood v. Kerr-McGee* as an example of a legal case based on an ancient doctrine of an ultrahazardous activity in which the "caged tiger rule" was applied to the very toxic radiation from plutonium. That case also illustrates an instance in which two areas of the law could address the same events in the world—Karen Silkwood becoming contaminated by plutonium. The major issue in that case was whether or not the regulations of the Nuclear Regulatory Commission (NRC) "preempted" or prevented pursuit of compensation for the family in the tort law. The NRC regulations may not have been sufficient to protect Silkwood from plutonium contamination. Recall, however, she died, not from radiation, but from a car accident. Yet her parents brought a tort suit against Kerr-McGee for injuries she did suffer from personal contamination and contamination of her apartment. She also would have suffered other injuries had she lived long enough for lung cancer to appear from her radiation exposures.

The relation between federal administrative law and state tort law is an area where there is some explicit legal guidance. Recall that the US Supreme Court upheld her parents' claim because compensation for injuries from nuclear plants was explicitly provided in federal law.

The Court found that the tort law explicitly backed failures of NRC regulations. To reach this conclusion, the Court had to incorporate several legal principles. Recall that the US Constitution has a supremacy clause: "federal law is 'the supreme Law of the Land' notwithstanding any state law to the contrary."[11] However, there is also a "canon of statutory construction known as the 'presumption against preemption,' which instructs that federal law should not be read as preempting state law "unless that was the clear and manifest purpose of Congress."[12] There are also some principles that further guide statutory interpretation (noted in *Silkwood*). Federal laws may preempt state laws that are "related to" some subjects, "concerning certain subjects 'covered' by federal regulations," and some where there are explicit or sufficiently implicit conflicts between federal and state law.[13]

In *Silkwood,* the Supreme Court recognized that the backup function of torts was implicitly recognized in the Price Anderson Act of 1957,[14] even though the nuclear regulations under the NRC could have protected Karen Silkwood and may not have done so, with workers' compensation providing minimal compensation at best for her injuries. In other instances, sometimes Congress may explicitly forbid tort

---

11 Jay B. Sykes & Nicole Vanatko (2019). Federal preemption: A legal primer. *Congressional Research Service*, July 23, 2019, citing U.S. CONST. art. VI, cl. At 3.

12 *Ibid.*, 3.

13 *Ibid.*, 3.

14 *Silkwood v. Kerr-McGee*, 104 S.Ct. 615 (1984), citing the Price-Anderson Act, amending the Atomic Energy Act. Pub.L. 85–256, 71 Stat. 576 (1957).

law actions, but at other times, if Congress is silent on the relations between administrative laws and tort law backup, it then is often left to the "presumption against [federal] prevention" because of concerns about the role of states in our federalist system.

We have also seen a criminal law–regulatory law interaction in *People v. O'Neil and Film Recovery Systems*. The Illinois Supreme Court endorsed the backup function of the criminal law because of a previous decision in *Chicago Magnet Wire*. That case follows next because it more explicitly provides a rationale for permitting criminal prosecutions when a company egregiously puts its employees at risk and OSH Act provisions do not provide adequate protection of sanctions for what they experience.

Note some of the major reasons the Illinois Supreme Court gives for its decision. Defendant was charged for "aggravated assault" by exposing their employees to "poisonous and stupefying" substances, but the opinion does not indicate any deaths. It began its analysis with the "assumption that the historic police powers of the States were not to be superseded by the Federal Act unless that was the clear and manifest purpose of Congress." It then held that the OSH Act cannot be reasonably "construed as explicitly preempting the enforcement of the criminal law of the States as to conduct governed by OSHA occupational health and safety standards."[15] In addition, Congress did not agree that the criminal law served the same purpose as the OSH Act. The "criminal charges here do not set any new or other standards for workplace safety but rather seek to impose an additional sanction for an employer's conduct that, if proved, would certainly violate the duty set out in section 5(a) of OSHA."[16] Finally, to decide differently would be to turn the federal OSH Act into a "grant of immunity" for ill treatment of employees. Consequently, it holds that there is no federal preemption of state criminal actions in this case, permitting the defendants to be prosecuted under the criminal law.

People v. Chicago Magnet Wire Corporation

Supreme Court of Illinois

126 Ill.2d 356 (1989)

Opinion: Justice WARD delivered the opinion of the court:

The issue we consider on this appeal is whether the Occupational Safety and Health Act of 1970 (OSHA) (29 U.S.C. § 651 et seq. (1982)) preempts the State from prosecuting the defendants, in the absence of approval from OSHA officials, for conduct which is regulated by OSHA occupational health and safety standards.

Indictments returned in the circuit court of Cook County charged the defendants, Chicago Magnet Wire Corporation, and five of its officers and agents, Anthony Jordan, Kevin Keane, Frank Asta, Gerald Colby and Allan Simon, with aggravated battery … and reckless conduct. The individual defendants were also charged with conspiracy to commit aggravated battery. In substance, the indictments alleged that the defendants **knowingly and recklessly caused the injury of 42 employees by failing to provide for them necessary safety precautions in the workplace to avoid harmful exposure to**

15 *People v. Chicago Magnet Wire et al.*, 126 Ill.2d 356, at 365.

16 *Ibid.*

"poisonous and stupifying substances" used by the company in its manufacturing processes. On the defendants' motion, the trial court dismissed the charges, holding that OSHA has preempted the State from prosecuting the defendants for the conduct alleged in the indictments. The appellate court affirmed … and we granted the State's petition for leave to appeal under Supreme Court Rule 315 […]

Defendant Chicago Magnet Wire Corporation is an Illinois corporation whose principal business is the coating of **wire** with various substances and chemical compounds. Anthony Jordan, Kevin Keane, Allan Simon, Frank Asta and Gerald Colby are officers or managerial agents of the corporation.

The indictments charged that the defendants unreasonably exposed 42 employees to "poisonous and stupifying substances" in the workplace and prevented the employees from protecting themselves by "failing to provide necessary safety instructions and necessary safety equipment and sundry health monitoring systems." […]

Counts of the indictments charging the defendants with aggravated battery alleged that the defendants exposed the employees to the toxic substances with "the conscious awareness that a substantial probability existed that their acts would cause great bodily harm" in violation of section 12-4(a) of the Criminal Code of 1961. … Other counts charging the defendants with aggravated battery alleged that the defendants knowingly committed acts "with the awareness that a substantial probability existed" that their conduct would cause the employees to "take by deception [of the employer], for other than medical purposes, poisonous and stupifying substances" in violation of section 12-4(c). … The defendants were charged with reckless conduct in that they exposed the employees to substances "in a reckless manner, which caused harm to and endangered * * * [their] bodily safety * * * by consciously disregarding a substantial and unjustifiable risk of harm * * * which constitute[s] a gross deviation from the standard of care which a reasonable person would exercise in this situation." The conspiracy counts alleged that the **individual defendants conspired with the intent to commit aggravated battery and charged that in furtherance of the conspiracy, the defendants committed certain overt acts**. […]

The circuit court dismissed the indictments, holding that OSHA preempts the States from prosecuting employers for conduct which is governed by Federal occupational health and safety standards, unless the State has received approval from OSHA officials to administer its own occupational safety and health plan. The court stated that because the conduct of the defendants set out in the indictments was governed by OSHA occupational health and safety standards, and the State had not received approval from OSHA officials to administer its own plan, it could not prosecute the defendants for such conduct.

The extent to which State law is preempted by Federal legislation under the supremacy clause of the Constitution of the United States is essentially a question of congressional intendment. … Thus, if Congress, when acting within constitutional limits, explicitly mandates the preemption of State law within a stated situation, we need not proceed beyond the statutory language to determine that State law is preempted. … Even absent an express command by Congress to preempt State law in a particular area, preemptive intent may be inferred where "the scheme of federal regulation is sufficiently comprehensive to make reasonable the inference that Congress 'left no room' for supplementary state regulation" … or where the regulated field is one in which "the federal interest is so dominant that the federal system will be assumed to preclude enforcement of state laws on the same subject" … Congressional intent to preempt State law may also be inferred where "'the object sought to be obtained by the federal law and the character of obligations imposed by it may reveal the same purpose.'" [...]

The declared purpose of OSHA is "to assure so far as possible every working man and woman in the Nation safe and healthful working conditions and to preserve our human resources." ... To this end, Congress gave the Secretary of Labor the authority "to set mandatory occupational safety and health standards" for the workplace and to secure compliance with those standards by imposing civil and criminal sanctions for their violation. ... An "occupational health and safety standard" is defined as "a standard which requires conditions, or the adoption or use of one or more practices, means, methods, operations, or processes, reasonably necessary or appropriate to provide safe or healthful employment and places of employment." ... OSHA also imposes a duty on employers, separate and independent from specific standards set by the Secretary, to provide a workplace "free from recognized hazards that are causing or are likely to cause death or serious physical harm to his employees." [...]

Congress also authorized the Secretary to conduct investigations and on-site inspections of workplaces and to institute enforcement proceedings for violations of OSHA standards. ... For violations of specific OSHA standards or section 5(a), OSHA authorizes the imposition of civil **fines ranging from $1,000 to $10,000** (29 U.S.C. §§ 666(a) through (c) (1982)). **Criminal fines of $10,000 may be imposed for giving unauthorized advanced notification of an OSHA inspection** or knowingly making false statements on any OSHA filing. (See 29 U.S.C. §§ 666(e), (f) (1982).) OSHA also provides for prison terms of up to six months for wilful violations of OSHA standards that result in an employee's death. [...]

The defendants read section 18(a) of OSHA ... that under it Congress explicitly provided that the States are preempted from asserting jurisdiction over any occupational health and safety issue that is governed by OSHA occupational health and safety standards unless the State obtains approval from OSHA officials to administer its own occupational health and safety plan under section 18(b). [...]

The defendants state that the conduct alleged in the indictments is governed by OSHA occupational health and safety standards. Specifically, they claim that OSHA standards define permissible exposure limits for the toxic substances which allegedly injured their employees and that OSHA also regulates the conduct that the prosecution says rendered the company's workplace unsafe. The defendants contend that therefore the trial court correctly held that, because the State had not received approval from OSHA officials pursuant to section 18(b) to prosecute the conduct set out in the indictments, the charges must be dismissed. **We disagree.**

... [T]he language of section 18 of OSHA [cannot] reasonably be construed as explicitly preempting the enforcement of the criminal law of the States as to conduct governed by OSHA occupational health and safety standards. ... Nowhere in section 18 is there a ... suggestion that the enforcement of State criminal law as to federally regulated workplace matters is preempted unless approval is obtained from OSHA officials.

The defendants argue, ... that the primary purpose of punishing conduct under criminal law is to deter conduct that society deems harmful and to secure conformity with acceptable norms of behavior. ... When applied to conduct in the workplace, the defendants argue, criminal law serves the same purpose as OSHA, i.e., to compel adherence to a particular standard of safety that will minimize the risk of injury.

It is the defendants' contention that in enacting OSHA, Congress intended to preempt all State laws to the extent that they regulate workplace safety. They cite regulations promulgated by the Secretary which they say so interpret OSHA. Specifically, they note that section 1901.2 provides: "Section 18(a) of [OSHA] is read as preventing any State agency or court from asserting jurisdiction under State law over any occupational safety or health issue to which a Federal standard has been issued." [...]

We cannot accept the defendants' contention that it must be concluded that Congress intended to preempt the enforcement of State criminal laws in regard to conduct of employers in the workplace because the State criminal laws implicitly enforce occupational health and safety standards.

Although the imposition of sanctions under State penal law may effect a regulation of behavior as OSHA safety standards do, regulation through deterrence, however, is not the sole purpose of criminal law. For example, it also serves to punish as a matter of retributive justice. Too, whereas OSHA standards apply only to specific hazards in the workplace, criminal law reaches to regulate conduct in society in general. In contrast, occupational health and safety standards are promulgated under OSHA primarily as a means of regulating conduct to prevent injuries in the workplace.

It is to be observed also that for the most part OSHA imposes strict liability for violation of its standards, and that the criminal charges here allege that the defendants knowingly or recklessly injured several of their employees by unreasonably exposing them to toxic substances in the workplace. In order to be convicted of the charges, the State must establish that the defendants not only committed acts causing injury but that they also had the charged mental state, i.e., that they recognized the risk of injury and nevertheless wilfully failed to take precautions to prevent injury. Thus, **the criminal charges here do not set any new or other standards for workplace safety but rather seek to impose an additional sanction for an employer's conduct that, if proved, would certainly violate the duty set out in section 5(a) of OSHA**. [...]

There is nothing in the structure of OSHA or its legislative history which indicates that Congress intended to preempt the enforcement of State criminal law prohibiting conduct of employers that is also governed by OSHA safety standards. We would observe that the **Supreme Court declared ... that "[w]here * * * the field which Congress is said to have pre-empted has been traditionally occupied by the States, * * * 'we start with the assumption that the historic police powers of the States were not to be superseded by the Federal Act unless that was the clear and manifest purpose of Congress.'"** [...]

Certainly, the power to prosecute criminal conduct has traditionally been regarded as properly within the scope of State superintendence. ... The regulation of health and safety has also been considered as "primarily, and historically" a matter of local concern. ... It cannot be said that it was the "clear and manifest" purpose of Congress to preempt the application of State criminal laws for culpable conduct of employers simply because the same conduct is also governed by OSHA occupational health and safety standards.

Although the provisions of OSHA are comprehensive, that Congress, in section 18, invited the States to administer their own occupational health and safety plans demonstrates that **it did not intend to preclude supplementary State regulation**. Indeed, section 2 of OSHA ... provides that the States are "to assume the fullest responsibility for the administration and enforcement of their occupational safety and health laws." It seems clear that the Federal interest in occupational health and safety was not to be exclusive.

Too, considering that until the recently increased interest in environmental safety charges were rarely brought under State law for conduct relating to an employer's failure to maintain a safe workplace, it would be unreasonable to say that Congress considered the preemption of State criminal law when enacting OSHA. … ("Our review of the legislative history of OSHA suggests that it is highly unlikely that Congress considered the interaction of OSHA regulations with other common law and statutory schemes other than worker's compensation").) Indeed, **OSHA provides principally civil sanctions and only a few minor criminal sanctions for violations of its standards**. Even for wilful violations of OSHA standards which result in an **employee's death an employer can be sentenced only to a maximum of six months' imprisonment**. There is no penalty provided for conduct which causes serious injury to workers. It seems clear that providing for appropriate criminal sanctions in cases of egregious conduct causing serious or fatal injuries to employees was not considered. Under these circumstances, it is totally unreasonable to conclude that Congress intended that OSHA's penalties would be the only sanctions available for wrongful conduct which threatens or results in serious physical injury or death to workers.

We judge that the purpose underlying section 18 was to **ensure that OSHA would create a nationwide floor of effective safety and health standards** and provide for the enforcement of those standards. … It was not *fear that* the States would apply more stringent standards or penalties than OSHA that concerned Congress but that **the States would apply lesser ones which would not provide the necessary level of safety**. The comment has been made: "Congress * * * sought uniform national standards not to facilitate commerce but to prevent the 'race for the bottom' that occurred when each state set its own standards. Congress favored a federal law 'so that those states providing vigorous protection would not be disadvantaged by those that did not.'" (See Note, Getting Away With Murder: Federal OSHA Preemption of State Criminal Prosecutions for Industrial Accidents, 101 Harv.L.Rev. (1987).) [T]here is nothing in OSHA or its legislative history to indicate that Congress intended to preempt the enforcement of State criminal law simply because of its incidental regulatory effect.

A question with resemblance to the one here was before the Supreme Court in Silkwood v. Kerr-McGee Corp. (1984). There, the Court addressed the issue of whether State courts are preempted under the Atomic Energy Act from assessing punitive damages against defendants that cause injuries by excessive radiation. In Pacific Gas & Electric Co. v. State Energy Resources Conservation & Development Comm'n (1983), the Court had held that under the Atomic Energy Act the States are precluded from regulating the safety aspects of nuclear energy. The defendant argued that a "State-sanctioned award of punitive damages * * * punishes and deters conduct relating to radiation hazards" and therefore should be preempted by the Atomic Energy Act. The Court upheld the award notwithstanding the fact that it would have an incidental regulatory effect, stating:

"In sum, it is clear that in enacting and amending the Price-Anderson Act, Congress assumed that state-law remedies, in whatever form they might take, were available to those injured by nuclear incidents. This was so even though it was well aware of the NRC's exclusive authority to regulate safety matters. No doubt there is tension between the conclusion that safety regulation is the exclusive concern of the federal law and the conclusion that a State may nevertheless award damages based on its own law of liability. But as we understand what was done over the years in the legislation concerning nuclear energy, Congress intended to stand by both concepts and to tolerate whatever tension there was between them. We can do no less. It may be that the award of damages based on the state law of negligence or strict liability is regulatory in the sense that a nuclear plant will be threatened with damages liability if it does not conform to state standards, but that regulatory consequence was something that Congress was quite willing to accept." Silkwood.

We note, too, that Congress expressly stated that **OSHA was not intended to preempt two bases of liability that, like criminal law, operate to regulate workplace conduct** and implicitly set safety standards—State workers' compensation and tort law. Section 4(b)(4) of OSHA provides:

"Nothing in this chapter shall be construed to supersede or in any manner affect any workmen's compensation law or to enlarge or diminish or affect in any other manner the common law or statutory rights, duties, or liabilities of employers and employees under any law with respect to injuries, diseases, or death of employees arising out of, or in the course of, employment." [...]

There is little if any difference in the regulatory effect of punitive damages in tort and criminal penalties under the criminal law. (See Restatement (Second) of Torts § 908 (1970).) We see no reason, therefore, why what the Court declared in Silkwood should not be applied to the preemptive effect of OSHA. Also, if Congress, in OSHA, explicitly declared it was willing to accept the incidental regulation imposed by compensatory damages awards under State tort law, it cannot plausibly be argued that it also intended to preempt State criminal law because of its incidental regulatory effect on workplace safety.

It is a contention of the defendants that it is irrelevant that the State is invoking criminal law jurisdiction as long as the conduct charged in an indictment or information is conduct subject to regulation by OSHA. The defendants argue that the test of preemption is whether the conduct for which the State seeks to prosecute is in any way regulated by Federal legislation. The defendants assert that because the conduct charged in the indictments is conduct regulated under OSHA, a State prosecution for that conduct is preempted by OSHA. The contention is not convincing.

Simply because the conduct sought to be regulated in a sense under State criminal law is identical to that conduct made subject to Federal regulation does not result in State law being preempted. When there is no intent shown on the part of Congress to preempt the operation of State law, the "inquiry is whether 'there exists an irreconcilable conflict between the federal and state regulatory schemes.'" ... A conflict arises where "compliance with both federal and state regulations is a physical impossibility" ... or when State law "stands as an obstacle to the accomplishment and execution of the full purposes and objectives of Congress" [...]

The defendants argue that the prosecutions here would conflict with the purposes of OSHA. They say that Congress intended that under OSHA the Federal government was to have exclusive authority to set occupational health and safety standards. ... The defendants correctly point out that although the States are given the opportunity to enforce their own occupational health and safety standards, the plan submitted must contain assurances that the State will develop and enforce standards "at least as effective" as OSHA's. (See 29 U.S.C. § 667 (1982).) Even after a State plan is approved, the Occupational Safety and Health Administration retains jurisdiction to enforce its own standards until it determines, based on three years of experience, that the State's administration of the plan is "at least as effective" as OSHA's. [...]

The defendants … say that the States would … be permitted to impose standards so burdensome as to exceed the bounds of feasibility or so vague as not to provide clear guidance to employers.

We believe the concern of the defendants is unfounded. … [because] prosecutions of employers who violate State criminal law by failing to maintain safe working conditions for their employees will surely further OSHA's stated goal of "assur[ing] so far as possible every working man and woman in the Nation safe and healthful working conditions."… State criminal law can provide valuable and forceful supplement to insure that workers are more adequately protected and that particularly egregious conduct receives appropriate punishment.

The defendants' statements that the State will now have the ability to enforce more stringent standards than OSHA's does not persuade. As stated, the **charges here are based on the defendants' alleged wilfull failure to remove workplace hazards which create a substantial probability that they will cause injuries to their employees**. Thus, employers are not left without guidance as to what standard of care they must meet. Too, in practical terms, if a defendant were in compliance with OSHA standards it is unlikely that the State would bring prosecutive action. […]

To adopt the defendants' interpretation of OSHA would, in effect, convert the statute, which was enacted to create a safe work environment for the nation's workers, into a grant of immunity for employers responsible for serious injuries or deaths of employees. We are sure that that would be a consequence unforeseen by Congress.

[…] The appellate court of Wisconsin … held that the State's authority to enforce its criminal laws in the workplace has not been preempted by OSHA: […]

"There is nothing in OSHA which we believe indicates a compelling congressional direction that Wisconsin, or any other state, may not enforce its homicide laws in the workplace. Nor do we see any conflict between the act and sec. 940.06, Stats. To the contrary, compliance with federal safety and health regulations is consistent, we believe, with the discharge of the state's duty to protect the lives of employees, and all other citizens, through enforcement of its criminal laws. Wisconsin is not attempting to impose a penalty for violation of any safety regulations. It is only attempting to impose the sanctions of the criminal code upon one who allegedly caused the death of another person by reckless conduct. […]

[O]n September 27, 1988, the congressional committee on government operations approved and adopted a report on the question of whether State criminal prosecutions for workplace safety violations are preempted by OSHA. The committee concluded …"OSHA should take the position that the States have clear authority under the Federal OSH Act, as it is written, to prosecute employers for acts against their employees which constitute crimes under State law." […]

[A] letter of the Department of Justice, responding to the report, states in part that the Department shared the concerns of the committee as to the adequacy of the statutory criminal penalties provided for violations of OSHA and also observes:

"As for the narrower issue … [whether] provisions of the OSH Act were intended to preempt criminal law enforcement in the workplace and preclude the States from enforcing against employers the criminal laws of general application, such as murder, manslaughter, and assault, it is our view that no such general preemption was intended by Congress. … [N]othing in the OSH Act or its legislative history which indicates that Congress intended for the relatively limited criminal penalties provided by the Act to deprive employees of the protection provided by State criminal laws of general applicability."

[...] For the reasons given, the judgments of the appellate court and circuit court are reversed and the cause is remanded to the circuit court of Cook County for further proceedings.

(Citations omitted)

JUDGMENTS REVERSED; CAUSE REMANDED.

A major takeaway from these points about different backup features of the laws vis-à-vis one another is that it is important for the legal system to be open to using a wide range of laws to protect the public from harm. Sometimes areas of law can be ineffective, elements of an offense may be difficult to establish to a required standard of proof; some areas of law, like administrative laws, may poorly provide protections, even though they were created to do something more atomistic areas of the law could not.

There are occasions when the tort law can have a surprising influence in holding (typically) individual companies or a small group of them accountable for harms to workers, the wider public, or the environment. David Rosenberg,[17] a Harvard tort law scholar, nicely outlines this issue in a review of David Brodeur's *Outrageous Misconduct: The Asbestos Industry on Trial*.[18] This book exposes the "failure of every other institutional safeguard [for employees]: the asbestos companies, of course, but also the medical and legal professions, the unions, the insurance carriers, and all manner of regulatory and legislative bodies." In contrast, "the tort system emerged as the uniquely effective and indispensable means of exposing and defeating the asbestos conspiracy, providing compensation to victims, and deterring future malfeasance."[19]

Even better, Rosenberg describes some notable virtues of the tort law: "the tort system was and remains the only institution capable of bringing justice to [those diseased asbestos] workers. ... [it was able to do this because] ... it operates on the basis of private incentives largely immune to political control and financial co-optation; it hunts for every useful scrap of material evidence; it calls upon the opinions of the most knowledgeable experts rather than relying on bureaucratic time-servers; and it values human life beyond monetary losses."[20]

For a more recent example, DuPont de Nemours, Inc. concealed many health and contamination effects of its C8 or PFOA chemical products (perfluorooctanoic acid), a critical surfactant ingredient in Teflon cookware, Gore-Tex, and stain resistant products, *inter alia*. Some of these diseases included testicular cancer, ulcerative colitis, deaths of experimental animals exposed to C8, and birth defects caused by pregnant women working on the "Teflon line." A tort case revealed DuPont's hiding of its own research results, deception of the US EPA and local communities, environmental contamination, and ultimately

---

17 David Rosenberg (1986). The dusting of America: A story of asbestos—carnage, cover-up and litigation. *Harvard Law Review*.

18 New York: Pantheon Books, 1985.

19 Rosenberg, *op. cit.*, 1696.

20 *Ibid.*, 1704.

citizens' adverse health effects.[21] It also produced substantial compensation to those who contracted diseases from C8 exposure.[22] DuPont and its corporate offshoot, Chemours, created for settling this case, compensated 3,500 people for $670 million in a class action.[23] It also set up a scientific panel to determine adverse health effects in affected communities, which in turn assisted compensation for those actually injured.[24] This case is the subject of a comparatively recent movie, *Dark Waters*.

This unusually successful tort action, perhaps torts at its best, which by means of discovery had the success just described. DuPont phased out manufacture of C8, choosing to pursue shorter-chain chemicals in its place. (Whether or not they will be less toxic is not clear.[25]) However, most tort cases typically cannot boast such wide-ranging success.

While Rosenberg is a tort law enthusiast, nonetheless the tort system is largely beyond immediate political control in individual cases. However, although often legislatures try to constrain its general directions and modify its provisions, the requirement for discovery of what each party knows about a case is quite important and often revelatory, and the tort law does something no other area does—it can provide various levels of compensation to those who have been harmed by the actions or products of others—neither the criminal law nor administrative law serves these aims. Improvements can be made in how it functions and Rosenberg reviews some of them. We should also note that when most legislatures provide "tort reform" (briefly discussed below), their goal is not to facilitate the law in providing better outcomes for plaintiffs, but rather making it more friendly to businesses or substantially constraining it.[26]

Internalizing the Negative Externalities of Harmful Activities

One motivation often seen in some areas of the law concerns what economists call preventing *negative externalities*. An externality is a *beneficial* or a *harmful/undesirable* spillover effect imposed on others for which they do not pay the full economic or social costs. A positive externality might be a lighthouse someone else erected from which all ship captains can benefit without paying to use it, or someone

---

21 Nathaniel Rich (2016). The lawyer who became DuPont's worst nightmare. *New York Times*, January 6, 2016. Located at https://www.nytimes.com/2016/01/10/magazine/the-lawyer-who-became-duponts-worst-nightmare.html; Sharon Lerner (2006). Teflon toxin contamination has spread throughout the world. *The Intercept*, April 19, 2006. Located at https://theintercept.com/2016/04/19/teflon-toxin-contamination-has-spread-throughout-the-world/; Cranor, *Tragic failures*, *supra*, note 5, p. 2; Robert Bilott (2019). *Exposed: Poisoned water, corporate greed, and one lawyer's twenty-year battle against Dupont*. Atria Books.

22 Denis Balibouse (2015). Teflon on trial: Ohio woman wins $1.6mn lawsuit alleging DuPont chemical led to cancer. *Reuters*, October 8, 2015. Available at https://www.rt.com/usa/318032-dupont-chemical-cancer-lawsuit/; Earl Rinehart (2016). DuPont loses another "bellwether" C8 law suit. *The Columbus Dispatch*, Wednesday, July 6, 2016. Located at http://www.dispatch.com/content/stories/local/2016/07/06/DuPont-C8-litigation.html.

23 DuPont reaches C8 settlement agreement for $670M (2017). *The Parkersburg News and Sentinel*, March 24, 2017. Located at http://www.newsandsentinel.com/news/local-news/2017/02/dupont-reaches-c8-settlement-agreement-for-670m/.

24 Stephanie J. Frisbee, A. Paul Brooks Jr., Arthur Maher, et al. (2009). The C8 Health Project: Design, methods, and participants. *Environmental Health Perspectives*, Vol. 117, No. 12, | December 2009, 1873–1882.

25 Laurel A. Schaider, Simona A. Balan, Arlene Blum, et al. (2017). Fluorinated compounds in U.S. fast food packaging, pp. 4, 105–111. *Environmental Science and Technology Letters*. https://doi.org/10.1021/acs.estlett.6b00435

26 *Ibid.*, 1706.

playing Chopin's Nocturnes at bedtime to which all can listen without paying a fee. In contrast, a *harmful, undesirable, or negative* externality is dumping trash on public lands or my property, instead of paying for proper trash disposal at a community trash dump. A consequence is that a public agency or citizens will have to pay to remove illegally dumped trash. Other negative externalities might be discharging air or water pollutants that cause diseases to the public that individuals must pay for. Or there could be workplace exposures to toxicants that cause diseases to employees for which the company does not pay and does not pay to prevent. Externalities distort economic markets and cause maldistributions of income and perhaps wealth compared with markets without externalities.

We should realize that to the extent economic activities produce negative externalities, such as illnesses, injuries, or deaths, these impose costs. If the costs are left on those harmed, they, their families, their insurers, or hospitals must absorb them. A number of legal institutions seek to prevent those costs from being left on the victims, but incorporated into the costs of the business that imposed the costs.

What we should realize from these examples is that when there are costs, someone has to pay for them—e.g., the victim, a victim's insurance company, a hospital, a health care system. Recall Justice Traynor's argument in *Escola*.

The criminal law seeks to prevent would-be assailants from harming members of the public by arresting and punishing the aggressors in an effort to deter others from similar activities. If assaulters escape prosecution, they have imposed an externality on the victims (with likely numerous additional monetary costs to repair any injuries, which could be minimal or quite substantial).

Causing diseases in the workforce imposes a negative externality on employees (a social cost) that may not be incorporated into the cost of the product. A major aim of creating workers' compensation was to ensure that "The cost of the product [produced by the workplace] should bear the blood of the workingman [who helped to produce the product]." To avoid externalities from toxic substances, occupational administrative laws could ensure that the costs of products reflect the prevention of the blood (diseases) of the workforce, but often poorly achieved in practice. This was an explicit aim of OSHA discussed in *Hodgson*. For another example, OSHA and the criminal law aimed to take action after the fact of Mr. Golab's death to deter other companies in the future from imposing toxic and life-threatening conditions on their employees. Similar motivations were behind the legal issues described in *Chicago Magnet Wire*.

Similarly, administrative laws that aim to reduce small particulate matter from causing lung and other diseases to the public are seeking to reduce the externalities imposed by pollution-caused illnesses. In *Whitman v. American Trucking,* the US EPA sought to reduce exposures to small particulate matter and take some steps toward reducing lung and related diseases (Chapter 5). If companies and automobiles produce fewer small air pollution particles, this will help reduce diseases and their costs, but the producers of the pollutants will have to bear somewhat larger costs of conducting their businesses.

The tort law is a legal institution that specifically permits injured parties to go to court (but they have to initiate legal action) and with a successful verdict shift the costs of their injuries back onto the defendants who caused them in the first place. Recall the argument given by Justice Traynor in *Escola v. Coca Cola* to modify the tort law for products liability. He argues that if the costs of injuries to Ms. Escola's hand were left to fall on her, this could be a notable cost in her life. Imposing strict liability (instead of negligence) on Coca Cola would more easily shift the costs to that company and use its product lines from Coke or other products to absorb the costs of her disease and would be a much better approach (see Chapter 4). Much more recently we have the example of tort litigation brought against DuPont that successfully revealed the company's law violations and shifted some externalities imposed on sick employees and citizens who had been exposed to DuPont's perfluorinated compounds.[27]

It is difficult to know what greater or lesser successes different areas of the law have had in preventing harm and in reducing externalities. I can provide only partial pictures in a short space. Consider the tort law. One major attempt to assess in a comprehensive manner what is known or not known about the tort law comes from Michael Saks.[28]

Some of what Saks reports, based on the limited evidence available, are: few people clearly tortiously injured even approach the tort law seeking redress of their harms;[29] few tort claims go to trial;[30] when there are jury awards, small losses are overcompensated, larger losses are undercompensated, and on average, jury awards undercompensate plaintiffs.[31] Judicial reviews at trial (trial judges) and afterward (appellate courts) tend to reduce jury awards even further with this, especially applying to punitive damages.[32] At nearly every stage, the tort system operates to *reduce* the likelihood that injurers will have to compensate their victims with only a small fraction of the costs of actionable injuries paid by injurers. And finally,

> From a compensation viewpoint, the ... tort system [does] not ... over-compensate or wildly compensate or impose undue costs on liable injurers. ... Its principal shortcoming [is]... that it usually provides no compensation at all or, when it does, it under-compensates.[33]

Saks sums up his view of torts: "So little compensation is achieved through the tort system that only as an act of hyperbole can it be said to be part of an injury compensation system."[34] (Despite this, he surprisingly notes that the "tort system may be a better and more effective deterrent than the above suggests, because it generates huge overestimates of its potency in the minds of potential defendants."[35]) Thus, to the extent he is correct, and this is one comprehensive effort to assess the tort system, the tort law seems to poorly repair externalities imposed on various victims, but we perhaps should be grateful that there may be greater deterrence of tortious actions than would be indicated by the average amount of compensation awarded.

---

27 Many costs were not shifted to DuPont because its perfluorinated substances are now all over the world in water systems and our bodies, and may well have costly consequences not easily traceable to the company.

28 Michael J. Saks (1992). Do we really know anything about the behavior of the tort litigation system—and why not?' 140 *Pennsylvania Law Review*, 1147–1292.

29 *Ibid.*, 1165, 1185.

30 *Ibid.*, 1214.

31 *Ibid.*, 1246.

32 *Ibid.*, 1261, 1281, 1287.

33 *Ibid.*, 1285, 1287, 1288.

34 *Ibid.*, 1286.

35 *Ibid.*, 1287.

Political Pressures

The brief excursion into externalities indirectly points to a major social concern that can make areas of the law less effective—individuals or businesses who have to pay costs to abide by the requirements of the law have incentives to oppose the areas of law. When the tort law functions well to hold defendants accountable for tortiously caused injuries, defendants must pay compensation to injured plaintiffs. Even if there is not litigation for particular injuries, the *threat* of litigation may cause potential tortfeasors some sleepless nights. As a consequence, the tort system draws considerable attention from potential defendants to modify the liability rules and even science rules[36] to make it more difficult for plaintiffs to succeed in court.

Bringing a tort litigation action does not face the same kinds of political pressures as we consider next for administrative agencies for a simple reason: it is up to individual plaintiffs and their lawyers when and if they will file a tort action (within boundaries otherwise set by legislation or appellate cases), as Rosenberg points out. However, the tort law is subjected to substantial pressures when legislators consider laws about torts, often during elections, and as part of continuing general public relations campaigns against torts.

This temptation to reduce the reach of torts began when it rose to greater prominence in the 19th century. Recall the discussion of Lawrence Friedman's history of American tort law in Chapter 3. Judges in the 19th century issued a number of rules over time to make it difficult for plaintiffs to recover from companies for workplace injuries, as well as from railroad companies whose actions burned houses or towns, caused prairie fires, and injured or killed ordinary people at crossings. Judges held that companies should only be held for fault—negligence—and did not even consider strict liability laws. In addition, there were a variety of liability rules that shielded companies from tortious injuries in the workplace. The courts' overriding concerns were threats to the economy and the burgeoning Industrial Revolution. Some of these emphases changed in intervening years as we have seen, with somewhat greater roles for strict liability and modification of legal rules to better align the law with complex and unusual causal events in the world (e.g., joint cause doctrines, *Stubbs*, eggshell skull principles, and *Sindell v. Abbott Labs*).

The business community still resists actions in torts and other areas of the law, including administrative law. Individuals and companies most likely to feel the threat of the tort law (and other areas) for injuries they might cause as recipients of these injuries seek to reduce or seek compensation of them. Businesses seek to reduce tort liability and to increase the difficulties for plaintiffs to establish liability. Thus, from time to time, there are spasms of "tort reform" led by politicians, seeking support from the business community, and those have had some successes. It is often a response to rising insurance rates in general or in the case of medical malpractice cases to the declining supply of physicians.[37]

We would have to penetrate too far into the weeds of some of these issues to represent various viewpoints, so we will not go there. However, in a recent review of "fourteen million actual cases filed

---

36 Carl F. Cranor (2016, 2017). *Toxic torts: Science, law and the possibility of justice* (2nd ed.). Cambridge University Press.

37 Scott DeVito & Andrew Jurs (2015). An overreaction to a nonexistent problem: Empirical analysis of tort reform from the 1980s to 2000s. *3 Stan. J. Complex Litig.* 62 63, 114–115.

between 1985 and 2009," Scott DeVito and Andrew Jurs found the "*necessity of tort reform has remained unproven* [emphasis in original]."[38]

> Our research and other studies together refute these arguments [regarding rising insurance rates and supplies of physicians], demonstrating that tort reform is often unnecessary (or at least, not necessary to reduce already dropping tort filing rates) and failing to achieve its intended goals of insurance premium reductions or increased physician supply. If so, tort reform remains solely as an anti-litigation political tool, disconnected from its initial justifications.[39]

In addition, the tort law is too often mischaracterized by opponents that distort the result of legal cases. Nearly 30 years after litigation, people still think Stella Liebeck was trying to make a quick buck off of McDonald's. In fact, that was a textbook negligence tort, decided by a jury. In part, the jury was likely impressed by the damage coffee at such high temperatures could do, and in part because McDonald's had failed to reveal many previous cases in which their hot coffee had burned patrons for which they had paid compensation.[40]

Consider analogous concerns from administrative law. Agencies such as OSHA or the EPA have been given legislative tasks to prevent harms to employees where they work (OSHA) or to prevent harms to the larger public (EPA) for which atomistic laws are not well suited. The aim of these institutions would be to spread the costs of prevention so they are incorporated into business activities up front and distributed to the community as a whole via regulated industries, insurance companies, or consumers who purchase associated products. Thus, such laws support the costs of trying to protect rights through preventive measures that in some respects, if regulatory laws function well, may be preferred to the tort law.

A more subtle issue arises with administrative agencies. In addition, to continually lobbying the agency, companies also seek to place former company officials in the agencies so that they have friendlier staff whom they can lobby for their preferred outcomes. Political scientists call this "industry capture." The Center for Public Integrity reports that

> Activity at the Environmental Protection Agency office that issues scientific reports on the toxicity of chemicals has nearly ground to a halt in recent years. ... The agency faces intense pressure from Congress and industry whenever it determines that a chemical poses a greater risk to public health than previously thought. Industry hires scientists who argue that known carcinogens such as arsenic, formaldehyde, and hexavalent chromium are generally safe at currently allowable levels. The scrutiny has made it difficult for the EPA to update chemical regulations.[41]

38 *Ibid.*, 63.

39 *Ibid.*, 114–115.

40 Alison Torres Bartka. Liebeck v. McDonald's: The Hot Coffee Case. Located at https://www.tortmuseum.org/liebeck-v-mcdonalds/.

41 Cranor, *Tragic failures*, 53, citing David Heath (2016). Meet the "rented white coats" who defend toxic chemicals. Center for Public Integrity, February 8, 2016. Available at https:// www.publicintegrity.org/2016/02/08/19223/

If these and other administrative agencies do not carry out the legislative mandates well and efficiently, costs that could be reduced will fall (invisibly) on employees or the general public as a result of workplace-caused illnesses or deaths on the one hand, or on the other hand, will pose costs from wider environmental health harms from toxicants such as particulate air pollution or ozone. These external costs fall on the obvious exposed populations, but it may be difficult for them to understand the causes of their maladies.

Of the three areas of the law we have considered, environmental health agencies in many respects are probably subjected to greater political pressures than the tort law. Because administrative agencies are creations of legislation, *at every step in the process* they are subjected to political pressures. When their birth is being considered in legislation, it is subjected to great political pressures. Once a law is enacted and seeks to carry out the legislative mandate by engaging in rule-making, it will be subjected to lobbyists both favoring and disfavoring the effort, typically with much greater pressures from businesses facing OSHA or EPA rule-making. Then, when it comes time to apply and enforce any successful rule-making, it will face resistance or obfuscation from the target of the rule. We often hear from politicians and general public relations anti-administrative law campaigns, that the staff that aims to administer the protective function of administrative agencies are often derisively referred to as mere "bureaucrats," making businesses and perhaps public life more expensive and possibly difficult. At one point in a national environmental health conference, I had an opportunity to ask an official of the US EPA about lobbying he faced; he reported that he is lobbied every week by affected businesses, and that when he returned from the conference we were attending, he had yet another of these meetings on the following Monday. In addition, at OSHA public hearings, when it was more active than at present, an auditorium would be dominated by affected businesses, their lawyers, and scientists with only one or two environmental or workplace public interest groups present.

Conclusion

In closing, recall that a major goal of the law is to reduce border violations that often result in harm to parties whose borders are crossed. This is clearly seen in many, but not all, criminal cases, in all actions when a citizen has acted tortiously toward others, and when administrative agencies, such as OSHA and the EPA, fail to do their legal jobs to protect employees or the wider public from toxicants. At this point, I often put the next concern in neon lights or in bolded texts, but I resist here.

When people are harmed by the border crossings of others, *there are costs, externalities*, imposed on the recipients of harm. A major question that must be addressed by the different areas of the law is, on whom should those costs fall? On the party that imposed them, as the tort law is available to do, and as at least in principle what the administrative law seeks to do, or should the costs be left to lie where they fall?

This book has sought to provide some basics about three areas of the law and how each functions. The aim has been to present the reader with some tools to guide his or her thinking about the parts of the legal system we considered. It also looked to compare some of the strengths and weaknesses of different aspects of the legal system, inviting readers to better assess the legal world around them.

---

meet-rented-white- coats-who-defend-toxic-chemicals.

APPENDIX

Procedural Timeline

Explanatory Notes on Procedural Points

Because the law has a number of formal rules guiding how trials are conducted, this commentary aims to provide a review of some of the main items in civil litigation.

Legal issues arise from events in the world, but of course, not all events between people raise legal issues; only some do. If someone believes that an injury they have suffered might raise issues the law could redress, they can file a **complaint** alleging what they believe is a legal claim against a party who may have contributed to their injury. For example, in *Sindell v. Abbott Labs*, Judith Sindell believed that her cervical cancer was caused by a pharmaceutical, diethylstilbestrol (DES), which her mother took while pregnant with her. The pharmaceutical companies she charged with selling DES had the legal right to **answer** her complaint. If both the complaint and answer are legally proper, a legal case is joined.

However, any legal issues between the plaintiff(s) and defendant(s) are subject to rules of law about whether or not they can be litigated at all or fully litigated at trial. In Ms. Sindell's case, very early in the steps of her alleged action, shortly after the complaints and answers had been filed, defendants asked the trial court to dismiss it. While good scientific evidence supported the claim that DES exposure of developing females *in utero* could cause cervical cancer, defendants claimed that Ms. Sindell could not sustain her suit because she could not show a legally needed element for recovery. She could not show which pharmaceutical firm made the pills her mother took that might have caused her disease. Consequently, defendants moved for a **demurrer**, arguing that her complaint should be dismissed because it **failed to state a legal claim that could be adjudicated**. In effect, there was no legal issue to be litigated. The trial court agreed, and the case was over shortly after it was instituted.

For another example, *Stubbs v. the City of Rochester*, Mr. Stubbs believed his typhoid fever was caused by contaminated drinking water from the city. He filed a complaint against the city, which answered it. However, after Mr. Stubbs presented his **case-in-chief** with all his evidence that implicated city water in his disease, Rochester argued that while contaminated water may have contributed to Stubbs's typhoid fever, several other exposures to the *Typhoid* bacillus could have caused it. In short, Stubbs failed to rule out enough other potential contributors to his illness to take his case to a jury. Rochester argued that Stubbs be **nonsuited** because the facts that he had presented in court were insufficient to have the jury consider the causal connection between his exposure to Rochester's water and his typhoid fever. The trial judge upheld their motion for a nonsuit. His case was at an end, even though the city had not yet presented its full legal case.

TABLE A.1 **Procedural Guide to Civil Litigation**

Pre-trial	Pre-trial	Pre-trial	Pre-trial	Trial
Event in world	Plaintiff files legal **complaint** in court.	Defendant files **Answer** in court.	**Discovery**	P's case in chief
		Does D file motion to **dismiss for failure to present legal claim** or a **demurrer**?	What does each party know about issues in case?	P's view of law & evidence. Does D file for **nonsuit for failure to prove causation?**
Stubbs contracts typhoid		**City of Rochester** answers	Other causes of typhoid	Stubbs **nonsuited:** facts were insufficient to show causation.
Anderson's house burned		**RR** answers	Other fires present	
Steinhauser in car accident		**Hertz** answers	**Ms. S** w/ psych condition	Routine
Evans in car accident		**Groves** answers	Ms. **Evans** w/brain issue	Routine
Summers shot		**Tice & Simonsen** answer	Who shot **Summers**?	Routine
Sindell contracted cervical cancer		**Abbott** Labs answers. **case dismissed**	**Sindell dismissed b/c** cancer not traceable for any D.	

Trial	Trial	Trial	Trial	Appeals
D's case in chief	Sides sum up, submit to jury	Post-verdict motions	Final judgment after verdict	Appellate court result
D's view of law & evidence. Does D file for **directed verdict based on balance of proof?**	Jury verdict	Does either party file for **JNOV** (often the D)?	Judge denies or grants **JNOV**	
In some instances, a legal case may result in a **directed verdict** if no reasonable jury could find for the opposing party. If this is granted, the case is over.	No jury; b/c of Stubbs' **nonsuit**		**Stubbs** appeals nonsuit.	**Stubbs** won; may take claim to jury
	Jury for **Anderson**		**RR** denied JNOV & appealed	**Anderson** won appeal
	Jury for **Hertz**		**Steinhauser** appealed	**Steinhauser** won appeal
	Jury for **Evans**		**Groves** appealed	**Evans** won appeal
	Jury for **Summers**		**Tice & Simonson** appealed	**Summers** won appeal
	Trial Ct: **Abbott Labs**-won on dismissal		**Sindell** appealed dismissal	**Sindell** won appeal

In other circumstances, both parties may present all their data and arguments on causal issues, but if one side's support for causation is so lacking compared with the other side's, the party with overwhelming evidence may seek a **directed verdict** against the opponent. Given the lopsided data presented, if **no reasonable jury could find for the opponent, a judge can issue a directed verdict,** and the case is over. For this ruling, a judge, who hears the same evidence as the jury, must compare one party's evidence with the other party's. When one party's evidence overwhelms the other party's, a judge may direct a verdict. Stubbs's issue in the previous paragraph was different. Rochester argued that his evidence was *incomplete* (he did not rule out other causes of typhoid), so the trial should not proceed.

Finally, after plaintiffs and defendants have presented their evidence and a jury has issued a verdict, one party, usually the defendant, may ask a judge to issue a **judgment notwithstanding the verdict**. In effect, this is a motion to overturn a jury decision. There are strong presumptions favoring a jury verdict; consequently, the basis of such a ruling is that **no reasonable jury** could have concluded that the evidence the jury considered supported the verdict they issued. A trial judge has heard the same evidence as the jury and is in a position to compare the balance of the evidence.

If a trial ends resulting from any of the rulings above, the losing party may appeal it to an appropriate appellate court. The text in Chapter 4 presents those cases and their outcomes at the appellate level.

GLOSSARY

Structure of the Legal System

Bench trial: A judge sitting at his or her bench in the courtroom both interprets (rules on) the law and serves as the jury in the case by making a factual finding under the law.

District or trial court: Typically the lowest level court in a state or federal legal system, presided over by a judge who runs a trial, with a jury of peers that adjudicates factual issues under the judge's interpretation of the law.

Highest appellate court in a state or the federal jurisdiction: In many state jurisdictions and in the federal system, this is called the "Supreme Court" of that jurisdiction. New York is an outlier, dubbing its highest court of appeal the "Court of Appeals."

Intermediate appellate court of appeals: Appellate courts, including supreme courts, only rule on the law or legal procedure as interpreted or applied by the trial judge at the district court level.

Burdens and Standards of Proof

Burden of proof: The **burden of proof**, properly so called, is the legal assignment of ***who* has to initiate legal action and change the legal status quo of the parties**, or **who** has to establish that a law has been violated and bring a legal case.

Burden of proof in the criminal law: An appropriate public official of a community—a public prosecutor, district attorney, or attorney general—*acting in the name of the represented community* must **initiate** legal action against a defendant suspected of violating the criminal law and bring a legal action against the suspect (see Chapter 1).

Burden of proof in the tort law: The **party who believes they have been injured by another must initiate** legal action against the defendant who is believed to have committed the injury (see Chapter 3).

Standard of proof: The **standard of proof** is the legal assignment within an area of law specifying how difficult it is **to change the legal status quo of the parties and hold a defendant accountable for a legal violation**.

Standard of proof in the criminal law: A public prosecutor, district attorney, or attorney general must establish **beyond a reasonable doubt** to the satisfaction of the *jury or finder of fact* that the quality and quantity of the evidence against the alleged defendant establishes defendant's guilt *for committing* the crime in question.

Standard of proof in the tort law: An injured party (plaintiff) who brings an action against a defendant(s) believed to have caused plaintiff's injury must establish to the satisfaction of the *jury* or *finder of fact* that the quality and quantity of the evidence against the alleged defendant(s) **more likely than not** supports plaintiff's claim. Alternative phrases are that defendant, based on the quality and quantity of the evidence, must be found liable **by a preponderance of the evidence or the balance of the probabilities,** or by **50% of the evidence "plus a feather."**

Sanctions for Legal Violations

For a violation of the criminal law, the typical sanction would be **a penalty** or **punishment** of the defendant whc has violated someone's legal borders that may involve jail or prison time, or a suspended sentence with parole, as well as a kind of social condemnation associated with the convicted defendant for the crime in question. For less serious offenses, the sanction may be a fine paid by the defendant to the state.

For a violation of the tort law, the typical sanction would require the defendant who violated the plaintiff **to put matters right (or make plaintiff whole** or **restore plaintiff as near as possible to their status quo ante)**, typically by **compensating** the plaintiff. Sometimes a plaintiff may request a different sanction than monetary damages, such as an injunction.

Generic Terms Often Used in Legal Cases

Border crossings: Violations of a person's legally authorized protected interests.

"Infirmities of human nature": A recognition of the limits to humans' abilities to control their behaviors, often referenced in voluntary manslaughter cases.

Moral turpitude: A term applying to differences in the extent to which offenders exhibit culpability in acting, or the needed degree of a guilty mind, especially in criminal cases.

Some Common Legal Terms That Appear in Cases

Affirm: Ordinarily used at the appellate level to agree that a trial court came to the correct decision.

Annulled decision: A lower court ruling is reversed.

Cause of action: A set of facts or legal theory that gives an individual or entity the right to seek a legal remedy against another.

Concur: Judge agrees with the result or decision but has his or her own or different reasons for the result.

Conviction quashed: To overthrow, annul, or vacate [British term].

Dissent: A judge disagrees with the majority decision in all or part of its opinion, typically in an appellate case.

Err: To make an error, usually referencing an action by a trial judge.

Exceptions: Term often used by a litigant to object to a trial court's alleged errors.

Grant a new trial: To authorize a new trial on some or all the issues addressed issued by a trial or appellate court, often based on a motion by one of the litigants.

Remand: To send back (to the trial court) for further action.

Remit: Send back to a trial judge.

Reverse: An appellate court vacates, sets aside, makes void, or annuls a judgment of a lower court.

Reversible error in the exclusion of evidence: A judgment that reasons for excluding evidence are in error and should be reversed.

Summary judgment: A final court decision made based on statements and evidence without going to trial.

Uphold or affirm: To ratify as correct a decision of a lower court.

Vacated: A court decision is rendered legally void.

BIBLIOGRAPHY

American Law Institute Model Penal Code Official Draft (1962). Section 2.09. In Sanford H. Kadish and Stephen J. Schulhofer, *Criminal law and its processes: Cases and materials* (5th ed.), p. 1190. Little, Brown and Company, 1989.

Balibouse, Denis (October 2015). Teflon on trial: Ohio woman wins $1.6mn lawsuit alleging DuPont chemical led to cancer. *Reuters*, October 8, 2015. Available at https://www.rt.com/usa/318032-dupont-chemical-cancer-lawsuit/.

Bilott, Robert (2019). *Exposed: Poisoned water, corporate greed, and one lawyer's twenty-year battle against Dupont*. Atria Books.

Black's Law Dictionary (5th ed.) (2004), p. 493. Bryan A. Garner, Ed. West Publishing.

Borel v. Fibreboard Paper Products Corporation et al., 493 F.2d 1076 (5th Cir., 1973).

Byrne v. Boadle (2 Hurl. & Colt. 722, 159 Eng. Rep. 299, 1863).

Clean Air Act, 42 U.S.C. §7401 et seq. § 109(b)(1) (1970).

Contact Team. (July 29, 2016) *Legal Dictionary*, "Executive Orders."

Cornell Law School, Intentional tort. Legal Information Institute. Located at https://www.law.cornell.edu/wex/intentional_tort.

Cornell Law School, The insanity defense. Located at https://www.law.cornell.edu/wex/insanity_defense.

Cranor, Carl F. (2017). *Tragic failures*. Oxford University Press

Cranor, Carl F. (2011). *Legally poisoned: How the law puts us at risk from toxicants*. Harvard University Press.

Cranor, Crystal A. Cardiac critical care nurse. Personal communication, April 8, 2021.

DeVito, Scott, & Jurs, Andrew (2015). An overreaction to a nonexistent problem: Empirical analysis of tort reform from the 1980s to 2000s. *3 Stan. J. Complex Litig.* 62.

Donovan, John (September 2019). How young is too young to be arrested? How Stuff Works, September 24, 2019. Located at https://people.howstuffworks.com/too-young-to-be-arrested.htm.

Feinberg, Joel (1970). The expressive function of punishment. In *Doing and Deserving*. Princeton University Press.

Finkel, Adam M. (March 13, 2019). Testimony of Adam M. Finkel Before the U.S. House of Representatives, Committee on Energy and Commerce, Environment and Climate Change Subcommittee, Hearing on "Mismanaging Chemical Risks: EPA's Failure to Protect Workers."

Friedman, Lawrence (1973). *History of American Law*, tort law. Simon & Schuster.

Frisbee, Stephanie J., Brooks Jr., A. Paul, Maher, Arthur, et al. (2009). The C8 Health Project: Design, methods, and participants. *Environmental Health*

Perspectives, Vol. 117, No. 12, December 2009, 1873–1882.

Gaffney, Jonathan M. "Executive Orders: An Introduction," *Congressional Research Service*, located at https://crsreports.congress.gov/product/pdf/R/R46738

Garvey, Todd (2017-03-27). A Brief Overview of Rulemaking and Judicial Review (PDF) (Report). Washington, DC: U.S. Congressional Research Service. R41546.

Heath, David (2016). Meet the "rented white coats" who defend toxic chemicals. Center for Public Integrity, February 8, 2016. Available at https://www.publicintegrity.org/ 2016/02/08/19223/meet-rented-white-coats-who-defend-toxic-chemicals.

Honore, Tony (1995). The morality of the tort law—Questions and answers. In *Philosophic foundations of tort law*, 73–95. David Owen, Ed. Clarendon Press.

Independent Particulate Matter Review Panel (June 2020). The need for a tighter particulate-matter air-quality standard. *The New England Journal of Medicine*, June 10, 2020. https://doi.org/10.1056/NEJMsb2011009

Jurs, Andrew, & DeVito, Scott (2013). The stricter standard: An empirical assessment of Daubert's effect on civil defendants. 62 *Cath. U. L. Rev.*, 675–731.

Kadish, Sanford H., & Schulhofer, Stephen J. (1989). *Criminal law and its processes: Cases and materials* (5th ed.). Little, Brown and Company.

Lectures in Tort Law, Yale Law School, 1980.

Legal Dictionary (March 16, 2016). "Strict Liability." Located at https://legaldictionary.net/strict-liability/.

Lerner, Sharon (2006). Teflon toxin contamination has spread throughout the world. *The Intercept*, April 19, 2006. Located at https://theintercept.com/2016/04/19/teflon-toxin-contamination-has-spread-throughout-the-world/.

Mashaw, Jerry L., & Merrill, Richard A. (1983). *Administrative law: The American public law system, cases and materials* (2nd ed.). West Publishing.

Morris, Herbert (1988). The decline of guilt. *Ethics*.

"Mrs. Onassis v. Mr. Galella" (1981). *Washington Post*. Located at https://www.washingtonpost.com/archive/politics/1981/12/25/mrs-onassis-v-mr-galella/27e9563d-a55f-4652-822b-97df1a392b2c/.

Murphy, Jeffrie, & Coleman, Jules (1984). *The philosophy of law: An introduction to jurisprudence*. Roman and Allenheld.

Occupation Safety and Health Act, Code of Federal Regulations, Chapter 16, OCCUPATIONAL SAFETY AND HEALTH, section 655 (b)(5).

Parkersburg News and Sentinel (March 24, 2017). DuPont reaches C8 settlement agreement for $670M. Located at http://www.newsandsentinel.com/news/local-news/2017/02/dupont-reaches-c8-settlement-agreement-for-670m/.

People v. Beardsley, 150 Mich. 206, 113 N.W. 1128 (Supreme Court of Michigan, 1907).

People v. Stamp, 2 Cal. App. 3d 203 (1969).

Physicians for Social Responsibility. *Coal's assault on human health*, 22–23.

Pope III, C. Arden, Burnett, Richard T., Thurston, George D., Thun, Michael J., Calle, Eugenia E., Krewski, Daniel, & Godleski, John J. (2004). Cardiovascular mortality and long-term exposure to particulate air pollution: Epidemiological evidence of general pathophysiological pathways of disease. *Circulation 109*:71–77. https://doi.org/10.1161/01.CIR.0000108927.80044.7F

Prosser and Keeton on Torts (5th ed.) (1984). W. Page Keeton et al., Eds. West Publishing.

Rich, Nathaniel (2016). The lawyer who became DuPont's worst nightmare. *New York Times*, January 6, 2016. Located at https://www.nytimes.com/2016/01/10/magazine/the-lawyer-who-became-duponts-worst-nightmare.html.

Rosenberg, David. (1986). The dusting of America: A story of asbestos—Carnage, cover-up and litigation. *Harvard Law Review*.

Roth, Lenny, & Blayden, Lynsey (2012). Provocation and self-defence in intimate partner and sexual advance homicides, NSW [New South Wales] Parliamentary Research Service, Briefing Paper No 5/2012, August 2012. Located at https://web.archive.org/web/20140623052433/http://www.parliament.nsw.gov.au/Prod/parlment/publications.nsf/0/F2BA1BFEED2D87EECA257A4800001BD7/%24File/briefing%20paperprovocation%20and%20self-defence.pdf.

Roueché, Berton (1982). The lemonade mystery. *The Saturday Evening Post* (May/June 1982).

Saks, Michael J. (1992). Do we really know anything about the behavior of the tort litigation system—and why not? 140 *University of Pennsylvania Law Review* 1147, at 1183–1184, citing Harvard Medical Practice Study, Patients, Doctors, And Lawyers: Medical Injury, Malpractice Litigation, And Patient Compensation In New York, The Report Of The Harvard Medical Practice Study To The State Of New York 3 (1990).

Schaider, Laurel A., Balan, Simona A., Blum, Arlene, et al. (2017). Fluorinated compounds in U.S. fast food packaging. *Environmental Science and Technology Letters, 4*, 105–111. https://doi.org/10.1021/acs.estlett.6b00435

Shouse California Law Group. California's new felony murder laws. Located at https://www.shouselaw.com/ca/defense/laws/felony-murder-rule/#:~:text=Under%20the%20new%20felony%20murder%20law%2C%20a%20person,principle%20set%20forth%20under%20Penal%20Code%2031%20PC.

Strong, J. W. (1992). *McCormick on evidence* (4th ed.). West Publishing.

Sykes, Jay B., & Vanatko, Nicole (2019.) Federal preemption: A legal primer. *Congressional Research Service*, July 23, 2019, citing U.S. CONST. art. VI, cl. At 3.

United States v. Park, 421 U.S. 658 (1975).

U.S. Environmental Protection Agency (2020). National ambient air quality standards for particulate matter. December 7, 2020. Located at https://www.epa.gov/pm-pollution/national-ambient-air-quality-standards-naaqs-pm.

U.S. Environmental Protection Agency (2020). Quality standards for particulate matter: EPA-452/R-20-002. Research Triangle Park, NC: Environmental Protection Agency, January 2020.

U.S. Environmental Protection Agency (2013). National ambient air quality standards for particulate matter, final rule. Federal Register, Vol. 78, No. 10. Tuesday, January 15, 2013. Rules and Regulations, 40 CFR Parts 50, 51, 52, 53 and 58 [EPA–HQ–OAR–2007–0492; FRL–9761–8] RIN 2060–AO47.

U.S. Environmental Protection Agency (1997). National ambient air quality standards for particulate matter. 40 CFR Part 50 [AD–FRL–5725–2] RIN 2060–AE66. Located at 38652 Federal Register, Vol. 62, No. 138. Friday, July 18, 1997. Rules and Regulations.

Yan Yan, Hong Xian, & Al-Aly, Ziyad (2018). The 2016 global and national burden of diabetes mellitus attributable to PM2·5 air pollution. *Lancet Planet Health*, 2: e301–312. Located at www.thelancet.com/planetary-health.

CPSIA information can be obtained
at www.ICGtesting.com
Printed in the USA
LVHW060913140922
728288LV00002B/6

9 781793 538475